INSIGHT GUIDES
LONDON

Discovery
CHANNEL
APA PUBLICATIONS
Part of the Langenscheidt Publishing Group
L

INSIGHT GUIDES
LONDON

Project Editor
Dorothy Stannard
Picture Editor
Hilary Genin
Art Director
Ian Spick
Cartography Editor
Zoë Goodwin
Production
Kenneth Chan
Editorial Director
Brian Bell

Distribution

UK & Ireland
GeoCenter International Ltd
Meridian House, Churchill Way West,
Basingstoke, Hampshire, RG21 6YR
Tel: +44 (0) 1256 817987
Fax: (44) 1256-817988

United States
Langenscheidt Publishers, Inc.
36–36 33rd Street 4th Floor
Long Island City, NY 11106
Fax: (1) 718 784-0640

Australia
Universal Publishers
1 Waterloo Road
Macquarie Park, NSW 2113
Fax: (61) 2 9888 9074

New Zealand
Hema Maps New Zealand Ltd (HNZ)
Unit D, 24 Ra ORA Drive
East Tamaki, Auckland
Fax: (64) 9 273 6479

Worldwide
Apa Publications GmbH & Co. Verlag KG (Singapore branch)
38 Joo Koon Road, Singapore 628990
Tel: (65) 6865-1600.
Fax: (65) 6861-6438

Printing

Insight Print Services (Pte) Ltd
38 Joo Koon Road, Singapore 628990
Tel: (65) 6865-1600.
Fax: (65) 6861-6438

First Edition 1989
Eleventh Edition 2008

www.insightguides.com
In North America:
www.insighttravelguides.com

ABOUT THIS BOOK

What makes an Insight Guide different? Since our first book pioneered the use of creative full-colour photography in travel guides in 1970, we have aimed to provide not only reliable information but also the key to a real understanding of a destination and its people.

Now, when the internet can supply inexhaustible (but not always reliable) facts, our books marry text and pictures to provide that more elusive quality: knowledge. To achieve this, they rely on the authority of locally based writers and photographers.

This book turns the spotlight on a city that been changing dramatically. Areas such as Southwark and the South Bank have been transformed and London's major museums (now free to visitors) magnificently revamped. Renewal continues with the resurgence of King's Cross and St Pancras, the site of the new Eurostar terminal, and the regeneration of the long-neglected East End, the main focus for the 2012 Olympics. *Insight Guide London* covers all this, and much more.

CONTACTING THE EDITORS

We would appreciate it if readers would alert us to errors or outdated information by writing to:

Insight Guides, P.O. Box 7910, London SE1 1WE, England.
Fax: (44) 20 7403-0290.
insight@apaguide.co.uk

THE CONTRIBUTORS

This edition of *Insight Guide: London* was edited by **Dorothy Stannard**, Executive Editor in Insight's London editorial office, implementing a vibrant new design by **Klaus Geisler**.

To ensure this new edition is as good as it looks, several members of Insight's editorial team trekked around their favourite areas of the city to identify and evaluate the latest attractions. They include **Alyse Dar** (St Paul's and the City), **Tom Le Bas** (Parliament and Buckingham Palace, and Holborn and the Inns of Court), **Clare Peel** (Trafalgar Square and Covent Garden, and Southwark and the South Bank), **Joanna Potts** (Soho and Chinatown) and **Sarah Sweeney** (Marylebone and Fitzrovia). Sweeney also helped ensure that the Travel Tips section contained the latest listings.

On the west side of town, **Siân Lezard** updated Knightsbridge and Kensington, while Chelsea was reworked by **Alexia Georgiou**, who also updated Mayfair.

The section on Village London, which takes a look at the city's more interesting suburbs, such as Greenwich, Kew, Hampstead and Spitalfieds, was updated by **Rachel Lawrence**, **Lesley Gordon,** Siân Lezard, and Dorothy Stannard.

This edition of the book builds on previous editions produced by **Brian Bell**, **Roger Williams** and **Andrew Eames**. Past contributors whose work is still evident here include **Roland Collins** (history), **Srinvasa Rao** (Who Lives in London?), **Allison Lobbett** and **Tim Grimwade**.

Many new images of London appear in this edition, taken in the main by **Glyn Genin** and **Britta Jaschinski**. The book was proof-read by **Sylvia Suddes** and indexed by **Isobel McLean**.

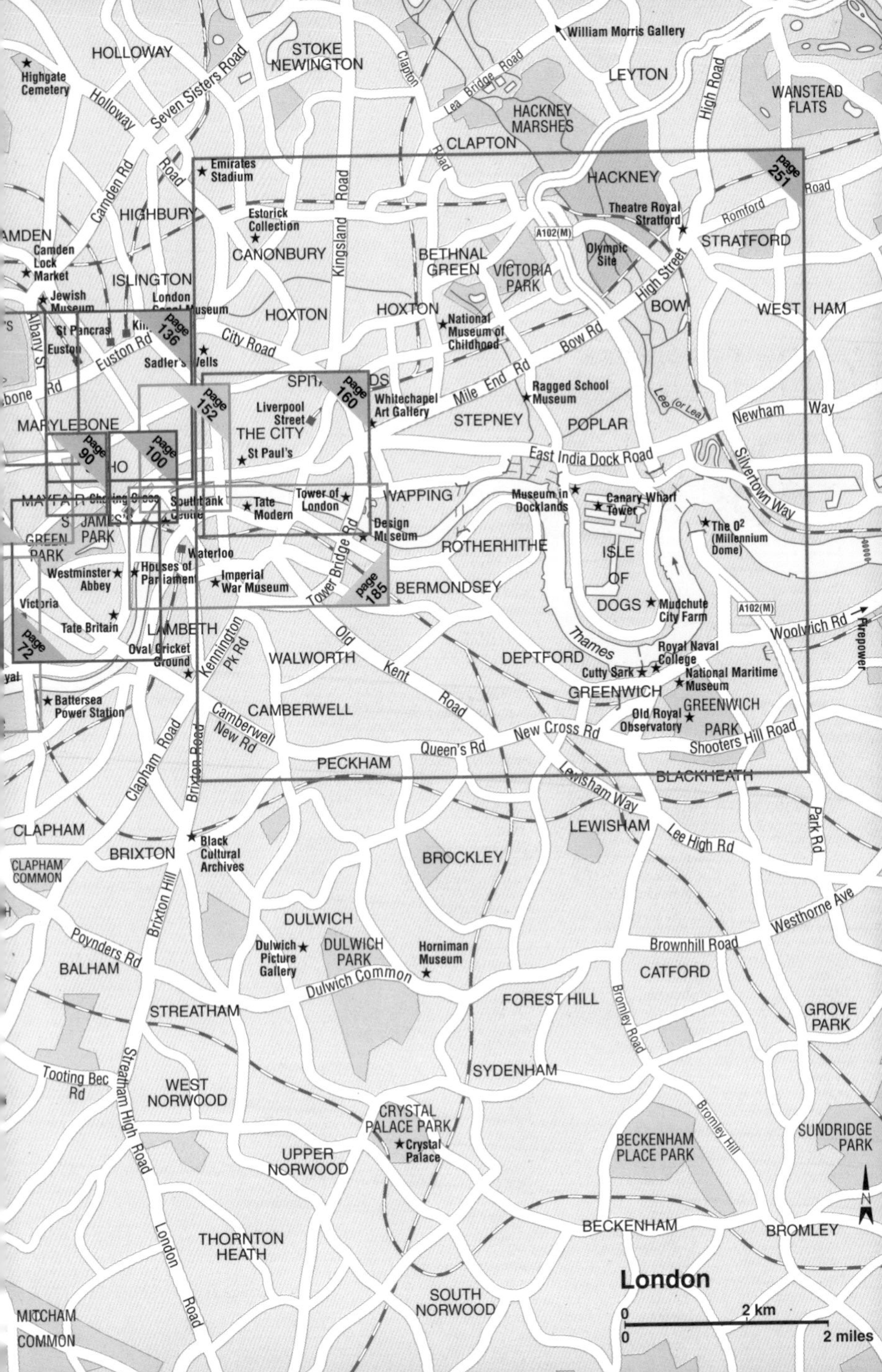

London
HOLLOWAY
Highgate Cemetery
Holloway
Seven Sisters Road
STOKE NEWINGTON
Clapton
William Morris Gallery
Lea Bridge Road
LEYTON
High Road
WANSTEAD FLATS
HACKNEY MARSHES
CLAPTON
Road
Emirates Stadium
Camden Rd
Road
Kingsland Road
HACKNEY
page 251
Road
Theatre Royal Stratford
Romford
HIGHBURY
Estorick Collection
A102(M)
STRATFORD
CAMDEN
Camden Lock Market
CANONBURY
BETHNAL GREEN
VICTORIA PARK
Olympic Site
High Street
ISLINGTON
Jewish Museum
London Canal Museum
HOXTON
HOXTON
BOW
WEST HAM
Albany St
St Pancras
Euston
Euston Rd
page 136
Sadler's Wells
City Road
National Museum of Childhood
Bow Rd
Mile End Rd
page 152
page 160
Whitechapel Art Gallery
Ragged School Museum
Lee (or Lea)
Newham Way
MARYLEBONE
Liverpool Street
THE CITY
STEPNEY
POPLAR
page 90
page 100
St Paul's
East India Dock Road
Silvertown Way
SOHO
Charing Cross
South Bank Centre
Tate Modern
Tower of London
WAPPING
Museum in Docklands
Canary Wharf Tower
ST JAMES'S PARK
GREEN PARK
Design Museum
The O^2 (Millennium Dome)
Waterloo
Tower Bridge Rd
ROTHERHITHE
ISLE OF DOGS
Westminster Abbey
Houses of Parliament
Imperial War Museum
page 185
BERMONDSEY
Mudchute City Farm
A102(M)
Victoria
Tate Britain
LAMBETH
Kennington Pk Rd
Old Kent Road
Thames
Woolwich Rd
Firepower
page 72
Oval Cricket Ground
WALWORTH
DEPTFORD
Royal Naval College
Cutty Sark
National Maritime Museum
GREENWICH
Battersea Power Station
CAMBERWELL
Camberwell New Rd
Old Royal Observatory
GREENWICH PARK
Clapham Road
Brixton Road
Queen's Rd
New Cross Rd
Shooters Hill Road
PECKHAM
BLACKHEATH
Lewisham Way
CLAPHAM
LEWISHAM
Lee High Rd
Park Rd
Black Cultural Archives
BRIXTON
BROCKLEY
CLAPHAM COMMON
Brixton Hill
DULWICH
Westhorne Ave
Poynders Rd
Dulwich Picture Gallery
DULWICH PARK
Horniman Museum
Brownhill Road
BALHAM
Dulwich Common
CATFORD
STREATHAM
FOREST HILL
Bromley Road
GROVE PARK
Streatham High Road
Tooting Bec Rd
SYDENHAM
WEST NORWOOD
CRYSTAL PALACE PARK
Crystal Palace
Bromley Hill
BECKENHAM PLACE PARK
SUNDRIDGE PARK
UPPER NORWOOD
N
BECKENHAM
BROMLEY
THORNTON HEATH
London Road
SOUTH NORWOOD
0
2 km
0
2 miles
MITCHAM COMMON

Other Insight Guides available:

Alaska
Amazon Wildlife
American Southwest
Argentina
Arizona & Grand Canyon
Asia, East
Asia, Southeast
Australia
Austria
Bahamas
Bali & Lombok
Baltic States
Barbados
Belgium
Belize
Bermuda
Brazil
Brittany
Buenos Aires
Bulgaria
Burgundy
Burma (Myanmar)
California
California, Southern
Canada
Caribbean
Caribbean Cruises
Channel Islands
Chile
China
China, Southern
Colorado
Continental Europe
Corsica
Costa Rica
Crete
Cuba
Cyprus
Czech & Slovak Republic
Denmark
Dominican Rep. & Haiti
East African Wildlife
Eastern Europe
Ecuador
Egypt
England
Finland
Florida
France
France, Southwest
French Riviera
Gambia & Senegal
Germany
Gran Canaria
Great Britain
Great Railway Journeys of Europe
Great River Cruises of Europe
Greece
Greek Islands
Guatemala, Belize & Yucatán
Hawaii
Hungary
Iceland
India
India, South
Indonesia
Ireland
Israel
Istanbul
Italy
Italy, Northern
Italy, Southern
Jamaica
Japan
Jordan
Kenya
Laos & Cambodia
Madeira
Malaysia
Mallorca & Ibiza
Malta
Mauritius Réunion & Seychelles
Mexico
Morocco
Namibia
Nepal
Netherlands
New England
New Mexico
New Orleans
New South Wales
New York State
New Zealand
Nile, The
Normandy
North American and Alaskan Cruises
Norway
Oman & the UAE
Pacific Northwest
Pakistan
Peru
Philippines
Poland
Portugal
Provence
Puerto Rico
Queensland & the Great Barrier Reef
Rajasthan
Romania
Russia
Sardinia
Scandinavia
Scotland
Sicily
South Africa
South America
South Korea
Spain
Spain, Northern
Spain, Southern
Sri Lanka
Sweden
Switzerland
Syria & Lebanon
Taiwan
Tasmania
Tenerife
Texas
Thailand
Thailand's Beaches & Islands
Trinidad & Tobago
Tunisia
Turkey
Tuscany
Umbria
USA: On The Road
USA: Western States
US National Parks: West
Utah
Venezuela
Vietnam
Wales

INSIGHT CITY GUIDES

Amsterdam
Athens
Bangkok
Barcelona
Beijing
Berlin
Boston
Bruges, Ghent & Antwerp
Brussels
Cairo
Cape Town
Chicago
Delhi, Jaipur & Agra
Dublin
Edinburgh
Florence
Glasgow
Hong Kong
Jerusalem
Kuala Lumpur
Las Vegas
Lisbon
London
Los Angeles
Madrid
Melbourne
Miami
Montreal
Moscow
New York
Oxford
Paris
Perth & Surroundings
Philadelphia
Prague
Rio de Janeiro
Rome
St Petersburg
San Francisco
Seattle
Singapore
Sydney
Taipei
Tokyo
Toronto
Vancouver
Venice
Vienna
Walt Disney World/Orlando
Washington, DC

INSIGHT HOTEL GUIDES

Asia's Best Hotels and Resorts
Australia & New Zealand's Best Hotels and Resorts

THE GUIDE AT A GLANCE

The book is carefully structured both to convey an understanding of the city and its culture and to guide readers through its attractions and activities:

◆ The Best Of section at the front of the book helps you to prioritise. The first spread contains the Top Sights, while Editor's Choice details unique experiences, the best buys or other recommendations.

◆ To understand London, you need to know something of its past. The city's history and culture are described in authoritative essays written by specialists in their fields who have lived in and documented the city for many years.

◆ The Places section details all the attractions worth seeing. The main places of interest are coordinated by number with the maps.

◆ A list of recommended restaurants, bars and cafés is printed at the end of each chapter.

◆ Photographs throughout the book are chosen not only to illustrate geography and buildings, but also to convey the moods of the city and the life of its people.

◆ The Travel Tips section includes all the practical information you will need, divided into five key sections: transport, accommodation, shopping, activities (including nightlife, events, tours and sports) and an A–Z of practical tips. Information may be located quickly by using the index on the back cover flap of the book.

◆ Two detailed street atlases are included at the back of the book, complete with a full index. On the second one, you will find all the restaurants and hotels plotted for your convenience.

PLACES & SIGHTS

Colour-coding at the top of every page makes it easy to find each area in the book. The colours correspond with those on the orientation map on pages 66–7.

A locator map pinpoints the specific area covered in each chapter. The page reference at the top indicates where to find a detailed map of the area highlighted in red.

Margin tips provide extra little snippets of information, whether it's a practical tip, a whimsical quote, an historical fact or advice on shopping and eating or things to do with children.

A four-colour map provides a bird's-eye view of the area covered in the chapter, with the main attractions co-ordinated by number with the main text.

PHOTO FEATURES

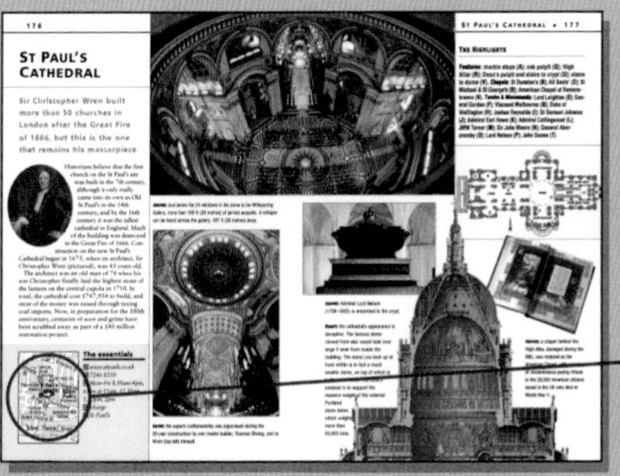
176

ST PAUL'S CATHEDRAL

Sir Christopher Wren built more than 50 churches in London after the Great Fire of 1666, but this is the one that remains his masterpiece

The essentials

ST PAUL'S CATHEDRAL ◆ 177

The Highlights

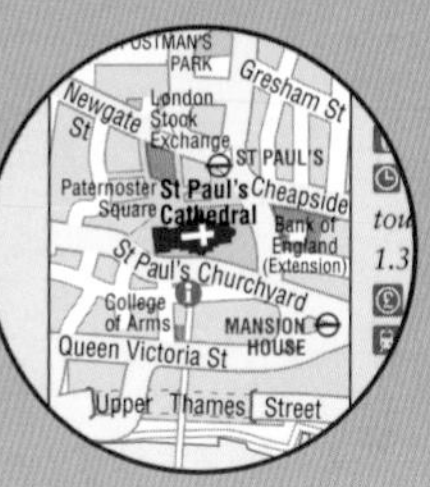

Photo Features offer visual coverage of London's major sights. The map shows the sight's location, while "The essentials" panel conveys practical information: address, contact details, website, opening times, and whether there's a charge.

RESTAURANT LISTINGS

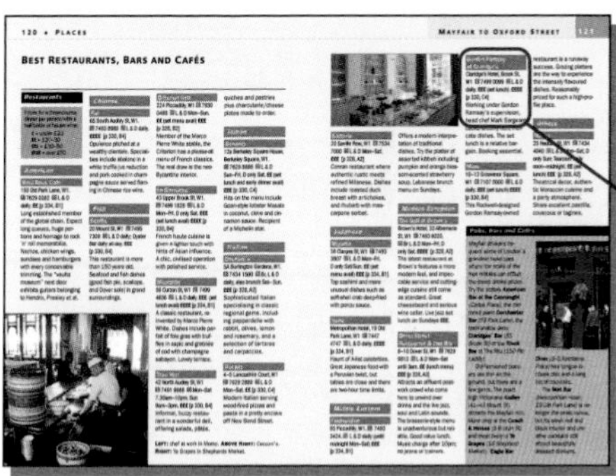
120 ◆ PLACES

BEST RESTAURANTS, BARS AND CAFÉS

MAYFAIR TO OXFORD STREET 121

Restaurant listings feature the best establishments within each area, giving the address, phone number, opening times and price category followed by a review. The grid reference refers to the atlas at the back of the book.

Gordon Ramsay at Claridge's

Claridge's Hotel, Brook St, W1 ☎ 7499 0099 ⓒ L & D daily. **£££** (set lunch). **££££** [p 330, C4]

Working under Gordon Ramsay's supervision, head chef Mark Sargeant

TRAVEL TIPS

298 ◆ TRAVEL TIPS

ACTIVITIES

THE ARTS, NIGHTLIFE, FESTIVALS, SHOPPING AND SPORTS

ACTIVITIES ◆ 299

...Operas are perform... ...ir original language and tick... ...ts are very expensive. Dressy affair. Tube: Covent Garden.

Classical Music

Barbican Arts Centre, Silk Street, EC2. Tel: 7638 8891. Home to the London Symphony Orchestra and the English Chamber Orchestra. This huge concrete complex built for the arts ... London's major class...

Advice-packed Travel Tips provide all the practical knowledge you'll need before and during your trip: how to get there, getting around, where to stay and what to do. The A–Z section is a handy summary of practical information, arranged alphabetically.

Contents

Best of London

Introduction

History

Features

Insights

Places

Restaurants & Bars

Travel Tips

Maps

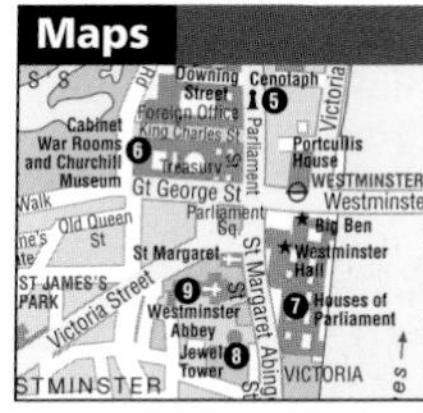

The Best of London: Top Sights

At a glance, everything you won't want to miss, from long-established icons like Tower Bridge and Big Ben to exciting new landmarks such as Tate Modern and the London Eye

▽**Big Ben and the Houses of Parliament**
The clock tower of this flamboyant Gothic-style building is a symbol of London. Guided tours of the Houses of Parliament can be arranged during the summer recess in August and September.
See page 75

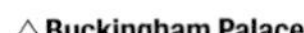

△**Buckingham Palace**
The best time to see the palace is during the Changing of the Guard. If you would like to see inside, then you must time your visit to coincide with the Queen's annual trip to Balmoral (late Jul–Sep) when some of the State Rooms of the palace open for guided tours.
See page 80

◁**The London Eye**
For the best views in London take a trip on the London Eye on the South Bank. The stately wheel takes 30 minutes to rotate, allowing plenty of time for picking out London's sights. On a fine day you will be able to see for 25 miles (40 km).
See page 186

◁**Trafalgar Square**
London's best-loved square has shooting fountains and Nelson's Column and is overlooked by the National Gallery.
See page 99

▷**Piccadilly Circus**
Presiding over this gateway to the West End and Theatreland is the famous statue of Eros.
See page 89

▽**Tate Modern**
For modern art in an inspired setting, visit this power station-turned-art-gallery on the South Bank.
See page 198

Tate Modern

◁**St Paul's Cathedral**
Built after the Great Fire of London of 1666, St Paul's is Christopher Wren's greatest work.
See page 176

▷**The British Museum**
This immense museum contains some of the world's most important treasures from antiquity.
See page 144

▷**Tower of London**
Established by William the Conqueror, the Tower has a long and bloody history. *See page 178*

▽ **Tower Bridge**
The famous bascule bridge is a triumph of Victorian engineering.
See page 195

THE BEST OF LONDON: EDITOR'S CHOICE

Here are our ideas on what to do once you've seen London's top sights, plus some tips and tricks even Londoners won't always know

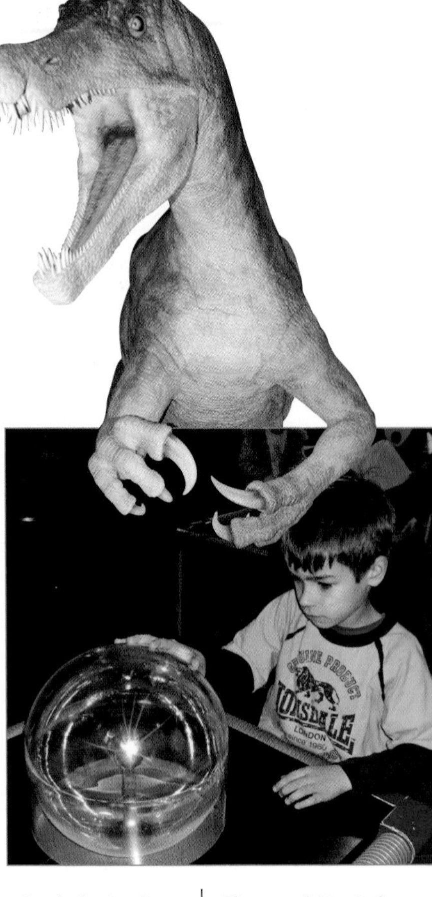

BEST FOR CHILDREN

- **Look and learn Investigate** in the **Natural History Museum** allows children to weigh, measure and examine specimens. Next door, the **Science Museum** has the **Launch Pad**, a great hands-on section. *See pages 218 and 214.*
- **Museum of Childhood** This outpost of the V&A appeals to adults and children alike. *See page 251.*
- **On the Wild Side** London Zoo in Regent's Park is one of the world's top zoos. *See page 128.*
- **The London Aquarium** Sharks, piranhas, touch pools and much more. *See page 185.*
- **The River Thames** Moored on the Thames, *HMS Belfast*, a World War II battleship, is suitable for older children *(see page 194)*. Younger ones will enjoy the piratical-looking ***Golden Hinde***, a replica of Sir Francis Drake's ship *(see page 192)*. Or take a tour on a **Duck**, an amphibious vessel used in World War II. *See page 315.*
- **Madame Tussauds** Teenagers love spotting their favourite celebrities, even if they are made of wax. *See pages 132–3*
- **London Dungeon** Scary fun ideal for 10–14-year-olds. *See page 194.*
- **London Transport Museum** A huge hit with younger children. *See page 105*
- **Ice-skating** In winter, ice rinks spring up outside the Natural History Museum and Somerset House. There is also a circular rink at Broadgate. *See pages 151 and 171.*
- **Playgrounds** Best is the Diana, Princess of Wales, Memorial Playground. *See page 211.*
- **Toy shops** Visit **Hamleys** in Regent Street or **Harrods**. *See pages 119 and 204.*

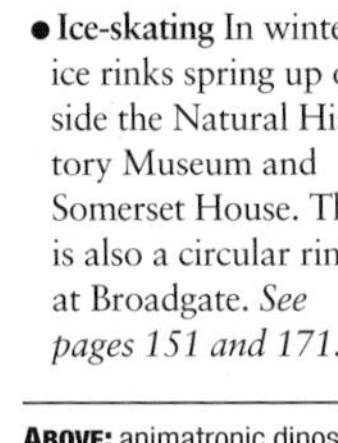

ABOVE: animatronic dinosaur in the Natural History Museum and hands-on fun at the Launch Pad in the Science Museum.

BEST VIEWS

- **The London Eye** Unbeatable vistas whichever way you look. *See page 186.*
- **Monument** Climb the 311 steps for views over the City. *See page 172.*
- **Waterloo Bridge** Panoramas day and night. *See page 187.*
- **Westminster Cathedral** Take the lift to the top of the 330-ft (100-metre) tower. *See page 79.*
- **Wellington Arch** The balconies offer sneak views into the gardens of Buckingham Palace. *See page 204.*
- **Richmond Hill** The view from here is protected by an act of Parliament. *See page 238.*
- **Parliament Hill** Far-reaching views across London. *See page 245.*
- **Restaurants and bars with views** include **Café 7** *(see page 197)* at Tate Modern, the **Oxo Tower** *(see page 196)*, **La Pont de la Tour** *(see page 197)*, **Babylon** *(see page 213)* and **Vertigo 42** *(see page 175)*

BEST WALKS

- **Old and new London** An introductory walk, starting from Westminster Abbey, crossing Westminster Bridge, strolling along the South Bank past the London Eye, Tate Modern and Shakespeare's Globe, and then crossing the Millennium Bridge to St Paul's Cathedral. *See pages 77–8, 184–190 and 159.*
- **Hampstead Heath** Meadows, woods, lakes and ponds, plus great views over London. *See page 245.*
- **Hyde Park and Kensington Gardens** Sculptures, fountains, gardens and playgrounds in the centre of the city. *See pages 210–11.*
- **Regent's Canal** Walk all or part of the 14 km (8½ miles) from Paddington to Limehouse, taking in Camden Lock and Little Venice. *See page 244.*
- **Richmond** Offers fabulous views, a deer park, interesting pubs and 17th-century Ham House. *See pages 238–9.*

BELOW: Pearly Kings and a Pearly Queen. **RIGHT:** crossing the Millennium Bridge.

ONLY IN LONDON

- **Harrods** The store that has everything. *See page 204.*
- **Shakespeare's Globe** The play's the thing, as in Elizabethan days. *See page 190.*
- **Royal Pageantry** The Changing of the Guard ceremony takes place at Buckingham Palace daily at 11.30am (alternate days in winter). *See page 82.*
- **Pearly Kings and Queens** You'll spot these colourful characters at East End festivals and markets. *See page 22.*
- **The V&A** The world's largest collection of decorative and applied arts. *See pages 206.*

HISTORIC PUBS

- **The George** This pub off Borough High Street, rebuilt in 1676, is London's only galleried coaching inn. *See page 197.*
- **Black Friar** Built in 1875 on the site of the Black Friars Monastery, this is London's only Arts and Crafts pub. The marble interior carries bronze friezes depicting the activities of monks. *See page 156.*
- **Lamb and Flag** Traditional pub tucked down a tiny alleyway in the heart of Covent Garden. *See page 106.*
- **The Grenadier** Hidden away in a quiet cobbled mews, this pub used to be the mess of the Duke of Wellington's officers. *See page 229.*
- **Jerusalem Tavern** Once an 18th-century coffee shop, this is now an intimate pub with cubicles, Georgian-style furniture and ales from Suffolk's St Peter's Brewery. *See page 175.*
- **The Mayflower** It was at this waterside pub in Rotherhithe that the Pilgrim Fathers moored their ship before setting off for Plymouth and thence the New World in 1620. *See page 195.*
- **Ye Old Cheshire Cheese** Famous olde-worlde pub off Fleet Street, rebuilt after the Great Fire but retaining a medieval crypt. Frequented by many well-known literary figures in the past, including Charles Dickens and Dr Samuel Johnson. *See page 155.*

DISTINCTIVE HOTELS

- **The Savoy** Grand riverside hotel, soon to be refubished, near Covent Garden. *See page 284.*
- **Browns** Intimate luxury in the heart of Mayfair. *See page 285.*
- **Blakes** One of the first boutique hotels. *See page 289.*
- **Hazlitt's** Early 18th-century property in the heart of Soho. *See page 285.*

ABOVE: the Black Friar's wonderfully ornate interior.
FAR RIGHT: dancer at Notting Hill Carnival held on the last weekend in August, and the Trooping of the Colour ceremony celebrating the Queen's official birthday in June.

SUMMER IN THE CITY

- **River Cruises** Cruise down to Greenwich or the Thames Barrier, or up to Hampton Court Palace. *See page 307.*
- **Open-air drama** Watch Shakespeare at the Globe Theatre on the South Bank or in Regent's Park. *See pages 190 and 128.*
- **The City in Bloom** See whole gardens recreated at the **Chelsea Flower Show** held in late May in Chelsea or visit the lovely **Rose Garden** (June through to late autumn) in Regent's Park. *See pages 225 and 127.*
- **Sporting Greats** See tennis played at Wimbledon and cricket played at Lord's. *See page 305.*
- **Cool off** Swim in the bathing ponds on Hampstead Heath or in the Serpentine in Hyde Park. Or join the regulars at the Oasis, a heated outdoor pool in Holborn. *See page 306.*
- **Notting Hill Carnival** Held on the last weekend in August, this is Europe's biggest carnival. *See page 304.*

BEST FESTIVALS

- **Notting Hill Carnival** This is Europe's biggest street festival, with Caribbean bands, extravagant costumes and floats. Last weekend in August.
- **Chinese New Year** Dancing dragons and exotic food in Soho's Chinatown. Late January/early February.
- **Trooping the Colour** The Queen rides out on Horse Guards Parade, with the Household Cavalry in red tunics and bearskin hats. The Saturday closest to 10 June.
- **Lord Mayor's Show** The Lord Mayor rides out in his gilded coach from the Guildhall to the Law Courts. Second Saturday in November.
- **Last Night of the Proms** Exuberant finale to annual BBC-sponsored Henry Wood Promenade Concerts in the Albert Hall and Hyde Park. Saturday night in mid-September.

For a full listing of festivals see pages 303

MONEY-SAVING TIPS

Half-price Theatre Tickets The 'tkts' booth in Leicester Square sells same-day tickets for West End shows at up to 50 percent off, plus a £2.50 service fee (Mon–Sat 10am–7pm, Sun noon–3pm). There is an another branch at Canary Wharf (Mon–Sat 10am–3.30pm). Tickets for some plays at the National Theatre can be purchased for £10 through the Travelex scheme (see page 44 for details).

Museums and Attractions The national museums and galleries (including Tate Modern, Tate Britain, the National Gallery, National Portrait Gallery, British Museum, Science Museum, Natural History Museum, the Victoria and Albert Museum, Imperial War Museum and National Maritime Museum) are free. Most other museums and attractions have entrance charges. The London Pass, allows free entry to some 56 attractions. At press time, prices for an adult pass ranged from £39/approx. US$77 for a one-day pass (including travel on Tube and bus) to £112/$220 for a six-day pass including travel (children under 15 £20/$40–£70/$140). Details: tel: 01664 485020; www.londonpass.com.

Public Transport The Underground (Tube) is expensive compared with most metro sytems in Europe, but money-saving Travelcards and passes are available and children under the age of 11 can travel free anywhere on the network (as well as the Docklands Light Railway and buses), providing they are accompanied by an adult *(see page 278)*. Buses are quite a bit cheaper than the Tube and offer a sight-seeing tour along the way. Alternatively walk – many places, especially in the West End, are closer than you might think.

WHITEREAD
ROUSSEAU
ROUSSEAU

HOLLYWOOD
PRODUCTION
DIRECTOR
CAMERA

LONDON'S ALLURE

What attracts millions of visitors is a potent mixture of continuity and tradition plus the excitement of never knowing what they're going to find round the next corner

Henry James described the capital as a "giant animated encyclopaedia with people for pages". With all its variety and history, it's hard to know where to start as a tourist, but James's emphasis is a good one. Even though the immensity of London makes it hard to embrace as a whole and you don't find long-time residents proclaiming their feelings through "I ❤ London" stickers, the people and the culture matter as much as the buildings. To most residents, the city is a collection of communities or villages, once independent but long since swallowed up, along with much of the surrounding countryside, by the expanding metropolis.

At the centre of this patchwork city is a common area of shared London, a London of work and play. This book deals primarily with shared London, the essential London of the West End, the City and South Bank, but it also covers some of the interesting local "villages" such as Hampstead, Islington, Greenwich and Brixton.

London, it is sometimes said, is as unrepresentative of the United Kingdom as New York is of the United States. There's some truth in this. Both cities have astonishingly cosmopolitan populations, their restaurants are almost as diverse as their immigrants, they are important centres of international finance, they pioneer the latest fashions, and their range of shops and theatres is absurdly disproportionate to their size.

But London is umbilically linked to the rest of Britain in some crucial respects. Unlike New York, it is a capital city, spawning governmental institutions. It is also an ancient city, dating back to Roman times. Foreign forces have not occupied it since the Normans arrived in 1066 and, although it was bombed during World War II, most of its iconic buildings survived.

As a result, it exudes a palpable sense of the nation's history. You can walk in the footsteps of Shakespeare, or Dickens, or Churchill. You can journey along the Thames, as Henry VIII did. You can visit the room in the Tower of London where Sir Francis Drake lived out his last days. You can drink in the pubs where Dr Samuel Johnson drank in the 18th century. You can sit in the reading room where Karl Marx studied. This book will show you how to do all these things, and more. ❑

PRECEDING PAGES: the Houses of Parliament; Tate Modern from the Millennium Bridge.
LEFT: a vintage magazine retailer in Soho.

WHO LIVES IN LONDON?

There have been racial tensions, even riots. But the city has absorbed many waves of immigrants and, with more than a quarter of central London's population born outside the UK, is a truly international metropolis

Celts, Romans, Saxons, Angles, Jutes, Danes and Normans were the first to tumble into London's melting pot. The first Far Eastern immigrants arrived in 1579, followed by Indians, Huguenots, Irish and the dispossessed of eastern Europe. And always there was the tide of new blood from the rest of Britain, drawn to London by hopes of fame, fortune, anonymity, or simply a new start. Today, nearly one in three of London's 7½ million residents is from a minority ethnic group, and around 300 languages are spoken.

The Cockney

Is there, then, any such thing as a "true" Londoner? Cockneys would seem to qualify, but being a cockney is as much a state of mind as it is a turn of phrase, and it is not exclusively genetic. Cockneys no longer need to be white and Anglo-Saxon; there are Italian, West Indian, Jewish and Pakistani cockneys. Nor do they necessarily have to be Londoners; the high cost of living has driven many out, and neighbouring towns such as Stevenage have large cockney populations. So what then makes a cockney? Certain traditions, being a member of an identifiable urban group, a distinctive language – and a quick sense of humour.

The original definition of a cockney – someone born within the sound of Bow bells, the clarion of St Mary-le-Bow in Cheapside in the City – would today exclude most Londoners.

Cockney is a London accent with no use of the aspirant "h", the "t" in the middle of words such as "butter", or the final "g" in words ending "ing". Cockneys traditionally spoke in a rhyming slang said to have originated among barrow boys who didn't want their customers to understand their conversations. A "whistle" is a suit, short for whistle and flute, "trouble and strife" means wife.

News vendors and market traders are often

LEFT: a butler poses for the camera in Chelsea. **RIGHT:** entering into the spirit of the Lord Mayor's Show, an occasion for lavish pageantry.

cockneys – they are shrewd, street-wise people, who prefer to work for themselves and who value freedom more than wealth. The aristocracy of the cockneys are the pearly kings and queens, whose suits are embroidered with mother-of-pearl buttons – a marketing gimmick in the 19th century and now worn at festivals (see www.pearlysociety.co.uk for upcoming events).

Century of immigration

In the 19th century the port of London was the largest in the world, and clippers such as the *Cutty Sark* had races to bring the year's first tea crops home from China. The Chinese community was in Limehouse, where Sherlock Holmes went to mull over his latest conundrums in the relaxing atmosphere of the opium dens. Ming Street, Peking Street and Mandarin Street are the sole legacy of the community that was heavily bombed in World War II. Today, Chinatown, called Tong Yan Kai (Chinese Street), is around Gerrard Street in Soho. Here resident Chinese opened restaurants during the war years to cater for British and US forces. Although the streets and annual New Year's festivities mark this out as the centre of London's Chinese population of 55,000, they live in all parts of the capital.

The traumas of 19th-century Europe led to

THE LONDON CABBIE

Perhaps the closest most visitors get to meeting a true Londoner is when they catch a cab. Taxi drivers, or cabbies, are experts on the city, and are essential to its life, coursing through its veins in their black cells (not that all the cabs are black any more: advertising has turned some of them into perambulating billboards).

Cabbies take pride in their job, knowing that nowhere else in the world does a taxi driver need to know so much in order to qualify for a licence to work. Would-be drivers must spend up to four years learning London in minute detail (called "doing the Knowledge"). They do this by travelling the streets of the metropolis on a moped, working out a multitude of routes from a clipboard mounted on the handlebars. Having acquired "the Knowledge", a driver must then pass a special driving test.

About 20,000 drivers work in London, of which half are owner-drivers. The others either hire vehicles from the big fleets or work night shifts in someone else's cab. In all, there are more than 15,000 vehicles. The classic cab, known as the FX4, was launched in 1959 and some models are still going strong. The newer Metrocab, although more spacious, has taken a while to find the same place in customers' – and cabbies' – affections.

Only a small proportion of drivers are women, though the number is increasing. It is also very much a white, working-class occupation, and traditionally a large percentage of drivers are Jewish. Whatever their origins, most London taxi drivers, particularly the older ones, have a reputation for being garrulous.

the mass exodus of Jews, and east London became England's Staten Island, with half a dozen refugee ships arriving every day. The Jews settled around the East End, giving it a dominant character. Since then, the community of around 250,000 has dispersed – to Stamford Hill, Golders Green and Finchley.

The Irish had been coming to Britain since the Anglo-Norman invasion of Ireland in the late 12th century. Mainly Catholic, they suffered for their faith in the Gordon riots of 1780, a dozen years before St Patrick's Catholic Church, which today holds services in Spanish and Cantonese, was built in Soho.

Irish immigration during the 19th century was brought about largely through the great famine of 1846–48, and many who came spoke only Gaelic. The Irish were a significant force in the 19th century's building boom, especially on the railways. Many settled in Camden and Kilburn, north of the rail termini at Euston and King's Cross. Today's 256,000 population is scattered across north and west London.

Londoners frequently complain about overcrowding. But the population was far higher in 1931 when it reached over 8 million, at least half a million more than today.

European settlers

Following the German invasion of Poland in 1939, the 33,000-strong Polish military in exile settled as a state-within-a-state in Mayfair and Kensington. Their pilots shot down one in seven German planes in the 1940 Battle of Britain. At the end of the war 150,000 were settled in London.

The Italians first settled around the church of St Peter's in Clerkenwell, in an area known to the residents as The Hill and to Londoners as Little Italy. The population was at its height from 1900 to 1930 but, when Italians living in Britain were interned during World War II, their role as restaurateurs began to be eroded

FAR LEFT: West African costumes are common in south and east London, especially Dalston, Peckham, New Cross and Woolwich. **ABOVE LEFT:** easy rider. **LEFT:** a classic London cab. **ABOVE:** Brick Lane in east London, centre of the Bangladeshi community.

by Greek Cypriots, who had been filtering into Britain since the 1920s. Disruptions on Cyprus caused further immigration in the 1950s and 1960s, with Greek and Turkish Cypriots amicably settling side by side in north London. The densest Greek community is around Green Lanes in Haringey, north London, where traditions are maintained in male-only cafés.

Where to Spot the Royals

On the second Saturday in June when the Queen's birthday is officially celebrated, she travels by carriage to Horse Guards Parade for the ceremony of Trooping the Colour. In November she is transported by state coach for the state opening of Parliament, escorted along the Mall by the Household Cavalry. Also in November, she attends the service of remembrance at the Cenotaph in Whitehall. In July a member of the family takes the salute at the Royal Tournament at Earl's Court. The engagements of the royal family are listed in the *Court Circular*, published daily in the better national newspapers.

If you are more interested in spotting princes William or Harry, you need to go (or get yourself invited) to one of the more exclusive nightclubs. Current royal favourites are Boujis (members only) in Thurloe Street, South Kensington, the Cuckoo Club (members only) in Swallow Street, Mayfair, and Mahiki in Dover Street, Mayfair.

Seasonal Arabs

In summer, when Middle East temperatures become too hot for comfort, London has traditionally attracted many Gulf Arabs, who spend much of their time enjoying the coolness of the parks and the shopping opportunities. First coming in the wake of the oil price hikes of the 1970s, they funded a mosque in Regent's Park, which can hold 1,800.

Seasonal Arabs are less common since the war in Iraq, but there are resident communities from Egypt, Iraq and Morocco, with a total of around 50,000. Most live in Kensington and Bayswater, and they congregate in Edgware Road, north of Marble Arch, where their restaurants, cafés and shops shine into the night. London is one of the largest Arab media centres.

Commonwealth immigrants

The 20th century saw immigration mostly from the Commonwealth, and the resulting ethnic influence extends as far as Heathrow. The airport itself was largely built by construction workers from India's Punjab. After the Sikhs came the Caribbeans, who found work on London's buses, Underground railway network and in the health service.

But while London likes to think of itself as a multicultural society, it has few black or Asian top administrators or civil servants. You can pass through the City or the Inns of Court or Docklands without meeting a business tycoon, leading lawyer or top editor from the settlers' communities. Until the general election of 1987, there were no ethnic-minority members of Parliament; that situation has since changed and there are now around a dozen.

Why there's a welcome

Partly because London's vast number of hotels, bars and restaurants have a chronic need for cheap but hard-working labour, immigration has been a less contentious issue in the capital than elsewhere in the country. Many caterers welcomed the expansion of the European Union in 2004 because it gave them legitimate access to affordable help from eastern Europe. But even in London there are worries about the pressures migrants place on public services.

LEFT: the Queen still draws the crowds when she is out and about. **TOP:** a favourite pastime. **ABOVE:** a Chelsea pensioner in St James's Park. **ABOVE RIGHT:** café scene in Knightsbridge.

Generally, though, London welcomes every type of visitor. Karl Marx and Mahatma Gandhi studied here. Charles de Gaulle lived in exile here. Writers Paul Theroux, Salman Rushdie and V.S. Naipaul chose to work here. Madonna made London her home. Even Harrods, the quintessentially English store, has been owned by an Egyptian, Mohamed Al-Fayed, since 1985, and it sells 40 percent of its merchandise to tourists. ❑

HOT PROPERTY

Over the past decade or so the dream of living in London has become unattainable for many young people unless they are prepared to rent with friends or live with family.

London's long overheated property market has pushed the average price of a London home to over £380,000, with properties in the posher areas, such as Kensington and Chelsea averaging £1,300,000, and seeing rises of up to £600,000 a year. A property crash has been predicted for at least five years, but a buoyant City and very wealthy international buyers (Russian, Arab and American) looking for a London base continue to keep it afloat.

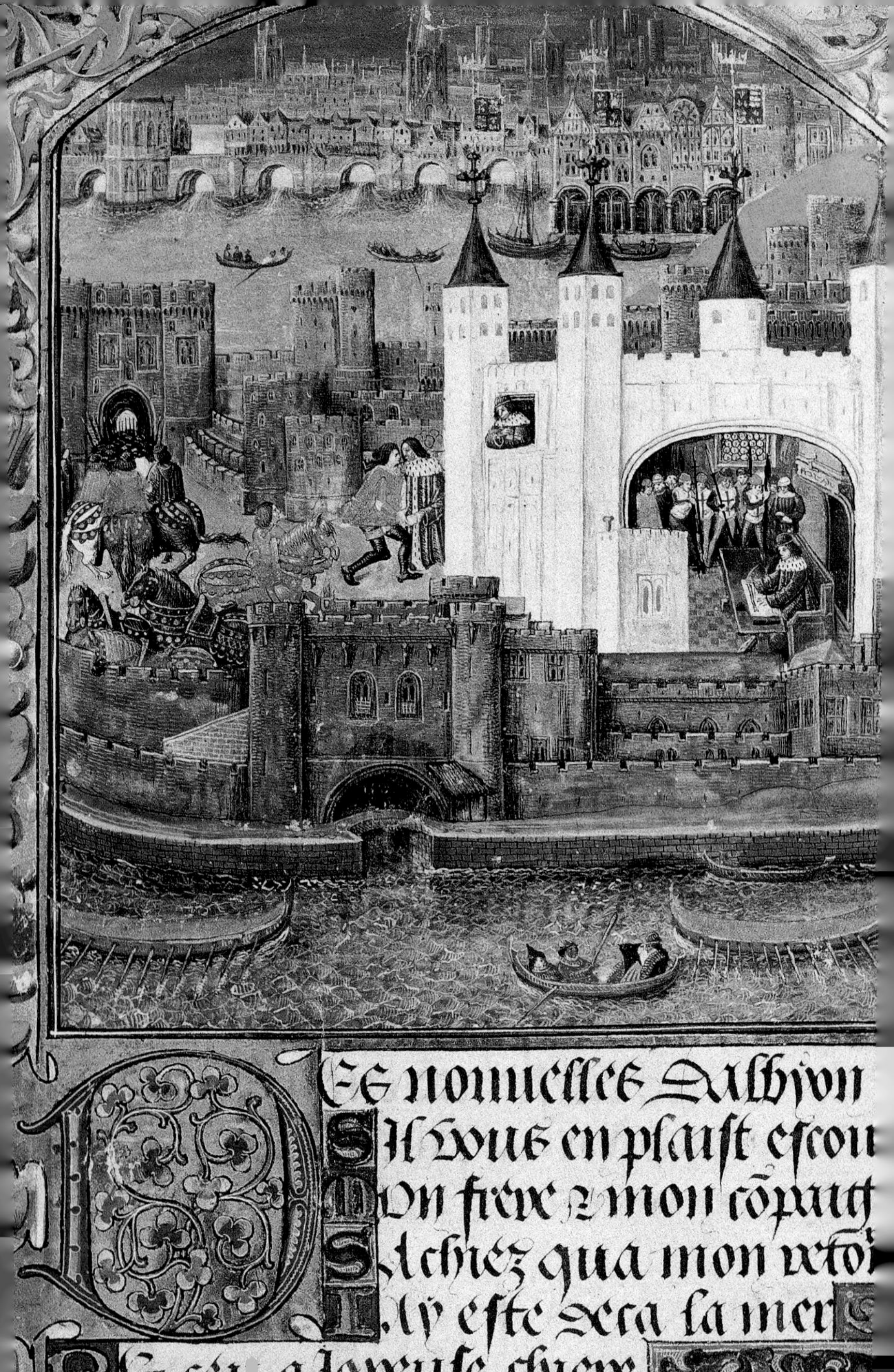
Des nouvelles dalbyon
Sil vous en plaist escou
Mon frere et mon copaig
Sachiez qua mon retou
Ay este deca la mer

THE MAKING OF LONDON

Fire, plague, population explosions, aerial bombing, economic recessions, urban blight, terrorism... London has survived everything history could throw at it, yet it has remained one of the world's most seductive cities

In AD 43 the invading Roman army chose gravel banks between what is now Southwark and the City as the site of a strategically important bridge. Roman London, the Celtic "Llyn-din", the fort by the lake, quickly took shape, but suffered a setback 17 years later when British guerrillas led by Queen Boudicca attacked and burned areas around Lombard Street, Gracechurch Street and Walbrook so completely that archaeologists have identified a change in the colour of the earth.

A rebuilt Londinium, as the Romans called it, had by AD 100 supplanted Colchester as the capital as well as the military and trading centre of Britain. But in 410, Rome itself was threatened by the Germanic races from the north and was forced to recall its garrison from England. Culture withered and the fabric of Londinium crumbled as the Anglo-Saxons allowed the alien Roman buildings to become derelict.

Roman Londinium had a timber bridge, quays, warehouses, a governor's palace, baths and amphitheatre. Roads radiated to Colchester, York, Chester, Exeter, Bath and Canterbury.

Recovery and expansion

But the city's position made it a natural trading centre and gradually it recovered its importance. In the 8th century the literary monk, the Venerable Bede, called it the "Market of the World". South of London Bridge, a residential area developed, later known as the Borough.

Two miles (3 km) upriver on Thorney Island, the Monastery of St Peter was established, later the great West Minster. Following his accession in 1042, Edward the Confessor moved his court from the City to Westminster, thereby creating the division of royal and mercantile power still in place today. In lieu of making the usual pilgrimage to Rome, he set about rebuilding the abbey, where succeeding kings were crowned, married and, until George III (d.1820), buried.

LEFT: view of London from the poems of Charles Duke of Orleans, 1394–1465. **RIGHT:** meeting Julius Caesar's invasion of Britain in 55 BC.

City landmarks

In 1066 William the Conqueror brought the laws of Normandy to England, and gave London privileges that are still honoured today. Self-direction in local affairs was satisfied by the election of a first mayor in 1192, with aldermen and a court. A new St Paul's Cathedral was started and the great keep of the White Tower completed in 1097. Westminster Hall was designed as a banqueting hall but, although the largest building of its kind in Europe, fell short of William's dreams – he said it was "a mere bedchamber" compared to what he had expected. By 1176 work had begun on a stone London Bridge, and the suburb on the south bank was growing.

Union and plague

The city had grown to 50,000 by the time of Geoffrey Chaucer, the "father of English poetry" – this in spite of the "Black Death" of 1348, when some 200 bodies a day were taken outside the city and buried in mass graves. This virulent bubonic plague, carried by rats and fleas, ravaged much of Europe but had a particularly devastating effect on London because of the city's narrow streets and insanitary housing.

London stopped growing in the 14th century. The City (now with a capital C) quite simply had no ambitions to get any bigger. Had it wanted to expand, it would have had to change its character, perhaps endangering in the process its hard-won privileges and sacrificing its unique position as a major European market and port. Whatever was happening outside the walls, the City maintained a blinkered detachment that was not disturbed until Queen Victoria's reign.

The Golden Age

The much married and celebrated divorcé Henry VIII (1491–1547) almost qualifies as the "father" of modern London, though the changes he brought about were the outcome of a bid for

personal freedom from the Church. In 1536, after the Pope refused to annul his marriage to Catherine of Aragon so that he could marry Anne Boleyn, Henry cut all ties with Roman Catholicism. He pronounced himself head of the Church of England and persuaded Parliament to authorise the dissolution of the monasteries, their property and revenues being granted to the Crown. Cardinal Wolsey's house was added to an expanding palace in Whitehall. Hyde Park and St James's were enclosed as deer parks.

Convent (now Covent) Garden and Clerkenwell, Stepney and Shoreditch, Kennington and Lambeth all expanded during this time, taking London's population to 200,000. A lasting monument to the era is Henry VIII's Hampton Court Palace, southwest of London *(see page 239)*.

Henry's daughter, Elizabeth I, whose mother, Anne Boleyn, had been beheaded for supposed adultery, came to the throne in 1558. She was truly London's queen and the "Golden Age" began, in commerce, education and the arts. William Shakespeare, a Londoner by adoption, was far from adulated by the authorities. When the Lord Mayor banned theatrical performances from London, he and his fellow playwright Ben Jonson moved outside his jurisdiction to new sites on the south bank of the Thames, an area notorious for bear pits, brothels and prisons.

TOP LEFT: William the Conqueror, miniature from *Flores Historiarum*, Matthew Paris (1250–52).
ABOVE LEFT: Westminster Hall, c.1460.
ABOVE: detail, *London from Southwark*, c.1630 by an unknown artist. **ABOVE RIGHT:** *Queen Elizabeth I*, attributed to George Gower.

Little survives of Tudor London's wood-framed houses with their oversailing upper storeys. But a flavour can be found in the Old Curiosity Shop near Lincoln's Inn (see page 154).

Revolution and style

Being childless, the "Virgin Queen" Elizabeth chose James VI of Scotland to succeed her as James I of England, thus launching the Stuart dynasty. Religious conflict continued, and a Catholic faction attempted to blow up Parliament in the infamous "Gunpowder Plot". On 5 November 1605, Guy (Guido) Fawkes was caught about to ignite barrels of gunpowder in the cellars. Fawkes was executed, but 5 November, Guy Fawkes Day, is still marked with fireworks and the burning of an effigy.

Against a background of conflict between the king and Parliament, London responded to a new influence: the Italian architecture of Palladio as seen through the work of Inigo Jones. The purity of Jones's style is best seen in the Queen's House at Greenwich, begun in 1613. Six years later came the Banqueting House in Whitehall.

Water, pestilence and fire

Great tragedies lay ahead for London. In 1665 the inadequate water supply and lack of sanitation brought the dreaded plague to the overcrowded city, and before it ran its course 100,000 inhabitants died. The Great Fire, less than a year later, came as if to cleanse the stricken city. From a baker's shop on Pudding Lane, Eastcheap, the flames raged for five days, watched and recorded by the great 17th-century diarist Samuel Pepys. Miraculously, only half a dozen people died.

After the fire, 13,000 houses and 87 parish churches lay in ruins, but rebuilding was immediately planned.

Bunhill Fields

Many victims of the Great Plague of 1665 were buried in plague pits in Bunhill Fields on City Road *(see page 164)*, where these days city workers eat their sandwiches among the tombstones. The cemetery, was specially built for plague victims, though the site had previously operated as a deposit for old bones from St Paul's churchyard where space was at a premium. The burial ground was not consecrated and was later associated with Nonconformists, including many notable ones such as Daniel Defoe, John Bunyan, author of *Pilgrim's Progress,* and the poet and artist William Blake.

Wren's dream

Christopher Wren, Surveyor General to the Crown, was inspired by Paris. London, too, he thought, should have *rond-points*, vistas and streets laid out in a grid pattern. But Wren's best ideas were never realised. Expediency dictated that the new should rise quickly on the sites of the old, with one prudent difference: new buildings were made of brick, not wood.

Wren turned his inventive powers to rebuilding 50 of the City's damaged churches. His achievements lie in the individuality of their soaring towers and steeples which rise above the rooftops. In 1675 work began on his masterpiece, a new St Paul's Cathedral.

House building spread through the green fields beyond Soho towards Hyde Park and across the Tyburn road. As the ripple of this 18th-century building ring moved outwards, the older centre was coming to the end of its

useful life. The need for better communications brought demands for another river crossing. Westminster Bridge was completed in 1751, but nearly 20 years passed before the City had its own second bridge, at Blackfriars. Whitehall was beginning to take on its 20th-century character. The palace of kings was replaced by the palaces of government.

Splendour and sweatshops

By 1800 London was poised on the brink of a population explosion. In the next 35 years it was to double in size – and the railways were yet to come. While Britain was at war with Napoleonic France, though, work on public buildings necessarily withered, but housing swelled with the increases in civil servants. Paddington and Marylebone, Camberwell and Kensington, Knightsbridge and Chelsea forged their identities.

Unlike the West End, the East End suffered ribbon building along the roads to Essex. Whitechapel High Street was "pestered with cottages", and Wapping with mean tenements. It was an area vulnerable to the impact of new developments in commerce following the Industrial Revolution. Canals had already linked the Thames with the industrial Midlands. Docks cruelly dismembered the riverside parishes. In 1825, 1,250 houses were swept away for St Katharine's Dock alone. The inhabitants were compressed, sardine-style, into accommodation nearby. The character of the modern East End was in the making. "Sweatshops" and the labour to go with them multiplied in this fertile soil of ruthless competition, poverty and immigration.

> *London became increasingly affluent in the early 19th century. Visiting in 1814, the Emperor of Russia asked, "Where are your poor?" Clearly he had not been east of the Tower of London.*

By the 1830s the Industrial Revolution was making its impact on the Thames below Wapping. The marshy pools of the Isle of Dogs, long used for duck shooting and hunting, were deepened to make the West and East India Docks. Wharves and shipyards lined the banks of the river itself in Blackwall, Deptford and Greenwich. With all this activity, London's air was dense with smog – smoke mixed with fog – although this word had not yet been coined.

LEFT: *The Great Fire of London*, 1666, by an anonymous artist, c.1675. **LEFT:** tomb in Bunhill Fields. **ABOVE:** portrait of Samuel Pepys by John Riley. **RIGHT:** *Gin Lane*, an engraving by William Hogarth, whose works vividly depict 18th-century London life.

Congestion and crime

By the early 19th century London was becoming impossibly congested, so bridges were built at Waterloo (1811–17) and Hammersmith (1824–27). London Bridge was rebuilt (1823–31) and foot passengers given a tunnel under the Thames at Wapping.

Courts of law and prisons responded to rising crime, while gentlemen's clubs met the Regency passion for gambling. In Bloomsbury's Gower Street, London University was born, and a fruit and vegetable market came to Covent Garden. Great collections were housed in the British Museum and National Gallery.

Londoners were on the move. In 1829 Mr Shillibeer introduced them to the omnibus, and the first steam train arrived with the London & Greenwich Railway of 1838. Terminal stations followed at Euston, King's Cross and Paddington by 1853; at Blackfriars, Charing Cross and St Pancras by 1871.

Cleaning up the Thames

At Westminster, the Houses of Parliament burnt down in 1834 when a furnace overheated, but soon Charles Barry and Augustus Pugin's Gothic extravaganza rose phoenix-like from the ashes: the House of Lords by 1847, the Commons and clock tower by 1858 and the Victoria Tower by 1860.

By this time, the "sights" of London had dropped into place. The British Museum gave a home to the Elgin Marbles in 1816, and Trafalgar Square gave a hero's welcome to Nelson's column. The City Corporation, meanwhile, made efforts to unlock the congested streets, cutting swathes through Holborn's houses and cemeteries for the viaduct to bridge the Fleet valley. Fleet Street, the Strand and Whitehall were by-passed by the grand boulevard of the Victoria Embankment. Tower Bridge opened in 1894, steel dressed up in stone to make it look historic.

By 1859 another problem had arisen, serious enough to cause the adjournment of the House of Commons: the unbearable stench from the Thames. Londoners still depended largely on the river for drinking water, and at the same

THE GREAT EXHIBITION OF 1851

In 1851 Queen Victoria opened the Great Exhibition of the Works of all Nations in Hyde Park, its magnificent glass building – dubbed "the Crystal Palace" – displaying Britain's skills and achievements to the world and attracting some 6 million visitors. With the profits of £186,000, Prince Albert, Queen Victoria's German-born husband, realised his great ambition: a centre of learning.

Temples to the arts and sciences blossomed in Kensington's gardens, nicknamed "Albertopolis". What was later named the Victoria and Albert Museum opened in 1857, followed by the the Royal Albert Hall in 1871, the Albert Memorial in 1872, and the Natural History Museum in 1881.

time disposed of all their sewage in it. Outbreaks of cholera were common until the City Engineer, Joseph Bazalgette, devised a scheme to take the sewage well downstream to Barking in Essex and release it into the river after treatment. His scheme is still the basis of the modern drainage system.

Dickens and social reforms

But London had become polarised. In the east, there was poverty and overcrowding, and in the west affluence and spacious living. The novelist Charles Dickens described the refuge of down-and-outs and penny-a-nighters in novels such as *Bleak House* (1853). Public conscience was aroused by his writings and those of the social reformer Henry Mayhew. This encouraged both political action and private philanthrophy.

The railways and new roads did some of the reformers' work for them, sweeping away many insanitary dwellings. Soon London's city's edge, opened up by the first suburban railway, the Metropolitan, in 1863.

ABOVE FAR LEFT: *Covent Garden*, by Phoebus Leven, 1864. **ABOVE LEFT:** detail from *A Street Scene with Two Omnibuses*, by James Pollard, 1845.
ABOVE: firefighting during the Blitz, World War II.
RIGHT: many thousands of London children were evacuated to the countryside during the Blitz.

> *By the end of the 19th century, London was throbbing with life and unloading the British Empire's fortunes across its wharves. Its docklands were called the warehouse of the world.*

World War II and the Blitz

Britain's capital has evolved piecemeal over centuries, without any overall plans. Twice in its history, however, it has had to be rebuilt. On the first occasion, after the Great Fire of 1666, and on the second, after World War II and the Blitz, which killed 29,000 London civilians and changed the face of the city.

World War II left Britain impoverished and without the empire that had provided so much of its wealth. Utilitarian buildings, often of charmless concrete, replaced those destroyed in the Blitz and were later condemned by critic Prince Charles, who said that modern town planners and architects did more damage than the Luftwaffe.

Swinging London

The 1950s were a time of post-war austerity with rationing still in place and efforts concentrated on regeneration in the face of a rapidly disintegrating empire. But there was also a massive baby boom and by the mid-1960s, as the post-war babies became teenagers, times were a-changing. While Paris became the centre of serious political action, London was the place to have fun, where old notions of deference, responsibility and hierarchy were swept away, cultural and sexual attitudes were liberated, and fashion and pop music prevailed. Swinging London centred on the King's Road in Chelsea, where Mary Quant's shop Bazaar epitomised the new fashions; Soho's Carnaby Street; and Barbara Hulanicki's store Biba in Kensington.

Meanwhile, many of the prewar slums of the East End were razed and replaced by new housing estates and tower blocks to meet the growing demand for decent public housing. The deep and divisive social problems created by the estates had yet to make an impact.

The roaring eighties

In the 1970s the pendulum swung the other way. Traditional industries collapsed all over Britain. Container ships made London's old wharves and warehouses redundant and the port that had once welcomed 14,000 vessels a year crumbled into dereliction.

By the time the economic boom of the 1980s

London's Mayor

In 1997 the UK elected a new Labour government led by Tony Blair, ending 17 years of Conservative rule under which the Greater London Council, which had administered London, had been abolished. The new Labour government decided to restore some self-government to the capital by creating a new post for the city: an elected mayor (as distinct from the ceremonial post of Lord Mayor, whose role is confined to the financial "square mile" of the City of London). The election was won by Ken Livingstone *(left)*, who had controversially led the Greater London Council hated and abolished by Margaret Thatcher (and by no means loved by Blair's New Labour).

One of Livingstone's first actions as mayor was to tackle the capital's chronic traffic congestion by imposing a congestion charge on vehicles entering the central zone on weekdays *(see page 279)*.

created a demand for taller office buildings, there was somewhere convenient to put them: the former docklands. The area became an adventure playground for architects and the area around the 850-ft (260-metre) Canary Wharf was dubbed Chicago-on-Thames. Meanwhile, for home buyers, the dream of living in London itself faded for many people as the strong economy pushed London house prices and rents well beyond the pockets of the lower paid.

The South Bank soars

The next area to be revived was Bankside, the south bank of the Thames where Shakespeare first staged his greatest plays and Dickens mined the material for many of his novels. Riders on the London Eye, the giant observation wheel erected to mark the millennium *(see page 186)*, looked down on a hive of building activity.

The area regenerated itself as the entertainments centre it had been 400 years previously. By the river, close to where a replica of Shakespeare's Globe Theatre was completed in 1997, a disused power station was transformed into Tate Modern, a mammoth museum of modern art attracting more than 5 million visitors in its first year. The Millennium Bridge, the first new river crossing in central London for more than a century, enabled pedestrians to walk from St Paul's Cathedral to Tate Modern in seven minutes.

ABOVE LEFT: male models pose in 1966. Second from left is clothes designer Ossie Clark, a leading figure in 1960s London. **LEFT:** London Mayor Ken Livingstone in a characteristically confrontational pose.
ABOVE: London introduces a Congestion Zone in 2005. **RIGHT:** the iconic arch of the rebuilt Wembley Stadium which opened in 2007.

An eye to the future

In July 2005, London surprised itself by winning its bid to host the 2012 Olympic Games. On the very next day terrorist bombs killed more than 50 people on three Tube trains and a bus, raising the question of how to make such a sprawling cosmopolitan city more secure.

> *The 2012 Olympics will be the catalyst for improvements to London's transport system and the development of East End brown field sites. The only uncertainty is who will pay the escalating cost.*

As preparations for the Olympics gain sail, long neglected parts of east London are being transformed to house the main stadia and Olympic Village. At the same time, the hitherto bleak area around King's Cross and St Pancras stations is being turned into a fitting setting for the new Eurostar terminal which opened in 2007. For once, perhaps, the city planners are beating London's age-old tendency to evolve in an organic, haphazard way. ❑

DECISIVE DATES

Early times

55 BC
Julius Caesar discovers Britain. In 55 BC he launches an invasion and defeats Cassivellaunus, a British chieftain. However, Roman forces do not stay.

AD 43
Londinium settled during second Roman invasion; a bridge is built over the Thames.

AD 61
Boudicca *(below)*, Queen of the Iceni tribe in East Anglia, sacks the city before being defeated.

c. 200
Three-mile (5-km) city wall built.

410
Troops are withdrawn to defend Rome.

449–527
Jutes, Angles and Saxons arrive in Britain, dividing it into separate kingdoms.

604
The first St Paul's Cathedral founded by King Ethelbert.

c.750
Monastery of St Peter is founded on Thorney Island, to become Westminster Abbey.

8th century
Shipping and manufacturing flourish on the river bank near today's Strand.

884
London becomes the capital of Britain under Alfred the Great.

1042
Edward the Confessor moves his court from the city to Westminster and rebuilds the abbey.

After the Conquest

1066
William I, Duke of Normandy and descendant of the Vikings, conquers Britain. He introduces French and the feudal system.

1078
Tower of London's White Tower built.

1154
The Plantagenets, descendants of the French House of Anjou, take over throne.

1176
A new London Bridge is built of stone.

1191
City's first mayor is elected.

1220
St Paul's Cathedral rebuilt.

1240
First parliament sits in Westminster.

1290
Jews are expelled from the city – a ban not lifted until the 17th century.

1381
Much of London is laid waste by the Peasants' Revolt.

1444
The Guildhall is rebuilt.

1485
The Tudor Age begins. Of Welsh descent, the Tudors preside over the English Renaissance, under Queen Elizabeth I (reigned 1558–1603).

1514
Hampton Court Palace begun.

1532
Henry VIII builds Palace of Whitehall, the largest in Europe. It catches fire in 1698.

1534
Henry VIII *(above)* declares himself head of the Church of England and dissolves monasteries.

1536
St James's Palace is built.

1588
William Shakespeare (1568–1616) begins his dramatic career in London.

1605
Guy Fawkes *(above)* tries to blow up Parliament.

1620
The Pilgrim Fathers set sail for America.

1642–9
Civil war between the Cavalier Royalists and the republican Roundheads. Royalists are defeated. Charles I is executed.

1660
After 11 years, monarchy is restored under Charles II.

1660–9
Samuel Pepys writes his famous diary.

1664–6
The Great Plague kills one-fifth of the population.

1666
The Great Fire destroys 80 percent of London's buildings.

1675
Sir Christopher Wren (1632– 1723) begins work on St Paul's Cathedral.

1694
The Bank of England is established.

1699
St James's Palace used as a royal court.

1714
The House of Hanover is ushered in by George I. The architectural style prevalent for the next 20 years is known as Georgian.

1732
George II makes 10 Downing Street available to Sir Robert Walpole, Britain's first prime minister.

1764
The Literary Club is founded by Samuel Johnson, compiler of the first English dictionary.

1783
Last public execution held at Tyburn (Marble Arch).

1811–20
The Prince Regent, later George IV, gives his name to the Regency style.

1820
Regent's Canal completed.

1824
The National Gallery is established.

1829
Prime minister Robert Peel establishes a police force (nicknamed "peelers").

1834
The current Houses of Parliament are built after the old palace of Westminster is destroyed by fire.

The Age of Empire

1837
Queen Victoria *(below)* comes to the throne at 18.

1840s
Trafalgar Square *(above)* laid out on the site of royal stables to commemorate Nelson's victory.

1849
Tea merchant Henry Charles Harrod takes over a small grocer's shop in Knightsbridge.

1851
The Great Exhibition is held in Hyde Park.

1859
A 13-tonne bell, nicknamed Big Ben, is hung in the clock tower of the Houses of Parliament.

1863
First section of the Underground railway is built between Paddington and Farringdon Street.

1888
Jack the Ripper strikes in Whitechapel.

1890
First electric railway to be built in deep-level tunnels, between the City and Stockwell.

1894
Tower Bridge is built.

1903
Westminster Cathedral is built. Marks & Spencer's first penny bazaar opens in Brixton.

1904
The first London motor taxi is licensed.

1909
The Victoria and Albert Museum opens in South Kensington

1914
World War I begins.

1915
Zeppelins and, later, Gotha airplanes begin dropping incendiary and explosive bombs on the city.

1922
British Broadcasting Company transmits its first programmes from Savoy Hill *(below)*.

1923
The first Football Association cup final is held at Wembley Stadium.

1926
London's first traffic roundabout is constructed at Piccadilly Circus.

1933
London's first automatic traffic lights are installed at Trafalgar Square.

1939–45
World War II. Children are evacuated, and London is heavily bombed.

Modern London

1951
Festival of Britain; new concert halls are built on South Bank near Waterloo.

1956
The Clean Air Act, introducing smokeless fuel, ends the asphixiating smogs.

1976
National Theatre opens.

1982
Flood-preventing Thames Barrier *(above)* finished.

1986
The Greater London Council is abolished.

1991
The first Canary Wharf tower is completed in Docklands.

1994
The first trains run through the Channel Tunnel to Paris and Brussels.

1997
Shakespeare's Globe opens on Bankside.

2000
Tate Modern opens on Bankside. The London Eye opens at County Hall.

2001
Greater London Authority is set up under mayor Ken Livingstone. Major museums drop entrance charge.

2002
The Millennium Bridge opens again after its unsettling wobble is cured.

2003
A £5 congestion charge is imposed on cars entering central areas.

2004
Planning permission is granted for what will be London's tallest building, the 1,016-ft (310-metre) London Bridge Tower.

2005
On 6 July London is chosen to stage 2012 Olympic Games. The following day bombs explode on three Tube trains and a bus, killing more than 50 people.

2006
In January a bottlenose whale is found swimming up the Thames in central London. Attempts to save it fail.

2007
The new Wembley Stadium opens four years late and more than £470 million over budget. In November the new Eurostar terminal opens at St Pancras.

THEATRELAND

Shakespeare, Sondheim, ABBA and a host of stars – the best (and the worst) of plays and musicals turn up in the West End. And theatre-lovers with a sense of adventure will find all kinds of innovative shows in fringe venues scattered around the city

The opening of Shakespeare's Globe on Bankside in 1997 was seen by some as a triumph of culture over commercialism. Here, for the price of a ticket, you can sit on rock-hard benches, squint through the sun slamming in through the large opening in the thatch roof, peer around pillars to try to catch lines from the acoustically challenged stage, and even, if the directors are to be taken at their word, cat-call and lob the occasional tomato if a performance is not to your liking.

This is theatre heritage to appeal to the tourist and even the purist, an Elizabethan playhouse risen from the rubble of time, and many make for its doors simply to savour the experience. The brainchild of American actor-director Sam Wanamaker, who didn't live to see it completed, the theatre is a replica of the 1599 auditorium in which William Shakespeare staged many of his plays. Like many theatres over the years, the original Globe was destroyed by fire.

That's Show Business

London's theatrical history goes back to a playhouse opened at Shoreditch in 1576 by James Burbage, the son of a carpenter and travelling player, and its development encompasses a strong tradition of taking sideswipes at social issues. In the *Roaring Girl* of 1611, for example, playwright Thomas Dekker dwelt at some length on London's traffic jams.

In modern times, live theatre was supposed to succumb first to movies, then to TV, yet it is still one of those essential attractions every visitor to London is supposed to experience, even if most opt for a blockbuster musical rather than anything more adventurous.

> *In spite of reports to the contrary, London's theatre scene is not declining. Theatres have broken their attendance records for several years running.*

In the days when *South Pacific* and *Camelot* dominated musical theatre no-one would have guessed the West End would hijack the genre from Broadway. Yet, in the 1970s Tim Rice and Andrew Lloyd Webber first demonstrated the possibilities of cunningly crafted rock-musicals

with *Jesus Christ Superstar* and *Evita*, and then Lloyd Webber moved on to dominate the stage musical with *Cats* (a collaboration with the late T.S. Eliot) and *Phantom of the Opera*.

Critics might scoff, but shrewd theatre brains saw that income from musicals could underwrite other work. Trevor Nunn masterminded the Royal Shakespeare Company's 1985 production of *Les Misérables*, which went on to conquer the world.

Musicals dominate the modern West End and are its biggest money-spinners – even though Lloyd Webber himself seems to have lost the urge to produce much new work and has been more prominent as the promoter of the Bollywood-based *Bombay Dreams* and a revival of *The Sound of Music* for which the starring role of Maria was cast via a reality TV show.

Broadway has reasserted its clout, whether in revivals of musical classics like *Guys and Dolls* or *Chicago* or recent successes such as *The Producers*, *Wicked* or *Monty Python's Spamalot*. The trend that gets critics tearing their hair, though, is for the pop-music musical, reprising the song catalogue of favourite artists. Begun by ABBA-based *Mamma Mia!*, this has continued with *Dancing in the Streets* (Motown), *We Will Rock You* (Queen) and even *Daddy Cool* (Boney M). The plots weaved around the songs are wafer-thin, but the crowds keep coming in.

PRECEDING PAGES: scene from the blockbuster musical *Phantom of the Opera*. **LEFT:** Shaftesbury Avenue is packed with options. **ABOVE:** a revival of the classic *Guys and Dolls*. **TOP RIGHT:** theatre in the round at Shakespeare's Globe. **ABOVE RIGHT:** *Blood Wedding* at the Almeida Theatre in Islington.

WHERE TO SIT

It's useful to know the terminology of English theatre layout. What in America is called the "Orchestra" (the seats at the lowest level) is in England called the "Stalls"; then, in ascending order, come the "Dress Circle" (or "Royal Circle"), and the "Upper Circle" (or "Grand Circle" or "Balcony"). The very top balconies, once known as "The Gods", are not recommended to anyone with vertigo or a hearing impediment.

If in a party, consider asking for a box, which can sometimes work out cheaper than seats in the stalls. You can doze off more privately, too.

Some claim musical-mania has squeezed out new drama, but a glance at the theatre pages in *Time Out* doesn't really bear this out. New productions of classics still appear each year, new writing still gets aired in fringe and mainstream venues, and writers such as Tom Stoppard or Mark Ravenhill do not lack audiences.

Ways to Buy Your Tickets

Despite the popular notion that everything in London is so successful that it sells out fast, most shows have some seats, especially early in the week. It's the more expensive tickets – generally for musicals – that are usually hardest to obtain.

The best way to get tickets is from the theatre itself, either by calling at the box office or online. This cuts out the sometimes extortionate fees of ticket agencies. Agencies and hotels are most handy for obtaining hard-to-get tickets.

Many theatres offer unsold tickets for performances the same day at reduced "standby" prices, although some are only available to students. Tickets for same-day performances are also available at around half-price from the tkts ticket booths in Leicester Square (Mon–Sat 10am–7pm, Sun noon–3pm) and at Canary Wharf DLR station. Matinees can be cheaper, but understudies may replace the stars. The National Theatre puts some same-day tickets on sale at 10am at its box office on the South Bank.

Tickets are offered outside theatres by touts for anything up to 10 times their face value. This isn't illegal, but check the ticket's face value and the position of the seat.

Hollywood-on-Thames

As well as locally grown stars such as Sirs Michael Gambon and Ian McKellen, and Dames Maggie Smith, Diana Rigg and Judi Dench, American actors have never been strangers to the West End – Dustin Hoffman played Shylock in *The Merchant of Venice* here in 1989 – but lately this flow has become a flood, as nearly every Hollywood name has seemed to feel a need to add a London stage appearance to their resumé.

Nicole Kidman caused a great stir when she appeared naked in David Hare's *The Blue Room* in 1998, and Val Kilmer, Woody Harrelson, Glenn Close and Christian Slater are among other famous faces seen on London stages, to varying reviews. Kathleen Turner won huge praise in a recent production of *Who's Afraid of Virginia Woolf*, but London's favourite American actor is Kevin Spacey. After scoring a massive hit in *The Iceman Cometh* in 1998, he accepted the job of part-time artistic director of the venerable Old Vic theatre, helping to raise funds to repair its leaky roof and promising to appear in two plays a year. His programmes as director have been sometimes eccentric, but seldom predictable.

National companies

London has two major state-subsidised companies: the National Theatre and the Royal Shakespeare Company. The National has the advantage of its own huge building

on the South Bank, with three auditoria. Its concrete exterior isn't to everyone's taste, but its technology is impressive – revolving stages are only the start of it. By contrast, the RSC gave up its London home at the unloved Barbican Centre in the City in 2001 (its main base is in Shakespeare's home town, Stratford-upon-Avon), and only recently returned to presenting a regular London season, at the Novello Theatre on Aldwych.

Criticisms levelled at the National have been its comparative lack of modern European plays and the prominence given during Trevor Nunn's directorship to big musicals such as *Oklahoma!* and *My Fair Lady* – felt by many to be more the concern of the commercial West End (to which these productions profitably transferred). The current director, Nicholas Hytner, has introduced more variety and innovation, and aided by business sponsorship has made many seats available for just £10.

FAR LEFT: Kathleen Turner and Bill Irwin in *Who's Afraid of Virginia Woolf?* – Turner is one of many Hollywood stars to have played on the London stage. **ABOVE LEFT:** Kevin Spacey, artistic director of the Old Vic. **ABOVE:** the National Theatre on the South Bank.

Off-West End to the fringe

In addition to 50 central theatres, there are over 60 smaller or "fringe" venues around London, from substantial theatres to tiny rooms above pubs. Their productions range from low-budget Shakespeare to political shows and international theatre. Much of new young British writing is dark, funny and well-observed.

> *Val Kilmer, Matt Damon and Madonna failed to impress on the London stage, but Kathleen Turner, Juliette Lewis and Jessica Lange have been acclaimed.*

The Royal Court, the Donmar Warehouse, the Young Vic, the Almeida in Islington and the Tricycle in Kilburn are the main outlets for new writing, which between them have pioneered many of London's most exciting recent productions. Lively pub theatres include the Bush (in Shepherd's Bush), the King's Head (Islington) and the Gate at Notting Hill Gate.

Every summer there is a very enjoyable open-air theatre season in Regent's Park, focusing on Shakespeare's comedies. ❑

EATING OUT

London's 12,000 restaurants and cafés offer some of the world's best culinary experiences – some even at a decent price. New eateries open as frequently as new movies, and are just as subject to the whims of fashion. So how do you find the good and avoid the bad?

London, once derided for mediocre cuisine, is today straining under a bombardment of Michelin stars. You can eat nachos and noodles, tapas and tempura, balti and bhajis; you can try pizza with Japanese toppings, choose from nearly 200 Thai restaurants or even eat English, a privilege reserved until a few years ago for diners at greasy-spoon cafés or, more tastefully, the traditional Rules or Simpson's in the Strand.

This revolution began in the 1980s, when the restructuring of London's financial world produced a legion of footloose brokers and traders looking for places to spend skyrocketing salaries. Innovative restaurants, like designer labels, were avidly sought out. At around the same time, the British discovered food. Cookery programmes proliferated on TV, book stores filled up with lavishly illustrated cook books and newspapers covered new restaurant openings with ever more excitement. The phenomenon of the "celebrity chef" was born.

Until then it had been *de rigueur* for chefs to be French, and the country's best-known were Albert and Michel Roux of Le Gavroche. Now local stars emerged: Rose Gray and Ruth Rogers, wife of the architect Sir Richard Rogers, opened their River Café alongside the architect's offices in Fulham, West London, presenting Tuscan Italian cooking with a metropolitan twist. At the same time Terence Conran, the style-maker whose Habitat stores had brought the earthy kitchenware of Provence to Britain, opened Bibendum restaurant in the splendid Art Deco Michelin tyre company building in Fulham Road, the first of a string of Conran venues in striking – sometimes giant – locations with emphatically stylish decor. Epitome of the style is Quaglino's, near Green Park, with a look that deliberately recalls a 1930s ocean liner. This was food as entertainment, out-to-impress dining

> *The Conran empire marked a shift of emphasis away from chefs and towards restaurateurs. Famous chefs took to running their restaurant chains rather than doing much cooking.*

that symbolised the early 1990s, but – though some have maintained high standards – these are not restaurants where you can generally expect much individuality or charm.

Current movers and shakers

Nowadays, London's food scene has settled down a little: it's still devoted to fads – Moroccan one year, Argentinian the next – but alongside them there's also a more consistent idea of quality, as the city has got used to the idea of being one of the world's dining capitals. Some stalwarts have absorbed new trends while sticking to what they know their clients want: the River Café remains inviolate, The Ivy and Le Caprice are ever-popular with the rich and famous, the Savoy Grill with businessmen, and Le Gavroche with traditionalist gourmands. The fashion for "mega-restaurants" has faded, as was indicated in 2007 when Terence Conran himself gave up control of his restaurant chain, passing it over to his former managers under a new name: the D&D Group.

Attention has shifted back from restaurant entrepreneurs to cooks, although London's current top chef, Gordon Ramsay, manages to be both. A former footballer whose cooking skills won Michelin recognition and whose short temper made him a TV star, Ramsay still cooks

LEFT: bastion of traditional British dining, Simpson's in the Strand. **ABOVE:** St John in Clerkenwell, the location of several notable new restaurants.
ABOVE RIGHT: Terence Conran's Bibendum occupies the former Michelin tyre company in Fulham Road.

FIRST, FIND YOUR TABLE

The downsides of London's top restaurants include terrifying prices, a growing air of exclusivity, and arrogance when it comes to dealing with anyone trying to make a reservation. Tables for dinner at Gordon Ramsay's main restaurant must be booked two months in advance, at the Ivy several weeks ahead; phone lines are often busy for hours, and when you do get through staff may be abrupt. One way to get around this is to go for lunch, and not bother booking but just turn up early, just after noon: Tom Aikens, The Wolseley, Le Gavroche and the Ivy are among the prestigious venues that often have lunchtime tables free.

himself (sometimes), instals talented young chefs in his restaurant stable and is an inescapable media face. London's grand hotels, traditional bastions of good cookery, have spruced up their restaurants to keep up with the dining boom, and Ramsay has taken astute advantage of this, taking over the Savoy Grill and Claridge's restaurant and installing Angela Hartnett at the Connaught. There are many other inventive young British chefs around town, though, with less media attention. Like Ramsay, most combine a classical, French-based training with an eclectic, adventurous approach; other stars of the moment include Chris Galvin, now in charge of the top-floor restaurant at the Hilton on Park Lane (as Galvin at Windows), and Tom Aikens, with his eponymous restaurant in Kensington.

Around the world, and back again

Many fans of eating out in London, however, say that what they enjoy most is the incredible variety of cuisines on offer. Its status as an international city attracts fine cooks from every

The Facts about Fish and Chips

A classic British dish, fish and chips originated in the 1850s. Today, only 8,600 fish and chip shops remain in Britain, compared with over 30,000 in the 1930s. Many of the best are run by immigrants, especially Italians (Rock & Sole Plaice in Covent Garden, with a branch in Swiss Cottage, and the Fryer's Delight in Theobalds Road, Holborn) and Greek Cypriots (the Golden Hind, in Marylebone Lane since 1914, and Costas in Notting Hill). Nautilus in Fortune Green Road, West Hampstead, is Jewish and coats its fish in matzo flour. You will also find fish and chip shops run by Chinese, Turkish Cypriots or central Europeans.

Other notable fish and chip addresses are the long-standing favourites the Sea Shell in Lisson Grove, and Geales (which changed ownership in 2007) in Notting Hill. Fish Central is a blessing to concert- and theatre-goers near the Barbican Centre, Seafresh in Wilton Road is handy for Victoria Station, and Masters Super Fish is convenient for Waterloo. Recently, too, there has even been a trendy newcomer in the old-fashioned world of fish and chips, with the opening of the all-new, stylish Fish Club in Battersea.

You generally get better value in a real fish and chip restaurant (attached to a takeaway shop) than in pubs or restaurants that offer fish and chips on their menus. One test, apart from truly fresh fish and crisp batter, is that they offer fresh lemon instead of just malt vinegar.

part of the world to work here. French chefs are still prominent, such as Eric Chavot (The Capital) or Morgan Meunier (Morgan M), and even France's grandest current chef has a London operation, L'Atelier de Joël Robuchon. Far Eastern or South Asian restaurants are no longer just cheap options either: London has some of the finest Indian (Rasoi, Café Spice Namaste), Japanese (Nobu) and Chinese (Bar Shu) restaurants in the world outside their countries of origin, and you can find regional variations, such as the superb south Indian vegetarian food of Rasa Samudra.

There has also been a re-evaluation of traditional British dishes, long dismissed as dreary. Pioneer of this new British style was Alastair Little in his Soho restaurant, but it was extended with still more zest by Fergus Henderson at St John, which has been hugely influential in showing that British favourites such as oxtail, smoked herrings and farm-reared pork can be delicacies if prepared with care and flair.

The middle ground

The ever-rising standard of fine dining in London may grab the headlines, but it has to be said that for most people who do not have limitless wallets or full mastery of the strategems used to get a table in restaurants such as Gordon Ramsay's, these are places that are only visited for a special occasion. Among more regularly accessible eating places, London's fad-chasing can be a source of disappointment, as time and again restaurant promoters have placed "concept" – decor, style, general trendiness – above quality of food, or value for money. This being so, it's pleasing to report that one of the best current trends has been for the new culinary flair at last to filter down into a wider range of restaurants at mid-range prices. Many "new-British" restaurants, especially, are decently priced: even

ABOVE LEFT: flavours of London – noodles at Wagamama, oysters at Bibendum, poppadums and spices at one of London's many excellent Indian restaurants. **ABOVE:** Gordon Ramsay, doyen of celebrity chefs. **ABOVE RIGHT:** Rasoi Vineet Bhatia, whose restaurant Rasoi has a Michelin star.

WHERE TO EAT

The biggest concentration of restaurants is in the West End, with Soho providing the most interesting choice. Chinatown, north of Leicester Square, has a bewildering array of Asian eateries, and Covent Garden good-value pre-theatre suppers. Kensington and Chelsea, with their abundance of wealthy residents, contain many expensive restaurants but also a good sprinkling of reasonably priced bistros.

Islington and Notting Hill also offer a good choice, and Clerkenwell and Shoreditch house some of the most interesting new restaurants. The City, whose oyster bars and restaurants cater to business lunchers, tends to be a ghost town in the evenings and at weekends.

the prestigious St John is not expensive, particularly for lunch, and recent arrivals such as Shoreditch's Canteen or Roast in Borough Market similarly offer flavour-rich modern food in stylish settings. Eating out in London may still be more expensive than in many cities, but at least the difference is getting a little less.

The trend for big institutions to re-examine their food has thrown up attractive novelties too: major museums such as the National Gallery, Tate Britain and Tate Modern all now have imaginative, good-value restaurants, and even the Royal Institute of British Architects has opened up its elegant Art Deco "canteen" as a smart modern brasserie, the RIBA Café.

> *The local gastropub has started to become London's equivalent of the Parisian street-corner bistro.*

The great pub renaissance

Another vital element in making good food more accessible – as well as the unstoppable growth of "ethnic" restaurants – has been the revolution in pub food. Realising there was more money to be made from food and wine than just beer and crisps, pub after pub has become a "gastropub", throwing out the limp sandwiches and plastic "ploughman's lunches" of old-style pub fare in favour of chalkboard menus that mix traditional British favourites with French, Italian or Oriental influences.

Old standards like sausage and mash have been given new life by the use of Toulouse sausages and mustard sauces, and imaginative salads have become a hallmark. This combination of good food and a relaxed feel that preserves a fair bit of the atmosphere of a London pub, typified by The Eagle (159 Farringdon Road, EC1), The Cow (89 Westbourne Park Road, W2) or trendier variants like the Lot's Road Pub & Dining Rooms (114 Lots Road, SW10), has been a real winner, with Londoners and visitors. The London gastropub can sometimes seem to have become a new cliché – every one has to have stripped floorboards and stressed furniture – but they're ideal for anyone looking for good-value interesting food in an informal setting.

The chain gang

As in every part of the world, in London plenty of restaurants, cafés, bars and pubs belong to chains. These can be an advantage when you're in unfamiliar territory and in search of something reliable; they're a disadvantage when a formula is replicated ad nauseam, and standards are low.

Some local London chains, though, are worth looking out for, especially if you're travelling with a family. Giraffes (South Bank and many more areas) are bright modern brasseries with "global fusion-food" (Mexico to Australia and more) that appeal equally to adults and children. For Italian standbys (snacks, pasta, pizza) Carluccio's Caffè, ASK and Strada are good bets, while Sofra branches provide enjoyable Turkish fare. The many Wagamama outlets are excellent, lively Japanese-style noodle houses, while in a higher price slot the six Royal Chinas in London are comfortable Chinese restaurants. ❑

FAR LEFT: Marylebone's stylish RIBA Café, at the Royal Institute of British Architects. **LEFT:** open kitchen at the Eagle, a gastropub on Farringdon Road.
ABOVE: The Cow in Notting Hill, one of many good gastropubs scattered around west London.

AFTERNOON TEA, AS IT SHOULD BE

Throughout the world there are people still convinced that everyone in England sits down for "afternoon tea" around 4pm every day, using best-quality porcelain. Sadly, this is a myth, and a full-scale, formal tea – with thin-cut sandwiches, a variety of cakes and a choice of fine teas – is nowadays a luxury. The venues that really keep up the tradition are the grand hotels, most typically Brown's, the Ritz and the Dorchester, all of which offer tea with all the trimmings in luxurious settings (reservations and smart dress are required).

Recently, too, there has been a bit of a tea revival, and several upscale restaurants now offer set afternoon teas, including The Wolseley and even the chic modern Asia de Cuba.

Retail Therapy

London's innovative department stores are redesigning the one-stop shopping experience

The past decade has seen dramatic changes in that most traditional of London shops, the department store. The stuffy image has gone and stores are now imaginatively designed spaces stocking everything from freshly cut flowers and organic food to cutting-edge designer clothes and bespoke jewellery. Their hairdressers have become on-site spas, and they offer a host of bars and restaurants.

Oxford Street has the greatest concentration of department stores, headed by Selfridges. Marks & Spencer and John Lewis provide a more traditional shopping experience, while round the corner on Regent Street, Liberty is both eccentric and chic. Head to Knightsbridge for Harvey Nichols, the fashionista's choice, and Harrods.

For a comprehensive listing of London's department stores, see page 295 of Travel Tips.

Above: Harvey Nichols has eight floors of the latest designer fashions in beauty, homeware and designer clothes, plus a Daniel Hersheon beauty salon and a small food court. The highlight is the store's much-rated restaurant Fifth Floor – a far cry from the days of the department store canteen.

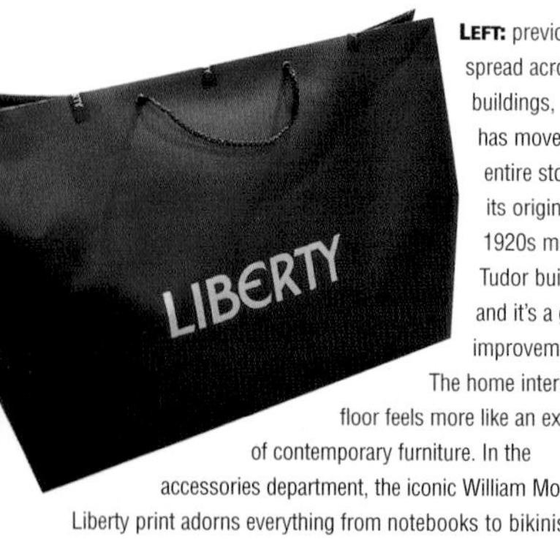

Left: previously spread across two buildings, Liberty has moved the entire store to its original 1920s mock-Tudor building and it's a great improvement. The home interiors floor feels more like an exhibition of contemporary furniture. In the accessories department, the iconic William Morris Liberty print adorns everything from notebooks to bikinis.

Above: opened as a grocer's shop in 1849, today Harrods is a tourist destination in its own right. Harrods sells pretty much everything you can think of in surroundings that range from the sublime to the ridiculous. But whatever you think of Harrods, no trip to London would be complete without a visit to its wonderfully extravagant food halls.

BRITISH DESIGNERS

Creativity and eccentricity mark out British designers from the international fashion pack

Stella McCartney's designs mix strong tailoring with feminine fabrics. Her popularity has sparked collaborations with Adidas and high-street chain H&M.

Vivienne Westwood's theatrical clothes never fail to cause a stir. She has shops at 430 King's Road, SW10, and in Conduit Street, W1.

Paul Smith is known for his tailoring and retro-inspired designs. Look out for his best-selling silk ties and signature striped accessories.

Philip Treacy' sculptural headgear can be found in the top department stores, including Harrods and Liberty.

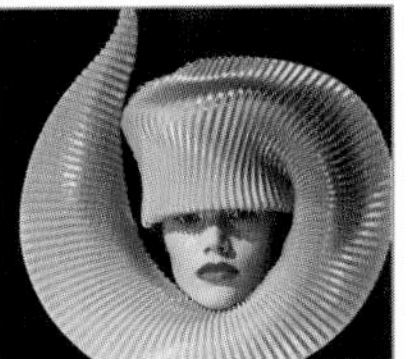

Mulberry is famous for its leather accessories – from personal organisers to weekend bags, all embossed with the classic tree logo.

Cath Kidston's distinctive floral and polka dot designs are used for everything from gifts, clothes and accessories to tents.

LEFT: Selfridges has become the ultimate London department store. Combining luxury-brands with high-street concessions, it manages to be both accessible and cool. The store has a changing programme of themed events to keep things interesting, as well as services ranging from leather repairs to ear piercing.

BELOW: for a department store specialising in fine food and beverages visit Fortnum and Masons at 181 Piccadilly.

MARKETS

There are few better introductions to London's rich mix of cultures and tastes than a visit to one of its markets

Many of the capital's markets have been in operation for centuries and a visit can conjure up images of an old London now largely lost to supermarket chains and developers. At the same time, London's markets are experiencing a revival, and alongside the traditional stalls selling fruit and veg you'll find organic meat and fish and specialist produce from all round the world.

The revival of markets has encouraged the renovation of surrounding areas and all kinds of independent shops and restaurants are popping up. For some this has gone a step too far – for example, there is little doubt that the creation of a restaurant and boutique precinct at Spitalfields has damaged something of its original haphazard appeal – and the high prices charged for goods have taken the edge off bargain-hunting.

Despite this, a wander around places like Borough Market, Broadway Market and Spitalfields continues to be a treat for all the senses – you just have to be prepared to brave the crowds.

ABOVE: markets are a great place for finding all manner of unusual hand-made items, such as these hand-knitted covers for mobile phones.

ABOVE: on Sunday mornings Londoners flood to Columbia Road Market in Hoxton *(see page 250)* for cut flowers, bulbs, shrubs, trees, and garden ornaments. The old-fashioned streets around the market offer funky shops and cafés too.

BELOW: the variety and quality of fresh produce at Borough Market is unrivalled in London, and some of the prices certainly reflect this. If you're happy to brave the lunchtime crowds, many of the stalls offer take-away snacks – a firm market favourite are the hot chorizo and rocket rolls from Spanish supplier Brindisa's stand.

ABOVE: the Sunday (Up)Market at Ely's Yard (Brick Lane) is a treasure-trove of second-hand clothing and one-off designs

BELOW: Leadenhall Market *(see page 171)* is a fine example of one of London's great 19th-century covered markets. It was used as a setting for Diagon Alley in the film *Harry Potter and the Philosopher's Stone.*

MARKET TREASURES

A wide range of clothing, crafts and trinkets are available at Camden's various markets.

The covered market at Greenwich is the place for hand-made jewellery and accessories. Quality varies and it's very crowded, but if it gets too much adjourn to the calmer antiques market a short walk away.

Portobello Road in Notting Hill is one of London's best-loved markets. For antiques explore the northern end of the street, for junk and offbeat fashions and arts and crafts head for the northern end (Fri–Sun only), under the Westway flyover.

THE ARCHITECTURAL LEGACY

Central planning played no part in London's haphazard development, and the city's organic growth, together with the contribution of men of genius such as Christopher Wren, John Nash and Inigo Jones, has given the capital its principal allure: infinite variety

Little remains of Roman Londinium, and even less of Saxon Lundenwic. Glimpses of the Roman city wall can be had at Tower Hill, and foundations of a Temple of Mithras have been exposed in Queen Victoria Street. The Saxons built mostly in timber, but were grateful for Roman stones. All Hallows-by-the-Tower has a Saxon arch, built with Roman tiles. Otherwise, they left little trace.

Norman to Gothic

The Norman Conquest of 1066 brought firmer resolution to the city, in the White Tower in the Tower of London, a sturdy box that showed the natives who was in control. Within it is St John's Chapel, with the squat pillars and round arches of Norman Romanesque architecture.

Medieval London grew out of the Gothic style, imported from France in the 13th century and in vogue until the 1550s. Far more delicate than Norman, it made outer walls thinner by supporting them with exterior buttresses, allowing larger windows. Southwark Cathedral is a fine example of simple, unadorned early English Gothic; Westminster Abbey, begun in 1245, was enhanced by royal mason Henry Yevele (1320–1400), London's first known architect. He also built the Jewel Tower and Westminster Hall in the Houses of Parliament, a vauntingly ambitious space with a timber roof by carpenter Hugh Herland.

> *The Tudor monarchs were great builders and brought the first real touches of grandeur and extravagance to London's buildings.*

Tudor London

The finest work of Gothic architecture in London is the lavish Henry VII's Chapel in Westminster Abbey, completed by his son, Henry VIII. The Tudor monarchs oversaw constant expansion and building in London. A hallmark of Tudor buildings – also called "Elizabethan", after Queen Elizabeth I – is the use of half-timbering and red brick. Staple Inn in High Holborn is the sole survivor from this time, but the era also saw the building of London's first theatres such as Shakespeare's Globe, now reconstructed near its original Southwark site.

Brickwork was confined to the rich, used to produce octagonal towers, fancy chimneys and patterns of colours and shapes. Royal palaces were built like this at Greenwich, Hampton Court, St James's, Lambeth and Westminster. London has only one example of the Jacobean style (from King James I): Prince Henry's Room (1610–11) above 17 Fleet Street. Its original ceiling, with geometric patterns, is still in place.

Inigo Jones and the Italian style

James I and his son Charles I brought a new elegance to London in the work of Inigo Jones (1573–1652). The court architect had studied in Italy, and brought Italian Renaissance ideas and introduced classical proportions in his Banqueting Hall in Whitehall and the Queen's House in Greenwich, and his original Palladian layout for Covent Garden, set out, with the neoclassical St Paul's church, around London's first true square.

FAR LEFT: the City of London. **LEFT:** early 19th-century terrace, Islington. **ABOVE:** John Nash's Park Crescent, off Portland Place. **ABOVE RIGHT:** St Paul's Cathedral. **RIGHT:** the "Gherkin" (the 30 St Mary Axe tower in the City) is open to the public once a year.

Wren and the Great Fire

Sir Christopher Wren (1632–1723) is undoubtedly London's greatest architect, but if there had been no Great Fire in 1666 his name would not be so well known. In three days 80 percent of London's buildings were destroyed: among the losses were the Guildhall and Old St Paul's, as well as over 100 churches.

Wren was a scientist and self-taught architect. His plans for the rebuilding of London were rejected, but he managed 52 churches (26 remain) as well as St Paul's. These very English

OPEN HOUSE

During London Open House weekends more than 600 buildings of architectural and historical interest that are usually closed to the public open their doors, for free. The main weekend is usually in mid-September, but more limited Open House tours are run all year. See www.londonopenhouse.org for details and lists of buildings. At some venues you need to book.

classical-baroque monuments eschewed earlier styles, their windows bathing white and gold interiors with light. His mastery of design is also displayed in the superb Greenwich and Chelsea hospitals, and several royal palaces.

John Nash and Georgian London

John Nash (1752–1835) is the man who gave the West End style. He gained his reputation designing country houses, and in 1811 was commissioned by the Prince Regent, later George IV, to turn his "Marylebone Farm" into Regent's Park, ringed by elegant neoclassical villas. Nash added theatrical terraces, colonnades and sculpted pediments, and his master plan included connecting the park with the Prince's residence – Carlton House Terrace, by The Mall – via Portland Place and Regent Street, London's first refined boulevards.

Nash's supremely elegant Regency style was the summit of Georgian architecture. The

The Sky's the Limit

Until the 1950s no new building in London was allowed to exceed the height of St Paul's Cathedral (365 ft/111 metres). Today the tallest tower is Canary Wharf's One Canada Square at 773 ft (235 metres). It is flanked by 700-ft (213-metre) blocks. Indeed, over the past few years the London skyline has been changed by a wave of giant-scale building, in the City of London in particular, and Mayor Ken Livingstone vocally favours the construction of yet more tall towers.

A new benchmark is due to be set by the controversial London Bridge Tower, also known as the "Shard of Glass", a 1,016-ft (310-metre) spire scheduled to be built next to London Bridge by 2011.

At a lower level, there has been a trend towards unusually shaped glass buildings such as City Hall (the "glass testicle"), housing the Greater London Authority by Tower Bridge and the 30 St Mary Axe building (dubbed the "Gherkin") in the City.

houses of Bedford Square are typically Georgian, with brick facades, sash windows and elaborate porticoes. As Italian influence waned, all things Greek became the vogue: Sir Robert Smirke (1781–1867) accordingly built the British Museum as a giant temple, to house Lord Elgin's plunder from the Parthenon.

Victorian revivals

Against this pagan Greek influence, Augustus Pugin (1812–52) contended it was time to return to "true Christian architecture", the Gothic. His chance to lead the revival came on 16 October 1834, when the old Palace of Westminster burnt down. His design for the new Houses of Parliament, carried out with Charles Barry (1795–1860), took as inspiration the Henry VII chapel in Westminster Abbey.

Gothic Revival was the cornerstone of Victorian architecture. It produced a distinctive Tower Bridge, while Sir George Gilbert Scott (1811–78) built St Pancras Station as a romantic castle. Victorian eclecticism even allowed a Tudor Revival, as in New Hall at Lincoln's Inn.

ABOVE LEFT: St Pancras Station *(far left)* and the Natural History Museum *(above and below)* typify Gothic Revival, a favourite of Victorian architects. **LEFT:** Canary Wharf. **ABOVE:** the "Gherkin" close up.

Modern architecture

Britain was virtually bankrupted by World War II, which accounts for the number of utilitarian blocks that had to be built quickly and cheaply in the 1950s and '60s and have not worn well. Buildings from the 1951 Festival of Britain such as the Royal Festival Hall, though, stand out beside more brutalist Modernist projects such as the all-concrete National Theatre (1967–77).

London's economic boom since the 1980s and the redevelopment of vast areas like Docklands have launched a whole new wave of construction, begun by Richard Rogers' futuristic Lloyds building in 1986. A city that resisted tall buildings has acquired skyscrapers, led by the mammoth Canary Wharf (since 1987).

The latest focus for new building is the Olympic Park in east London, site of the 2012 Games. London's new architecture is a mix of provocative styles – a playful giant wheel, Norman Foster's tapering City tower the "Gherkin" – reflecting a new openness and a readiness to add still more to London's endless variety. ❑

ORIENTATION

The Places section details all the attractions worth seeing, arranged by area. The areas are shown on a colour-coordinated map on pages 66–7. Main sights are cross-referenced by number to individual maps

For a cosmopolitan city of 7.2 million people, London is quite parochial. Each neighbourhood, each street corner, is proud of its own identity. Central London is the shared London of all these groups and of nearly 20 million visitors a year as well. Symbols of London – the Beefeaters, the bobbies, the cabbies, the cockneys, the pageantry, the Royal Family, the Houses of Parliament – all are here, along with the stock market, motorcycle messengers, dirty air, and crawling traffic.

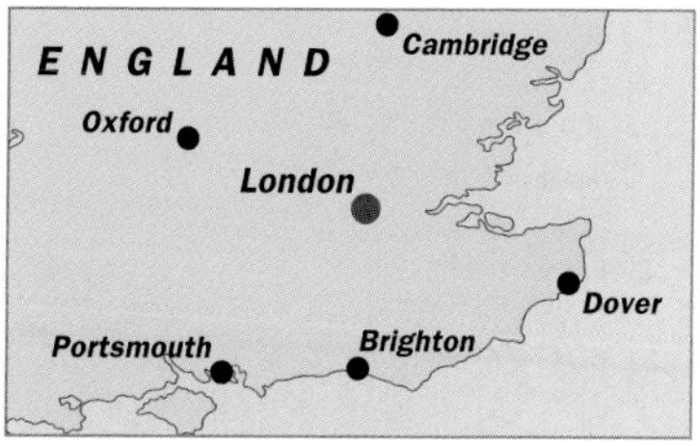

After an initial tour by boat or on an open-top bus to orientate yourself, the best way to see Central London is on foot. Although Greater London sprawls for 610 sq. miles (1,580 sq. km), the central area is surprisingly compact. Walkers have time to appreciate the infinite variety of architectural detail that traces the city's long development. What's more, they will be treading in the footsteps of some of history's most celebrated citizens – to aid the imagination, blue plaques *(see page 138)* show where the great, the good and the notorious once lived.

We begin the Places section by focusing on the royal and ruling heart of the city, Parliament and Buckingham Palace. The ensuing chapters cover the remainder of the central area, from Piccadilly to Chelsea, and cross the river to explore the vibrancy of Southwark and the South Bank. Village London *(pages 233–263)* tours some of the most interesting local communities outside the central area, usually reached by bus or Underground. Day Trips *(pages 267–273)* suggests a range of convenient excursions from London.

All the sites of special interest are numbered on specially drawn maps to help you find your way around, and a street atlas begins on page 317.

As a visitor, you may be one of the 72 percent who visit the Tower of London, or the 92 percent who make their way to Piccadilly Circus. But you will probably also be one of the millions who find some small, distinctive corner of this remarkable city to be enthusiastic about. ❑

PRECEDING PAGES: Tower Bridge and HMS *Belfast*; aerial view of Trafalgar Square.
LEFT: view down Whitehall towards Big Ben.

Central London
Top Sights

British Museum
pages 144–49

Piccadilly Circus
page 89

Trafalgar Square
page 99

Buckingham Palace
page 80

Big Ben
page 76

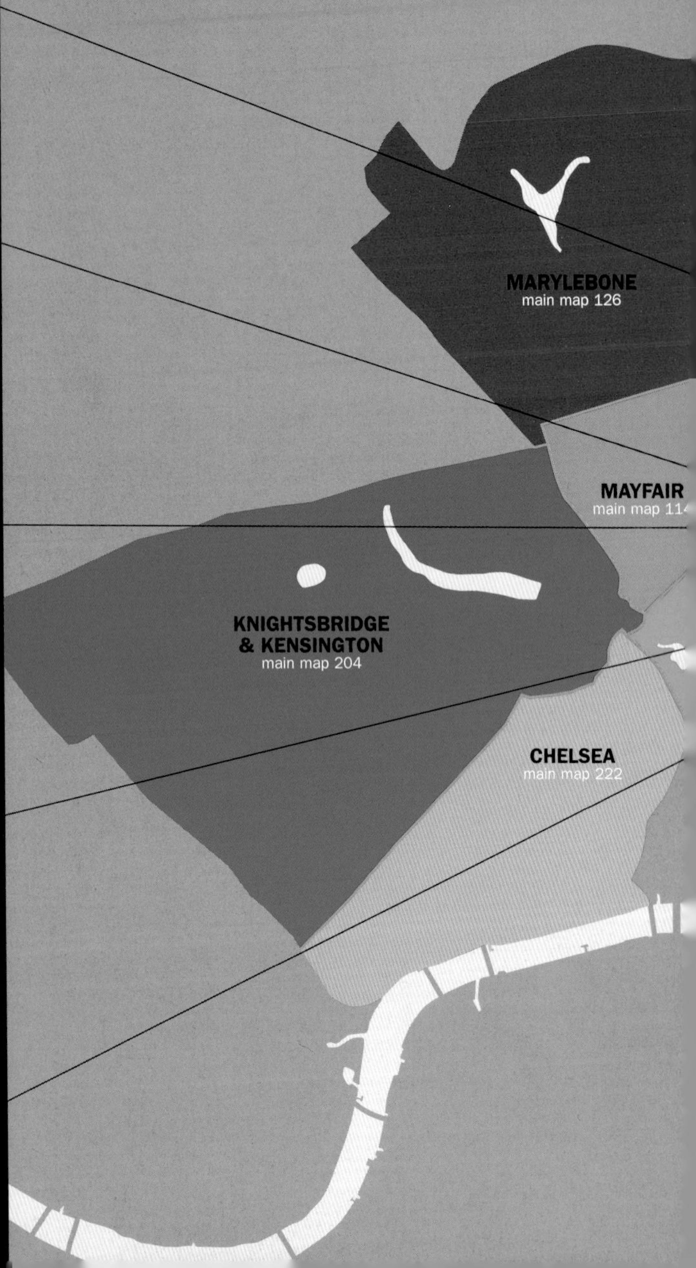

MARYLEBONE
main map 126

MAYFAIR
main map 114

KNIGHTSBRIDGE & KENSINGTON
main map 204

CHELSEA
main map 222

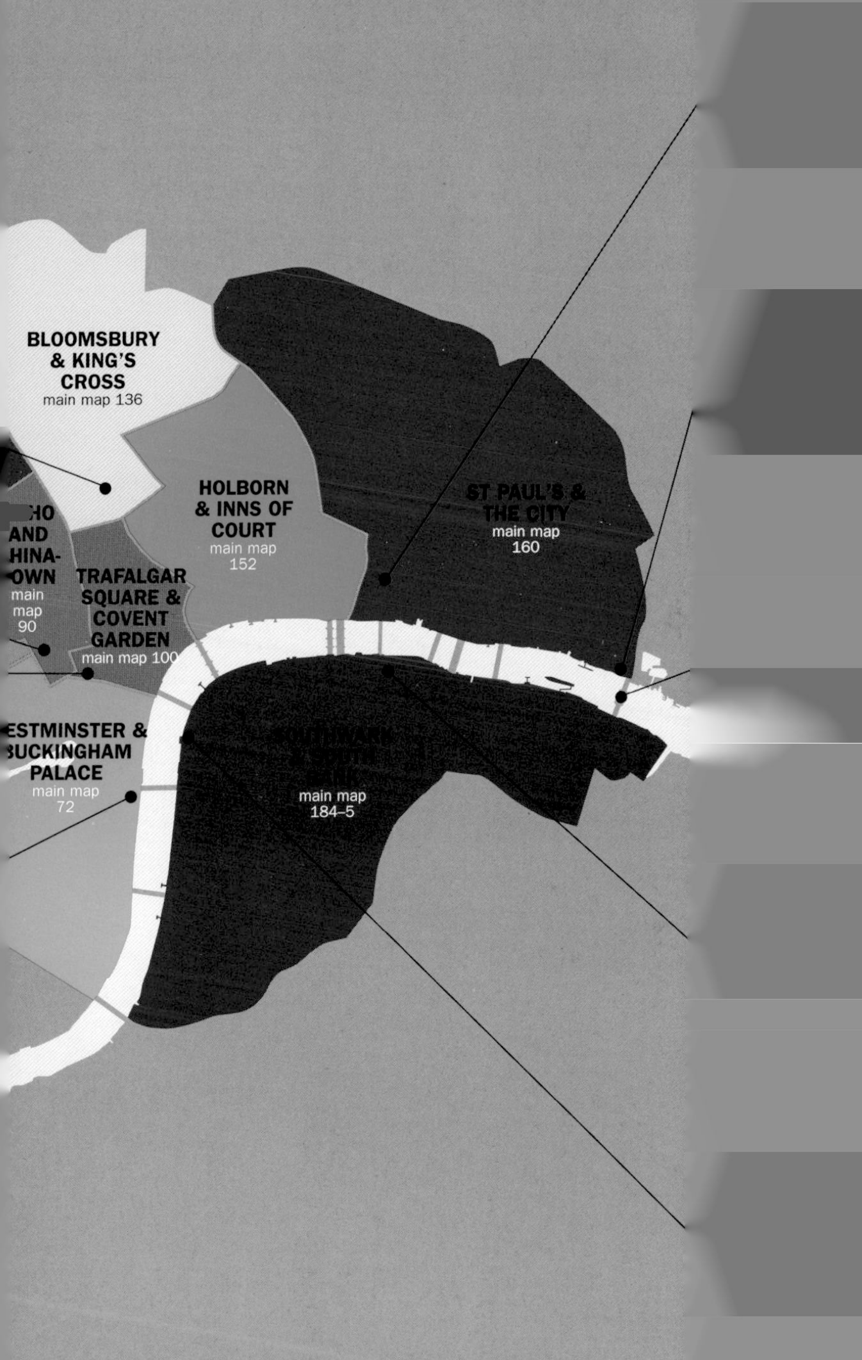
BLOOMSBURY & KING'S CROSS
main map 136
HOLBORN & INNS OF COURT
main map 152
ST PAUL'S & THE CITY
main map 160
main map 90
TRAFALGAR SQUARE & COVENT GARDEN
main map 100
PALACE
main map 72
main map 184–5

Central London

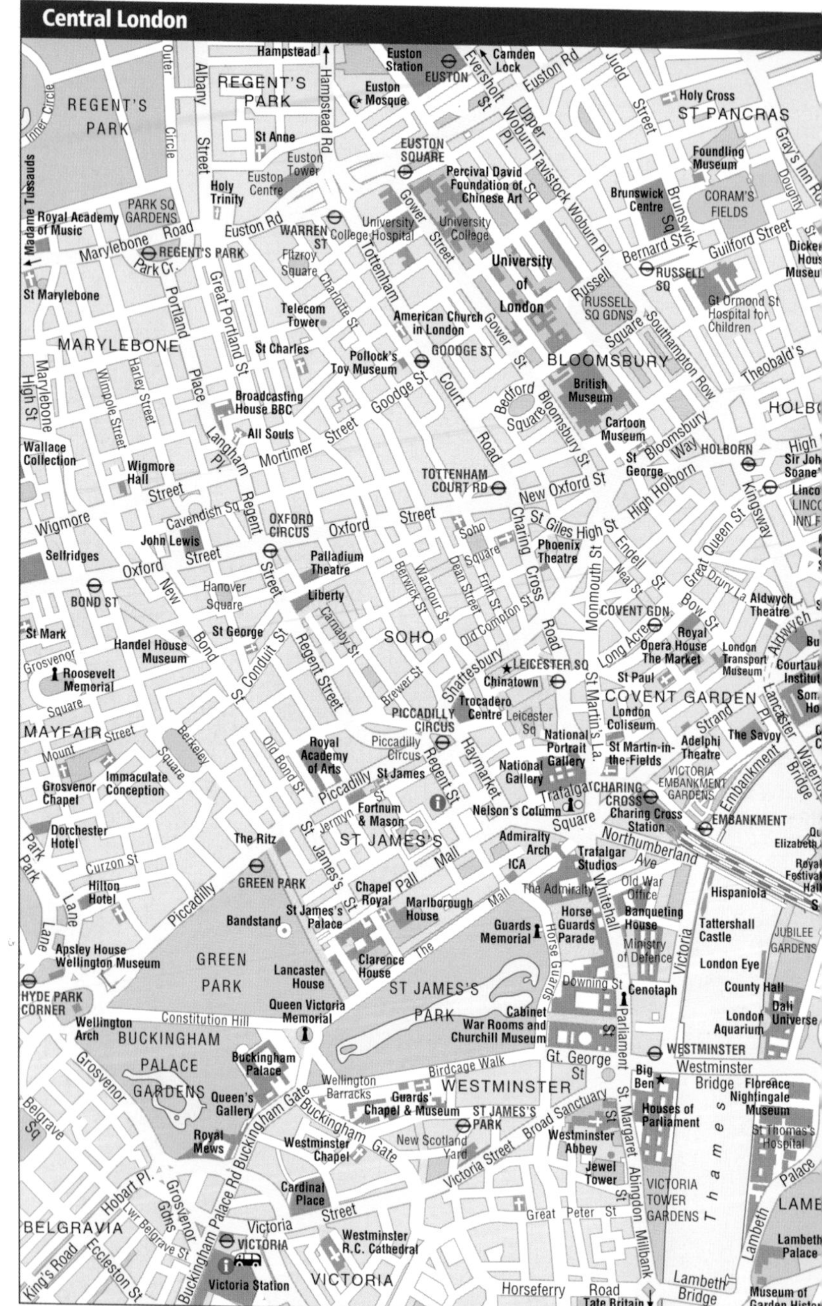

Central London

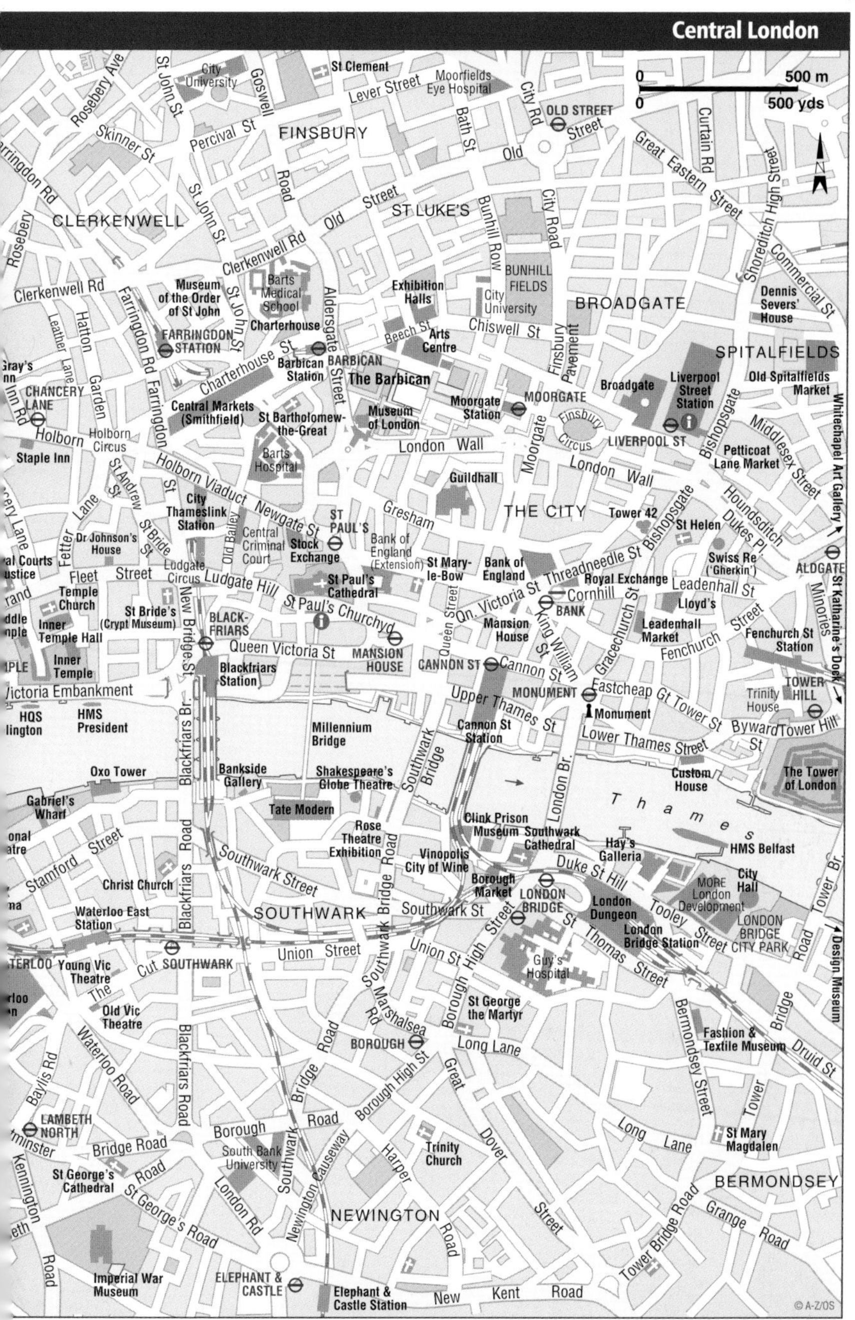

Recommended Restaurants, Bars & Cafés on page 85

WESTMINSTER AND BUCKINGHAM PALACE

Westminster is the centre of official London. Parliament meets here, the Queen and the prime minister have their London homes here, and state funerals are conducted in Westminster Abbey

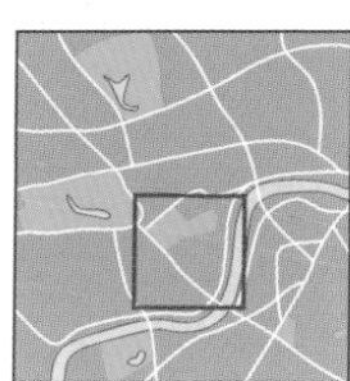

As the focus of government and the monarchy, Westminster contains within its ancient and easily walked boundaries the headquarters of the nation's policy-making civil servants, the prime Minister and the Cabinet, and the royal family. Many kings and queens are buried in Westminster Abbey, founded by the last Saxon ruler, Edward the Confessor (1042–66).

WHITEHALL

Official London begins immediately south of **Trafalgar Square** *(see page 99)*, where the broad and unmistakably official thoroughfare of **Whitehall** ❶ stretches imperiously southwards towards the Houses of Parliament. Most buildings along here are government offices, built from Portland stone in an imposing classical style.

On the right, beyond the Trafalgar Studios, are the offices of the Admiralty, for centuries the headquarters of the Royal Navy until the Ministry of Defence took over in 1964, and those of the Armed Forces Commander-in-Chief, known as the **Horse Guards** ❷. Outside this colonnaded building are two mounted Life Guards in fancy uniforms, white gloves, plumes and helmets, rigidly oblivious to the throng of camera-toting tourists. Changed every hour from 10am to 4pm, they guard the site of the main gateway to what was the Palace of Whitehall, used by King Henry VIII in the 16th century and burnt to the ground in 1698. Through the archway of Horse Guards and opening out on to St James's Park is the huge **Horse Guards Parade.** Here in June the Queen's birthday is honoured by a splendid pageant called **Trooping the Colour**; the name is

Main attractions

- HORSE GUARDS
- BANQUETING HOUSE
- CABINET WAR ROOMS
- HOUSES OF PARLIAMENT
- WESTMINSTER ABBEY
- TATE BRITAIN
- WESTMINSTER CATHEDRAL
- ST JAMES'S PARK
- BUCKINGHAM PALACE
- THE MALL

LEFT: the Thames from Westminster.
RIGHT: Buckingham Palace.

A member of the Life Guards outside the entrance of the former Palace of Whitehall.

derived from the regimental colours which are paraded.

Banqueting House 3

✉ Whitehall; www.hrp.ork.uk ☎ 0870 751 5178 ⏲ Mon–Fri 10am–5pm; £ charge 🚇 Embankment

Opposite Horse Guards, on the other side of Whitehall, is the Renaissance-style **Banqueting House**, built in 1620 by Inigo Jones, the man responsible for bringing this Italian style of architecture to England. It is the only surviving fragment of the palace destroyed by fire in 1698. Inside the huge hall upstairs, the ceiling is divided into nine large panels filled with rich baroque paintings by Rubens. They were commissioned by Charles I to glorify (or deify) the House of Stuart (Rubens was paid £3,000 and knighted for his work), but the Civil War followed and Charles I was beheaded on a scaffold outside the building. The hall is still used for official state banquets.

The prime minister's home

London's most famous address, **Downing Street 4**, just off Whitehall, is little more than a terrace of four 18th-century houses, sealed off behind a heavy gate. The street is

Westminster and Buckingham Palace

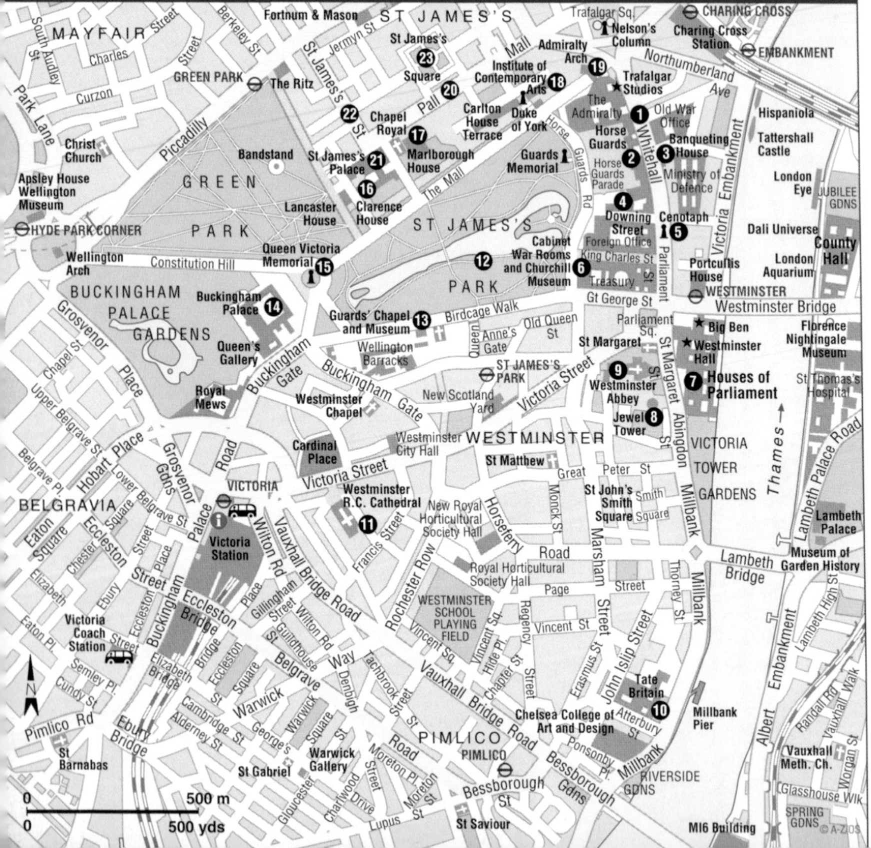

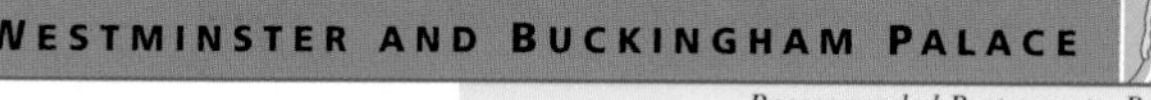

Recommended Restaurants, Bars & Cafés on page 85

named after the diplomat Sir George Downing who went to America with his parents in 1638 and became the second student to graduate from Harvard University. No. 10 is the official residence of the Prime Minister, and the venue for Cabinet meetings.

The plain black door and net-curtained windows suggest nothing of stylish rooms or of the state business conducted inside. Successive prime ministers have lived here since 1732. The Chancellor of the Exchequer has his official residence at No. 11.

Across Whitehall from Downing Street are the offices of the Ministry of Defence. Just south of here, the **Cenotaph** ❺, the national war memorial designed by Sir Edwin Lutyens, breaks Whitehall's monotony. On Remembrance Sunday in November it is the focal point of a service attended by the Queen and political leaders to remember the dead of two world wars and other conflicts.

Beyond the Cenotaph, Whitehall becomes **Parliament Street.** The stolid buildings on the same side as the Horse Guards house the Foreign and Commonwealth offices; its designer, Sir George Gilbert Scott, described it as "a kind of national palace."

Turn right into King Charles Street, which runs between the **Foreign Office** and the **Treasury** and **Cabinet offices** before reaching **Clive Steps** and a statue of Robert Clive (1725–74), a key figure in the establishment of British power in India. Beside the steps is a small wall of sandbags, the only above-ground sign of the Cabinet War Rooms, one of London's best small museums.

The statue of Robert Clive (1725–74), who rose from being a humble scribe in the East India Company to become governor of the Bengal Presidency, laying the foundations for British rule in India. His suicide at the age of 49 was linked to opium use and depression.

ABOVE LEFT: No. 10 Downing Street.
BELOW: Horse Guards.

How Parliament Works

Widely known as the mother of parliaments, the British Parliament has been a model for democracies all over the world

The Houses of Parliament consist of the House of Commons and the House of Lords. The Commons, the House of locally elected Members of Parliament (MPs), known as the Lower House, wields virtually all the power but inhabits only half the building. Jutting out towards Parliament Square is Westminster Hall, with the offices, dining rooms and libraries of the Commons; in the centre is the Commons' debating chamber.

To the right of Westminster Hall is the domain of the Lords, whose role is to examine and sometimes block bills proposed by the Lower House, although a bill can be reintroduced. Until recently, most lords governed by birthright, as descendants of the previous ruling classes, but the voting rights of many hereditary peers have been abolished and the make-up of the Lords has changed. Most members are now life peers, ennobled for services to the nation, and their titles can't be passed to their children. Former members of the Commons are often made peers for years of service.

There are 651 elected MPs, yet the Commons seats only about 450. This is not usually a problem since MPs attend sessions when they wish. The governing party sits on one side, facing the opposition. Cabinet ministers sit on the front bench, opposite the "Shadow Cabinet". The Cabinet, consisting of up to two dozen ministers and chaired by the prime minister, meets at 10 Downing Street weekly to review major issues.

Major parties represented are the Conservatives, Labour and the Liberal Democrats. General elections are run on the basis of local rather than proportional representation. Therefore a party's presence in the house may not reflect its overall national standing. A party, however, needs an overall majority in the house to push through its bills. The procedure of lawmaking is so complex that a bill usually takes more than six months to be enacted. If it is still incomplete at the end of the parliamentary year, it is dropped. Various techniques are employed by the opposition to delay a bill.

The press can report on Parliament and the business of both houses is televised. A select group of journalists ("lobby correspondents") have daily informal "background" briefings with ministers or government officials.

Parliament meets from October to July. In November, the government's plans for the year are announced in the Queen's Speech at the State Opening of Parliament, held in the chamber of the Lords. From the Strangers' Gallery, the public can watch the House of Commons at work, though seats are limited and security precautions introduced since a flour-filled condom thrown from the gallery hit Tony Blair in 2004, have made access more difficult. The weekly Prime Minister's Question Time – an unruly affair – usually attracts a full house. ❑

LEFT: the Queen arrives for the State Opening of Parliament. **ABOVE:** the Commons in action.

Recommended Restaurants, Bars & Cafés on page 85

The Cabinet War Rooms and Churchill Museum 6

✉ Clive Steps, King Charles Street; www.cwr.iwm.org.uk ☎ 7930 6961 ◷ daily 9.30am–6pm Ⓔ charge 🚇 Westminster

This was the wartime bunker from which Sir Winston Churchill conducted World War II. Many of the 21 rooms were abandoned in 1945 and left untouched until the museum opened in 1984; others have been meticulously restored to their wartime condition, "down to the last paper clip". The Central Map Room and the rooms that served as a round-the-clock typing pool illustrate the problems of communications in the 1940s. A converted broom cupboard housed a pioneering hotline to the White House, enabling Churchill to have confidential talks with President Roosevelt.

The **Churchill Museum** within opened in 2005 and includes a selection of letters and other memorabilia.

LEFT: the entrance to the Cabinet War Rooms. **BELOW:** "Big Ben" behind Boudicca's statue.

PARLIAMENT SQUARE

Parliament Street empties out into **Parliament Square**, with its tall trees and lawns lined with statues of illustrious statesmen. This, the country's first official roundabout, is surrounded by national landmarks.

The Houses of Parliament 7

✉ www.parliament.uk ☎ 0870 906 3773 ◷ see panel, page 76 Ⓔ free except for Aug–Sep guided tours 🚇 Westminster

The clock tower of the **Houses of Parliament** has become a symbol of London. Its elaborately fretted stone sides rise up nearly 330 ft (100 metres) to a richly gilded spire and a 13.5-tonne hour bell supposedly nick-

The Cabinet War Rooms' Central Map Room.

The name Big Ben, commonly used for the clock tower of the Houses of Parliament, properly refers only to the 13-ton bell. If you want to climb the 393 steps to see it, and enjoy a fantastic view, you will need to be a UK resident and contact your MP to arrange a tour. Children under the age of 11 are not admitted. Tours last around 1 hour.

BELOW RIGHT: The Union flag on top of Victoria Tower indicates that Parliament is in session. Night sessions are indicated by a light shining over the clock tower.

named **Big Ben** after a rather fat government official called Sir Benjamin Hall who was commissioner of works when the bell was installed. Its chimes first rang out across Westminster in 1859, after an earlier bell was damaged while being tested three years previously. Hoisting Big Ben to its lofty perch took around 20 hours.

Facing Big Ben is the odd-looking **Portcullis House**, a £250-million office block for members of Parliament; its prominent and much criticised "chimneys" form part of the air-conditioning system.

The oldest part of the Houses of Parliament and one of the oldest buildings in London is **Westminster Hall**, begun in 1078. The thick buttressed walls are spanned with a magnificent hammer-beamed oak roof. This hall has witnessed many seminal events in British history: coronation celebrations, lyings-in-state and treason trials. Among those condemned to death were Sir Thomas More, who fell foul of King Henry VIII; King Charles I, accused of treason against Parliament; and the 17th-century revolutionary Guy Fawkes, who tried to blow up the buildings *(see page 29)*.

Fire and reconstruction

In 1834 a fire achieved what Guy Fawkes had failed to do and most of the ancient Palace of Westminster was destroyed. Westminster Hall, a small crypt chapel and the Jewel Tower *(see page 77)* survived. Following this conflagration, the current purpose-built structure was created in exuberant Gothic style by Sir Charles Barry and Augustus Pugin.

The houses are embellished with gilded spires and towers, mullioned windows and intricate stone carving and statues. The complex, which took some 30 years to complete, covers 8 acres (3.2 hectares); there are 11 courtyards and more than 1,100 rooms. Apart from the ceremonial state rooms and the two main debating chambers, the House of Lords and the House of Commons, there are libraries, dining rooms and tearooms and offices and secretarial facilities for government ministers, opposition leaders and ordinary members of Parliament.

Visiting the Houses of Parliament

Guided tours of the Houses of Parliament are held during Parliament's summer recess in August and September (Mon, Tue, Fri, Sat 9.15am–4.30pm; Wed, Thur 1.15–4.30pm). To watch parliamentary debates at other times of the year from the public galleries overlooking the Commons or Lords chambers, queue by St Stephen's Gate on the western side of the building. Note that Parliament is also in recess at Christmas and Easter.

Entry times vary depending on when parliament is in session, but normal sitting times for the Commons are Mon–Tue 2.30–10.30pm; Wed 11.30am–7.30pm; Thur 10.30am–6.30pm. The Commons does not normally sit on Friday, but when it does the hours are 9.30am–3.30pm. Expect to queue for between 1 and 1½ hours, less in the evenings. The longest queues are for Prime Minister's Question Time (held at noon on Wednesday); UK residents should contact their MP for an advance ticket.

Recommended Restaurants, Bars & Cafés on page 85

Main points of interest

St Stephen's, on the western side of the building, is the main entrance to the House of Commons, and anyone can watch debates from the visitors' gallery, though there are almost always queues *(see page 76)*. Beneath **St Stephen's Hall** is the ancient crypt chapel that survived the 1834 fire. Members can take their marriage vows and have their children baptised here. The **Commons chamber** was bombed in 1941; the current chamber only opened in 1950.

The immense **Victoria Tower** marks the grand entrance to the House of Lords. It is also the entrance used by the Queen when opening a new session of government.

Opposite Parliament is the moated **Jewel Tower** ❽, a relic of the Palace of Westminster dating from 1365. Its small museum of Parliament Past and Present (Apr–Oct 10am–5pm, Nov–Mar 10am–4pm; charge) has more information panels than artefacts.

Beyond Victoria Tower and overlooking the Thames are the **Victoria Tower Gardens**, containing memorials to suffragettes Emmeline Pankhurst and her daughter, and Auguste Rodin's powerful statue group, *The Burghers of Calais*.

The Jewel Tower has had several functions over the centuries. It was used to test official standards of weights and measures from 1869 until the 1930s. Its moat once supplied fish for the sovereign's table.

Westminster Abbey ❾

www.westminster-abbey.ork
7222 5152 Mon–Fri 9.15am–3.45pm, most Weds until 6pm (7pm in summer), Sat 9am–1.45pm
charge; guided tours extra
Westminster

The most historic religious building in Britain is **Westminster Abbey**. It is also an outstanding piece of Gothic architecture, which is probably more

LEFT: sightseeing from the top of a tour bus.
BELOW: the opulent House of Lords.

For art lovers in a hurry, a 220-seat catamaran runs every 40 minutes between Tate Britain on the Thames' north bank and Tate Modern on the south bank. It stops at the London Eye. Tel: 7887 8888.

ABOVE AND BELOW Rodin's *The Kiss* and *The Cholmondeley Ladies*, artist unknown, in Tate Britain.
RIGHT: the towers of Westminster Abbey.

striking from the detail on the inside than from its outward aspects. So many eminent figures are honoured in this national shrine that large areas of the interior have the cluttered appearance of an overcrowded sculpture museum. *For full coverage of the abbey, see pages 86–7.*

St Margaret's Church

On the northeast side of Westminster Abbey facing the Houses of Parliament is **St Margaret's Church,** used by MPs for official services and for high-society weddings. Sir Walter Raleigh (1552–1618), the sea captain, poet and favourite of Queen Elizabeth I, who established the first British colony in Virginia and introduced tobacco and potatoes to Britain, was interred here after his execution. William Caxton (c.1421–91), who ran the first English printing presses nearby, is also buried here.

Beyond Westminster Abbey and Victoria Gardens a short street leads to one of London's most unobtrusive but notable concert halls, **St John's Smith Square**. This former 18th-century church has fine acoustics

and a reputation for classical music. In the crypt is a good wine bar-cum-restaurant *(see page 85)*.

Tate Britain ⑩

Millbank; www.tate.org.uk/britain 7887 8888 daily 10am–5.50pm, until 10pm first Fri of each month free, but charge for feature exhibitions Pimlico

A 10–15-minute walk along Millbank from the Houses of Parliament

Recommended Restaurants, Bars & Cafés on page 85

is **Tate Britain,** founded in 1897 by Henry Tate, of the Tate & Lyle sugar empire, and today the storehouse for the Tate's collection of British art from 1500 to the present. It is complemented by Tate Modern, further down the river on Bankside, which houses most of the Tate's modern and contemporary international collection *(see pages 198–199).*

The galleries within Tate Britain are arranged by date and theme. The only criticism is that there isn't enough space: the majority of the collection has to be kept in storage out of the public view. A much-needed extension is being considered.

Among the British paintings are portraits by William Hogarth (1697–1764) and Thomas Gainsborough (1727–88), views of the English countryside by John Constable (1776–1837) and, in the Clore Gallery, seascapes and landscapes by J.M.W. Turner (1775–1851). Turner bequeathed the paintings to the nation on his death, with the stipulation that they should all be hung in one place, and should be available for the public to see, without charge.

The most popular 19th-century painters represented are the Pre-Raphaelites, including Millais, Holman Hunt, Rosetti and Burne-Jones. Modern British artists represented include Stanley Spencer, Francis Bacon and David Hockney. Sculptures include works by Jacob Epstein, Barbara Hepworth and Henry Moore. The Tate also stages free lectures and film shows, and has a reputation for the avant garde, with the award of an annual Turner Prize. Its Rex Whistler-designed restaurant is a great place to have lunch *(see page 85).*

Across the river from Millbank, to the right, the modern green-and-cream building is **Vauxhall Cross,** headquarters of MI6's spymasters; this secret services building, designed by Terry Farrell, is built in a "Faraday Cage" which stops electro-magnetic information passing in or out.

VICTORIA STREET

The west door of the Westminster Abbey opens on to **Victoria Street,** important commercially but, since its re-building, a long grey canyon of undistinguished office blocks. Down this street, close to the Victoria Station end, is **Westminster Cathedral.**

Westminster Cathedral ⓫

7798 9055 tower 9.30am–12.30pm and 1–5pm charge for tower Victoria

This is the most important Catholic church in London. Its bold red-and-white brickwork makes it look like a gigantic layer cake. Built at the end of the 19th century in an outlandish Italian-Byzantine style not seen elsewhere in London, it has a 330-ft (100-metre) tower incorporating a lift. The views from the top are superb. The interior is sumptuous, with many chapels clad in coloured marble, but the decor was never finished; the numerous mosaics included in the original designs are

Fine views from the top of Westminster Cathedral's tower.

BELOW: the Italian-Byzantine-style facade of Westminster Cathedral.

A carved canopy on one of the elegant terraced houses in Queen Anne's Gate.

absent, and the ceiling is largely bereft of decoration.

On the north side of Victoria Street behind St James's Park Underground station is **Queen Anne's Gate**, a small, quiet street which has retained much of its 18th-century atmosphere. Lord Palmerston, who became prime minister in 1855, was born at No. 20.

St James's Park and Buckingham Palace

The formal arrangement of lakes and flora at **St James's Park** ⓬ is one of the most delightful in London. Formerly the grounds of St James's Palace acquired by Henry VIII in 1531, it was laid out in 1603, then re-landscaped in formal style by John Nash in 1827. It has always had a collection of ducks and water fowl, including black swans and pelicans, fed every day at 3pm. Another entertainment is the lunch-time concerts played in the bandstand.

Continuing the ornithological theme is **Birdcage Walk**, which takes its name from an 18th-century aviary, running along the south side of the park from Parliament Square to Buckingham Palace and dividing the park from the drilling ground of the **Wellington Barracks**, the home of the Royal Grenadier Guards and the Coldstream Guards. Here the **Guards' Chapel and Museum** ⓭ (daily 10am–4pm, tel: 7930 4466; www.army.mod.uk; charge) are on the site of a former chapel which was hit by a bomb in 1944, killing 121 members of the congregation.

There are five of these aristocratic infantry regiments of Guards, first formed during the English Civil War (1642–9), and the museum provides a social history in uniform (including a uniform worn by the Duke of Wellington), as well as a large collection of toy soldiers.

ABOVE RIGHT AND BELOW: St James's Park.

Buckingham Palace ⓮

✉ Buckingham Palace Road; www.royal.gov.uk ☎ 7766 7300 ⏲ late July–late Sep only, 9.45am–6pm; tickets are timed, and a visit lasts 2–2½ hours £ charge 🚇 Green Park, Hyde Park Corner, Victoria

Buckingham Palace has been the main London home of the royal family since Queen Victoria acceded to the throne in 1837. Her grandfather, George IV, employed John Nash (responsible for many of the grander parts of central London) to enlarge the building which had been built in the 17th century for the Duke of Buckingham (it originally

Recommended Restaurants, Bars & Cafés on page 85

became the property of the Crown when George III bought it for his wife in 1761). Nash added two wings that were later enclosed in a quadrangle, while the main facade came later still, being designed by Aston Webb in 1913.

A tour of the palace

The sumptuous **State Rooms** are open to the public for a few weeks in late summer when the Queen is not in residence. These include the Dining Room, Music Room, White Drawing Room and Throne Room, where there are paintings by Vermeer, Rubens and Rembrandt. The tour includes a stroll through part of the 40-acre (16-hectare) Palace Gardens where the cream of society mingles with the good and the worthy from all walks of life at the celebrated garden parties. The guests are invited because of some commendable contribution made to the nation, but few of the 8,000 people a year get to shake the Queen's hand.

Only the invited get further into the 600-room palace, although one enterprising intruder penetrated as far as the Queen's bedroom one night in 1982. She talked to him quietly while managing to summon palace security. The Queen and the Duke of Edinburgh occupy about 12 of the 650 rooms, on the first floor of the north wing, overlooking Green Park. If the Queen is in residence, the royal standard flies from the centre flag pole.

Next to the Royal Mews on Buckingham Palace Road, the **Queen's Gallery** (daily 10am–5.30pm; tel: 7839 1377; charge, combined tickets with admission to Buckingham Palace and the Royal Mews are available late July–late Sep) was

The palace garden parties have long been a quaint way of keeping the "right" sort of young people in each other's company; guests are requested not to bring married sons and daughters.

ABOVE: Buckingham Palace. **BELOW LEFT AND RIGHT:** the Blue Drawing Room and the Grand Staircase at the palace.

The gift shop next to the Queen's Gallery on Buckingham Palace Road is the place to buy souvenirs such as "God Save the Queen" pillowcases, Queen Victoria china, Buckingham Palace biscuits, and a variety of Windsor-endorsed luxury foodstuffs.

refurbished in 2002 to coincide with the Queen's Golden Jubilee. The Queen has one of the top private art collections in the world, including an exceptional collection of Leonardo da Vinci drawings, portraits by Holbein and Rubens, sketches by Hogarth, and a superb series of watercolour views of Windsor by Paul Sandby. Exhibitions are changed periodically.

RIGHT: *Portrait of Agatha Bas* (1641) by Rembrandt, the Queen's Gallery. **BELOW:** ornamental gate to Green Park on the Mall.

The adjoining **Royal Mews** contain royal vehicles, from coaches to Rolls-Royces. The Gold State Coach, built for George III in 1762, is still used by the Queen on major state occasions (late July–late Sep daily 10am–5pm; late March–late July, late Sept–Oct Sat–Thur 11am–4pm; charge).

Most of the everyday crowds come to see the **Changing of the Guard** which takes place outside the palace on alternate mornings at 11.30am, and daily in May, June and July. The New Guard, which marches up from Wellington Barracks, meets the Old Guard in the forecourt of the palace and they exchange symbolic keys to the accompaniment of regimental music. The Irish Guards are distinctive for their bearskin hats (now made from synthetic materials).

The **Queen Victoria Memorial** ⓯, in front of the palace was built in 1901. It encompasses symbolic figures glorifying the achievements of the British Empire and its builders.

THE MALL

The Mall, the wide thoroughfare leading from Buckingham Palace to Trafalgar Square, was laid out by Charles II as a second course for the popular French game of *paille maille*, a kind of croquet, when the one in Pall Mall *(see page 83)* became too rowdy. The Mall is the venue for the autumn **State Opening of Parliament,** when the Queen rides in a gold stage coach surrounded by more than 100 troopers of the Household Cavalry wearing armorial breastplates. A further eccentricity are two farriers who accompany the procession, bearing spiked axes to kill any horse lamed in the parade and then chop off its hooves to prevent the horse flesh being sold to a butcher.

The Mall is lined with a succession of grand buildings and historic houses reflecting different styles and periods. The ducal palaces have been used as royal residences: **Clarence**

Recommended Restaurants, Bars & Cafés on page 85

House ⓰ is home to Prince Charles; at **Lancaster House** Chopin gave a recital for Queen Victoria; and **Marlborough House** ⓱, designed by Sir Christopher Wren, was the home of Queen Mary, consort of George V (1865–1936) until her death in 1953. Now it is a Commonwealth conference and research centre. The brick Tudor **St James's Palace** faces on to Pall Mall *(see below)*.

Near the end of the Mall is **Carlton House Terrace**, built by John Nash, part of which houses the headquarters of **The Royal Society**, a learned body for the promotion of natural sciences. The oldest society of its kind, it was founded in 1660.

At the Trafalgar Square end, the terrace incorporates the **Mall Gallery** and the **Institute of Contemporary Arts** ⓲, a venue for avant-garde exhibitions, cinema and theatre, held in the restored Nash House. The cinema shows a wide range of art house movies, and there is a book shop.

The reinforced concrete structure across the Mall on the corner of the park is a bomb-proof shelter built for the Admiralty and nicknamed the Citadel, or Lenin's Tomb.

Admiralty Arch ⓳, leading from The Mall to Trafalgar Square, is a five-arched gateway commissioned by King Edward VII in memory of his mother, Queen Victoria, and completed in 1911. Traffic passes through the two outer arches: the central arch is opened only for state occasions, letting royalty in and out of the city.

PALL MALL AND ST JAMES'S

Along elegant **Pall Mall** ⓴ exclusive gentlemen's clubs mingle with the grand homes of royalty, with their lofty book-lined rooms, elegant, picture-lined dining rooms and chan-

The central section of Admiralty Arch, a ceremonial gateway leading from The Mall to Trafalgar Square.

LEFT: Horse Guards on the Mall. **BELOW:** the Queen Victoria Memorial in front of Buckingham Palace.

The bronze statue of Frederick, the Duke of York, at the top of the Duke of York Steps.

RIGHT: St James's Palace. **FAR RIGHT:** Boisdale (top), the Cinnamon Club (bottom).

deliered lounges can be seen from the street. The area has been the haunt of men of influence since the 17th century and it is reassuring to learn that, for the most part, the clubs enjoy a reputation for dull food and boring, snobbish company.

In **Waterloo Place**, at the east end of Pall Mall and the bottom end of Regent Street, the statue of Frederick, the "grand old" Duke of York (whose 10,000 men are fruitlessly marched up and down hill in a popular nursery rhyme), overlooks the Mall and St James's Park from its 124-ft (37-metre) column. The cost of his monument was met by extracting a day's wages from every man in the armed services.

One building that is unmistakable in Pall Mall is the red-brick **St James's Palace** ㉑ at the western end, built by Henry VIII in 1540 in a style that echoes his palace at Hampton Court. The state apartments are not open to the public and the chief relic of the original Tudor palace, the **Gatehouse** or **Clock Tower**, one of the finest examples of Tudor architecture in the city, is best viewed from the street. Clarence House, part of the complex, is the London home of Prince Charles.

North of St James's Palace **St James's Street** ㉒ leads into an area traditionally associated with gentlemen's tailors and shoe-makers. The characterful shop frontages include **Berry Bros and Rudd**, at No. 3, which could be straight out of a Dickens novel. **James Lock and Co**, at No. 6, is the birthplace of the bowler hat. A few doors up is **Lobb's**, shoemakers to Queen Victoria.

St James's Square

Also off the north side of Pall Mall is **St James's Square** ㉓ laid out by Henry Jermyn, the first Earl of St Alban in about 1660. The Dukes of Norfolk had a town house in the square from 1723 until 1938. The building was used by General Eisenhower when he was preparing to launch the invasions of North Africa and northwest Europe in World War II. Also here is the London Library, an independent subscription library whose past members have included Dickens and George Eliot. ❑

Club Land

Each of London's clubs has its own character and attracts a certain type of person. It is said that bishops and Fellows of the Royal Society join the Athenaeum (see picture), the foremost literary club, while actors and publishers opt for the Garrick or Saville Club. Diplomats, politicians and spies prefer Brooks', the Traveller's, Boodles or White's, while journalists gather at the Groucho Club in Soho. The novelist Jules Verne used the Reform Club (Pall Mall), the leading liberal club, as the setting for Phileas Fogg's wager that he could travel around the world in 80 days.

The majority of London's clubs are the near-exclusive preserve of men. Their continuing influence in the social, commercial and political life of the capital should not be underestimated. Dukes join the Turf Club, while top Tories like to dine together at the Carlton on St James's Street.

BEST RESTAURANTS, PUBS AND BARS

Restaurants

Prices for a three-course dinner per person with a half-bottle of house wine:

£ = under £20
££ = £20–30
£££ = £30–50
££££ = over £50

British

Boisdale
15 Eccleston St, SW1 7730 6922 L Mon–Fri, D only Sat. **£££** [p 334, B3]
Scottish dishes such as lobster bisque, haggis, and Aberdeen Angus steaks. There is always fresh fish and game and a full malt whisky line-up.

The Footstool
St John's, Smith Square, SW1 7222 2779 L & D Mon–Fri, D on weekday concert evenings and weekends. **££–£££** [p 335, D3]
Beneath one of London's top concert venues, this brick-vaulted restaurant offers good food and excellent service. Sandwiches and snacks are also on offer, and there is a long wine list.

Goring Dining Room
Goring Hotel, Beeston Place, SW1 7390 9000 L & D Sun–Fri, D only Sat. **£££** [p 334, B3]
Traditional fare such as lobster omelette thermidor, roast beef and Yorkshire pudding, filet of venison and proper puddings. Sunday roast lunch is a speciality.

Tate Britain Restaurant
Millbank, SW1 7887 8877 L daily. **££** (set menu) **£££** (à la carte) [p 335, D4]
Traditional fare such as fish of the day, veal escalope and steak-and-kidney pudding are well prepared and reliably good. There is also an excellent wine list.

Indian

The Cinnamon Club
Old Westminster Library, Great Smith St, SW1 7222 2555 L & D Mon–Fri, D only Sat. **££** (set lunch) **££££** [p 335, D2]
Set in a beautifully refurbished Victorian library, with a clubby feel. The menu has a fine selection of specialities from Nile perch to Keralan curry.

Quaglino's
16 Bury St, SW1 7930 6767 L & D Mon–Sat, D only Sun. **£££** [p 328, A3]
Glamorous Conran brasserie. Live music on Fridays and Saturdays (when it closes at 1am) add to the laid-back atmosphere.

Le Caprice
Arlington House, Arlington St, SW1. 7629 2239 L & D Mon–Sat, D only Sun. [p 328, A3]
Chic, buzzy bistro with Art Deco decor. The food – sophisticated salads, seafood and wonderful desserts – is more for picking over than wolfing down. Last-minute seating at the bar sometimes possible.

PUBS AND BARS

As one might expect, Westminster has a good choice of pubs, including **St Stephen's Arms** *(10 Bridge St, SW1)* and the **Red Lion** *(48 Parliament St, SW1)*, both popular with politicians. There are also wine bars aplenty. **Tapster** *(3 Brewers Green, Buckingham Gate SW1)*, offer a traditional wine bar setting and menu, as does **Balls Brothers** *(50 Buckingham Palace Road)*. For a sleeker environment, try **Cinnamon Club Bar**, the high-tech downstairs bar of the restaurant *(see main listings)* or **Zander** *(45 Buckingham Gate, SW1)*. For speciality wiskies, as well as cocktails, try **Millbank Lounge** *(30 John Islip St, SW1)*, a modern bar decked out in red and chrome.

WESTMINSTER ABBEY

More than 3,300 notable people are buried here. The clutter of monuments make it seem like an ecclesiastical Madame Tussauds, with stone replacing wax

Monarchs were interred here until George II in 1760, and they are still crowned here. Among the royal tombs, look out for those of Elizabeth I, her half-sister Queen Mary, and Mary Queen of Scots, all in the Lady Chapel. Never fond of one another in life, they are united in death.

Poets lie close by, beginning with Geoffrey Chaucer in 1400, who had been Clerk of Works to the Palace of Westminster.

Other tombs include those of the naturalist Charles Darwin, the explorer David Livingstone and the scientist Sir Isaac Newton.

The Tomb of the Unknown Warrior *(above)* houses a body brought back from France at the end of World War I, along with the soil for the grave. As the national shrine, Westminster Abbey was the natural resting place for this anonymous representative of the countless war dead.

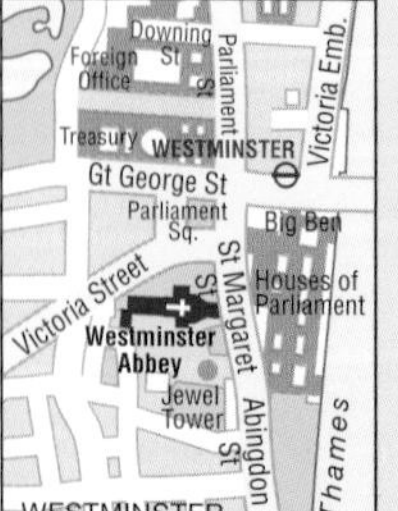

The essentials

www.westminster-abbey.org

7222 5152

9.15am–3.45pm, most Weds until 6pm (7pm in summer), Sat 9am–1.45pm

charge; guided tours extra

Westminster

ABOVE: much of the present abbey, the third on the site, was built in the 13th century in early English Gothic style by Henry III. In the 16th century, Henry VII added the chapel in the late Gothic Perpendicular style. During the 18th century, Nicholas Hawksmoor designed the towers at the main west entrance.

ABOVE: the abbey organ was originally built in 1733 but has been much rebuilt and redecorated since. Famous organists who played here include Henry Purcell, who is also buried in the abbey. Other composers buried here include Ralph Vaughan Williams.

SOME HIGHLIGHTS

Poet's Corner. The remains of Chaucer, Edmund Spenser, Samuel Johnson, Dryden, Sheridan, Browning, Tennyson, Dickens and Kipling lie here. Ben Jonson is buried standing up because he didn't wish to occupy too much space.
Coronation Chair. This has been used for every coronation in the Abbey since 1308.
Henry VII's Chapel. Contains exquisite fan-vaulting and the statues of nearly 100 saints.
Chapter House. Parliament met here in the 14th century. It has a fine tiled floor from 1259 and some lurid wall paintings based on the Apocalypse.
Undercroft Museum. This 11th-century room contains many of the Abbey's treasures as well as waxworks and death masks of various monarchs.
Sculptures. There are superbly carved angels in the south transept, and the chapels of Henry V and Henry VII are packed with saints and philosophers.
Brass band concerts are held in a garden off the Cloisters during Thursday lunchtime in Jul–Aug.

ABOVE: some of the monuments are worth the price of a ticket to the Abbey. On the left, the actor-manager David Garrick (1717–79) takes a final curtain call. In the middle, the husband of a noblewoman, Elizabeth Nightingale, tries to fend off the skeleton of Death as it comes to claim her in 1731 ("more theatrical than sepulchral", said one critic). On the right is the toga-clad Admiral Clowdisley Shovell who, washed up on a beach in 1707 after surviving a shipwreck, was killed for his emerald ring by a passing fishwife.

THE RED LION SOHO
THE RED LI
Melati Restaurant
STAURANT

Recommended Restaurants, Bars & Cafés on pages 95–7

SOHO AND CHINATOWN

Soho, Chinatown and Leicester Square form London's main entertainment centre, where you'll find abundant clubs, pubs, cinemas and theatres, and cuisines from all over the globe

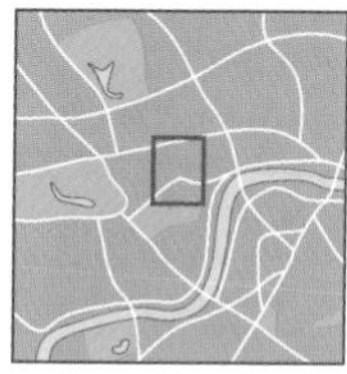

Main attractions

- PICCADILLY CIRCUS
- OLD COMPTON STREET
- SOHO SQUARE
- BERWICK STREET MARKET
- CARNABY STREET
- CHINATOWN

The West End has long been seen as the place to head for a night out in London. Piccadilly Circus is a springboard for London's theatreland while Leicester Square is the gateway to Chinatown and the location of the Empire cinema, the venue for UK film premieres. Over the past few decades, however, as tacky shops and chain restaurants have muscled in on these famous squares, their glamour has begun to look a little tarnished. Neighbouring Soho, on the other hand, has largely shed its once-dubious image as London's dark underbelly to become one of the capital's foremost destinations for drinking and dining.

PICCADILLY CIRCUS

At the heart of the West End is **Piccadilly Circus ❶**, star of millions of postcards. The first illuminated advertising signs appeared here in 1890, offering lucrative rental income to shopkeepers but contrasting harshly with the elegant architecture of neighbouring Regent Street. The statue of Eros, Greek god of love, was erected in 1893 as the Angel of Charity in honour of the philanthropic seventh Earl of Shaftesbury (1801–85) who drove the broad thoroughfare bearing his name through the squalid slums that had grown up to the northeast.

Adding to Piccadilly's bright lights are the refurbished Criterion theatre on the south side, a huge branch of Virgin Megastore on the west and the 19th-century facade of the London Pavilion, a former music hall, on the east, which is now part of the **Trocadero Centre ❷**, a complex of shops and restaurants on Holland Street. It includes **Amora: the Academy of Sex and Relationships**

LEFT: a sunny day in Soho.
RIGHT: sitting under Eros, Piccadilly Circus.

The Hungarian **Pâtisserie Valerie** (open until 11pm) at No. 44 Old Compton Street sells mouthwatering sweet and savoury pastries. If you're in need of a caffeine fix but don't like London prices, the **Algerian Coffee Shop** on Old Compton Street serves great coffee at low prices. It also sells freshly roasted coffee. Take your pick from the jars of beans that line the shelves like an old-fashioned sweet shop.

BELOW: Bar Italia in Soho's Frith Street.

(11am–midnight; over-18s only), a museum, shop, bar and exhibition space that aims to inspire, educate and entertain.

The Trocadero also contains **Funland**, a huge indoor entertainment complex (10am–midnight weekdays, 10am–1am weekends) – five floors of video games, slot machines, dodgems, 10-pin bowling, a sports bar, and a pool hall, all of which have seen better days.

BUSTLING SOHO

On the north side of Shaftesbury Avenue lies **Soho,** a bustling area of narrow streets long popular with immigrants. Flemish weavers, French Huguenots, Greeks, Italians, Belgians, Maltese, Swiss, Chinese and Russian Jews have sought refuge here at various times.

Their influence is still felt in the patisseries, delicatessens, restaurants and shops. Four hundred years ago Soho was an area of open fields, and its name is said to come from a hunting cry: "So-ho, so-ho!".

Bars and clip joints

Once infamous as the centre of London's sex industry, Soho occupies a middle-ground between the edgy, seedier Soho of its past and the tourist-friendly hotspot of smart bars and restaurants that populate the area today. "Anything you like, sir" is still a phrase murmured to passers-by, but most of the strip joints and sex shops have been pushed towards the side streets. There are also venues for drag artists and transvestites that have been going long enough to have become almost respectable, and several of the attractive late-night bars and restaurants designed for the discerning gay crowd draw visitors of all persuasions.

Old Compton Street ❸

This is Soho's main artery, where a few of the celebrated continental food stores, cafés and specialist shops

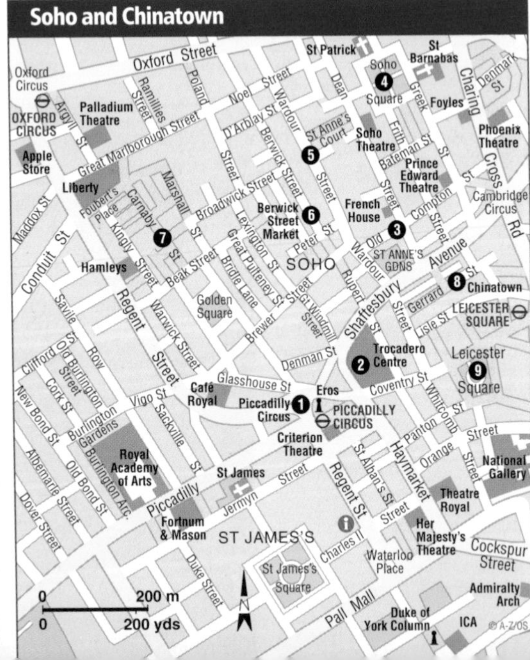

Recommended Restaurants, Bars & Cafés on pages 95–7

which once dominated the street, live on. Most have been replaced by modern coffee shops, bars and more outlandish establishments, such as the body-piercing shop.

Situated at the Charing Cross Road end of Old Compton Street, the **Prince Edward Theatre** has guided behind-the-scenes tours (Thur 11am; tel: 0870-850 9191; charge) of its current production, *Mary Poppins*.

Just off Old Compton Street are the French House in Dean Street, the centre of the Free French in World War II, an artists' haunt and still fiercely French. Artists such as Francis Bacon and Lucian Freud used to take advantage of the liberal licensing arrangements at the Colony Club in Dean Street. At 22 Frith Street, opposite Ronnie Scott's jazz club, is Bar Italia, a narrow café-bar with pavement seating and a retro Italian feel, which serves the best cappuccino in town and is open 24 hours a day. It is also a great place to watch international football matches; the large screen at the back of the bar is visible from the street.

Soho Square ❹

At the top of Frith Street, **Soho Square** was one of London's best addresses when it was built in the 17th century. Today various film, new media and design companies are based here, their minimalist receptions lit up by plasma screens or statement art. During the summer the garden at the heart of the square is crowded with office workers grabbing a bit of sun with their sandwich. In the centre of the square are a 17th-century statue of Charles II and a 19th-century mock-Tudor gardeners' tool shed from which steps lead down to an underground cavern, used as a

A few of Soho's bars and pubs are still exclusively gay: two examples are the Admiral Duncan and Comptons in Old Compton Street. Among the clubs is Candy Bar, a lesbian venue in Carlisle Street *(also see page 302)*.

TOP LEFT: Candy Bar in Carlisle Street. **BELOW LEFT:** Karl Marx wrote *Das Kapital* in his house at 26 Dean Street. **BELOW:** Old Compton Street.

Historic Streets

Many famous people are associated with Soho, from the painters Thomas Gainsborough (1727–88) to Francis Bacon (1909–92), from Casanova (1725–98) to Oscar Wilde (1854–1900). The restaurant Aperitivo at 41 Beak Street was the home of Antonio Canaletto, the Venetian painter, from 1749 to 1751. In 1926 John Logie Baird transmitted the first television images from an attic at 22 Frith Street (now Bar Italia), next door to where Mozart stayed as a boy. The house at 26 Dean Street, now Quo Vadis restaurant, is where Karl Marx wrote *Das Kapital*.

A Night on the Town

Ah, London! London! our delight,
Great flower that opens but at night.
— Richard Le Gallienne, French poet

The make-up of any major city seems to change at night as offices empty into pubs and trains drain the centre of workers and replace them with players. The West End, a shopping and office centre by day, is the heart of London at night.

Who goes where?

Soho is still the most fashionable area, and is still the sex centre of London, although smut is on the retreat. Some of the best food and the trendiest clubs are here, including Ronnie Scott's jazz club in Frith Street and for clubbers with a sense of fun, Madame Jo Jo's on Brewer Street. Soho entertains a real cross section of Londoners, from the casually-dressed lager drinkers packing out the more traditional pubs, to the city boys swilling champagne in their private members' bar before hitting a lap-dancing club such as Stringfellow's in Upper St Martin's Lane.

Old Compton Street is the centre of the gay scene, with pubs such as the Admiral Duncan and Comptons drawing big crowds. Around the corner on Wardour Street, Village Soho is another popular gay venue with unthreatening clientele and a sprinkling of glam.

Most of the so-called "super-clubs" in the area have now closed down but one hanger-on is Cirque at the Hippodrome (Cranbourne Street). The celebrated gay disco: G-A-Y (the Astoria, 157–65 Charing Cross Road) continues to entertain, sometimes with live pop acts that have included the Spice Girls, Kylie Minogue and Madonna.

With the new late-licensing laws many bars stay open until at least 3am, which has removed much of the 11pm rush towards neighbourood clubs. Some bars can be difficult to get into, but this tends to be because of capacity rather than the dress codes of old. Many of the cafés also stay open into the small hours and do a roaring trade in the *de rigueur* post-bar coffee and snack.

The evening promenade

Londoners get a buzz from being in the company of the countless nationalities that throng Leicester Square, Piccadilly Circus, Trafalgar Square and Covent Garden. These are the best-known central areas for evening promenading. London may not seem to offer a conducive climate, but 84 percent of all overseas visitors describe their evening activities as "just walking around".

Further Afield

Apart from Soho, the King's Road in Chelsea, Notting Hill and Queensway, Camden and Islington are lively in the evenings. More offbeat places can be found in the east end of town, such as Farringdon, Brick Lane and Hoxton Square. For a glamorously old-fashioned evening, head for Mayfair and St James's. Here you'll find discreet restaurants and exclusive nightclubs such as Annabel's in Berkeley Square, appealing to an older crowd which doesn't need to ask the price. ❑

LEFT: an evening in Ronnie Scott's.
ABOVE: the Admiral Duncan, a popular gay pub on Old Compton Street.

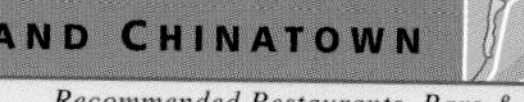

Recommended Restaurants, Bars & Cafés on pages 95–7

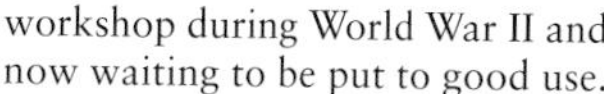

workshop during World War II and now waiting to be put to good use.

The red-brick tower of St Patrick's Catholic Church lends a bit of variety to the architectural proceedings. Established in 1893 on the site of an earlier church, St Patrick's was a refuge for the area's poor Irish immigrant community.

A hint of Soho Square's former glory can be seen in the 18th-century house of charitable works, caring for the destitute, **St-Barnabas-in-Soho**, on the corner of Greek Street. In 2006 St-Barnabas ceased its role as hostel to homeless women and is currently reviewing its status. Its elegant interior of fine woodcarvings, fireplaces and plasterwork is still open to the public but it is worth telephoning in advance just in case (open first Monday of the month; tel: 7437 1894).

Wardour Street ❺

Continuing west from Soho Square past Dean Street, the next main road is **Wardour Street**, once sarcastically known as the only street in the world which was shady on both sides. It is still the heart of London's film and recording industries, and during weekday lunch times the surrounding bars and restaurants are full of 30-something media bods discussing the next big thing.

Wardour Street has become something of a restaurant hotspot in recent years, and venues such as Busaba Eathai and Floridita ensure the street is busy long after office hours.

At the Shaftesbury Avenue end of Wardour Street, a tower is all that remains of Sir Christopher Wren's church of **St Anne's**, bombed in the war, though its beautifully kept gardens provide some shade and benches for a rest on a hot day.

Berwick Street Market ❻

The fruit and vegetable market in parallel **Berwick Street** is well laid out and inexpensive, and its stalls also sell cheese and flowers. The traders represent the most dense concentration of cockneys in central London apart from the taxi cafés, and their language is colourful.

Carnaby Street ❼

A detour away from Soho via Broadwick Street will take you towards **Carnaby Street**. The street now hosts up-market branches of

A detail from the exterior of the French Protestant Church of London at Soho Square, which holds an archive of books and records related to the French Huguenots.

LEFT: the mock-Tudor 19th-century tool shed in the centre of Soho Square. **BELOW:** Berwick Street Market.

SHOP

The 1920s mock-Tudor facade of Liberty is visible at the end of Carnaby Street (turn onto Great Marlborough Street for the main entrance). In recent years, it has shed its slightly stuffy image to combine eccentric English charm with edgy, high-fashion clothing and decor. It is well worth a look *(also see page 52)*.

RIGHT: the Empire Leicester Square is one of seven cinemas on the square. **BELOW:** Gerrard Street in Chinatown. **BELOW RIGHT:** the statue of Charlie Chaplin on Leicester Square.

some of the hipper high-street chains (Office, Fornarina and Lee Jeans, for example). You will still find examples of the sort of fashion creativity that first put the area on the map, but for this you'll need to leave Carnaby Street itself and explore the pedestrianised streets to the east.

CHINATOWN 8

Returning to Soho and continuing down Wardour Street, walk along the south side of Shaftesbury Avenue to **Gerrard Street** and parallel **Lisle Street**, home of Chinese grocers, restaurants and stores. Kitsch Chinese street furniture, lamps and archways in Gerrard Street make this the heart of Chinatown. Some of the Oriental cuisine here is the best in town, although quality varies.

There are also herbal and medicine shops. On Sundays, a family outing day for the city's Chinese, there is a Chinese food market. Chinese New Year in late January or early February is celebrated in style, with massive papier-mâché lions dancing through the streets.

LEICESTER SQUARE 9

Just south of Chinatown, Leicester Square is home of the big cinemas and host to the capital's film premieres. Until the 17th century, this was the garden of Leicester House and at the four corners of the garden are busts of famous people associated with the square. At the centre is the **Shakespeare monument** (1874), surrounded by brass plates in the ground giving distances to cities all over the world. Facing the bard is a **statue of Charlie Chaplin**, born in Southwark, south London, in 1889. Around the square is a regular contingent of caricature artists, buskers, Bible-thumpers and, on special occasions, a funfair roundabout and amusement rides. ❑

BEST RESTAURANTS, BARS AND CAFÉS

Restaurants

Prices for a three-course dinner per person with a half-bottle of house wine:

£ = under £20
££ = £20–30
£££ = £30–50
££££ = over £50

American

Ed's Easy Diner
Old Compton St, W1 ☎ 74394 4439 ⏲ daily, all day. **£** [p 328, B1]
Beefburgers, veggie burgers, chicken burgers dished up in 1950s American-style surroundings. There is another Ed's diner at the Trocadero on Rupert Street.

British

Lindsay House
21 Romilly St, W1 ☎ 7439 0450 ⏲ L & D Mon–Fri, D Sat. **£££** (set menu), **££££** [p 328, B1]
Chef Richard Corrigan delivers a Michelin-starred culinary experience. Sample dishes include roast squab pigeon and saddle of rabbit with black pudding.

Chinese

Harbour City
46 Gerrard St, W1 ☎ 7439 7859 ⏲ daily, all day. **£–££** (set menu), **££** [p 328, B2]
A recommended choice with a window table overlooking Gerrard Street. Dim sum noon–5pm.

Joy King Lau
3 Leicester St, WC2 ☎ 7437 1133 ⏲ daily, all day. **££** (set menu). **£££** [p 328, B2]
This is a popular choice for those who know Chinese food well. Set menus from around £28 feature sizzling veal with black-pepper sauce, a range of noodle dishes, and dim sum until 4.45pm.

Mr Kong
21 Lisle St, WC2H ☎ 7437 7341 ⏲ daily, all day to 2.45am, Sun until 1.45am. **£–££** (set menu), **££** [p 328, B2]
This is one of the more authentic (and claustrophobic) Chinese restaurants in the area. Offers many unusual dishes such as Kon Chi baby squid with chilli sauce, and sand-storm crab. Has a lively vegetarian selection too.

Royal Dragon
30 Gerrard St, W1 ☎ 7734 1388 ⏲ daily, until 3am. **££** [p 328, B2]
This is noisy and sizzling with quick- fire dishes that descend from on high. Set menus are reliable. Dim sum noon–5pm

Yauatcha
15 Broadwick St, W1 ☎ 7494 8888 ⏲ daily, all day. **£££** [p328, B2]
This stylish new tearoom and dim sum emporia offers delicious, if expensive, dim sum from noon until midnight (until 10.30pm on Sun).

Fish

Randall & Aubin
16 Brewer St, W1 ☎ 7287 4447 ⏲ L & D daily. **£££** [p 328, B1]
Piles of lobster, crab and oysters greet you as you enter this bustling place.

Zilli Fish
36–40 Brewer St, W1V. ☎ 7734 8649 ⏲ L & D Mon–Sat. **£££** [p 328, B2]
Not cheap, but a great lunch venue. Try the lobster spaghetti or the salmon stuffed with spinach. The banana spring rolls and chocolate sauce are divine.

ABOVE: dim sum in Chinatown. **RIGHT:** the Gay Hussar, a long-established Soho eaterie.

French

L'Escargot Marco Pierre White

48 Greek St, W1 ☎ 7437 6828 ⌚ L & D Mon–Fri, D only Sat, Sat lunch in the Picasso room. **£££** (set menu) **££££** [p 328, B1]

The *grand-père* of London's French restaurants, with its lovely 1920s decor, is now run by Marco Pierre White. It offers a choice between the exciting hubbub of the ground floor or the more intimate Picasso room upstairs, with à la carte and set menus.

La Trouvaille

12A Newburgh St, W1 ☎ 7287 8488 ⌚ L & D Mon–Sat. **££** (set menu) **£££** [p 328, B1]

Small and intimate restaurant. The impeccably sourced and creatively conceived dishes include monkfish and mango. The wine list is also quirky and quite exotic.

Hungarian

Gay Hussar

2 Greek St, W1 ☎ 7437 0973 ⌚ L & D Mon–Sat. **££** (set menu), **£££** [p 328, B1]

In polished, gentleman's club surroundings, a mix of hearty British and Hungarian dishes are served. Pork and potatoes are prominent.

Indian

Indian Masala Zone

9 Marshall St, W1 ☎ 7287 9966 ⌚ L & D daily. **£–££** [p 328, A1]

Bright and always busy, this offers reasonably priced, if slightly sanitised Indian food in fast-paced surroundings

International

Balans

60 Old Compton St, W1. ☎ 7439 2183 ⌚ daily, all day (Mon–Thur 8am–5am, Fri, Sat 8am–6am, Sun 8am–2am). **££** [p 328, B1]

Sets out to bring a buzz and glamour to gay eating in Compton Street with its range of New York brunch-style dishes – including melt-in-your-mouth eggs benedict – and an extensive all day menu.

Café Emm

17 Frith St, W1 . ☎ 7437 0723 ⌚ L & D daily. **£** [p 328, B1]

Buzzy, intimate and exceptionally good value, Café Emm is packed out every night. Portions are large, and dishes range from salmon fish cakes to lamb shank with ratatouille and mash. Be prepared for boisterous birthday parties.

Floridita

100 Wardour St, W1. ☎ 7314 4000 ⌚ Mon–Wed 5.30pm–2am, Thur–Sat 5.30pm–3am. **££** (set menus) **£££**. £6 music charge after 8.30pm, £10 after 10pm. [p 328, B1]

Eat to a Latin beat in this Cuban-themed restaurant – a reincarnation of the cavernous Mezzo that used to occupy the site. Loud and lively.

Italian

Amalfi

29–31 Old Compton St, W1 ☎ 7437 7284 ⌚ L & D daily. **££** [p 328, B1]

The cooking is of the 1970s bistro variety, but pizzas, vegetable pastas and other Italian fare are filling and you can be sure of quick service and a table without reservation.

Kettners

29 Romilly St, W ☎ 7734 6112 ⌚ daily, all day. **££** [p 328, B1]

This sprawling *grande dame* fuses an extensive champagne list with a pizza menu. Piano bar too. Always busy.

Quo Vadis

26–29 Dean St, W1 ☎ 7437 9585 ⌚ L&D Mon–Fri, D only Sat. **££££** [p 328, B1]

Prices for a three-course dinner per person with a haf bottle of house wine:
£ = under £20
££ = £20–30
£££ = £30–50
££££ = over £50

A venerable institution in the one-time home of Karl Marx serving high-end modern Italian food. Brit art on the walls, and an expensive but excellent wine list.

Spiga

84–6 Wardour St, W1 ☎ 7734 3444 ◷ L Mon–Sat D only Sun. £££ [p 328, B1]
A contemporary Italian restaurant that has a cool and airy atmosphere conducive to chatting over a crisp pinot and a tasty stone-fired pizza. Try and get a booth if you can.

Japanese

Satsuma

56 Wardour St, W1 ☎ 7437 8338 ◷ daily, all day. ££ [p 328, B1]
This is fast food but well presented with some very tasty *udon* and *ramen* noodle dishes, plus sushi.

Mediterranean

Hummus Bros

88 Wardour St, W1 ☎ 7734 1311 ◷ L & D Mon–Sat. £ [p 328, B1]
As the name suggests, the focus is hummus. Choose from a selection of tasty, Mediterranean-influenced toppings and mop up with flat bread. Simple, but it works.

Modern European

Alastair Little

49 Frith St, W1 ☎ 7734 5183 ◷ L & D Mon–Fri, D only Sat. £££ [p 328, B1]
Its eponymous chef no longer mans the stoves, but the service and cooking remain excellent.

Aurora Soho

49 Lexington St, W1. ☎ 7494 0514 ◷ L & D Mon–Sat. £££ [p 328, B1]
The courtyard garden is great for a chatty lunch or an intimate evening for two. The accent is on fresh fish.

Bar du Marché

19 Berwick St W1 ☎ 7734 4606 ◷ all day, Mon–Sat. £ (set menu ££) [p 328, B1]
Tucked behind Berwick Street market, this is a surprisingly unpretentious Soho hangout. Serves a mix of French brasserie style food, salads and seafood.

Mildred's

45 Lexington St, W1 ☎ 7494 1634 ◷ noon–11pm Mon–Sat. ££ [p 321, B1]
This is a friendly, laid-back place. The food is a surprising range from veggie burgers to tofu stir fries and a delicious ale pie, accompanied by organic

Above Left: Amalfi on Old Compton Street.
Left: a beacon of good tastes on Dean Street.
Right: the French House, also on Dean Street.

Pubs, Bars and Cafés

Bars

If you're in search of a hip hang-out, head for West Soho and **Alphabet** *(61–3 Beak St)*. Arranged over two floors, it caters for a media in-crowd. A quality martini and an excellent selection of wines can be found at **Café Boheme** *(13–7 Old Compton St)*. For a touch of class, the very grand **Atlantic Bar & Grill** *(20 Glasshouse St)* in the refurbished ballroom of the Regent Palace Hotel, is perfect for a champagne cocktail.

Pubs

If it's Soho history you're after, **the French House** *(49 Dean St)* offers a decadent and beautiful old bar that was the centre of the French resistance in London during World War II, and the regular haunt of painter Francis Bacon and writer Samuel Beckett. The upstairs restaurant serves good French fare *(tel: 7437 2799)*. **Couch** *(97–9 Dean St)* is a popular post-work pub with plenty of seating (but only three couches) and superior bar food. **Bar Code** *(3–4 Archer St)* is a late-night funky gay dance and cruise bar.

For those who like their ale from a barrel and not a bottle, Soho has plenty of classic Victorian pubs – **The Argyll Arms** *(18 Argyll St)*, **the Coach & Horses** *(29 Greek St)*, **the Dog & Duck** *(18 Bateman St)* are just three.

Cafés

The best in Soho are found in and around Compton Street. **Bar Italia** *(22 Frith St)* is a Soho legend, which serves great Italian coffee and snacks 24/7. The most wonderful, boho French café this side of the Channel is **Maison Bertaux** *(28 Greek St)* where the surroundings appear as if they'll crumble to the touch, just like their exquisite cakes; and for a gentle French experience amid the bustle of gay Compton Street, **Patisserie Valerie** *(44 Old Compton St)* belongs to another age.

TRAFALGAR SQUARE AND COVENT GARDEN

With its shooting fountains and soaring column, Trafalgar Square is one of London's most popular open spaces. It is also a short hop from vibrant Covent Garden

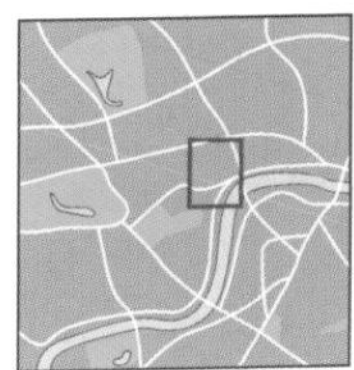

South of Leicester Square is Trafalgar Square, from where the Strand heads east, flanked on one side by Covent Garden and on the other by the river-side Victoria Embankment leading down to Waterloo Bridge.

TRAFALGAR SQUARE ❶

The closest that London has to the kind of large public square common in other European capitals was designed in 1838 by Sir Charles Barry. In 1841 it was named **Trafalgar Square** to commemorate Admiral Lord Nelson's 1805 victory against Napoleon's navy at Trafalgar, off the Atlantic coast of Spain.

At the centre of the square is **Nelson's Column**, a 167-ft (50-metre) Corinthian column topped by a 12-ft (3.6-metre) statue of Horatio Nelson, battle-scarred with only one arm but without a patch on his blind eye. He is gazing towards the Mall, inspecting the fleet of model ships attached to pillars on the avenue.The four iconic lions (1847) are by Edwin Landseer.

Around the square, Canada House, South Africa House and Uganda House are memories of distant Empire days. Also celebrating the old Empire are statues of General Charles Napier and Major General Sir Henry Havelock, on the plinths in the two southern corners of the square. The statue in the northeast corner depicts George IV.

Controversy over who should occupy the northwest-corner's fourth plinth – left empty after plans in 1841 to erect an equestrian statue collapsed through lack of funds – has recently caught Londoners' imaginations. Suggestions for a suit-

Main attractions

- TRAFALGAR SQUARE
- NATIONAL GALLERY
- NATIONAL PORTRAIT GALLERY
- ST MARTIN-IN-THE-FIELDS
- COVENT GARDEN MARKET
- ROYAL OPERA HOUSE
- ST PAUL'S, THE "ACTOR'S CHURCH"
- LONDON'S TRANSPORT MUSEUM
- LONDON COLISEUM
- CHARING CROSS BOOKSHOPS

LEFT: Nelson's Column and one of Edwin Landseer's iconic lions in Trafalgar Square. **RIGHT:** the National Gallery and Trafalgar Square's pools and fountains.

Museum shops are big business these days, and the ones at the National Gallery and National Portrait Gallery (both immediately accessible from the main entrances) do a great range of art-themed merchandise, from books to mugs, clothing, jewellery and items for children.

able occupant ranged from, inevitably, Diana, Princess of Wales to footballer David Beckham. A committee was formed to commission works of art that could take their turn, each for 18 months, on the plinth, with *Alison Lapper Pregnant* and Thomas Schütte's *Hotel for the Birds* the first two installations.

The square has long been the site of public gatherings, political demonstrations and New Year celebrations. A mayoral campaign to rid it of its traditional plague of pigeons was largely successful, and in 2003 the north side of the square was pedestrianised to give people a sporting chance of reaching the fountains without being mown down by traffic.

In the southwest corner of the square, Admiralty Arch marks the start of The Mall, leading to Buckingham Palace *(see page 82)*. Whitehall, the other exit, leads to the Houses of Parliament *(see page 75)*.

The National Gallery ❷

✉ Trafalgar Square; www.nationalgallery.org.uk ☎ 7747 2885 ⏲ Mon, Tue, Thur–Sun 10am–6pm, Wed 10am–9pm Ⓔ free except some special exhibitions 🚇 Charing Cross

Dominating the north side of Trafalgar Square is the neoclassical **National Gallery**, designed by William Wilkins in 1838 with a modern wing by

RIGHT: Holbein's *The Ambassadors* in the National Gallery.
BELOW: the entrance of the National Gallery, seen from the side.

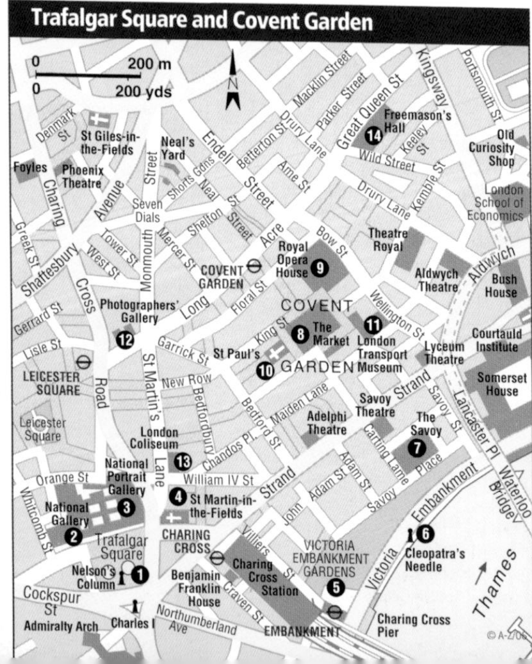

Recommended Restaurants, Bars & Cafés on pages 106–7

Robert Venturi completed in 1991. This is the country's most important art gallery, home to around 2,000 west European masterpieces, including works by Rembrandt, Rubens, El Greco, Vermeer and Van Gogh to name but a few. *For full details, see pages 108–9.*

The National Portrait Gallery ❸

St Martin's Place; www.npg.org.uk; 7312 2463 free except some special exhibitions Mon–Wed, Sat, Sun 10am–6pm, Thur, Fri 10am–9pm free except for some special exhibitions Charing Cross

Behind the National Gallery is the **National Portrait Gallery**, housed in a Florentine Renaissance building originally designed by architect Ewan Christian and opened in 1896. Only a fraction of the collection's 10,000 paintings, drawings and sculptures, plus half a million photographs of the nation's illustrious men and women is on display at any one time. *For full details, see pages 110–11.*

St Martin-in-the-Fields ❹

Trafalgar Square; www.stmartin-in-the-fields.org box office (evening concerts): 7839 8362 daily 8am–6pm free except evening concerts Charing Cross

Across the road is the church of **St Martin-in-the-Fields**, the oldest building in Trafalgar Square, built in 1724 by a Scottish architect, James Gibbs, when this venue was in fields outside the city. Nell Gwynne, the mistress of Charles II, is one of several famous people buried in this parish church of the royal family, which was so chic in the 18th century that pews were rented out on an annual basis. The royal box is on the left of the altar. The crypt, which houses a soup kitchen for the homeless, a café and the London Brass Rubbing Centre, was used as an air-raid shelter during the bombing blitz of World War II.

Regular classical music concerts are held in the church on Thursday, Friday and Saturday and alternate Tuesdays, at 7.30pm. There are also free lunch-time concerts.

The spire of St Martin-in-the-Fields behind a statue of Charles I by the French sculptor Hubert Le Sueur (1633).

BELOW: soaking up the sunshine on Trafalgar Square.

Nelson's Column

Horatio Nelson (1758–1805) is the country's greatest naval hero. A tiny figure, he was partially blinded in his right eye in Corsica, had his right arm amputated at Santa Cruz and was pacing the deck of HMS *Victory*, when he was fatally shot by a French sharpshooter off Cape Trafalgar. He could be insubordinate, famously putting a telescope to his blind eye at the Battle of Copenhagen and pretending he could not read an order to disengage from battle. He is also remembered for his affair with Emma Hamilton, the wife of the British Ambassador to Naples. The three shared a *ménage à trois.*

It took until 1878 before Cleopatra's Needle was towed in a specially constructed pontoon to London, where its intended site outside parliament was not strong enough to bear the 180-tonne weight. Buried beneath it are newspapers from the day it was erected, a set of coins, four Bibles in different languages, a railway timetable and photographs of the 12 best-looking Englishwomen of the time.

Around the Strand

The mundane modern architecture in the Strand, the main thoroughfare connecting the West End with the City, camouflages the fact that it was once a very fashionable street, home in the 18th and 19th centuries to the actress Sarah Siddons, the poet Samuel Taylor Coleridge and the novelist George Eliot. Although the street is well past its glory days, a sense of history is not altogether lost: you can still dine in traditional style at Simpson's, opened in 1848, or take tea in the Thames Room of the Savoy.

At the Strand's western end, near Trafalgar Square, is **Charing Cross** railway station. In front of it is a replica of the last of 12 crosses set up by Edward I in 1291 to mark the funeral procession of his queen, Eleanor of Castile, from Nottinghamshire to Westminster Abbey. "Charing" is from "*chère reine*" (dear queen) Eleanor.

Victoria Embankment

At this point, cut down Villiers Street, which for a while was home to Rudyard Kipling, author of *The Jungle Book* (a blue plaque marks the spot). Nearby is Craven Street, where the Founding Father of the USA, Benjamin Franklin, lived 1757–75. His Georgian mansion is now a museum, the **Benjamin Franklin House** (36 Craven Street; www.benjaminfranklinhouse.org; tel: 7839 2006; Wed–Sun noon–5pm; charge).

Back on Villiers Street, at its southern end, is **Victoria Embankment**, built in 1870 to ease traffic congestion and carry sewage pipes needed to improve London's crude sanitation system. In the **Victoria Embankment Gardens** ❺ a restored **Water Gate** once marked the river entrance to York House, London home of the archbishops of York, birthplace of philosopher and statesman Francis Bacon (1561–1626) and home of the dukes of Buckingham.

On the river front is **Charing Cross Pier**, a starting point for boats heading east to Greenwich. This is also the site of the 60-ft (18-metre) **Cleopatra's Needle** ❻, carved in Aswan, Egypt, c.1475BC and presented to Britain in 1819 *(see margin note, left)*. The needle is flanked by two bronze Sphinxes.

BELOW: one of the Sphinxes flanking Cleopatra's Needle. (**RIGHT**) on the Victoria Embankment.

Recommended Restaurants, Bars & Cafés on pages 106–7

The Savoy

Back on the Strand are several theatres, including the **Adelphi**, opened in 1806 and quickly followed by others. Richard D'Oyly Carte (1844–1901), sponsor of Gilbert and Sullivan operas at the splendid Art Deco **Savoy Theatre**, also financed the building of the **Savoy Hotel** ❼, which opened in 1889 as one of the first in London with private bathrooms, electric lights and lifts (elevators). From the Strand, the Savoy is unimposing, but it is grand enough to have its own private forecourt and the only road in Britain where traffic drives on the right.

D'Oyly Carte is commemorated in a stained-glass window in the **Queen's Chapel of the Savoy** (daily except Mon; services: Sun 11am, Wed 12.30pm; www.duchyoflancaster.co.uk), behind the hotel. It was founded in the 16th century when the former Savoy Palace became a hospital. Built by Peter, ninth Count of Savoy, in 1246, the palace had its heyday under John of Gaunt (1340–99), when it was "the fayrest manor in Europe, big enough for a large part of an army."

COVENT GARDEN ❽

Named after a convent whose fields occupied the site, **Covent Garden** was for centuries the principal market in London for vegetables, fruit and flowers, and the workplace of Eliza Doolittle, the flower girl in George Bernard Shaw's *Pygmalion*, who later burst into song in the film and musical *My Fair Lady*. The main piazza was originally laid out with colonnaded town houses designed by Inigo Jones c.1630, and inspired by the 16th-century Italian architect Andrea Palladio. A small market was founded here as early as 1661.

After the market moved out in 1974, the area became a blueprint

TIP

Hitch a ride with one of Covent Garden's rickshaw bicycles *(left)*. They're not cheap, but they offer a novel, ecologically efficient and dry method of transport for short trips.

Charing Cross is the spot from which distances to and from London are measured.

BELOW LEFT: inside the market. **BELOW:** bird's-eye view of Covent Garden Market.

KIDS

On the second Sunday in May a service at St Paul's commemorates the Punch and Judy puppet tradition, first noted here in 1662 by diarist Samuel Pepys. There's a brass band procession around the area at 10.30am and puppetry performances in the afternoon. For adults, the Punch & Judy pub inside the market marks the spot where the puppet show was first mounted.

ABOVE RIGHT: old-fashioned telephone boxes near the Opera House. **BELOW:** the Transport Museum. **BELOW RIGHT:** the fashionable face of Covent Garden, in Neal's Arcade off Shorts Gardens.

for turning old commercial buildings into a mall of stores and stalls. Restaurants, cafés and shops occupy the old warehouses in the streets around the market square. There is a good line in street entertainers, who undergo auditions before they are granted a licence to perform here.

Royal Opera House ❾

Bow Street; www.royaloperahouse.org 7304 4000 Mon–Sat 10am–3.30pm free except for tours Covent Garden

In 1733, a theatre was established in the northeast corner of Covent Garden, on the site now occupied by the **Royal Opera House.** A fire ravaged the first building in 1808, consuming Handel's organ and many of his works. The Opera House has had to contend with unimpressed audiences: price riots were common in the 19th century, and in 1809 lasted 61 nights. The Floral Hall, which acts as a reception space prior to performances and during intervals, is spectacular.

St Paul's ❿

Bedford Street; www.actorschurch.org 7836 5221 Mon–Fri 9am– 4.30pm, Sun 9am–12.30pm and for services free Covent Garden

The portico of **St Paul's**, the actors' church, built in 1633 by Inigo Jones, and used as a backdrop in *My Fair Lady*, dominates the western end of the square. The vaults and grounds of this Tuscan-style church are said to contain the remains of more famous people than any other church except Westminster Abbey. The headstones

have long been removed, but residents include master wood-carver Grinling Gibbons (died 1720), the composer of *Rule Britannia*, Thomas Arne (1778), the caricaturist Thomas Rowlandson (1827) and the actress Ellen Terry (1928).

London Transport Museum ⓫

Covent Garden Piazza; www.ltmuseum. co.uk daily 10am–6pm 7565 7299 charge for adults; free to accompanied children under 16 Covent Garden

The old flower market, in the south-eastern corner of the square, is now occupied by **London Transport Museum**, which has a large collection of horse-drawn coaches, buses, trams, trains and rail carriages. It effectively traces the social history of modern London, whose growth was powered by transport, and deals with issues such as congestion and pollution. This is a great museum for children.

Around Drury Lane

Neighbouring **Drury Lane** is closely linked with the theatre. Its principal venue is the Theatre Royal, which, when it opened in 1663, was only the second legitimate playhouse in the city. The mistress of Charles II, Nell Gwynne, depicted by cartoonists as a voluptuous orange seller, trod the boards here. Its stage is large enough to mount blockbuster musicals.

Opposite its white Corinthian portico is the former **Bow Street police station**, home in the 18th century of the scarlet-waistcoated Bow Street Runners, the prototype policemen.

Long Acre and St Martin's Lane

Long Acre cuts through Covent Garden, from Neal Street to Leicester Square tube station. At 12–14 Long Acre is Britain's best travel bookshop, **Stanford's**. Nearby, at 5 and 8 Great Newport Street, is the **Photographers' Gallery** ⓬ (Mon–Sat 11am–6pm, Thur until 8pm, Sun noon–6pm; free). South of Long Acre is St Martin's Lane, home of the English National Opera's **London Coliseum** ⓭ *(see page 299)*, where productions are sung in English, with surtitles.

As it runs northeast, Long Acre becomes Great Queen Street, site of the **Freemasons' Hall** ⓮ (Mon–Fri 10am–5pm; tel: 7395 9257), an imposing white behemoth that is home to a museum on the history of freemasonry, a library and tavern.

CHARING CROSS ROAD

Monmouth Street leads to **Charing Cross Road**, a centre for rare and second-hand books. Britain's largest book shop, **Foyles**, is a maze of more than 4 million volumes but has become much better organised, if duller, since the death of its eccentric former owner, Christina Foyle. **Zwemmer's** is known for fine art and photography books. Music shops cluster around Denmark Street, known as **Tin Pan Alley**, a home of early British rock 'n' roll. ❑

The iconic revolving globe on top of the London Coliseum measures 12ft (4 metres) in diameter and weighs around 5 tonnes.

BELOW: second-hand books on Charing Cross Road.

Best Restaurants, Bars and Cafés

Restaurants

Prices for a three-course dinner per person with a half-bottle of house wine:

£ = under £20
££ = £20–30
£££ = £30–50
££££ = over £50

American

Christopher's

18 Wellington St, WC2 7240 4222 L & D Mon–Sat, Br Sat/Sun. **££** (set menus), **£££** [p 329, D1]
The dishes on the contemporary American menu are imaginative and usually well prepared, but the elegant dining rooms are the main attraction. Good-value pre- and post-theatre menus.

Hamburger Union

4–6 Garrick Street, WC2 7379 0412 L & D daily. **£** [p 328, C2]
Laid-back diner serving a great range of gourmet hamburgers freshly prepared on the premises using quality beef (other meats also available). Excellent chunky chips and traditional touches such as squeezy sauce bottles add to the appeal.

Joe Allen

13 Exeter St, WC2 7836 0651 noon–midnight Mon–Sat, D only Sun. **££** (brunch, pre-theatre and late supper menus. **£££** [p 329, D2]
Tucked away below street level, this relaxed diner has a predictable enough menu – salads, steaks, spareribs, pecan pie – and average-quality food, but it's ever popular with diners, who sip cocktails until 12.45am.

British

Rules

35 Maiden Lane, WC2 7836 5314 L & D daily. **££** (pre-theatre menu) **££££** [p 329, C2]
Rules (est. 1798) is London's oldest restaurant, and the decor, notably the wonderful Art Nouveau stained-glass ceiling and the wood panelling, reflects its heritage. The robust food is very English, with beef, lamb and a variety of game from Rules' own estate in the Pennines.

Simpson's-in-the-Strand, Grand Divan

100 The Strand, WC2 7836 9112 L & D daily, B Mon–Fri. **£** (breakfast), **££** (set menu), **££££** [p 329, D2]
This bastion of Britishness retains all the grandeur of bygone days – chandeliers, oak panelling and tail-coated waiters – while managing a surprisingly relaxed atmosphere. The menu is traditional (beef fillet, calves' liver, duck and Dover sole); for many the famed roast beef, wheeled in on a silver-domed carving trolley is the only choice. A good place to breakfast like a king. Also at the Savoy are Gordon Ramsay's 1950s' American diner-style **Banquette** and the traditional **Savoy Grill**.

Fish

Le Palais du Jardin

136 Long Acre, WC2 7379 5353 L & D daily. **£££** [p 329, C2]
The oval bar, glossy wooden partitions and brass bannisters of this huge brasserie are reminiscent of a ship's polished interior, while lush greenery and skylights give the mezzanine an alfresco feel (pavement seating in summer). Fresh fish and seafood platters are the focus.

J. Sheekey

28–32 St Martin's Court, WC2 7240 2565 L & D daily. **££** (weekend lunch menu), **££££** [p 328, C2]
Think chargrilled squid with gorgonzola polenta, Cornish fish stew and New England baby lobster, followed by rhubarb pie, or the famed Scandinavian iced berries with white-chocolate sauce. Impressive wine list. Chic. Booking essential.

Left: Asia de Cuba. **Right:** J. Sheekey, famous for fish.

French

L'Estaminet

14 Garrick St, WC2 ☎ 7379 1432 ⓒ L & D Mon–Fri, D only Sat. **££** (pre-theatre menu), **£££** [p 328, C2]

Offers old-fashioned charm plus terrine, *escargot* and *saucisson* starters, followed by classic meat dishes.

International

Asia de Cuba

St Martin's Lane Hotel, 45 St Martin's Lane, WC2 ☎ 7300 5500 ⓒ L & D daily. **£££** (pre-theatre menu), **££££** [p 328, C2]

Attached to one of London's hippest hotels is this buzzing restaurant. with eccentric decor and fusion menu. Lobster parcels, pot-roast pork and melt-in-your-mouth tuna are a few of the treats on offer.

Modern European

Belgo Centraal

50 Earlham Street, WC2 ☎ 7813 2233 ⓒ L & D daily **£/££** [p 328, C1]

Belgian fare of mussels and chips and excellent beers. Long benches, shared tables and waiters dressed as monks add to the atmosphere. The "Beat the Clock" option offers great value from 5pm to 6.30pm.

The Ivy

1 West St, WC2 ☎ 7836 4751 ⓒ L & D daily. **££** (Sat–Sun lunch menu), **££££** [p 328, C1]

The menu at the Ivy, one of London's best-known celebrity haunts, is British plus international favourites. The wine list is strong and the surreptitious star-spotting irresistible. The only problem is getting a table – reserve months, not just days, ahead.

The Portrait Restaurant

National Portrait Gallery, St Martin's Place, W1 ☎ 7312 2490 ⓒ L daily, D Thur–Fri. **£££** [p 328, C2]

When it comes to location, few can beat the top floor of the National Portrait Gallery. It offers views of Trafalgar Square, Big Ben, and the Millennium Wheel. The food is above average by gallery restaurant standards.

Sarastro

126 Drury Lane, WC2 ☎ 7836 0101 ⓒ L & D daily. **£** (set-lunch menu), **££** [p 329, D1]

"The show after the show" is this restaurant's slogan. The flamboyant decor, with velvet drapes, golden chairs, opera boxes, chandeliers and props, is a stage set in itself. The menu is more straightforward, offering basic fish, meat and vegetarian options.

Vegetarian

Food for Thought

31 Neal St, WC2 ☎ 7836 9072 ⓒ Br, L & D Mon–Sat, L only Sun. **£** [p 329, C1]

This pleasant eatery does an imaginative selection of affordable dishes, with a daily changing menu. Tom-yam soup might be followed by gnocchi with gorgonzola and oyster mushrooms. A BYOB (no corkage) policy keeps the cost down.

Pubs, Bars and Cafés

Cafés, wine bars and pubs are ten a penny in the Covent Garden area – ideal for a relaxed lunch or a night on the town, with happy hours/late closing hours commonplace.

For location, it's hard to top. **The Portrait Bar** *(National Portrait Gallery)*, with wonderful views over Trafalgar Square, or **The Opera Terrace Bar** *(Royal Opera House)* above the Piazza.

Londoner's old favourites, such as the **Cork & Bottle** *(44–46 Cranbourn St)*, pull in the crowds for their comfort factor and excellent wine lists, while venues such as **Browns** *(4 Great Queen St)* and **Denim** *(4a Upper St Martin's Lane)* appeal to trendy urbanites. If beer is your thing, try the **Freedom Brewing Company** *(41 Earlham St)*, with huge copper tanks in situ, or the **Lowlander** *(36 Drury Lane)*, boasting an impressive lager and ale list.

Historic pubs around Covent Garden include the Lamb and Flag *(33 Rose Street)*, tucked away down the tiniest of alleyways, and **The Punch & Judy**, on the upper level of the Market itself. Villiers Street, which leads to Embankment tube, shelters the wonderful **Gordon's Wine Bar**, where drinkers take shelter under the arches on chilly nights and sit out on the terrace in summer. Sherry and port are specialities here.

Some of the most exclusive bars are found in hotels, from classics such as the **American Bar** *(Savoy Hotel, Strand)* to the ultra-fashionable **Lobby Bar** at One Aldwych.

THE NATIONAL GALLERY

Dominating Trafalgar Square is one of the world's finest art collections, bringing together masterpieces from over seven centuries – and entry is free

The National Gallery was founded in 1824, when a private collection of 38 paintings was acquired by the British Government for the sum of £57,000 and exhibited in the house of the owner, banker John Julius Angsterstein, at 100 Pall Mall. Included in the collection were *Bacchanal* by Poussin, *St Ursula* and *The Queen of Sheba* by landscape master Claude, paintings by Van Dyck, two admirable Rembrandts, a superb Aelbert Cuyp, and William Hogarth's narrative, *Six Pictures called Marriage à la Mode*.

As the collection grew, a new building was needed. William Wilkins' long, low construction, with its neoclassical facade and dome, opened in 1834 in the then-recently created Trafalgar Square. The building has been remodelled in various ways. The most prominent addition is the Sainsbury Wing, added by the American architect Robert Venturi in 1991.

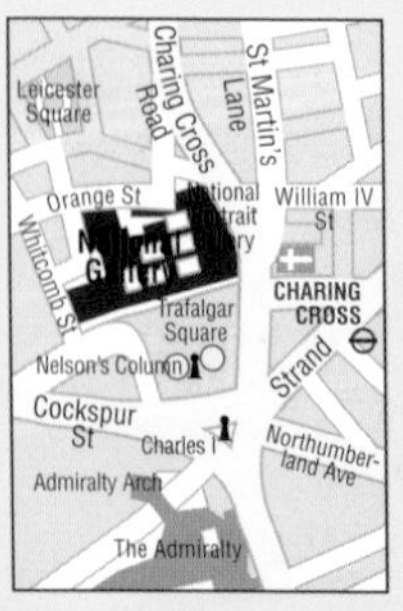

The essentials

Trafalgar Square; www.nationalgallery.org.uk

7747 2885

Mon, Tue, Thur–Sun 10am–6pm, Wed 10am–9pm

free except some special exhibitions

Charing Cross

ABOVE: the **West Wing** contains paintings from 1500–1600, including Raphael's *Saint Catherine of Alexandria* (c.1507), above, Michelangelo's *The Entombment* (c.1500–1), Leonardo's *The Virgin of the Rocks* (1491–1508) and Titian's *Bacchus and Ariadne* (1523). Also here is Holbein's double portrait of *The Ambassadors* (1533).

ABOVE: J.M.W Turner's *The Fighting Téméraire*, voted the nation's favourite picture in a 2005 poll.

GALLERY LAYOUT

The National Gallery's collection is arranged chronologically, from the 13th century to the end of the 19th century, through four wings, starting in the Sainsbury Wing containing works from the 13th–15th century.

Many people enter the gallery through its grand main entrance, however, from where a magnificent flight of stairs offers you a choice of three directions. Take the left flight to the West Wing and the Renaissance galleries. Go straight ahead, through the Central Hall, for the North Wing, where you will find several portraits by Rembrandt as well as Velázquez's *Rokeby Venus*, the Spanish painter's only surviving nude, or turn right for the East Wing. Here you will find portraits and landscapes, including work by Gainsborough, Constable (see *The Hay Wain* above), Turner and Stubbs.

For special exhibitions held in the main wing of the gallery, it is best to take the Getty Entrance, which opened in 2006.

ABOVE LEFT: among the gallery's Post-Impressionist works is Georges Seurat's *Bathers at Asnières*. **LEFT:** Boticelli's *Venus and Mars* (c.1485) in the Sainsbury Wing.

National Portrait Gallery

A showcase for five centuries of top British portraiture

A British Historical Portrait gallery was founded in 1856, the initiative of the 5th Earl of Stanhope. With no collection as such, it relied on gifts and bequests, the first of which was the "Chandos" picture of William Shakespeare, attributed to John Taylor, c.1610, and arguably the only portrait of Britain's most famous playwright done from life. From the start, additions to the collection (initially comprising traditional paintings, drawings and sculpture, with photography a later addition) were determined by the status of the sitter and historical importance of the portrait, not by their quality as works of art; these criteria still pertain today. Portraits of living people were not admitted until 1968, when the policy was changed to encourage younger artists and a fresh exploration of the genre.

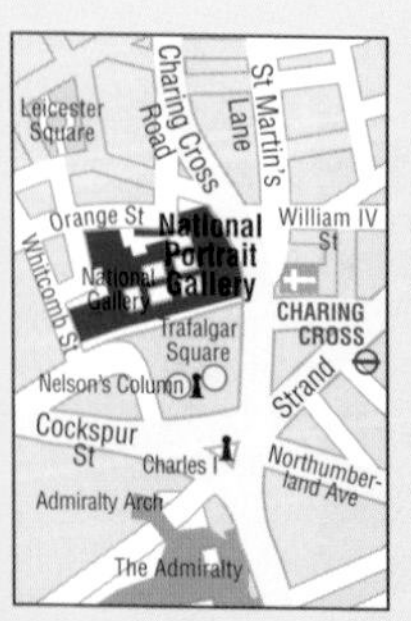

The essentials

St Martin's Place; *www.npg.org.uk*
7312 2463
Mon–Wed, Sat–Sun 10am–6pm, Thur 10am–9pm
free except for some special exhibitions
Charing Cross

LEFT: this portrait of Elizabeth I by an anonymous artist was almost certainly painted from direct observation, when she was about 40. There are about 50 portraits of Elizabeth II in the collection.

SPECIAL EXHIBITIONS

Changing exhibitions are held on the ground floor, and it is worth checking the website to see if anything interesting is on. Recent examples include Face of Fashion, showcasing the work of five European and American fashion photographers, including Paolo Roversi, whose dreamy 2002 *Natalia,* featured above, shows the influence of 19th-century photographer Julia Margaret Cameron.

GALLERY LAYOUT

The displays are broadly chronological, starting on the second floor (reached by the vast escalator from the main hall) and ending on the ground floor. There are thematic sub-divisions within

each period: the Tudors, 17th-century and 18th-century portraits on the second floor; the Victorians and 20th-century portraits until 1990 (including special displays on the Balcony Gallery and landing) on the first floor, and, on the ground floor, the ever-popular British portraits since 1990 and temporary shows.

ABOVE: The Rolling Stones (Bill Wyman, Mick Jagger, Keith Richards, Charlie Watts and Brian Jones) taken by Norman Parkinson in 1964 for a fashion spread in *Queen* magazine. The Stones are wearing clothes designed by Mary Quant's Ginger Group.

LEFT among the 17th and 18th-century portraits on the second floor is this one of Lady Emma Hamilton, the wife of the British Ambassador to Naples and the mistress of Lord Nelson *(see page 100)*, painted by George Romney in 1785. Emma Hamilton was known for her great beauty and vitality; there are 17 portraits of her in the gallery's collection.

RIGHT AND BELOW: the official portraits of the Victorian and Edwardian periods, which fill the bulk of the first floor, are some of the last examples of stylish formality. Works are organised by theme, from the arts, in Room 24, home to this Romantic portrait of poet Alfred Tennyson by Samuel Laurence (above right) to science and technology, featuring evolutionist Charles Darwin (right), to politics and expansion and empire.

Recommended Restaurants, Bars & Cafés on pages 120–1

MAYFAIR TO OXFORD STREET

Mayfair has consistently retained its social prestige since the building of its great estates began in the 1660s. With its Georgian residences, gentlemen's clubs and exclusive shops, it is synonymous with wealth

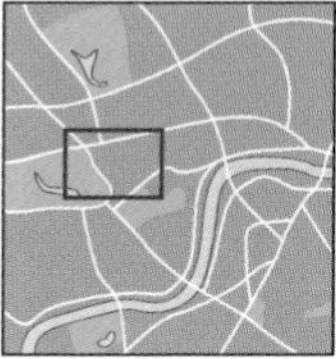

West of Trafalgar Square and Piccadilly Circus is Mayfair the smartest part of town. This is where a broom cupboard costs as much as a house in the country, where shoes are hand-made and where life is bespoke.

The area is divided in two by Piccadilly. To the south of this famous thoroughfare lies St James's *(see page 84)*, which grew up around the life of the royal court; to the north Mayfair, the most expensive place to land on the English Monopoly board. The second most expensive, Park Lane, forms the western boundary of the area, while Oxford Street, the capital's most famous shopping street, is on its northern side.

PICCADILLY

Court fops and dandies were a source of moneymaking for London's traders. In the 18th century Robert Baker grew rich by selling them "pickadils", fashionable stiff collars, and built a mansion on what was then Portugal Street. It became known as **Piccadilly**, and it remains a fashionable street and a favourite location for airline and national tourist offices.

LEFT: Burlington Arcade, a classy place to shop off Piccadilly.
RIGHT: a gentleman's outfitters.

Royal Academy of Arts ❶

Burlington House, Piccadilly; www.royalacademy.org.uk 7300 8000 daily 10am–6pm, Fri until 10pm; John Madejski Fine Rooms Tue–Fri 1–4.30pm, Sat & Sun 10am–6pm charge except for permanent collection Green Park

Behind the imposing Renaissance-style facade of **Burlington House** on the north side, fronted by a handsome courtyard, the Academy stages big, thematic exhibitions and is famous for

Main attractions

- ROYAL ACADEMY OF ARTS
- FORTNUM AND MASON
- THE RITZ
- BURLINGTON ARCADE
- BOND STREET
- CORK STREET GALLERIES
- HANDEL HOUSE MUSEUM
- SHEPHERD MARKET
- OXFORD STREET
- SELFRIDGES
- LIBERTY
- HAMLEYS

The Royal Academy is famous for its Summer Exhibition, the largest open contemporary art exhibition in the world.

its Summer Exhibition to which any artist may present work for selection. The fun of this massive assemblage of paintings is that it ranges from the sublime to the risible.

In the **John Madejski Fine Rooms**, tucked to the rear of the main staircase, much of the RA's little-known permanent collection is rotated on a yearly basis. In contrast to the Academy's top-lit galleries, these smaller rooms have been restored to reveal heavy gilding and panelled doors crowned by plaster putti – the *gusto italiano* as interpreted by William Kent in the 1720s. The Academy's most famous bequests include Michelangelo's marble *Taddei Tondo* (in the high-tech Sackler wing), Constable's *The Leaping Horse* and Gainsborough's *A Romantic Landscape*.

Fine living

At No. 181 Piccadilly is **Fortnum and Mason ❷**, grocers to the Queen and famous for its food hampers, food hall and shop assistants in tails. A tercentenary refurbishment has seen the food hall expand into the basement, with a new wine bar and plans for an ice-cream and soda fountain. The hourly changing of the guard on the mechanical clock above the shop front is a free attraction.

A little further along Piccadilly is

RIGHT: entrance to the Ritz Hotel.

Mayfair to Oxford Street

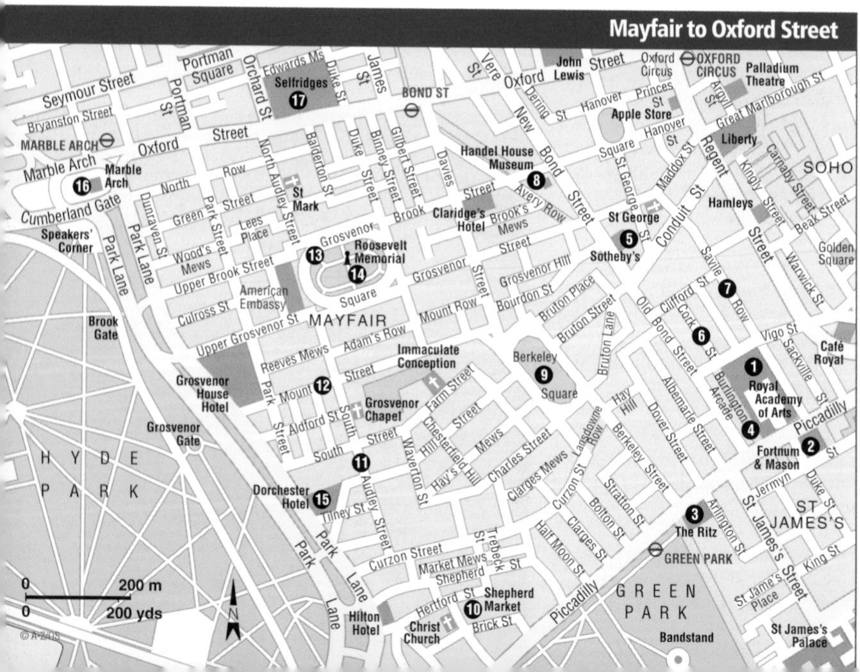

Recommended Restaurants, Bars & Cafés on pages 120–1

The Ritz ❸, where afternoon tea in the Palm Court is a tradition. The hotel, built in 1906, was fashionable in the 1930s, but lacks the cachet it used to have. In 1995 it was bought for £75 million by the low-profile Barclay brothers, David and Frederick. Its casino, probably the city's classiest, remains popular. The elegant Louis XVI dining room overlooks Green Park.

Piccadilly Arcade, known for its glass and chinaware shops, has graceful, bow-fronted Regency windows which belie the fact that it was built in 1910. Almost opposite and beside the Academy, **Burlington Arcade** ❹ was built in 1819.

MAYFAIR

The region bounded by Piccadilly and Park Lane, Oxford and Regent streets, has been a place of wealth and power since the early 18th century, when it was first laid out by the Grosvenor family, dukes of Westminster. **Mayfair** takes its name from the fair which was held annually on the site of what is now Shepherd Market. In the best British tradition, it clings to its exclusivity, although many of the magnificent Georgian homes of business barons and princes of property are now overrun with hotels, luxury offices, embassies and clubs.

The high street of Mayfair is **Bond Street**, divided into Old Bond Street at its southern end leading north to New Bond Street. Here are London's most exclusive couturiers and designer boutiques, jewellery shops, antiques emporia and art galleries.

The headquarters of **Sotheby's** ❺, the auctioneers founded in 1744 and now American-owned, is at No. 34. World record prices for art works are notched up here, but not every sale is for millionaires. Admission is free, as long as you look reasonably presentable, and there is a small café.

Asprey the jeweller and Fenwick's the department store are also part of Bond Street's fabric and are worth checking out. Art galleries proliferate in Bond Street and adjacent Bruton Street, but the best place for art is **Cork Street** ❻, parallel to Bond Street to the east, with such prestigious premises as Waddington's and The Gallery in Cork Street, where Britain's top artists are represented.

Just beyond is **Savile Row** ❼, the home of several gentlemen's outfitters, where even off-the-peg items are highly priced. The offices of Apple, the Beatles company, were at No.3 Savile Row, and in 1969 the group staged what was to be their last ever live concert from its roof, included in the film *Let It Be*.

Handel House Museum ❽

✉ 25 Brook Street; www.handelhouse.org ☎ 7495 1759 ⏲ Tue–Sat 10am–6pm, Thur until 8pm, Sun noon–6pm Ⓢ charge except Sat Ⓤ Bond Street/Oxford Circus

On **Brook Street**, which runs from the west side of New Bond Street, stands the house in which Handel wrote his *Messiah*. His home for 35

The Burlington Arcade was built in 1819. This Regency promenade of Lilliputian shops is patrolled by Beadles. In their top hats and livery, they ensure good behaviour, with "no undue whistling, humming or hurrying". Only a Beadle knows what constitutes undue humming.

BELOW: an auction in progress at Sotheby's.

KIDS

On Saturday afternoons at Handel House children (5 yrs upwards) can drop in for free guided craft activities led by a volunteer, a tour of the house, and the chance to dress up in Georgian costume. Special sessions with the Composer in Residence are sometimes also geared towards children; past events have included "Handel's Watering-can Music".

years until his death in 1759, it has been refurbished in early 18th-century style. While the composer's life and work is well documented with information sheets, CD listening posts, and paintings, prints and old musical scores, the sparsely furnished rooms come into their own as evocative settings for intimate chamber music concerts – often with the Handel House harpsichord as their focus – and other special events.

Another musical resident here was Jimi Hendrix, who occupied a flat at No.23 from 1968 to 1969 (now the museum's private offices, although tours are available once a year). A small corner of the museum is given over to a series of photographic portraits showing the guitar legend at home.

Smart addresses

Brook Street is also home to **Claridge's Hotel**, one of London's premier luxury hotels, built in the 1890s, though mostly in art deco style. Here also is the **Savile Club**, haven of the literary establishment.

RIGHT: the entrance to Claridge's. **BELOW:** Shepherd Market.

BERKELEY SQUARE ❾

Nightingales rarely sing in **Berkeley** Square, though they may have done when the song was written in 1915, and this once highly aristocratic square has been much spoilt by dull office buildings. In 1774 Lord Clive of India committed suicide at No. 45. The Earl of Shelburne, the prime minister who conceded the independence of the United States in 1783, lived in Lansdowne House, now the site of the private-members Lansdowne Club. And Berkeley Square House is built on the site of the house where Queen Elizabeth II was born in 1926.

SHEPHERD MARKET ⑩

From Berkeley Square, Curzon Street leads to Shepherd Market, Mayfair's "village centre", by way of a side-passage. This small pedestrian enclave is incongruous amid the grand town houses and exclusive hotels. Built in around 1735 by the architect Edward Shepherd, it was established to supply the daily needs of local residents and obliterated the open space which had accommodated the May Fair – commemorated by a blue plaque at 7 Trebeck Street – whose riotousness offended the well-off residents.

Even today Shepherd Market maintains a quaint air. There are specialist shops, pubs and restaurants, all on a village scale. At night, the area is a haunt of up-market prostitutes.

SOUTH AUDLEY AND MOUNT STREETS

Along **South Audley Street** ⑪ is the former residence of Charles X, the last Bourbon king of France, who lived here 1805–14. At No.19, **Thomas Goode & Co**, the china, silverware and crystal shop once almost exclusively the preserve of international royalty, has occupied its own block here since the 1840s.

Behind neat miniature hedges, a marble colonnade frames the window displays. Stealing the show are the pair of howdah-bearing ceramic elephants, 7 ft (2.1 metres) tall in their regalia, which are the establishment's trademark. Produced by Minton for Thomas Goode, they took the Paris Exhibition by storm.

The shop incorporates a design archive and museum section.

The original wood pannelling and chandeliers of the Audley pub set the tone for the unbridled Victoriana of **Mount Street** ⑫, whose eastern portion especially, lined with fine shops, is strikingly homogeneous: wholly rebuilt from 1880–1900 in the pink terracotta Queen Anne style, its red-brick façades are enthusiastically decked out with terracotta features.

GROSVENOR SQUARE ⑬

A pleasing, friendly statue of General Eisenhower and Winston Churchill having a chat on a bench

In 1875 architects Messrs Ernest George Peto were commissioned to design a frontage for Thomas Goode and Co. Many of the unusual features they incorporated still remain. One is the mechanical front door, which opens automatically under the weight of anyone standing on the platform. This rare piece of Victorian design is believed to be the only example still in use in the world.

ABOVE LEFT: pretty Shepherd Market has a village feel. **BELOW:** the window of Thomas Goode & Co.

The entrance to Selfridges on Oxford Street. The store opened in 1909. The present American neoclassical emporium was completed in 1926.

BELOW RIGHT: shoppers on Oxford Street.

in Bond Street is a sign of the interest Americans have always had in Mayfair. In 1785 John Adams, the first United States Minister to Britain and later the nation's president, took up residence at **9 Grosvenor Square**. No fewer than 31 of the 47 households in the square then belonged to titled families. In 2007 plans were made to move the embassy to a larger and more secure suburban location. The building here may become a hotel.

The cost of the statue of **Franklin D. Roosevelt** ⓮ in the gardens was met by grateful British citizens after World War II.

PARK LANE

Park Lane, running from Hyde Park Corner to Marble Arch, forms the western boundary of Mayfair. Its once magnificent homes overlooking Hyde Park *(see page 211)* have largely been replaced by modern hotels and apartments. These include the **Hilton Hotel** and the **Dorchester Hotel** ⓯, General Dwight D. Eisenhower's HQ in World War II, and popular with visiting film stars. To the north, the residence of the Grosvenor family (owners of a 300-acre/120-hectare estate covering Mayfair and Park Lane) was knocked down in 1928 to make way for the **Grosvenor House Hotel**, whose Great Room is London's largest banqueting hall.

MARBLE ARCH AND OXFORD STREET

At the top of Park Lane, the **Marble Arch** ⓰, designed by John Nash and based on the Arch of Constantine in Rome, was placed here, then known as Tyburn, in 1850 after being removed from the front of Buckingham Palace because it proved too narrow for the State coaches to pass through. It now sits in the middle of a busy traffic island.

Crowds first came to **Oxford Street** to see the condemned being taken to Tyburn *(see box below left)*: this produced a ready clientele for shopkeepers, and stores first appeared along "Ladies' Mile" between Tottenham Court Road and Marylebone Lane, just short of Bond Street Underground station. This

Hangman's Haunt

A stone slab on a traffic island opposite Marble Arch at the west end of Oxford Street, London's principal shopping thoroughfare, marks the spot where a triangular gallows known as the Tyburn Tree stood from 1388 to 1783, each of its three beams being capable of hanging seven people at once. Up to 50,000 convicted felons died here. The site of London's main place of execution took its name from Tyburn Brook, which flowed into the Westbourne River at what is now the Serpentine in Hyde Park. The condemned were transported here along what is now Oxford Street (formerly Tyburn Street) from Newgate Prison or the Tower of London.

Hanging days were public holidays: the victims dressed in their best, carried nosegays of flowers and took a last mug of ale. Felons were allowed to speak to the crowd before being hanged.

Recommended Restaurants, Bars & Cafés on pages 120–1

was where the first department stores were built. One of the finest to this day, **Selfridges ⓱**, was built further west by Gordon Selfridge, a Chicago retail millionaire. Marks & Spencer, the drapers, opened their largest shop next door in 1930, still the site of their flagship store.

Only buses and taxis are allowed to drive down most of Oxford Street and its widened pavements are usually packed with tourists. Near Bond Street Underground station, designer boutiques in St Christopher's Place – with its pavement cafés and hanging baskets – offer an escape from the masses, as do Bond Street and South Molton Street on the south side.

At Oxford Circus, Oxford Street crosses over **Regent Street** which continues north, part of Nash's scheme to connect the Prince Regent's home at Carlton House with his newly acquired property at Regent's Park. Among Regent Street's restaurants are **Veeraswamy's** (entrance on Swallow Street), London's first Indian restaurant, and the **Café Royal**, at No. 68, which was used by *belle-époque* figures such as George Bernard Shaw, Oscar Wilde, James Whistler and Aubrey Beardsley.

The Café Royal was also a haunt of the high-living Edward VIII and George VI when they were Prince of Wales. Nowadays, it exudes a less refined atmosphere, although usually the most you'll see is a glimpse of the gilded foyer: beyond, its seven floors of conference and banqueting rooms, bars, and production suites cater solely to private functions. ❑

Oxford Street is known for its department stores and chain stores, but Regent Street is also worth exploring. Shops include **Hamleys**, the world's biggest toy store, at Nos. 188–196, **Aquascutum**, legendary for creating the trench-style raincoat, at No. 100, and the gigantic **Apple Store** at No. 235. **Austin Reed**, at No. 100, has an Art Deco barber's in its basement (now a beauty salon). Just off Regent Street on the fringes of Soho is **Liberty's** *(see pages 52 and 94)*.

LEFT: Angelina Ballerina in Hamleys toy shop on Regent Street (**BELOW**).

BEST RESTAURANTS, BARS AND CAFÉS

Restaurants

Prices for a three-course dinner per person with a half-bottle of house wine:

£ = under £20
££ = £20–30
£££ = £30–50
££££ = over £50

American

Hard Rock Café
150 Old Park Lane, W1. 7629 0382 L & D daily. ££ [p 334, B1]
Long established member of the global chain. Expect long queues, huge portions and homage to rock 'n' roll memorabilia. Nachos, chicken wings, sundaes and hamburgers with every conceivable trimming. The "vaults museum" next door exhibits guitars belonging to Hendrix, Presley et al.

Chinese

Kai
65 South Audley St, W1. 7493 8988 L & D daily. ££££ [p 330, B4]
Opulence pitched at a wealthy clientele. Specialities include abalone in a white truffle jus reduction and pork cooked in champagne sauce served flaming in Chinese rice wine.

Fish

Scotts
20 Mount St, W1 7495 7309 L & D daily; Oyster Bar daily all day. £££ [p 330, B4]
This restaurant is more than 150 years old. Seafood and fish dishes (good fish pie, scallops, and Dover sole) in grand surroundings.

Criterion Grill
224 Piccadilly, W1 7930 0488 L & D Mon–Sun. ££ (set menu avail) £££ [p 328, B2]
Member of the Marco Pierre White stable, the Criterion has a please-all menu of French classics. The real draw is the neo-Byzantine interior.

Le Gavroche
43 Upper Brook St, W1. 7499 1826 L & D Mon–Fri, D only Sat. £££ (set lunch avail) ££££ [p 330, B4]
French haute cuisine is given a lighter touch with hints of Asian influence. A chic, civilised operation with polished service.

Mirabelle
56 Curzon St, W1 7499 4636 L & D daily. £££ (set lunch avail) ££££ [p 334, B1]
A classic restaurant, re-invented by Marco Pierre White. Dishes include parfait of foie gras with truffles in aspic and gratinée of cod with champagne sabayon. Lovely terrace.

Truc Vert
42 North Audley St, W1 7491 9988 Mon–Sat 7.30am–10pm, Sun 9am–3pm. £££ [p 330, B4]
Informal, buzzy restaurant in a wonderful deli, offering salads, pâtés, quiches and pastries plus charcuterie/cheese plates made to order.

Indian

Benares
12a Berkeley Square House, Berkeley Square, W1. 7629 8886 L & D Sun–Fri, D only Sat. ££ (set lunch and early dinner avail) £££ [p 330, C4]
Hits on the menu include Goan-style lobster Masala in coconut, clove and cinnamon sauce. Recipient of a Michelin star.

Italian

Cecconi's
5A Burlington Gardens, W1. 7434 1500 Br, L & D daily, also brunch Sat–Sun. £££ [p 328, A2]
Sophisticated Italian specialising in classic regional gems, including pappardelle with rabbit, olives, lemon and rosemary, and a selection of tartares and carpaccios.

Rocket
4–5 Lancashire Court, W1 7629 2889 L & D Mon–Sat. ££ [p 330, C4]
Modern Italian serving wood-fired pizzas and pasta in a pretty enclave off New Bond Street.

LEFT: chef at work in Momo. **ABOVE RIGHT:** Cecconi's. **RIGHT:** Ye Grapes in Shepherds Market.

Sartoria
20 Saville Row, W1 ☎ 7534 7000 ⓒ L & D Mon–Sat. **£££** [p 328, A2]
Conran restaurant where authentic rustic meets refined Milanese. Dishes include roasted duck breast with artichokes, and rhubarb with mascarpone sorbet.

Japanese

Miyama
38 Clarges St, W1 ☎ 7493 3807 ⓒ L & D Mon–Fri, D only Sat/Sun. **££** (set menu avail) **£££** [p 334, B1]
Top sashimi and more unusual dishes such as soft-shell crab deep-fried with ponzu sauce.

Nobu
Metropolitan Hotel, 19 Old Park Lane, W1 ☎ 7447 4747 ⓒ L & D daily. **££££** [p 334, B1]
Haunt of A-list celebrities. Great Japanese food with a Peruvian twist, but tables are close and there are two-hour time limits.

Middle Eastern

Fakhreldine
85 Piccadilly, W1. ☎ 7493 3424. ⓒ L & D daily (until midnight Mon–Sat) **£££** [p 334, B1]
Offers a modern interpretation of traditional dishes. Try the platter of assorted kibbeh including pumpkin and orange blossom-scented strawberry soup. Lebanese brunch menu on Sundays.

Modern European

The Grill at Brown's
Brown's Hotel, 33 Albemarle St, W1 ☎ 7493 6020. ⓒ Br L & D Mon–Fri, D only Sat. **££££** [p 328, A2]
The latest restaurant at Brown's features a more modern feel, and impeccable service and cutting-edge cuisine still come as standard. Great cheeseboard and serious wine cellar. Live jazz set lunch on Sundays **£££**.

Dover Street Restaurant & Jazz Bar
8–10 Dover St, W1 ☎ 7629 9813 ⓒ L & D Mon–Sat until 3am. **££** (lunch menu) **£££** [p 328, A3]
Attracts an affluent post-work crowd who come here to unwind over drinks and the live jazz, soul and Latin sounds. The brasserie-style menu is unadventurous but reliable. Good value lunch. Music charge after 10pm; no jeans or trainers.

Gordon Ramsay at Claridge's
Claridge's Hotel, Brook St, W1 ☎ 7499 0099 ⓒ L & D daily. **£££** (set lunch). **££££** [p 330, C4]
Working under Gordon Ramsay's supervision, head chef Mark Sargeant cooks dreamy rich, intricate dishes. The set lunch is a relative bargain. Booking essential.

Maze
10–13 Grosvenor Square, W1 ☎ 7107 0000 ⓒ L & D daily. **£££** (set lunch) **££££** [p 330, B4]
This Rockwell-designed Gordon Ramsay-owned restaurant is a runaway success. Grazing platters are the way to experience the intensely flavoured dishes. Reasonably priced for such a high-profile place.

Others

Momo
25 Heddon St, W1 ☎ 7434 4040 ⓒ L & D Mon–Sat, D only Sun; Tearoom daily noon–midnight. **££** (set lunch) **£££** [p 328, A2]
Theatrical decor, authentic Moroccan cuisine and a party atmosphere. Share excellent *pastilla*, couscous or tagines.

Pubs, Bars and Cafés

Mayfair drinkers frequent some of London's grandest hotel bars where the scale of the free nibbles can offset the steep drinks prices. Try the stately **American Bar at the Connaught** *(Carlos Place)*, the mirrored piano **Dorchester Bar** *(53 Park Lane)*, the fashionable deco **Claridges' Bar** *(55 Brook St)* or the **Rivoli Bar** at The Ritz *(150 Piccadilly)*.

Old-fashioned boozers are thin on the ground, but there are a few gems. The posh, high Victoriana **Audley** (41–43 Mount St) attracts the Mayfair rich. More cosy is the **Coach & Horses** *(5 Bruton St)* and most lively is **Ye Grapes** *(16 Shepherd Market)*. **Eagle Bar**

Diner *(3–5 Rathbone Place)* has tongue-in-cheek chic and a long list of cocktails.

The **Met Bar** *(Metropolitan Hotel, 19 Old Park Lane)* is no longer *the* celeb venue, but its sleek red and black interior and creative cocktails still attract beautifully dressed drinkers.

London's Parks

The city has more green spaces than any comparable conurbation – and they're used for everything from sunbathing to speechmaking

London's eight major parks – Hyde Park, Kensington Gardens, Regent's Park, St James's Park, Green Park, Greenwich Park, Richmond Park and Bushy Park – are all owned and run by the Crown. Many were once royal hunting grounds, and they retain an elegant air.

The largest park is Hyde Park (350 acres/140 hectares), a vast open space only a few paces away from bustling Oxford Street. The corner of the park near Marble Arch is known as Speaker' Corner, where freedom of speech is given full rein on Sunday afternoons.

Hyde Park adjoins Kensington Gardens, which have the air of a Victorian children's playground, with model boats on the Round Pond. The oldest park is St James's, beautifully landscaped with fountains and views of Buckingham Palace and Whitehall. Regent's Park, in Marylebone, houses London Zoo and has a very fine Rose Garden.

In addition there are several fine suburban parks, some of them established in the 19th century to alleviate the unhealthy living conditions of the poor. The other great open space is Hampstead Heath in north London.

Right: making a point at Hyde Park's Speakers' Corner.

Above: the Royal Botanic Gardens at Kew *(see page 236)* cover 300 acres (121 hectares), among the most extensive in the world. As well as being a public garden, Kew is a world centre for scientific research.

Below: one of London's more unusual rituals takes place at 9am on Christmas Day, when dozens of men and women dive into the Serpentine Lake in Hyde Park. They are competing for the Peter Pan Cup, first presented by children's author J.M. Barrie

ABOVE: the tidal River Thames is too hazardous for leisure activity, and so the Serpentine Lake in Hyde Park is London's largest boating centre. Rowing boats can also be hired in Regent's Park and Battersea Park.

RIGHT: Richmond Park *(see page 238)* was once a royal hunting ground, but today more than 600 red and fallow deer graze in peace. The 2,470-acre (1,000-hectare) park has extensive facilities for horse riders, cricketers, golfers and footballers. Adam's Pond is used for model boats, and two Pen Ponds are reserved for anglers.

MUSIC AND THEATRE IN THE PARK

The sight of people sitting in striped deckchairs in a park on a warm summer's day listening to a brass band is reassuringly English. Five of the royal parks have their own bandstands and hold regular, free afternoon concerts at weekends. Musical entertainment is laid on throughout the summer. Jazz and woodwind recitals are given at Kensington Gardens and the last night of the Proms (the summer Henry Wood Promenade Concerts in the Albert Hall) spills over into Hyde Park. Concerts in Greenwich Park are held in a special park arena by the Royal Observatory. The evening concerts are held in mid-July and feature well known musicians.

Great houses provide other venues for music and theatre. Although the future of the much loved and long-established orchestral concerts at Kenwood House is uncertain, concerts are also held in the grounds of Holland House in Holland Park, west London, and make a delightful evening. But possibly the best place to be on a dry summer evening is watching an open-air Shakespeare production in Regent's Park (left).

BT
Marylebone
West End
New Traffic
Scheme Ahead
Street

Recommended Restaurants, Bars & Cafés on pages 130–1

MARYLEBONE AND FITZROVIA

North of Oxford Street lies Marylebone, a characterful area of elegant squares and terraces bordered by Regent's Park. Among its attractions are Madame Tussauds, London Zoo and the Sherlock Holmes Museum

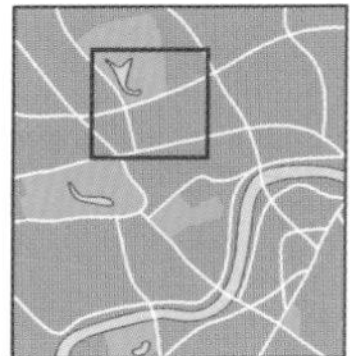

The residential area of **Marylebone** (pronounced *mar-le-bun*) lies between Oxford Street and Regent's Park. It is largely Georgian in character, its streets and squares named after the Cavendish, Harley and Portland families, who progressively developed the district from the beginning of the 18th century. The need to relieve congestion in Oxford Street inspired the creation of a new road running from Paddington to Islington through the parish of St Mary-by-the-bourne.

Today, Marylebone still retains an air of genteel village dwelling, an oasis framed by multicultural Edgware Road to the west, Oxford Street to the south and Tottenham Court Road to the east. The section known as Fitzrovia, traditionally an artists' enclave and retaining a bohemian atmosphere, nestles around the Telecom Tower.

NORTH OF OXFORD STREET

St Christopher's Place, a pedestrian enclave lined with boutiques and cafés, is accessible through a narrow passageway on Oxford Street *(see pages 118–9)* and leads via cobbled James Street to Wigmore Street containing several good restaurants as well as various medical specialists spilling over from **Harley Street**, the preferred haunt of private physicians since the 1840s.

On the north side of the road stands **Wigmore Hall** ❶ *(see page 300)*, a delightful concert venue, particularly at lunchtimes. BBC Radio 3 broadcasts live from here on Monday and on Sundays. The Art Nouveau building, which has notable acoustics, was erected in 1901.

Main attractions
- WIGMORE HALL
- WALLACE COLLECTION
- SHERLOCK HOLMES MUSEUM
- REGENT'S PARK
- LONDON ZOO
- LORD'S CRICKET GROUND
- MADAME TUSSAUDS
- ROYAL ACADEMY OF MUSIC
- LONDON CENTRAL MOSQUE
- TELECOM TOWER
- MARYLEBONE HIGH STREET
- FITZROY TAVERN
- CHARLOTTE STREET

LEFT: Fitzrovia's Telecom Tower rises over 18th- and 19th-century terraces.
RIGHT: the entrance to Wigmore Hall, a fine Art Nouveau concert hall.

Sir Joshua Reynolds' Miss Jane Bowles *(1775), the Wallace Collection.*

Wallace Collection ❷

✉ Hertford House, Manchester Square, W1;
www.wallacecollection.org
☎ 7563 9500 ◷ daily 10am–5pm
€ free 🚇 Bond Street

This remarkable display of art ranges from 17th- and 18th-century English and European paintings to Sèvres porcelain. In addition to pictures by Velázquez, Boucher and Fragonard, it contains Rembrandt's *Self-Portrait in a Black Cap*, Rubens' *Rainbow Landscape*, Franz Hals's *Laughing Cavalier*, Poussin's *Dance to the Music of Time*, and Gainsborough's *Lady Robinson as "Perdita"*. The collection was bequeathed to the British nation by the widow of Richard Wallace, the illegitimate son of the fourth Marquess of Hertford, who originally amassed these works.

MARYLEBONE VILLAGE

Tucked amongst quiet residential terraces, **Marylebone High Street** ❸ is a hub of homeware shops, boutiques and restaurants, its urban village atmosphere providing a cosy oasis from the surrounding bustle. It also has several specialist food shops,

Marylebone and Fitzrovia

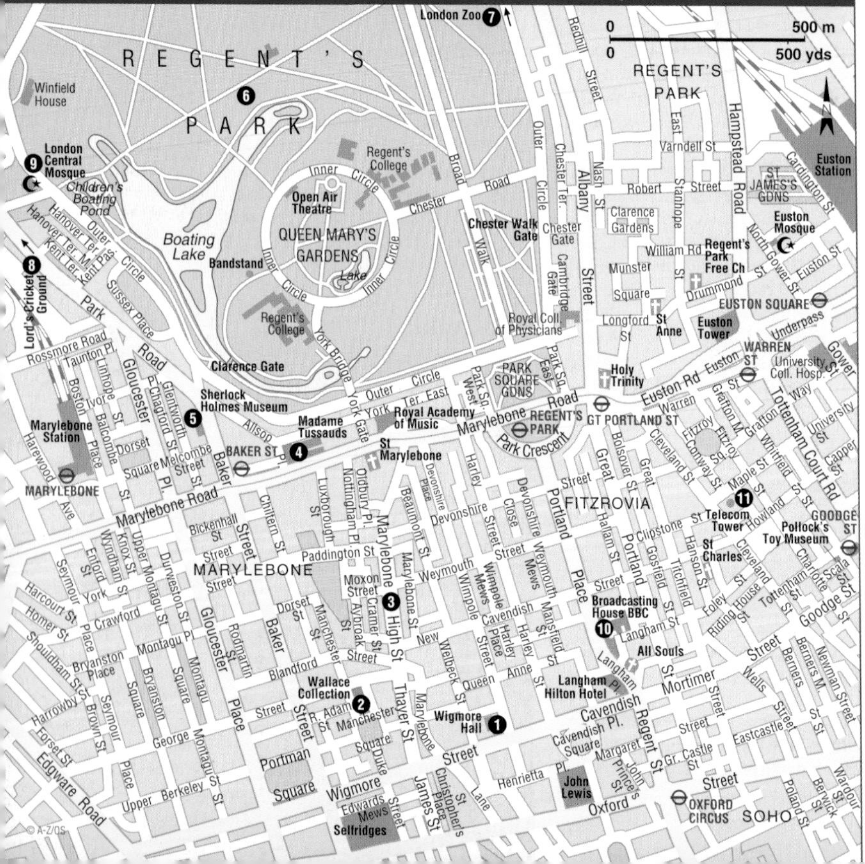

Recommended Restaurants, Bars & Cafés on pages 130–1

from charcuteries to fishmongers. On Sundays there is a **farmers' market** (10am–2pm) on Moxon Street.

More pubs and small shops are dotted along narrow **Marylebone Lane**, which winds along the course of the subterranean River Tyburn.

MARYLEBONE ROAD AND BAKER STREET

Marlebone Road is one of London's busiest east-west thoroughfares. Its intersection with north-south Baker Street is marked by two well-known attractions, Madame Tussauds and the Sherlock Holmes Museum.

Madame Tussauds ❹

Marylebone Road; www.madame-tussauds.co.uk 7935 6861 daily 9am–6pm charge Baker Street

With its high-tech special effects and increasing emphasis on contemporary celebrities, Madame Tussauds wax-work museum is one of London's top attractions, especially for teenagers. *For more information, see the photo feature on pages 132–3.*

Not far past the scrum outside Madame Tussauds is the **Royal Academy of Music**, which hosts daily recitals, workshops, seminars and concerts, most of which are free (tel: 7873 7300). Opposite the Academy stands **St Marylebone Parish Church**, which was depicted by Hogarth in the wedding scene of *A Rake's Progress*. Lord Byron (1788) and Charles Wesley (1707) were baptised here.

Sherlock Holmes Museum ❺

239 Baker Street, NW1; www.sherlock-holmes.co.uk 7935 8866 daily 9.30am–6.30pm charge Baker Street

On Baker Street, north of the intersection with Marylebone Road, this museum re-creates the Victorian home of Arthur Conan Doyle's fictional detective. Some rooms are detailed representations of his living quarters, others contain waxwork tableaux of characters and scenes described in the stories. A Victorian "maid" is on hand to answer questions.

REGENT'S PARK

Baker Street, Marylebone High Street and Portland Place all lead to **Regent's**

Regent's Park's rose garden in the heart of the Inner Circle contains some 20,000 roses. They bloom from June through to Christmas.

LEFT: falconry display in Regent's Park Zoo. **BELOW:** exhibits in the Sherlock Holmes Museum.

An alternative and more romantic route to London Zoo is to take a canal boat from Camden Lock or Little Venice along Regent's Canal. The London Waterbus Company runs regular services in summer (tel: 7482 2660; www.londonwaterbus.com) with a reduced service during winter.

In 1964 several scenes in the Beatles film A Hard Day's Night *were filmed at Marylebone station*

Park ❻, an elegant 470-acre (190-hectare) space surrounded by John Nash's Regency terraces. Shakespeare plays are performed at the Open Air Theatre in summer. The boating lake is a tranquil spot, and Regent's Canal runs through the north of the park.

London Zoo ❼

Outer Circle, Regent's Park, NW1; www.zsl.org/london-zoo 7722 3333 daily Mar–Oct 10am–5.30pm, Nov–Feb 10am–4pm charge Camden Town

Increasingly placing an onus on conservational breeding, London Zoo has launched two new projects: the Gorilla Kingdom and Clore Rainforest Lookout displaying South American mammals, birds and reptiles. On a more tactile level, the children's enclosure allows visitors to handle animals such as rabbits and llamas.

Aside from the variety of wildlife on show, the Penguin Pool by the Russian architect, Berthold Lubetkin, and the Aviary by Lord Snowdon are of architectural interest.

RIGHT: the legendary W.G. Grace at Lord's Cricket Ground.
BELOW: the dome and minaret of London Central Mosque.

Around the Park

On the northwest side of the park is **Lord's Cricket Ground** ❽ (nearest tube: St John's Wood), belonging to the Marylebone Cricket Club, which runs the English game. To access the ground and the portrait-packed Long Room through which players walk on their way to the field, see the honours boards in the players' dressing rooms and visit the **museum**, you must take the 100-minute tour (daily except

Recommended Restaurants, Bars & Cafés on pages 130–1

on major match or preparation days, noon, 2pm, also 10am Apr–Sept; tel: 7432 1033).

Nearby is the **London Central Mosque ❾** and Islamic Cultural Centre. The site for the mosque was a gift from the government to the Muslim community during World War II, in recognition of the substantial Islamic population of the British Empire, although the building of the mosque was not completed until 1977. Visitors are welcome but note that clothing to below the knee is required; women can borrow headscarves from the bookshop.

PORTLAND PLACE

The eastern stretch of Marylebone leads to Park Crescent and **Portland Place**, conceived by the Adam brothers as a home for the rich. John Nash included it in his grand design to connect Regent's Park with St James's but the plan was never realised. The Adam houses in Portland Place house several embassies, institutes and learned societies, such as the Royal Institute of British Architects (RIBA).

Langham Place, which curves round to connect Portland Place with Regent Street, has a trio of dramatic buildings: the circular **All Souls' Church** built by Nash in 1822–24, the Langham Hilton hotel and **Broadcasting House ❿**, headquarters of the BBC, where the first public television transmission was made in 1932. The TV studios are now at White City in west London, but the corporation's main radio studios are still here.

FITZROVIA

Dominating the skyline of this former bohemian enclave is the **Telecom Tower ⓫**, which at more than 600 ft (180 metres) high is one of the tallest structures in London. **Fitzroy Square** is central to the area's literary heritage *(see below)*; George Bernard Shaw, Virginia Woolf and more recently Ian McEwan have all lived here.

Cosmopolitan **Charlotte Street** used to be known mainly for Greek eateries but now has a variety of chic restaurants. Running parallel is **Tottenham Court Road**, home to many electrical goods and home furnishing stores such as Heal's, and the eastern boundary of Fitzrovia. ❑

KIDS

Pollock's Toy Museum (tel: 7636 3452; Mon–Sat 10am–5pm) has a great variety of toy exhibits and puppet theatres, spread over an eccentric building accessible by a small entrance on Scala Street. There is an old-fashioned toy shop on the ground floor.

ABOVE: Victorian doll in Pollock's Toy Museum. **BELOW LEFT:** All Souls' Church, Langham Place.

Fitzrovia's Legacy

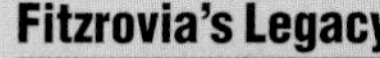

Fitzrovia has long attracted countercultures; in the mid-19th century, for example, it was a hub of working-men's clubs and Chartist activity. However, it is most famous for attracting a bawdy bohemian set between the 1920s and 1950s. Welsh poet Dylan Thomas and the painter Augustus John frequented the Fitzroy Tavern, while writer Julian Maclaren-Ross drank away his publishing advance at The Wheatsheaf, ultimately becoming better known for his "King of Fitzrovia" persona, complete with silver-topped cane, than for his short stories.

George Orwell was another regular and the Newman Arms on Rathbone Street features in his novels *Nineteen Eighty-Four* and *Keep the Aspidistra Flying*. Others included Anthony Powell, Wyndham Lewis and Francis Bacon. The scene dissolved in the 1950s. Today creativity comes in other forms: many media companies are based here.

BEST RESTAURANTS, BARS AND CAFÉS

Restaurants

Prices for a three-course dinner per person with a half-bottle of house wine:

£ = under £20
££ = £20–30
£££ = £30–50
££££ = over £50

British

Langan's Bistro
26 Devonshire St. W1
7935 4531 L & D Mon–Fri, D only Sat. **££** [p 330, B2]
Old-timer and former celebrity haunt serving simple, old-fashioned bistro fare with considerable aplomb. No culinary fireworks in the kitchen but good for more sedate romantic occasions.

Stanley's
6 Little Portland St, W1
7462 0099 L & D Mon–Sat. **££** [p 331, C3]
Beer and sausage restaurant offering imaginative food and a choice of ales.

Fish

Back to Basics
21a Foley St, W1 7436 2181 L & D Mon–Sat. **£££** [p 331, C2]
A blackboard menu has a dozen or so fish dishes in this excellent neighbourhood venue.

Fishworks
89 Marylebone High St.
7935 9796 L & D Mon–Fri, D only Sun. **££** [p 330, B2]
Member of a well-regarded chain selling fresh fish and seafood in the front and with a restaurant behind.

Golden Hinde
73 Marylebone Lane, W1
7486 3644 L & D Mon–Fri, D only Sat. **£** [p 330, B3]
Vintage chippie (1914), with a magnificent 1930s fryer now purely decorative. Fabulous glisteningly fresh fish in crispy golden batter. BYOB. No corkage.

French

Galvin Bistrot de Luxe
66 Baker Street, W1
7935 4007 L & D daily. **£££** [p 330, B3]
Critically adored brasserie serving traditional Gallic dishes. Has a reasonable set menu 6–7pm.

Italian

Caldesi
15–17 Marylebone Lane, W1 7935 9226 L & D Mon–Fri, D only Sat. **£££** [p 330, B3]
This is a quiet gem. A sample dish is monkfish with prawns, tomato, wild fennel and basil . Caffè Caldesi at 118 Marylebone Lane is a cheaper, buzzier alternative.

Da Paolo
3 Charlotte Place, London, W1 7580 0021 L & D Mon–Fri, D only Sat–Sun. **££** [p 331, D2]
Italian village atmosphere and dishes that include linguine with langoustines and beef fillet with blue cheese.

Japanese

Roka
37 Charlotte Street, W1
7580 6464 L & D daily. **£££** [p 331, D2]
See and be seen at this uber-stylish place, where the food is based on *robatayaki* cuisine (cooked on an open charcoal grill).

Modern European

Odin's Restaurant
27 Devonshire St, W1
7935 7296 L & D Mon–Fri. **£££** [p 330, B2]
Grand antique-filled dining room that's good for an intimate dinner as tables are hidden behind old-style screens. Dishes include crab bisque and grilled Dover sole.

Orrery
55 Marylebone High St, W1
7616 8000 L & D daily. **£££** (set menu) **££££** [p 330, B2]
Dinner here is a romantic

LEFT: Fishworks on Marylebone High Street.
ABOVE RIGHT: frying tonight at the Golden Hnd.

gastro experience. Barbary duck with *pain d'épice*, foie gras *tarte tartin* and *banyuls* jus are typical dishes.

O'Conor Don

88 Marylebone Lane, W1. 7935 9311 L & D Mon–Fri. ££ [p 330, B3]
Elegant yet homely dining room over a pub. Modern Irish menu including oysters and beef in Guinness.

Spanish

Navarro's

67 Charlotte St, W1 7637 7713 L & D Mon–Fri, D only Sat. ££ [p 331, D2]
A choice of some 50 Spanish *tapas* in a restaurant with a bright blue frontage and colourful interior. Seafood dishes generally excel.

The Providores and Tapa Room

109 Marylebone High St, W1 7935 6175 L & D daily. Tapa Room ££, Provi dores £££ [p 330, B2]
Interesting ingredients are used to create exciting fusion dishes. The downstairs Tapa Room is more informal. Don't leave without sampling the chocolate, raisin and sherry brownie.

Six-13

19 Wigmore St, W1 7629 6133 L & D Sun–Thur, L only Fri, D only Sat. ££ (set lunch). ££££ [p 330, C3]
A smart kosher restaurant serving modern reinterpretations of classic Jewish cuisine and Mediterranean fish dishes in Art Deco-style surroundings. The name refers to the 613 Jewish rules for living. All wines are kosher too. There's a cheaper diner downstairs.

Middle Eastern

Fairuz

3 Blandford St, W2 7486 8108 daily. ££ [p 330, B3]
There are nearly 50 meze on the excellent menu but the mains are good too, the charcoal grills generous and cooked to perfection. Helpful staff, warm decor and outdoor seating in summer.

North African

Original Tagines

7a Dorset St, W1 7935 1545 L & D Mon–Fri, D only Sat. £ (set lunch), ££ [p 330, B2]
This is a buzzy little restaurant which specialises in deliciously spiced Moroccan tagines including tender lamb in black-pepper sauce with caramelised pepper. Laid-back atmosphere.

Vegetarian

Eat and Two Veg

50 Marylebone High St, W1. 7258 8595 daily, all day. ££ [p 330, B2]
Stylish formica-and-leatherette diner.

Manna

Erskine Road, NW3 7722 8028 D only Mon–Sat, L & D Sun. ££ [p 330, C1, off map]
Good vegetarian restaurant in Primrose Hill.

Pubs, Bars and Cafés

At the **Fitzroy Tavern** *(16 Charlotte St)* they still display George Orwell's journalists' union card. The **Newman Arms** *(23 Rathbone St)* is famed for its pies and **The Marquis of Granby** *(2 Rathbone St)* offers many varieties of British sausage.

Modish bars range from the **Long Bar** in the Sanderson Hotel *(50 Berners St)* to the cultish basement **Jerusalem** *(33–34 Rathbone Place)*, and the conspiratorial **Bradley's Spanish Bar** *(42–44 Hanway St)*. **Coco Momo** *(79 Marylebone High St)* is a good gastro-bar.

For sheer indulgence, visit the **Tsar's Bar** at Langham Hilton *(1 Portland Place)* and choose from the 100+ vodkas to go with your caviar. For a Scottish experience try a Nessie's monster sandwich and a choice single malt at **The Gunmakers** *(33 Aybrook St)*.

Cafés

Quiet Revolution *(62–64 Weymouth St)* is an organic haven. For a daytime treat, tuck into a gâteau at **Patisserie Valerie** at Maison Sagne *(105 Marylebone High St)* or visit **Café Bagatelle** *(The Wallace Collection, Manchester Sq)* for a civilised lunch or tea break, in an airy glass-roofed courtyard. In Fitzrovia, **Squat & Gobble** (69 Charlotte Street) offers hefty portions of tasty sandwiches, salads, and daily specials.

Seeing Stars at Madame Tussauds

When computer animation creates miraculous images on cinema screens, what is the appeal of a collection of mute effigies with glass-fibre bodies and wax heads?

A key ingredient in the success of Madame Tussauds is that the models are no longer roped off or protected by glass cases. You can stroll right up to them – an impertinence their body-guards would never permit in real life. You can give George Bush a piece of your mind. You can be photographed with your arm around the Queen (pictured) or Tom Cruise. Whatever impulse draws crowds to see a minor television personality declare open a supermarket is at work here in overdrive, and the reactions are similar. Is Mel Gibson really that short? Is Beyoncé's skin really that perfect? An additional talking-point is provided by the fact that, while the best models are astonishingly lifelike, a surprising proportion just aren't all that good.

To ring the changes, Tussauds mounts temporary groupings based on films such as *Pirates of the Caribbean* or TV shows such as *Big Brother*.

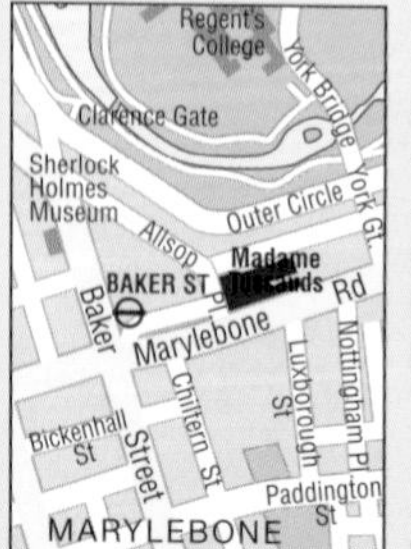

The essentials

Marylebone Road; www.madame-tussauds.co.uk

daily 9am–6pm

tel: 020-7935 6861

Admission fees are at West End theatre levels (as much as £25 for an adult and £21 for a child).

Baker Street

ABOVE: it can take 500 hours of specialist sculpting to create figures such as Princes William and Harry. If the subjects are willing, a cast of their teeth is taken to ensure accuracy. Some donate clothing for their waxwork – Nicholas Cage provided a pair of jeans, Kylie Minogue a mini-dress and Tony Blair a suit.

RIGHT: a "bizarrely comical collection of extra-terrestrials" from the Wallace and Gromit animation stable is projected on the dome of the former planetarium. The premise of the dimwitted 10-minute film is that their great desire is to visit Earth, which they believe is inhabited exclusively by celebrities. You will enjoy this experience only if you subscribe to Tussauds' dictum about celebrities: "Our lives are enriched by them and the things they do."

ABOVE: the Beatles – age cannot wither them, nor will they be melted down while fans want to pose with them.

RIGHT: Humphrey Bogart's likeness is passable, though Marlon Brando and Alfred Hitchcock fare less well. You can hug Marilyn Monroe as her skirt billows up as it did in *The Seven Year Itch*.

THE WOMAN BEHIND THE WAXWORKS

The story began during the French Revolution in 1789 when Marie Grosholtz, trained by a doctor in modelling anatomical subjects in wax, was asked to prepare death masks of famous victims of the guillotine. She married a French engineer, François Tussaud, in 1795, but left him in 1802 to spend the next 33 years touring Britain with a growing collection of wax figures. The London waxworks began in Baker Street and moved to the Marylebone Road in 1884.

Today those gory beginnings are echoed in the waxworks' Chamber of Horrors, which contains the blade that sliced off Marie Antoinette's head and re-creates various none-too-scary tableaux of torture.

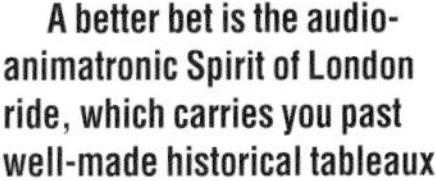

At extra cost, you can enter a dark section of the chamber where actors portraying deranged serial killers lunge at you and yell in your face. Since you are forewarned that this will happen and assured that they won't touch you, it's hard to be seriously terrified.

A better bet is the audio-animatronic Spirit of London ride, which carries you past well-made historical tableaux.

BELOW: sport is represented mainly by soccer celebrities such as Wayne Rooney, pictured, and David Beckham.

ELIZABETH II A.D. 2000 THIS GREAT COURT

Recommended Restaurants, Bars & Cafes on pages 142–3

BLOOMSBURY AND KING'S CROSS

Home to the British Museum and the traditional base of publishing in London, Bloomsbury has an intellectual reputation. But a new wind is blowing through the area with the regeneration of neighbouring King's Cross and the opening of the Eurostar rail terminal at St Pancras

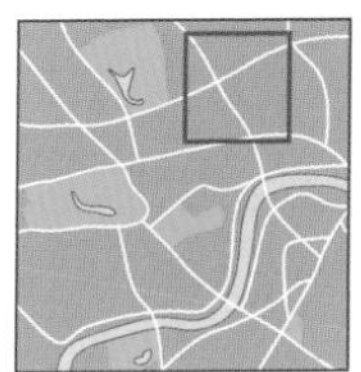

The eastern side of Tottenham Court Road marks the beginning of Bloomsbury, London's literary heart, and home to the British Museum and the University of London. The area was laid out in the late 17th and early 18th centuries, initially by the Earl of Southampton and later by Wriothesley Russell, the third Duke of Bedford, both commemorated in the place names of the area.

Publishing houses occupy many of the fine Georgian properties lining the streets and squares. Bloomsbury is blue plaque territory *par excellence (see page 138)*. Charles Dickens lived in Doughty Street between 1837 and 1839 *(see the Dickens House Museum, page 139)* and in the early part of the 20th century it nurtured the Bloomsbury set, a group of writers who laid the foundations for modernism in Britain. Virginia Woolf, Vanessa Bell, Duncan Grant, Dora Carrington, E.M. Forster, Roger Fry, Maynard Keynes and Queen Victoria's biographer, Lytton Strachey, all lived at addresses in the area. They probably had more influence as a body than as individuals, and were bookish men and women in a bookish world.

LEFT AND RIGHT: the glass-roofed Great Court and the Greek-style facade of the British Museum.

The British Museum ❶

✉ Great Russell Street, WC2; www.thebritishmuseum.ac.uk ☎ 7323 8299 ⏲ daily 10am–5.30pm, until 8.30pm Thur & Fri Ⓢ free except some special exhibitions Ⓜ Russell Square

The British Museum on Great Russell Street is the nation's greatest treasure house. It opened in 1759, in smaller premises in South Kensington, and now owns more than 6½ million items, ranging from the oldest neolithic antiquities to 20th-century

Main attractions

THE BRITISH MUSEUM
CORAM'S FIELDS
THE FOUNDLING MUSEUM
DICKENS HOUSE MUSEUM
KING'S CROSS
ST PANCRAS STATION
LONDON CANAL MUSEUM
THE BRITISH LIBRARY

> *London thou art a jewel of jewels, a jasper of jocundity, music, talk, friendship, city views, publishing, something central & inexplicable, all this is within my reach...*
>
> Virginia Woolf 1924

manuscripts *(see separate feature on the museum, pages 144–5)*.

Access to the collections is via the **Great Court,** roofed with a steel and glass canopy in 2000 and one of the most spectacular spaces in London. The museum's famous circular Reading Room, where Karl Marx did much of his research for *Das Kapital,* is now open to all as an information centre, its library having moved to Euston Road *(see page 141)*.

Near the museum

From the museum three short streets (**Museum Street, Coptic Street** and **Bury Place**) lead to Bloomsbury Way. Among their antiquarian bookshops and cafés look out for the **London Review Bookshop** (14 Bury Place), which regularly hosts author readings and interviews; **Blade Rubber** (12 Bury Place), selling a huge range of rubber stamps as well as everything needed to make home-made greetings cards; and, next door to one another at the northern end of Bury Place, **It's All Greek** and **Parthenon**, both selling quality replicas of ancient artefacts (though the British Museum's own shop is also very good for these).

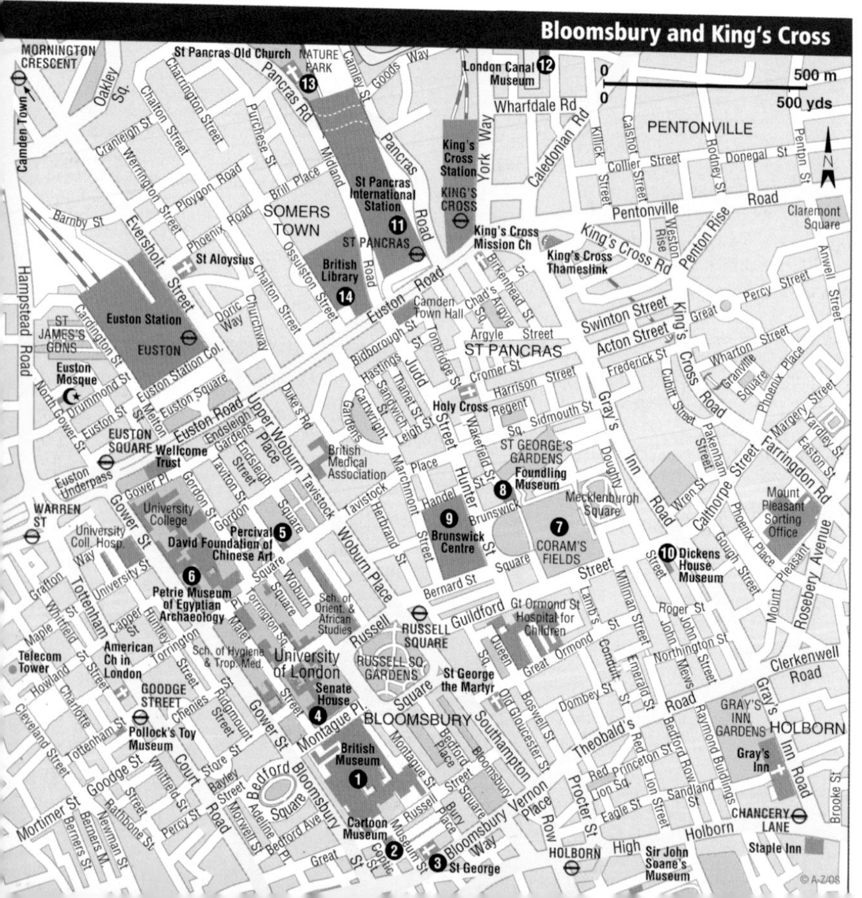

Bloomsbury and King's Cross

In Little Russell Street, running between Museum Street and Coptic Street, the **Cartoon Museum** ❷ (Tue–Sat 10.30am–5.30pm, Sun noon–5.30pm; 35 Little Russell St; tel: 7580 8155; charge) charts the history of British cartooning from Hogarth and Bateman to Steve Bell and Gerald Scarfe, taking in comic-book characters such as Dennis the Menace and comic postcards by Donald McGill.

The British Museum's collection had an effect on the architecture of the area. Nicholas Hawksmoor's **Church of St George** ❸ (1730) in Bloomsbury Way was inspired by the Mausoleum of Halikarnassus, one of the Seven Wonders of the Ancient world, remnants of which can be seen in the museum *(see page 146–7)*. This is best appreciated by looking at its unusual stepped tower with lions and unicorns at its base and a statue of George I wearing a toga on top. The church often holds free choral performances on Sunday afternoons (www.stgeorgesbloomsbury.org.uk).

THE UNIVERSITY OF LONDON

Just north of the British Museum is the University of London, identified by the grey turret of **Senate House** ❹, built in 1936, on the western side of Russell Square. Among the university buildings, the School of Oriental and African Studies houses the **Percival David Foundation of Chinese Art** ❺ (Mon–Fri 10.30am–5pm; 53 Gordon Square; tel: 7387 3909; free), one of the finest Chinese ceramic collections in the West, with 1,700 works from the 10th to the 18th century.

Close by, at 46 Gordon Square, is the house to which Virginia Woolf and her siblings moved after their

TIP

The Tavistock Hotel on Tavistock Square has a wonderful retro-look bowling alley in its basement (entrance Bedford Way). This is a great option for children on a wet day, but be aware that they are not admitted after 4pm. In the evenings and at weekends it is essential to book (tel: 7153 1979).

LEFT: a few of the thousands of rubber stamps for sale at Blade Rubber on Bury Place. **BELOW LEFT:** Nicholas Hawksmoor's tower on the Church of St George.
BELOW: literary bookshop on Bury Place.

Blue Plaques

Numerous famous writers, artists and intellectuals have made Bloomsbury their home. Commemorating their presence are scores of blue plaques

One of many pointers to London's varied past are the blue plaques slapped on sundry sites to commemorate famous people, events and buildings. There are plenty in Bloomsbury, but they are strewn all across London. Almost 900 have appeared on the former homes of the famous and the long dead, and about 20 new ones are added each year. The first plaque was erected by the Royal Society of Arts in memory of the poet Lord Byron in 1867. In 1901 the London County Council took over the service, which is today administered by English Heritage.

Bona-fide plaques are ceramic with white lettering on a circular blue base. They are bald statements of fact, giving little biographical information – simply the name, dates, profession and usually the period he or she lived in the building.

The awarding of a plaque is almost haphazard: there is no overall register of famous people who have lived in London. Many plaques are put up because descendants or adherents of the deceased put forward the suggestion to English Heritage. Thus plaques function as a barometer of public taste, as notions change about what constitutes fame. The range has been dominated by 19th-century politicians and artists, but in 1997 the first plaque to commemorate a rock star – Jimi Hendrix – went up in Brook Street.

A plaque-spotting tour would not lack variety. Captain William Bligh of Bounty fame lived at 100 Lambeth Road, SE1; Charlie Chaplin lived at 287 Kennington Road, SE1; Sir Winston Churchill lived at 34 Eccleston Square, SW1; Benjamin Franklin lived at 36 Craven Street, WC2; Charles Dickens lived at 48 Doughty Street, WC1; Henry James lived at 34 De Vere Gardens, W8; Karl Marx lived at 28 Dean Street, W1; George Bernard Shaw lived at 29 Fitzroy Square, W1; and Mark Twain lived at 23 Tedworth Square, SW3.

Most candidates for traditional plaques are submitted to lengthy scrutiny. They must have been dead for at least 20 years; they must be regarded as eminent by luminaries in their profession; they should have made an important contribution to human welfare; the well-informed passer-by should recognise their name; and they should, by the kind of infuriatingly nebulous "general agreement" that has characterised British decision-making, deserve recognition.

More recently the borough of Southwark began placing its own blue plaques to locals who received most votes in a public poll. This enabled the living as well as the dead to be commemorated murally. ❑

ABOVE: Bloomsbury hostess Lady Ottoline Morrell lived at 10 Gower Street. **LEFT:** the Borough of Southwark recognises the living as well as the dead.

father's death in 1904, thus becoming a magnet for other Bloomsberries.

The **Petrie Museum of Egyptian Archaeology** ❻ (Tue–Fri 1–5pm, Sat 10am–1pm; University College London, Malet Place; free) is a two-room collection of treasures of interest mainly to students and academics.

CORAM'S FIELDS ❼

East of the British Museum, across **Russell Square**, the area is dissected by Southampton Row. On the east side of the square, just beyond the children's hospital in Great Ormond Street, are Coram's Fields, where children rule the roost (adults may only enter the park if accompanied by children). As well as playgrounds, sports facilities, and a nursery, it has rabbits, chickens and sheep.

Thomas Coram was a sea captain who started a hospital and school for foundling children and persuaded artists of the day, including William Hogarth, to donate works of art to raise funds. The collection, which includes paintings by the great 19th-century portraitists Thomas Gainsborough and Joshua Reynolds, is displayed in the **Foundling Museum** ❽, in the old Foundling Hospital on the north side of Coram's Fields (Tue–Sat 1.30–4.30pm, Sun noon–6pm; 40 Brunswick Square; tel: 7841 3600; www.foundlingmuseum.org.uk; charge; children free).

The ground floor traces the history of the hospital and of the philanthropic movement set against the background of 19th-century social conditions. Upstairs, in a fine rococo drawing room, are items belonging or related to George Frideric Handel, one of the hospital's benefactors.

Shopping and eating

The **Brunswick Centre** ❾, a 1960s shopping-cum-housing development on the west side of Coram's Fields, has recently been given a makeover. It includes several good eating options as well as the Renoir, an art-house cinema. Alternatively, south of Coram's Fields is **Lamb's Conduit Street**, a characterful street with interesting shops and the Lamb pub.

DICKENS HOUSE MUSEUM ❿

47 Doughty St, WC1 7405 2127 Mon–Sat 10am–5pm charge Russell Square

A five-minute walk southeast of Coram's Fields is the house-museum where Dickens lived with his family between 1837 and 1839 and wrote

BELOW LEFT: portrait of Dickens in a window of the Dickens House Museum.
BELOW: Dickens House Museum.

Among the many eating and shopping options in St Pancras is the longest champagne bar in Europe. It is situated just below the clock inside the station.

Oliver Twist and *Nicholas Nickelby*. In a reverential atmosphere visitors can inspect a huge collection of furniture, memorabilia, paintings, books and documents. The displays on the upper floors illustrate his one great passion besides literature – the plays, which he produced, directed and acted in at various times.

South of Dickens House, **John Street**, lined with handsome Georgian properties, some with a full complement of 18th-century ironwork, leads to Theobald's Road and Holborn *(see pages 150–1)*. North of Coram's Fields, and best reached along Hunter Street, lies the newly booming area of King's Cross and St Pancras.

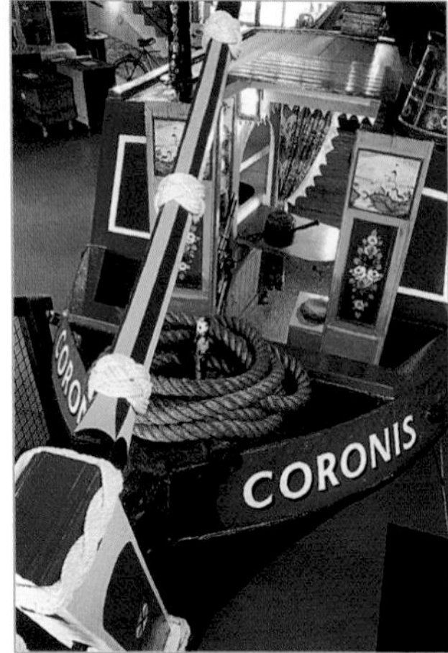

RIGHT: inside the Canal Museum. **BELOW:** St Pancras, brought back to life by the new Eurostar terminal. **BELOW RIGHT:** opposite Euston Station, on Euston road, look out for St Pancras New Church. Its eight caryatids (four on each side) were inspired by the Erechtheum on the Acropolis in Athens.

KING'S CROSS AND ST PANCRAS

Just as Southwark and Bankside became the focus for redevelopment in the late 20th century, the area around St Pancras and King's Cross stations, for many years run-down and sleazy, are undergoing massive regeneration in the first decade of the 21st century. Triggered by the construction of the Eurostar rail terminal, which opened in November 2007, the area is fast becoming a new cultural zone, attracting creative industries and organisations, contemporary art galleries, as well as bars, restaurants and luxury apartments.

Housing the new terminal, **St Pancras Station** ⓫, an immense red-brick edifice by Sir Gilbert Scott, the

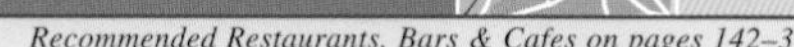

Recommended Restaurants, Bars & Cafes on pages 142–3

master of Victorian Gothic, has been superbly restored after several decades of neglect and uncertainty.

Regent Quarter

The area behind the two stations, for long an industrial backwater crossed by roads and railway lines, is also being regenerated, especially the so-called Regent Quarter, near the Regent Canal. Occupying an old icehouse on the wharf of **Battlebridge Basin**, is the **London Canal Museum** ⓬ (Tue–Sun 10am–4pm; 12–13 New Wharf Road, accessed from Wharfdale Road; www.canalmuseum.org.uk; tel: 7713 0839; charge). As well as portraying canal life, the museum tells the hard story of London's 19th-century ice trade, when ice was imported from Norway. One of two ice pits is open to view.

Camley Street

Behind St Pancras Station, Camley Street leads north towards Camden. On the left is **St Pancras Old Church** ⓭, one of the oldest Christian sites in London. Its cemetery contains the graves of several notable figures, including the celebrated architect and art collector Sir John Soane *(see page 153)* and his wife.

Also on Camley Road, opposite the cemetery and flanking the canal is a slim **nature park** (free) with a trail, wildlife pond and child-friendly activities on weekends.

The British Library ⓮

96 Euston Road; www.bl.uk
7412 7332 Mon–Sat 9.30am–6pm, until 8pm Tue, Sun 11am–5pm, tours available free
King's Cross

Back on Euston Road, next door to St Pancras, is the British Library, which moved here from the British Museum in 1998. It houses 16 million books and periodicals, including a Gutenberg Bible, the Magna Carta and original texts by Shakespeare, Dickens and da Vinci. In addition to guided tours of some of the highlights, the library holds temporary exhibitions. The spacious courtyard (with café) is a peaceful refuge from busy Euston Road. ❑

Opposite Euston Station is the excellent new Wellcome Collection (183 Euston Road, www.wellcomecollection.org; Tue–Sat with late opening Thur; free), a museum-cum-art space devoted to medicine and its relationships with art and society. It mixes items from Henry Wellcome's (1853–1936) eclectic collection of objects, interactive exhibits, paintings and much more. Other draws include a stylish café and a bookshop.

Using the British Library

Researchers can use the reading rooms by applying in person or through the website (www.bl.uk) for a reader's pass. Two forms of identification, including proof of home address and proof of signature must be produced. Your need to use the library will be ascertained, and so documentation or a business card supporting your application is useful. Free 45-minute induction sessions help users find their way around the vast resources.

Members of any local library in the UK can also access the collection, if the book required cannot be obtained from any other library. This is done through the local library service.

BELOW: the gates of the British Library with a statue of Newton by Eduardo Palaozzi.

BEST RESTAURANTS, BARS AND CAFÉS

Restaurants

Prices for a three-course dinner per person with a half-bottle of house wine:

£ = under £20
££ = £20–30
£££ = £30–50
££££ = over £50

American

All Star Lanes
Victoria House, Bloomsbury Place, WC1 ☎ 7025 2676. ⌚ L & D Mon–Wed & Sat, D only Thur & Sun **£** [p 331, E2]
Smart American-style diner serving good steaks, burgers, crab cakes etc with 10-pin bowling on the side. Red leather cocktail bar adds to the glamorous 1950s effect.

Chinese

Sheng's Tea House
68 Millman St, WC1. ☎ 7405 3697 ⌚ L & D Mon–Fri, D only Sat. **£** [p 331, E2]
Freshly made stock and no MSG are welcome features at this cheerful and inexpensive Chinese noodle shop behind Coram's Fields. There is a menu for vegetarians.

Fish

North Sea Fish Restaurant
7–8 Leigh St, WC1 ☎ 7387 5892 ⌚ L & D Mon–Sat. **£–££** [p 331, E1]
Veteran chippie serving big portions of straightforward fish and chips, plus traditional British puddings.

French

La Brasserie Townhouse
24 Coptic St, WC1 ☎ 7636 2731 ⌚ L & D Mon–Sat, D only Sun. **£££** [p 331, E3]
Well-conceived short French menu, properly executed. Very convenient for the British Museum.

Cosmoba
9 Cosmo Place, off Southampton Row, WC1 ☎ 7837 0904 ⌚ L & D Mon–Sat. **££** [p 331, E2]
A hidden gem in an alley connecting Southampton Row and Queen Square. Plain, family-run and specialising in homely Italian food.

Indian

Malabar Junction
107 Great Russell St, WC1 ☎ 7580 5230 ⌚ L & D daily. **£££** [p 331, D3]
Much classier than its frontage suggests, this elegant Indian restaurant specialises in spicy and nutty Keralan cuisine. Lovely atrium for light-filled dining.

Salaam Namaste
68 Millman St, WC1 ☎ 7405 3697 ⌚ L & D daily. **££** [p 332, A1]
A light and modern restaurant Excellent pan-Indian cuisine with a special emphasis on

seafood. Lots of familiar Indian dishes, but many inventive options too

Italian

Carluccio's

1 The Brunswick Centre 7833 4100 L & D daily. £–££ [p 331, E1]
Member of the popular Italian chain, serving light lunches, suppers, breakfasts and pastries, with a small Italian deli-cum bakery attached.

Pizza Express

30 Coptic St, WC1 7636 3232 L & D daily. £ [p 331, E3]
This branch of the quality pizza-pasta chain occupies a fabulous old dairy decorated in art nouveau tiles. A stone's throw from the British Museum.

Japanese

Abeno

47 Museum St, WC1. 7405 3211 L & D daily. ££ [p 331, E3]
Oriental pancake house specialising in okonomiyaki, tasty, if messy, omelettes and pancakes crammed with meat, vegetables or fish, cooked on a hotplate at the table.

Wagamama

4a Streatham St, WC1. 7323 9223 L & D daily. £ [p 331, E3]
This was the original of the chain. Canteen-like basement with communal tables and bench seating, serving wholesome budget noodles and garnishes such as dumplings, salads, soups and juices.

Spanish

Cigala

54 Lamb's Conduit St, WC1 74051717 Mon–Sun L&D. £££ [p 332, A1]
Set up by Jake Hodges, founder of Moro, Cigala serves real Spanish food in an attractive modern dining room. Excellent Spanish wine list, including many sherries. Tapas are served in the basement.

Others

Kobe Jones

St Giles Hotel, 112 Russell St, WC1 7300 3250 L & D Mon–Fri, D only Sat & Sun. £££ [p 330, D2]
Member of a small sophisticated chain with branches in Sydney and Melbourne specialising in tasty pan-Pacific dishes, including plenty of fish options.

Konaki

5 Coptic St, WC1 7580 9730 L&D Mon–Fri, D only Sat. £–££ [p 331, E3]
Long-established and popular Greek restaurant near the British Museum. Well prepared Greek staples. A small terrace for summer dining

Perseverance

63 Lamb's Conduit St, WC1. 7405 8278 L & D Mon–Sat, L only Sun. £££ [p 332, A1]
Popular gastro-pub offering light, inventive, tasty and well-presented dishes in a crowded bar or the more secluded first-floor dining room.

The Brunswick Centre

This shopping mall [p 331, E1] in the heart of Bloomsbury has several of the better chain restaurants, offering good-value dining. They include **Strada** *(Nos 15–17; tel: 7278 2777; £)* for good wood-oven pizzas), **Hare & Tortoise** *(Nos. 11–13, tel: 7278 9799)*, for good-value Asian; and **Giraffe** *(£–££)*, a café-bar with a global menu including great breakfasts and healthy options for children. Also popular with families is **Nando's** *(No. 3, tel:7713 0351; £)* serving spicy Portuguese-style chicken with salads, rice or chips, followed by frozen yoghurts, cheesecake, etc for pudding.

LEFT: chef at work in Wagamama.

Pubs, Bars and Cafés

Bloomsbury has several traditional pubs tucked into its quiet corners. One of the best sources is pedestrianised Lamb's Conduit Street where **The Lamb**, a classy old-timer serves Young's beer, pub food and has a small pavement terrace. Also see **Perseverance** *(see main listings)*, a gastro-pub at No. 63.

Just along the street is another long-time favourite, **Vats Wine Bar**, offering a convivial atmosphere, quality food (fish, hearty casseroles, home-made pies, etc) and a lengthy wine list. Closer to the British Museum, Pied Bull Yard, just off Bury Place, offers **Truckles** (Mon–Fri only), wine bar with a light and airy ground floor, a sawdust-sprinkled basement, and a large courtyard.

For afternoon tea, try the British Museum's **Court Restaurant**, high up under the spectacular glass roof, with views into the circular Reading Room for some tables. Also nice for lunch.

The British Museum

Founded in 1759, this world-class institution on Great Russell Street contains some 6½ million objects

Devote just 60 seconds to each object owned by the British Museum and you'd be there, without sleep or meal breaks, for more than 12 years. Even though only 50,000 objects are on display at any given time, this is not a place to "do" in a couple of hours. It is a treasure house that caters for scholars as well as tourists and, as the scholars do, it is best to concentrate initially on what interests you most. A tour of the highlights is a good start (see right-hand column or join one of the organised tours). As you seek out any particular objects in the 100 or so galleries, you will be diverted by enough intriguing displays to justify future visits.

The British Museum is the most traditional of institutions, with most objects in glass cases and few buttons and levers for children to manipulate, but it is rarely boring. The best time to visit is soon after opening. This is also an ideal time to appreciate the Great Court, a dramatic glassed-over space in the heart of the complex, added for the millennium, and the round Reading Room, where Marx and Lenin once studied, which now functions as an information and research centre.

The essentials

Great Russell Street, WC2; www.thebritishmuseum.ac.uk

7323 8299

daily 10am–5.30pm, until 8.30pm Thur & Fri

free except some special exhibitions

Russell Square

British Museum

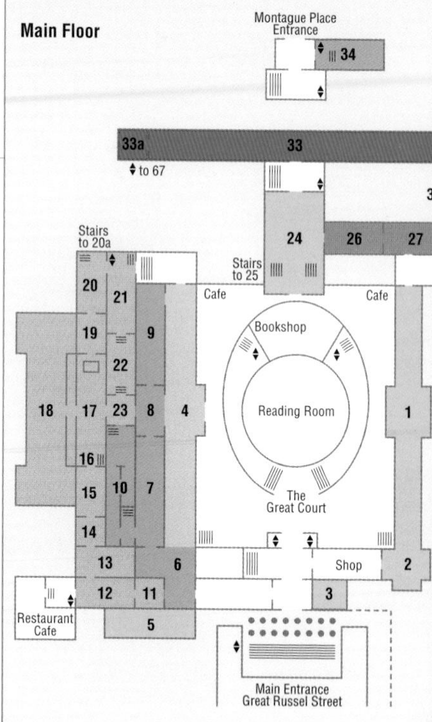

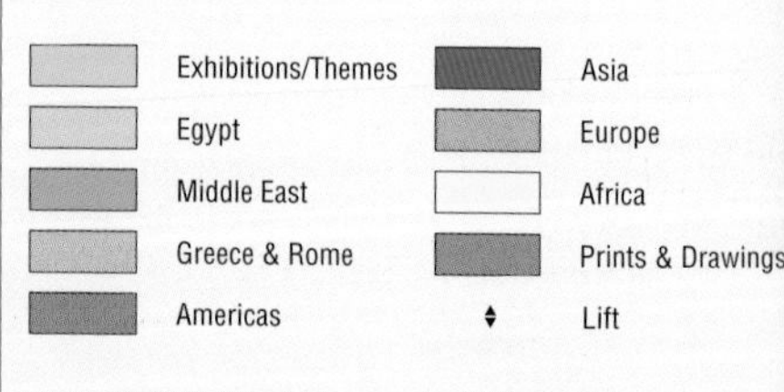

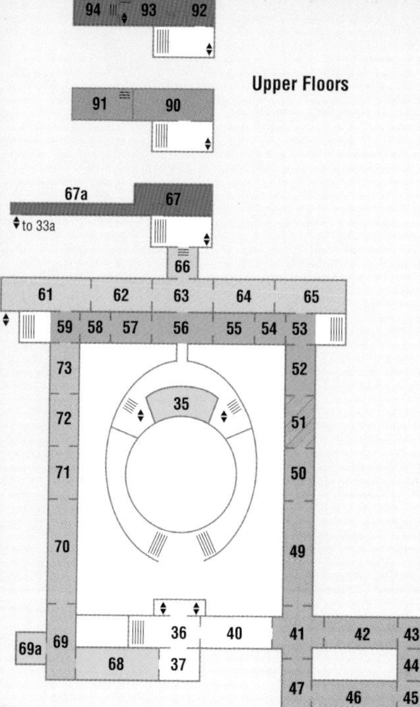

Lower Floors

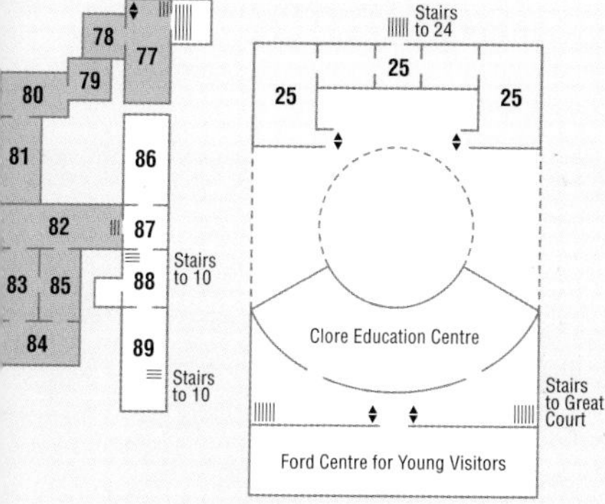

LEFT: the Portland Vase, a superbly crafted cameo-glass vessel from the early 1st century.

TOP RIGHT: the gilded wooden inner coffin of Henutmehyt, a Theban priestess, dating from c.1290 BC.

RIGHT: the 12th-century Lewis Chessmen, found in the Outer Hebrides

TOP 10 HIGHLIGHTS

The Egyptian mummies
This is the richest collection of Egyptian funerary art outside Egypt.

The Sculptures of the Parthenon
Commonly known as the Elgin Marbles, these 5th century BC sculptures have a wondrous muscular detail.

The Rosetta Stone
This granite tablet from the 2nd century BC provided the elusive key to deciphering ancient Egypt's hieroglyphic script.

The Nereid Monument
The imposing facade of this 4th-century monument from Xanthos in Turkey was reconstructed after an earthquake.

The Mausoleum of Halikarnassos
This giant tomb, finished around 351 BC in southwest Turkey, was one of the seven wonders of the ancient world.

The Sutton Hoo Ship Burial
The richest treasure ever dug from British soil, an early 7th-century longboat likely to have been the burial chamber of an East Anglian king.

The Lewis Chessmen
82 elaborately carved 12th-century chess pieces, found in the Outer Hebrides, off the Scottish coast.

Lindow Man
A well preserved 2,000-year-old body found in a peat bog in England and dubbed Pete Marsh.

The Benin bronzes
Brass plaques found in Benin City, Nigeria, in 1897. They depict court life and ritual in extraordinary detail.

The Cassiobury Park Turret Clock
This intricate 1610 weight-driven clock, is part of a remarkable collection of timepieces.

The Main Collections

Greece and Rome

The museum's vast holdings from the Classical world are divided between Rooms 11–23 on the ground floor (off the left-hand side of the Great Court as you enter the museum), where the larger objects are found, and Rooms 69–73 on the first floor.

Room 18, the **Parthenon Gallery**, is lined with an exquisitely detailed frieze from the colonnade of the Parthenon *(see right)*, removed from the Acropolis by Lord Elgin, British Ambassador in Constantinople, at the end of the 18th century. The Parthenon was dedicated to the goddess Athena Parthenos and the frieze is said to depict the Great Panathenaia, a procession held every four years in honour of the goddess. It was carved under the direction of the master sculptor Pheidias.

Nearby, in Room 17, is the **Nereid Monument**, a magnificent Lycian tomb (c.390–380 BC) from Xanthos, and, in Room 21, fragments and sculptures from the **Mausoleum of Halikarnassos** (modern-day Bodrum; mid-4th century BC), the tomb of Maussollos, considered to have been one of the Seven Wonders of the Ancient World. A large-scale model of the mausoleum shows how it would have looked in its splendid entirety.

Above: head of a horse of Selene (the Moon) from the Parthenon (5th century BC). **Main Picture:** a section from the north frieze of the Parthenon

Ancient Near East

This section covers the ancient civilisations of Mesopotamia, Anatolia and the Levant. Among the highlights are tablets containing the inscription of Nebuchadnezzar II, King of Babylon, found in the ruins of Babylon in the early 19th century . Other highlights are the carved Assyrian reliefs and gateway figures from the palaces at Khorsabad, Nineveh and Nimrud.

Below: human-headed winged bull, one in a pair of marble bulls that guarded either side of a gateway at Khorsabad, Assyria (710 BC), in modern-day Iraq.

TREASURES OF ANCIENT EGYPT

The Roxie Walker Galleries of Egyptian funerary archaeology (Rooms 62–63, on the upper floor) are the rooms to see first, simply because they can get wildly overcrowded as the day goes on – 98 percent of visitors want to see the Egyptian mummies. They're worth seeing, too: thanks to the enthusiastic plundering of 19th-century explorers, this is the richest collection of Egyptian funerary art outside Egypt.

The size and ornamentation of the coffins and sarcophagi are immediately striking. The richly gilded inner coffin of the priestess Henutmehyt *(see page 145)*, for example, dating from 1290 BC, is a work of considerable art. Scans displayed beside the coffin of Cleopatra (not the Cleopatra) show how well the body inside is preserved, and the process of embalming is explained in detail. Apart from the noble humans who were destined to spend their afterlife in London's Bloomsbury, there are various mummified cats, dogs, fish and crocodiles, plus amulets and assorted jewellery.

Look out, too, for the paintings from the Tomb of Nebamun, a Theban official, dating from the 18th Dynasty (c.1450 BC).

TOURS WORTH TAKING

Ninety-minute tours of the museum's highlights (charge payable) take place daily at 10.30am, 1pm and 3pm. Free "eye-opener" tours (30–40 minutes) are also held, and a variety of audio sets can be hired, including one for children.

Early Europe

As well as highly crafted Celtic artefacts and Roman treasures, look out for Lindow Man, a 1st-century man discovered in a peat bog in Cheshire.

Medieval and Modern Europe

Apart from the Sutton Hoo treasure, objects include richly decorated ecclesiastical artefacts such as an intricately decorated 12th-century gilt cross from Germany.

ABOVE: the ceremonial helmet from the Sutton Hoo treasure.
TOP RIGHT: Nebamum hunting birds in the marshes (1450 BC).
ABOVE RIGHT: Lindow Man, the 1st-century bog man.

Africa

The Sainsbury African Galleries in the basement combine ancient and modern, showing how cultural traditions are still alive today. This is one of the most colourful and vibrant collections in the museum.

Of special interest are the Benin Bronzes, from the Kingdom of Benin (now in Nigeria), a powerful state in West Africa between the 13th and 19th centuries. As well as the beautifully detailed bronze plaques depicting life in the royal court are bronze heads and figures.

Other highlights of this section include Asante goldwork, from the gold-rich Ghanaian kingdom of Asante, Afro-Portuguese ivories, African textiles and funerary screens from the eastern Niger Delta.

Top and Above: two of the free-standing Benin bronzes. The bronzes were discovered, languishing in an outbuilding, by British forces making a retaliatory attack on Benin following the massacre of a British diplomatic mission there. Only some of the bronzes found their way to Britain; others were sold to museums around the world.

Right: an ivory mask, also made by the Edo peoples of Benin.

The Americas

The museum has superb collections from Central and North America in Rooms 26–27 on the ground floor (far-right corner off the Great Court). There are a number of impressive Olmec statues and other works from around 1000 BC, plus magnificent carved Mayan slabs from the 8th century AD. Relics from the Aztec civilisation include turquoise mosaic work that may have been given to Hernán Cortés by Moctezuma II and a very rare pre-Conquest manuscript painted on deer skin.

Prints and Drawings

For conservation and space reasons, only a fraction of the museum's 3 million works on paper are displayed at any one time. Highlights include Old Master prints and drawings, and satires of the 18th and 19th centuries.

RIGHT: Raphael's *Virgin and Child* cartoon, one of numerous drawings by Raphael held by the museum.

Asia

The museum's collections of Chinese, Japanese and Korean artefacts are astonishingly large, with a series of vast galleries given over to them (33–34 on the ground floor; 67 and 91–94 on the first floor). Exhibits from India include the Amaravati Sculptures (1st–3rd century AD) that adorned a stupa (Buddhist temple) in Andhra Pradesh, southeastern India, and exquisite Mughal miniatures (16th–17th century).

Money and Medals

A collection of 750,000 coins dates from the 7th century BC to the present day, and there are notes dating back to 14th-century China (Room 68).

MAIN PICTURE: double-headed serpent (1400–1521), Mexico. It is carved in wood and covered with turquoise mosaic. Turquoise was highly prized as a symbol of fertility by the Aztecs.

LEFT: Assistant to a Judge of Hell, stone figure from the Ming Dynasty (16th century), China. The figure is holding a bundle of scrolls recording the sins of the deceased.

REFRESHMENTS

The ground level of the Great Court has two refreshment areas, but for something more special head up the stairs to the Court Restaurant. Breakfast, lunch and tea are served. Try to get a table looking down upon the circular Reading Room.

HOLBORN AND THE INNS OF COURT

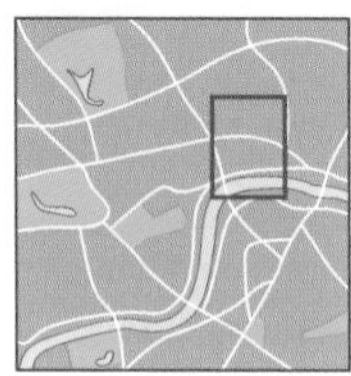

Once the haunt of Samuel Johnson, Dickens and Thackeray, this area on the cusp of the City is packed with history. It has long been the centre of the legal profession and was for centuries the irrepressible hub of Britain's newspaper industry

Main attractions
SOMERSET HOUSE
THE INNS OF COURT
LINCOLN'S INN FIELDS
SIR JOHN SOANE'S MUSEUM
DR JOHNSON'S HOUSE
ST BRIDE'S CHURCH

BELOW: lawyers near the Royal Courts of Justice.

Holborn encompasses what can be termed legal London, with landmarks such as the Royal Courts of Justice, the Old Bailey and the historic Inns of Court clustered around Fleet Street, the former centre of the national newspaper industry. The area is wedged in between London's financial and political centres, and is markedly different from both: away from the busy thoroughfares, quiet courtyards, leafy parks and some of the city's oldest buildings lend a sense of a bygone London.

KINGSWAY AND THE EASTERN STRAND

Somerset House ❶

The Strand; www.somersethouse.org.uk 7845 4600 galleries daily 10am–6pm charge for each gallery (combined tickets available), but Courtauld Institute free Mon 10am–2pm Temple

Somerset House became the city's first office block in 1775 when the original 16th-century palace was rebuilt. For many years it housed the official registry of births, marriages and deaths; the inland revenue offices remain, but the northern and southern wings now accommodate a series of galleries and museums. The complex is divided into two main sections by its large courtyard, which in December and January is turned into a **skating rink**, the classical facade providing a magical setting.

Entering from the Strand, you'll come to the **Courtauld Institute**, home to a collection of 20th-century European art, notably some major Impressionist paintings, and London University's art-history studies centre. Cross the courtyard, passing the fanciful statue of George III wearing a toga, to the southern wing, where there are two further galleries: the **Hermitage Rooms**, where artworks

Recommended Restaurants, Bars & Cafés on page 157

from the Hermitage museum are shown in temporary exhibitions, and, downstairs, the **Gilbert Collection**, a treasure trove of European silverware, clocks, jewellery, mosaics and other decorative arts.

The Seamen's Hall gives access to the splendid **River Terrace**, which in summer has a café with great views.

Across the Strand from Somerset House is **Bush House** ❷, the headquarters of the BBC's World Service, which broadcasts across the world in a babelesque variety of languages. To the north, **Kingsway** marks the western boundary of Holborn and legal London. It was named after George V, and its tunnel, opened in 1906 for trams to dive beneath the buildings of Aldwych before emerging at Waterloo Bridge, was a miracle of urban engineering in its day.

Two baroque churches sit on traffic islands in the Strand: by Bush House is **St Mary le Strand**, built by James Gibbs from 1715; a short distance further east by a statue of Gladstone is **St Clement Danes** ❸, completed by Wren in 1682. The name is a reference to the first structure on the site, built by the Vikings in the 9th century. The church has an association with the Royal Air Force.

At the end of the Strand on the left are the **Royal Courts of Justice** ❹, which deal with libels, divorces and all civil cases. The courts moved here from Westminster Hall in 1884. The neo-Gothic confection of towers and spires has around 1,000 rooms, and newspaper and television journalists often hang around its entrance awaiting verdicts. Visitors are free to sit in the public galleries of the 58 courts when trials are in session.

If you are visiting more than one gallery in Somerset House, it's worth buying a combination ticket. Free guided tours of the buildings (excluding the galleries) are available on the first Saturday of the month at 1.30 and 3.45pm.

LEFT: Swiss snuffbox from the Gilbert Collection. **ABOVE AND BELOW:** winter ice skating and summer fun in the courtyard of the Courtauld Institute.

The Inns of Court buildings were originally leased as hostels to trainee lawyers by the Knights Hospitaller (who succeeded the Templars, earlier owners of this land).

THE INNS OF COURT

All around this area are the **Inns of Court**, home of London's legal profession. The "Inns" were once, much as they sound, places of rest and comfort for trainee lawyers. From the 19th century onward, law was taught at King's College, next to Somerset House in the Strand, and at University College in Gower Street. Before then, the only way to obtain legal training was to serve an apprenticeship in one of the Inns.

Four still remain, and still function as accommodation and offices for the legal profession: **Middle Temple** ❺ and **Inner Temple** ❻ between Fleet Street and the Embankment, and **Gray's Inn** *(see page 154)* and **Lincoln's Inn** further north. With their cobbled lanes and brass plaques bearing Dickensian names, they are atmospheric places to stroll around. Note that the entrances to Middle Temple Lane and Inner Temple Lane are easily missed – the gates are usually closed and access is via a small side passageway.

These Inns take their name from the crusading Knights Templar, who bought land here in the 12th century and built the **Temple Church**, inspired by the Church of the Holy Sepulchre in Jerusalem. There are a number of the knights' tombs inside, and a tiny punishment cell by the altar. Sloping down to the Embankment, the grassy swards of the Temple Gardens are a pleasant place to take a break from sightseeing.

BELOW: buying London's evening paper. **RIGHT:** Temple Gardens.

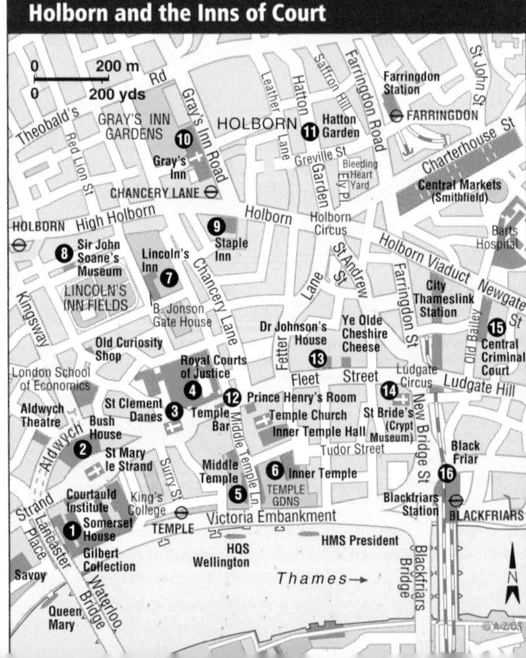

Recommended Restaurants, Bars & Cafés on page 157

North of the Royal Courts of Justice, between Kingsway and Chancery Lane, is **Lincoln's Inn** ❼, alma mater of Oliver Cromwell, and the two great 19th-century prime ministers, William Gladstone and Benjamin Disraeli.

Lincoln's Inn Fields were created for the students' recreation, but the best sport was watching the early city planners try to outmanoeuvre each other: Inigo Jones sat on a 17th-century Royal Commission to decide the area's fate. Today, visitors can puzzle out the significance of Barry Flanagan's sheet-steel sculpture in the northeast corner, watch the lunch time netball games or pass on to one of London's gems, Sir John Soane's Museum.

Sir John Soane's Museum ❽

13 Lincoln's Inn Fields; www.soane.org 7405 2107 Tue–Sat 10am–5pm and 6–9pm first Tues of each month free except Tue evenings Holborn

This marvellous museum is a self-endowed monument to John Soane (1753–1837), one of London's most

important architects and collectors, who left his house and collection much as they had been during his lifetime. He built his private home on three sites along the edge of Lincoln's Inn Fields (No.13) and it is a delight to visit, like being in a miniature British Museum.

Among the highlights are an Egyptian sarcophagus, Hogarth's *Rake's Progress* and some fine Canalettos, but much of the pleasure of visiting is derived from the building itself.

TIP

Prince Henry's Room (Mon–Sat 11am–2pm, free) is a little-known gem of a museum on the first floor of 17 Fleet Street (opposite the end of Chancery Lane), one of London's few surviving timber-framed buildings. It has an elaborate plasterwork ceiling and some fine wood panelling. It also contains artefacts and paintings relating to the diarist Samuel Pepys (1633–1703).

ABOVE: *An Election Entertainment,* part of William Hogarth's Election sequence painted in 1754–55. **BELOW:** Sir John Soane's Museum.

A sign outside a Fleet Street opticians. This part of London has retained a core of shops selling a particular item; opticians and other optical-related goods (such as camera lenses) as well as watch repair shops along Fleet Street, and diamonds in Hatton Garden.

BELOW: the Old Curiosity Shop. **BELOW RIGHT:** the spire of St Bride's, said to have inspired the first tiered wedding cake.

Dickens's world

The ghost of the great Victorian writer Charles Dickens (1812–70) haunts the streets of Holborn. Just south of Lincoln's Inn Fields is the **Old Curiosity Shop**, a tiny 16th-century structure – now functioning as a shoe shop – likely to have been the inspiration for Little Nell's antiques shop.

On the other side of Lincoln's Inn, Dickens's first marital home was on the site of the neo-Gothic Prudential Assurance building in Holborn, opposite a half-timbered row of shops at the bottom of Gray's Inn Road. This is **Staple Inn** ❾, one of the former Inns of Chancery that dealt with commercial law. Dating from 1586 and a survivor of the Great Fire of London, it shows how much of the city must have looked before 1666.

Dickens underwent his legal apprenticeship at **Gray's Inn** ❿ (Mon–Fri 10am–4pm), one of Holborn's four Inns of Court. Dating from the 14th century, its grounds lie just to the west of Gray's Inn Road. The magnificent garden was laid out by Francis Bacon, the Elizabethan essayist. With an irony that must have tickled Dickens's sense of the law's ridiculousness, Gray's Inn Hall saw the first production of Shakespeare's *Comedy of Errors*.

Further east is **Bleeding Heart Yard**, scene of much of the domestic action in *Little Dorrit* . Only a step or two away is **Hatton Garden** ⓫, the centre of London's diamond trade, and **Leather Lane**, where market stalls sell fresh food and household goods.

FLEET STREET

Just beyond the Temple Inn and the Royal Courts of Justice is **Temple Bar** ⓬, where a mean-looking griffin *(see picture on page 156)* marks the boundary between Westminster and the City of London, beyond which, theoretically, the monarch cannot pass without the Lord Mayor's permission.

Stretching eastwards is **Fleet Street**, home of Britain's national newspapers from 1702, when the first daily newspaper, the *Courant*, was published here, until the 1980s,

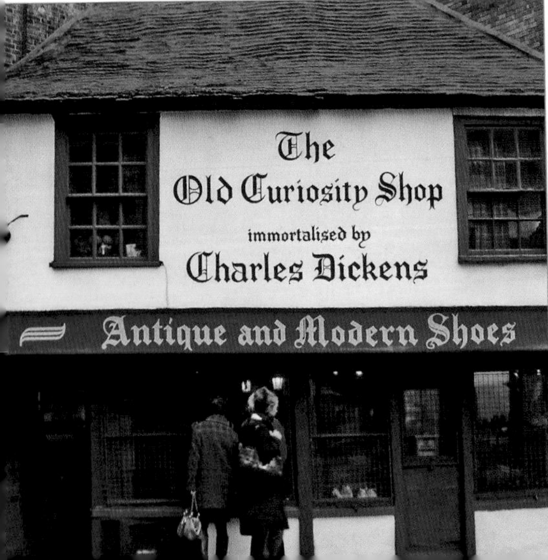

when new technology enabled the press barons to move to cheaper sites in Docklands and elsewhere.

There is still evidence of the street's illustrious past. Dr Samuel Johnson ("A man who is tired of London is tired of life") lived in the back courts at 17 Gough Square from 1748 to 1759 where, with the help of six assistants, he compiled the first comprehensive English dictionary. **Dr Johnson's House** ⓭ is an evocative museum of this great man of letters (Mon–Sat 11am–5.30pm, Oct–Apr until 5pm; charge). The creaky old building dates from 1700; Johnson paid rent to the tune of £30 per year, equivalent to around £3,000 today. (The alleyway leading to Gough Square is immediately east of No.167 Fleet Street.)

The crime writer Edgar Wallace (1875–1932) is immortalised on a plaque on the northwest corner of **Ludgate Circus**, at the far end of Fleet Street near St Paul's. He had his first newspaper job in the building that stands on this site.

Wedged in behind the **Reuters Building** designed by Sir Edwin Lutyens in 1935 is "the journalists' and printers' church", **St Bride's** ⓮. It was near here that the aptly named Wynkyn de Worde, an associate of William Caxton, set up the street's first press. There is a small museum of Fleet Street in the crypt, where a magpie collection of Roman mosaics from a villa on this site, Saxon church walls, William Caxton's *Ovid* and a large

Drinkers in Ye Olde Cheshire Cheese pub on Fleet Street (the entrance is on an alleyway called Wine Office Court) close to Dr Johnson's House can raise a glass to the great man's memory. This is one of London's oldest inns – Johnson and later Dickens and Thackeray all came here. *For details see page 157.*

LEFT: Ye Olde Cheshire Cheese in Wine Office Court. **BELOW LEFT:** Johnson portrayed in a window of his former home

Dr Johnson's Dictionary

Samuel Johnson (1709–84) was one of the great figures of the Enlightenment, rising from a humble background to become a member of London's intellectual elite. Having arrived in the city in 1737, he was commissioned in 1746 to produce a dictionary for a fee of £1,575 – a large sum at the time, but the work ended up taking 10 years, and Johnson had to pay for his staff and materials out of it. In 1762, however, his financial stability was assured with the award of a £300 annual pension by the king in recognition of his efforts (and thanks to some very influential friends).

While some words in the dictionary have changed in meaning over the years (for example, "nice" was defined as "superfluously accurate"), many of his pithy definitions still fit the bill. One of the more oblique entries is for "lexicographer", which Johnson ruefully defined as "a harmless drudge".

On top of the Old Bailey's dome, a golden figure of justice stands with a sword in her right hand and, in her left, scales to weigh the evidence.

BELOW: the griffin at Temple Bar. **RIGHT:** the Arts and Crafts interior of the Black Friar.

number of coffins are stored – much was revealed when the building was bombed in World War II. Samuel Pepys was baptised at St Bride's (he was born in 1633 in Salisbury Court, off Fleet Street) and he records in his diary how he had to bribe the sexton to find room for his brother's corpse here. The church's elegant spire makes it Sir Christopher Wren's tallest church and it is said to have inspired the first tiered wedding-cake. Lunch-time concerts are often held here during the week.

LUDGATE HILL

The River Fleet, which once marked the division between Westminster and The City, used to be a "disembouging stream" according to the 18th-century poet Alexander Pope, which "rolls the large tribute of dead dogs to Thames". Acting as a sluice for Smithfield Market, and notorious since the 14th century for its foetid ague-spreading stench, it was bricked over in the 18th century, although the subterranean waters still have the propensity to make their presence felt by periodi-

cally flooding basements in the area.

The Fleet Prison for debtors was on the Fleet's right bank, Newgate Prison on the left. Executions took place here after 1868, when a law brought an end to the rowdy public spectacles they had become.

On the site of the former prison, just beyond Ludgate Circus, is the **Central Criminal Court** ⓯, universally known by the name of the street in which it is located, **Old Bailey**. Some of the country's most unpleasant criminals have been brought to account here, and in the forbidding No. 1 Court, until the abolition of the death penalty in 1965, convicted murderers were sentenced to be hanged, the judges placing black caps on their heads as they passed sentence. You can still watch cases from the visitors' gallery (Mon–Fri 10.15am and 1.45pm, closed Aug). Queues are long for high-profile trials.

BLACKFRIARS

The underground river enters the Thames at Blackfriars Bridge, named after a monastery that was here from 1278 to 1530. A fine monument to this monastic order is the 1905 **Black Friar** ⓰, on the corner of Queen Victoria Street: a most spectacular Arts and Crafts pub.

Heading west along Victoria Embankment from Blackfriars takes you back to Somerset House past the permanently moored ships *HMS President* and *HQS Wellington*, with function rooms for private hire, opposite the gardens of the Inns of Court. ❑

BEST RESTAURANTS, PUBS AND BARS

Restaurants

Prices for a three-course dinner per person with a half-bottle of house wine:

£ = under £20
££ = £20–30
£££ = £30–50
££££ = over £50

Asian

Chi Noodle and Wine Bar
5 New Bridge St, Bride Court EC4 ☎ 7353 2409 ⊙ L & D Mon–Fri. ££ [p 332, B3]
Airy restaurant and take-away offering pan-Asian noodle and rice dishes.

Pu's Thai Brasserie
10 Gate St WC2 ☎ 7404 2126 ⊙ L & D Mon–Fri, D only Sun. £ [p 332, A3]
Reasonable Thai restaurant around the corner from Soane's Museum.

Wagamama
109 Fleet St EC4 ☎ 7583 7889 ⊙ L & D Mon–Fri. £ [p332, B3]
Branch of the popular chain offering inexpensive noodles, soups and salads at communal tables.

British

Ye Olde Cheshire Cheese
145 Fleet St ☎ 7353 6170 ⊙ L &D Mon–Sat, L only Sun. £££ [p 332, B3]
This is easily dismissed as a tourist trap, but its age and history are impressive: it was frequented by Dickens and Samuel Johnson. The cosy chop room serves good roast beef, steak and kidney pies, game pies, etc.

French

Bleeding Heart Restaurant and Bistro
Bleeding Heart Yard, Greville St, EC1 ☎ 7242 2056 for restaurant ⊙ L & D Mon–Fri, D only Sun. £££ [p 332, B2]
Comprises three establishments: the tavern, the bistro (No. 7) and the restaurant, each in separate premises. The latter is the place to go for superb French cuisine as well as alfresco dining in the cobbled courtyard.

Modern European

Northcliffe House
26–28 Tudor St, EC4 ☎ 7583 8399 ⊙ L & D Mon–Fri ££ [p 332, B3]
Situated in a former newspaper office just off Fleet Street , this is a comfortable establishment serving tasty modern cuisine plus a few more imaginative options. A good-value fixed-price menu is available.

ABOVE RIGHT: courtyard of Bleeding Heart.

Other

Gaucho
125–126 Chancery Lane, WC2 ☎ 7242 7727 ⊙ B, L & D Mon–Fri. £££ [p332, B3]
Argentinian-style chain specialising in steaks, but good fish and chicken are also available. Good for special breakfasts too.

Pubs and Bars

This area has several historic pubs. Two of the most atmospheric are **Ye Olde Cheshire Cheese** off Fleet Street *(see restaurants)* and **Black Friar** *(174 Queen Victoria St)*, whose Arts and Crafts interior (stained glass, wood panelling, marble and mosaics) is worth a visit in itself, but it is also known for its good choice of ales.

Another opulent interior, this time high Victorian, is offered by **La Grand Marque**, in a former bank on Ludgate Hill, where City types come to quaff good wines and champagnes. (There is another branch with a better line in food, in Middle Temple Lane.) Another ex-bank turned boozer is the opulent **Old Bank of England** on Fleet Street.

Also worth mentioning are **Davy's of Creed Lane** *(100 Creed Lane)*, offering quality wines and wine-bar fare, and **El Vino** *(47 Fleet St)*, once the favourite wine bar of hard-drinking journalists and now of lawyers. Its cellar restaurant serves traditional British food.

Offering a different ambience is **Alibi** *(18 Lime Office Court, Shoe Lane)*, a lounge bar serving wines and cocktails plus snacks, platters and daily specials.

17406
East London
26
DOMINION THEATRE
Victoria
Aldwych
11
Chelsea

Recommended Restaurants, Bars & Cafés on pages 174–5

St Paul's and the City

The City, covering just one square mile, is Britain's main financial centre. This was the original London, once contained by Roman walls, and it retains its own government and police force

The City, London's financial quarter, is a world apart from the rest of the capital. It runs its own affairs, has its own police force and a distinct set of hierarchies. Even the Queen treads carefully here: on her coronation drive in 1953, she was obliged – if only by tradition – to stop at Temple Bar and declare that she came in peace. The name "Square Mile" is given to this financial district that was at one time regarded as "the clearing-house of the world", but it signifies far more than a limited geographical area. For most of its 2,000-year history, the City *was* London.

Today, more than 300,000 workers stream into the City every weekday. Known for their work-hard-play-hard attitude, they are driven by competition and substantial annual bonuses. On weekends, the 9,000 City residents are left to savour the stillness that settles across the Square Mile, an area where a strong sense of tradition has helped a potentially faceless financial world retain a certain degree of character.

The City has been devastated twice. In 1666 the Great Fire devoured four-fifths of the area, and during the winter of 1940–1 Germany's Luftwaffe left one-third of it in ruins.

LEFT: St Paul's from Ludgate Hill.
RIGHT: view of the City from the South Bank.

St Paul's Cathedral ❶

www.stpauls.co.uk 7246 8350
Mon–Fri 8.30am–4pm, tours at 11am, 11.30am, 1.30pm, 2pm
charge St Paul's

At the top of Ludgate Hill, the western approach to the City, stands St Paul's, the first purpose-built Protestant cathedral and Sir Christopher Wren's greatest work. A tablet above his plain marble tomb reads: *Lector, si monumentum requiris, circumspice* ("Reader, if you wish to see his

Main attractions

- St Paul's Cathedral
- Bart's Hospital
- St Bartholomew the Great
- Smithfield Meat Market
- Charterhouse Square
- St John's Gate
- Bunhill Fields
- Museum of London
- Guildhall
- Bank of England
- Leadenhall
- Monument
- Tower of London

Like any closed world, the City doesn't open up easily to outsiders. Peering out of a tourist bus at acres of glass and concrete is far too superficial an examination; time and legwork in the network of alleys and backstreets which thread through the office blocks will reveal much more.

memorial, look around you"). *For full coverage of St Paul's, see the feature on pages 176–7.*

Paternoster Square

St Paul's needs room to breathe, but the area around it – in particular the ancient market site known as **Paternoster Square** – has been intensively developed. In spite of recent remodelling, it forms a disappointing setting for Wren's masterpiece.

In 2004 the **London Stock Exchange** abandoned its long-held base near the Bank of England in Threadneedle Street for new premises

St Paul's and the City

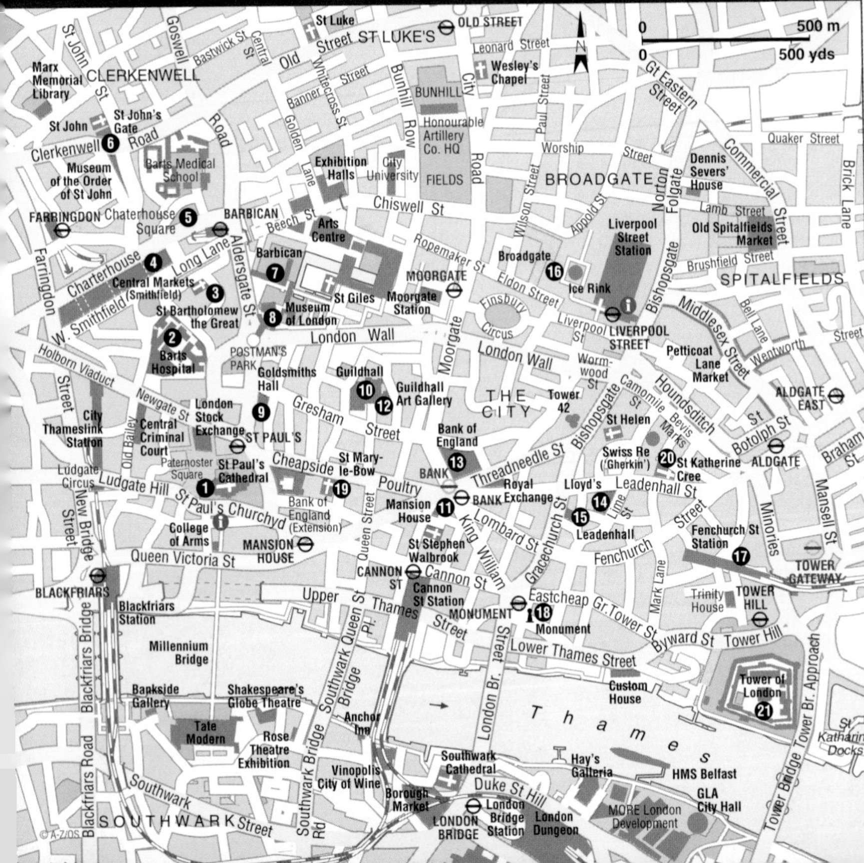

in Paternoster Square that were better suited to electronic trading.

Formed by merchants trying to raise money for a Far Eastern trip in 1553, the Stock Exchange has changed enormously since the Big Bang reforms of 1986 when it agreed to radically change its practices. Fixed commission systems were abolished, jobber and broker functions were merged and transferred to a computerised quotation system. The trading floor, once crowded with frantic pin-striped figures engaged in open outcry, fell silent. As a result, the Stock Market is a fairer but duller place. It is no longer open to the general public.

Historic churches

In the warren of roads that lead from St Paul's to the river, there are several Wren churches. **St Andrew-by-the-Wardrobe** in St Andrew's Hill, was named because it stood near a royal furniture store. **St Nicholas Cole Abbey** is followed by **St Benet's**, which serves as the Metropolitan Welsh Church.

On the other side of Queen Victoria Street is the **College of Arms** (entrance hall open when receptionist is present Mon–Fri 10am–4pm, free; Record Room tours by arrangement, charge; tel: 7248 2762; www.college-of-arms.gov.uk), which has a handsome, recently refurbished 17th-century interior by William Emmett and a library of heraldry and genealogy which, for a fee, deals with genealogy enquiries.

Other Wren churches in the vicinity include **St James Garlickhythe** on busy Upper Thames Street, which

The Stock Market trading floor has vanished but a new spectacle, The Source, *now spans the height of the building's atrium. Composed of rising and falling spheres suspended on cables, this computer-controlled kinetic sculpture is said to represent market forces.*

LEFT: setting up an outside office.
ABOVE: sign on The College of Arms.
BELOW: neo-baroque archway on Paternoster Square

A carved wooden figure in the Museum of St Bart's Hospital.

BELOW: tomb of the monk Rahere, founder of St Bartholomew's Hospital, in St Bartholomew the Great.

was disastrously struck by a crane that demolished its rose window in 1991, and **St Michael Paternoster**, the burial place of Dick Whittington (1423), a Lord Mayor of London, who, with his cat, Puss-in-Boots, has gone into British mythology as a pantomime figure. This rags-to-riches story sets out to prove that even country bumpkins could be elected Lord Mayor of the City, though the real Whittington came from a wealthy county family and amassed a fortune as a merchant.

West Smithfield

Northwest of St Paul's is the great block of St Bartholomew's Hospital.

Bart's Hospital ❷

museum, North Wing 7601 8152 Tue–Fri 10am– 4pm, tours by arrangement Fri 2pm free, charge for tour Barbican or St Paul's

Founded in1123, St Bartholomew's Hospital is the oldest in London. Like many early hospitals, it was founded as a monastery offering "hospitality" to pilgrims and the needy. The care provided was initially a combination of shelter, comfort, food and prayer, and only in later centuries evolved into medical treatment. Patients were tended by monks and nuns (hence the term "sister" still in use today).

The hospital includes an interesting little **museum** on changes in medicine over the centuries. A door at the rear of the museum opens to reveal two William Hogarth murals dressing the staircase of the entrance hall of the North Wing. Some of the figures are belived to have been modelled on patients. For a closer look, book one of the guided Friday tours.

Opposite the hospital, on the wall at the corner of **Giltspur Street** and **Cock Lane**, is a golden figure of a urinating boy, symbolising the extinguishing of the 1666 Great Fire at this point. Just beyond, in **West Smithfield**, are memorials to the Scottish hero William Wallace, victim of a spot of judicial butchery here in 1305, and to the 270 "Marian martyrs", Protestants burned at the stake for religious heresy by Queen Mary in the 1550s.

Recommended Restaurants, Bars & Cafés on pages 174–5

St Bartholomew the Great ❸

West Smithfield; www.greatstbarts.com 7606 5171 Tue–Fri 8.30am–5pm (4pm mid-Nov–mid-Feb), Sat 10.30am–1.30pm, Sun 8.30am–1pm and 2.30–8pm Barbican

One of the oldest and finest churches in the City stands in a corner of the square, perhaps a trifle shocked by what has passed before, for this was also the site of the Bartholomew Fair, immortalised in Ben Jonson's play of the same name. Film-makers, too, have been drawn to this corner of London: scenes in *Four Weddings and a Funeral* and *Shakespeare in Love* were filmed inside the church. The monk Rahere, who founded St Bartholomew's Hospital is buried here.

SMITHFIELD TO CLERKENWELL

The unlikely confection of iron and plaster adjacent to St Bartholomew's is **Smithfield Central Markets ❹**, at its busiest early in the morning. Here the porters and workers known as "bummarees" thunder about with barrow loads of carcasses and the knife grinders shower sparks out of the backs of their vans. Through all the commotion, it's still possible to hear "backchat", Smithfield's equivalent of Billingsgate profanity, designed to fool unwanted listeners.

The last of the great markets still on its original site, Smithfield is now one of the most modern meat markets in the world, thanks to a £70 million overhaul. The renovation was accomplished without sacrificing the Victorian shell of the Central

As late as the mid-19th century cattle were still being driven through the streets of London to be slaughtered in Smithfield meat market. Some unruly animals would charge into shops and houses if the doors were open, hence the probable origin of the phrase "bull in a china shop".

ABOVE LEFT: St Bartholomew's the Great. **BELOW LEFT:** Smithfield butcher.

A Street by Any Other Name

Smithfield meat market originally traded in live animals herded in from the country. But the gore of slaughter proved too much for the Victorians, and they moved the industry outside the city, leaving Smithfield to deal in carcasses only. They also changed the names of the area's lanes, so that Stinking Lane became Newgate Street and Blow Bladder Lane King Edward Street.

Other street names hark back to the livery companies who plied their trades in the area. A flavour of the City's trading past remains in the main shopping thoroughfare, Cheapside, behind St Paul's. In medieval times, Cheapside (from the old English word ceap – to barter) was the City's mercantile heart: the names of the side streets, Bread Street, Milk Street and Wood Street, give an idea of the merchandise. Just beyond Cheapside was the poulterers' area, now known as Poultry. Cannon Street (a corruption of candlewick) was the candlemakers' area. Garlick Hill could be smelled from Cheapside.

Tombstones in Bunhill Fields, where many famous people are buried, including John Bunyan, author of The Pilgrim's Progress.

BELOW: City workers enjoy an evening drink.

Markets. Although Smithfield has resisted becoming a shopping piazza like Covent Garden, the area has gone up-market, with a number of good-quality restaurants in St John Street.

Just north of Smithfield is Georgian **Charterhouse Square** ❺. With its gas lamps and cobbles, it is a favourite location for period film-makers. The Carthusian order **London Charterhouse** still has around 40 residents, some of whom conduct guided tours between April and August (tel: 7251 5002; charge).

St John's Gate ❻

St John's Lane; www.sja.org.uk
7324 4005 Mon–Fri 10am–5pm, Sat 10am–4pm, tours Tue, Fri–Sat 11am, 2.30pm free Farringdon

To the left of London Charterhouse, approached through the medieval St John's Gate off Clerkenwell Road, is **St John's Priory**, founded by the crusading Order of the Knights of St John. Little remains of the buildings dissolved by Henry VIII, but there is a small **museum** in the Gate House, and there are guided tours of the Grand Hall and remains of the Priory Chapel which, like the Temple Church off Fleet Street, was round.

Clerkenwell

Further north, beyond Old Street is **Clerkenwell**, historically a district of immigrants (notably Italian) and revolutionary traditions, as well as the traditional centre of the city's watchmaking industry. In the 19th century, Chartists and campaigners for Home Rule collected around Clerkenwell Green.

Guiseppe Mazzini, the Italian revolutionary, lived at No. 10 Laystall Street and Lenin edited a newspaper in what is now the Marx Memorial Library at 37a Clerkenwell Green (open to the general public Mon–Thur 1–2pm only; tel: 7253 1485; www.marx-memorial-library.org).

To the east, just south of Old Street Underground station on City Road, is **Bunhill Fields**, the burial ground for many notable nonconformists including Daniel Defoe, William Blake and John Bunyan. Across the road is **Wesley's Chapel** (Mon–Sat 10am–4pm, Sun 12.30–

2pm, closed Thur lunch time; tel: 7253 2262; www.wesleychapel.org.uk), built by the founder of Methodism, John Wesley, in 1778. Wesley's house (charge) is also open to the public and there is a museum in the crypt. In the men's public toilets are original Victorian fixtures manufactured by Thomas Crapper.

The Barbican

Based around three 42-storey towers, the **Barbican Centre** ❼ is the only residential block in the City. With an arts centre and business space, it was devised by the Corporation of London in the 1950s to attract residents and boost a falling City population. It took more than 20 years to build and is renowned for its its inaccessibility and maze-like design.

The community ideal was never realised as the flats were sold at exorbitant prices. Nevertheless, it is a cultural cornucopia, including an art gallery, a cinema, a theatre and the London Symphony Orchestra.

Beside the Barbican Centre, on the site of a Roman fort, is the Museum of London.

Museum of London ❽

London Wall; www.museumoflondon.org.uk 0870 444 3852 Mon–Sat 10am–5.50pm, Sun noon–5.50pm free Barbican

With more than a million objects in its stores, this is the world's largest urban-history museum and an essential stop for understanding how the City developed.

Aside from important prehistoric and Roman collections, it has a vast archaeological archive, a costume and decorative arts collection, a photo-

TIP

During the day there are often foyer performances and live music on the terrace of the Barbican's Waterside café overlooking the fountains.

ABOVE: detail from Edward Penny's *A City Shower* (c.1764), the Museum of London.
LEFT: John Wesley, the father of Methodism.
BELOW: the Barbican.

The Romans

The Romans established the City in AD 45, but there are few remains of the original Roman settlement. The Roman Wall, which was 2 miles (3 km) long, 20 ft high and 9 ft wide (6 by 3 metres) and had six magnificent gates (Ludgate, Aldersgate, Cripplegate, Newgate, Bishopsgate and Aldgate) is now found only in fragments. Good sections can still be seen at London Wall, Noble Street, Cooper's Row and the Museum of London. There are also remains on the approach to the Tower of London from Tower Hill Underground station. The wall's course can be traced with the help of maps which have been set up on the City's pavements.

KIDS

The Museum of London holds a good range of free activities and workshops for children, especially during school holidays.

It is a myth that the City walls halted the Great Fire of 1666. In fact, the flames leapt across the Fleet River, destroying around 63 acres (25.5 hectares) outside of the walled area.

BELOW: the Lord Mayor's Parade.

graphic archive of 280,000 images and more than 5,000 hours of oral life- story recordings.

The lower galleries are closed for redevelopment and most of the museum's collections, including all post-1914 exhibits, are in storage. When they open in winter 2009, the new galleries will give considerably greater access to the vast collection.

London's history is presented chronologically from prehistory to the early Stuarts. The same thematic threads run through each period: architecture, trade and industry, transport, health, multiculturalism, religion, fashions, leisure pursuits. There are many detailed information panels; you may find that, an hour into your visit, you're still with the Romans.

Here are some highlights:

London Before London

This surveys life in the Thames Valley from 450,000 BC–AD 50. The centrepiece of the exhibition is the "River Wall" displaying 300 artefacts that have beeen found in the Thames.

Roman London

This gallery has a hoard of gold coins (1st–2nd century AD) found buried in a safety deposit box near Fenchurch Street, and the gilded arms of what must have been a life-size statue of a god or emperor.

Tudors to the early Stuarts

The civil war collection includes Oliver Cromwell's death mask and Bible, but more captivating is the cabinet filled with the glittering Cheapside Hoard. In 1912, a workman digging in London hit on a box containing 230 pieces of finely crafted jewellery set with precious stones. The treasure may have belonged to a goldsmith who hid his stock during the civil war of 1642–49.

London's Burning

This tells the story of the Great Fire of 1666, and its aftermath, through the experiences of the city's inhabitants. Objects include primitive fire-fighting equipment and fire-damaged floor tiles from Pudding Lane. This exhibition will be open until the new galleries are unveiled.

THE GUILDS

Craftsmen with the same trade tended to congregate in small areas, and clubbed together to form medieval guilds. Like trade unions, the guilds operated to ward off foreign competition and established an apprenticeship system. They set standards for their goods and ran mutual-aid schemes which helped members in difficulty. The more prosperous guilds built halls to meet and dine in and wore lavish uniforms or "liveries", in due course becoming livery companies.

Down the centuries the livery companies shed their Mafia image and joined the establishment, promoting charities and founding some of England's better educational institutes, including Haberdashers' College and Goldsmiths' College.

The Livery Halls

Today some of the most impressive portals in the City belong to livery halls. Behind their gleaming paintwork and elaborate carvings members dine as lavishly as ever.

Most spectacular is **Goldsmiths Hall** ❾ in Foster Lane (tel: 7606 7010; www.thegoldsmiths.co.uk/hall), between the Museum of London and St Paul's, where the integrity of gold and silver issued the previous year is checked in an annual ceremony. The use of the word "hallmark" as a seal of value originated here. Unfortunately, visitors are not usually allowed inside the livery halls, except in special circumstances.

While the 107 livery companies today have little connection with their original crafts, they still exert influence in their home territory. The City is governed by the City Corporation, chaired by the **Lord Mayor** (whereas the rest of the capital comes under the wing of the Mayor of

Postman's Park delivers a soothing antidote to the high walkways and municipal signage of the over-scale Baribican. Small, secluded and a short walk from the Museum of London walkway exit, this is a good place to take a break. Rows of hand-lettered Doulton plaques placed in an open gallery by radical socialist George Watts (1817–1904) commemorate fatal acts of bravery by ordinary people. The General Post Office, from which the park derives its name, closed long ago.

LEFT: gold leopard, Skinners Hall.
BELOW: the ceiling of the Livery Hall of the Drapers Company.

At Sixes and Sevens

For years there was fierce rivalry between the craftsmen's guilds. In 1515 the Lord Mayor interceded and named a top 12 based on wealth: Mercers (dealers in fine cloth), Grocers, Drapers, Fishmongers, Goldsmiths, Skinners, Merchant Taylors, Haberdashers, Salters, Ironmongers, Vintners and Clothworkers. Competition between the Skinners and Merchant Taylors, who both claimed the number six slot, was particularly fierce. The Lord Mayor, with Solomon-like decisiveness, decreed they should alternate positions six and seven every year. His action originated the expression "at sixes and sevens", meaning "uncertain".

*Behind Mansion House is **St Stephen Walbrook**, the Lord Mayor's church, dating from 1696 and considered by many to be Christopher Wren's best. Its dome is believed to be a dry run for St Paul's and its controversial "cheeseboard" altar is by Henry Moore.*

London, who presides over the Greater London Authority). The office of Lord Mayor dates from 1189 and since then a number of colourful and sometimes bizarre ceremonies have become attached to the job. The new Mayor is elected each year on Michaelmas Day, 29 September, when the reigning Lord Mayor and his aldermen parade through the streets carrying posies of flowers to ward off the stench which filled the City when the ceremony began.

Guildhall ⑩

Gresham Street; www.cityoflondon.gov.uk 7606 3030 daily 9am–5pm free St Paul's

In November the mayor is sworn in here, taking up his symbols of office in a ceremony known as the Silent Change, so called because no words are spoken. The Guildhall is the best place to glimpse the guilds' past. Dating from the 15th century, and several times restored, the Great Hall is decorated with the liveries' banners and shields. A small, well-ordered museum in a room adjacent to the Library displays the timepieces owned by the Clockmakers' Company. This splendid collection is the oldest and largest of its kind. (Mon–Fri 9.30am–4.30pm; free).

The Lord Mayor's Show is held a day after his swearing in. This colourful parade starts at the Guildhall and passes through the City, culminating at **Mansion House** ⑪, opposite the Bank of England. This is the Lord Mayor's official residence, designed by George Dance the Elder in 1785, but its magnificent rooms are not open to the public.

Guildhall Art Gallery ⑫

Guildhall Yard; www.guildhall-art-gallery.org.uk 7332 3342 Mon–Sat 10am–5pm, Sun noon–4pm charge Mansion House or St Paul's

Established in 1885, the Guildhall's gallery was destroyed in the Blitz and reopened in 1999. John Singleton Copley's immense *The Defeat of the Floating Batteries at Gibraltar*, around which the new gallery was designed, commands

BELOW: the Guildhall. **BELOW RIGHT:** a Guildhall member in traditional regalia.

Recommended Restaurants, Bars & Cafés on pages 174–5

attention, but allow time to linger over the smaller-scale works depicting London life.

Shortly before work began on the present building, the remains of a **Roman amphitheatre** were discovered under the yard. The arena, including well-preserved timber drains bearing original carpentry tool marks, may now be viewed in a lower-level gallery as the centrepiece of an imaginative display on the age of the gladiator.

BANK AND BEYOND

The triangular intersection known as **Bank** can intimidate. Imposing civic architecture abounds, with Sir Edwin Lutyens' HSBC building on the north-west side, the Mansion House on the western corner, the **Royal Exchange** building to the east and Sir John Soane's implacable facade of the Bank of England to the north.

All the City's great institutions grew from the fulfilment of the most basic needs and only later acquired their grandiose headquarters. Banking first came to the City in the 17th century when Italian refugees set up lending benches (*banca* in Italian) in **Lombard Street,** running eastwards from the Bank of England.

The Bank of England ⓭

✉ museum entrance in Bartholomew Lane; www.bankofengland.co.uk
☎ 7601 5545 ⏲ Mon–Fri 10am–5pm
£ free 🚇 Bank

The **Bank of England** dominates the Bank square as it does the British financial scene. Popularly known as the Old Lady of Threadneedle Street, a nickname which probably originates from a late 18th-century cartoon depicting an old lady (the bank) trying to prevent the then prime minister, Pitt the Younger, from securing her gold. The name stuck because it aptly describes the conservative, maternalistic role the bank played in stabilising the country's economy – a role strengthened in 1997 when the new Labour government freed it from direct government control.

The Bank of England was set up in 1694 to finance a war against the Dutch. In return for a £1.2 million loan, it was granted a charter and became a bank of issue (with the right to print notes and take deposits). Today it prints 5 million notes daily,

One of several striking ornamental signs on Lombard Street. The signs were put up in 1902 to mark Edward VII's coronation.

ABOVE LEFT: Rosetti's *La Ghirlandata* (1873), Guildhall Art Gallery. **BELOW:** an ornate memorial to Admiral Horatio Nelson (1758–1805), the Guildhall.

The Royal Exchange, where animated young traders in traditional garish blazers once shouted and waved instructions, is now occupied by a clutch of luxury retailers including Cartier, Bulgari, Tiffany, Hermes, De Beer and Chanel. To round off a spree here, head for one of the Exchange's posh restaurants or bars.

destroys another 5 million and stores the nation's gold reserves. Its present home was largely rebuilt between 1925 and 1939.

It covers 3 acres (1.2 hectares) and contains the **Bank of England Museum.** While waxwork mannequins of clerks and customers carry on their business, the presentations narrate how the bank helped to finance Britain's war effort against France in 1688, how it became one of the first institutions in the City to employ women and how it controlled government borrowing during World War II. There is also an interactive display illustrating the bank's role in setting official interest rates.

RIGHT: the Bank of England Museum. **BELOW LEFT AND RIGHT:** exterior and interior of the Lloyd's of London building.

Lloyd's of London

The Big Bang brought immediate demands for new office buildings which would be purpose-built for modern communications and, by 1991, 1.7 sq. miles (4.4 sq. km) of office space had been built in the City. One of the first, and the most dramatic, was the 1986 **Lloyd's of London** ⓮ building in Lime Street, designed by Sir Richard Rogers (now Lord Rogers).

For so long the biggest insurance group in the world, Lloyd's started in the 17th-century coffee house of Edward Lloyd, where underwriters, shippers and bankers gathered and began to strike deals. Its practices remained largely unchanged for 300 years, but in the late 1980s sundry international disasters led to some huge payouts and millions of pounds were lost. Many of the "names" – investors who shouldered the insurance risks, often through syndicates, and who had always thought their investment as safe as the Bank of England – lost life savings and owed more than they could ever possibly pay; a few committed suicide.

Recommended Restaurants, Bars & Cafés on pages 174–5

The building is no longer open to visitors, but the exterior, where glass elevators whisk employees to their offices is a highlight of the City. Hidden from site on a magnificent marble floor is a wooden rostrum housing the **Lutine Bell**, which was rung once for bad news and twice for good. The huge **Casualty Book** contains a record of all ships lost at sea.

Beside this modern building is the more accessible **Leadenhall** ⓯, once the wholesale market for poultry and game, and now a handsome commercial centre. The magnificent airy Victorian cream and maroon structure has a collection of upmarket chain shops, sandwich bars, stylish restaurants, and food and book shops, attracting City workers at breakfast and lunch time.

Grand stations

London's other steel-and-glass Victorian constructions – the railway stations – were also given facelifts during the 1980s building boom. **Liverpool Street** was overhauled along with neighbouring **Broadgate** ⓰, one of the most ambitious developments in the City, with 13 office-block buildings around three squares including, at Broadgate Square, an ice rink with sushi, coffee and sandwich stalls dotted around the perimeter. Fernando Botero's hugely voluptuous *Broadgate Venus* is a high point.

A few minutes west of Liverpool Street station is the pleasant open space of **Finsbury Circus** (8am–7pm

Broadgate's circular ice rink is open from October until early April. Snacks and drinks are sold at stalls nearby. Lessons are available, tel: 7505 4068; www.broadgateice.co.uk.

LEFT: Leadenhall Market. **BELOW:** Broadgate ice rink.

Monument, commemorating the Great Fire of London. Climb its 311 steps for superb views.

or dusk; closed weekends Oct–Mar). Embraced by elegant terraces and centuries-old plane trees, this is a popular lunchtime spot. You can grab a sandwich and sit amidst the throngs of suited City workers.

Fenchurch Street ⓱ with its arched roof and graceful windows was the City's first railway station. Originally situated in the Minories, it moved in 1854 to its present location and has since acquired the 1930s Manhattan-style office building, **1 America Square**, over its railway lines.

To stand out in such an architectural playground, new buildings have to be innovative. One recent example is the distinctive **Swiss Reinsurance building** in St Mary Axe, a 40-storey tapering glass tower designed by Lord Foster and known affectionately as "the erotic gherkin". The only piece of curved glass used in the structure forms the tip of the dome, under which is an exclusive restaurant giving 360-degree views over London.

RIGHT AND BELOW: summer in the City – bowls in Finsbury Square and lunch in Finsbury Circus.

Monument ⓲

Monument Yard; www.towerbridge.org.uk 7626 2717 viewing gallery daily 9.30am–5pm; closed until spring 2008 charge Monument

Erected according to Wren's designs to commemorate the fire, this Roman Doric column stands 202 ft (61 metres) high. The height is exactly the same as the distance between the monument's base and the king's baker's house in Pudding Lane where the fire began.

The Great Fire lasted five days and spread through 460 streets, destroying 89 churches and more than 13,000 houses. At the base of the column is a relief depicting the king and his citizens fighting the

Recommended Restaurants, Bars & Cafés on pages 174–5

blaze. Inside, 311 steps wind giddily up to a small platform, from which the view is spectacular. Appropriately enough, the gallery affords a chance to appreciate the remarkable vision Wren imposed on the City through his spires, but it will be closed for major works until spring 2008. There are 56 Wren spires, and you risk severe Wren-fatigue if you attempt to see them all. Selected visits reveal the work of the artist at the height of his powers.

St Mary-le-Bow ⓳ is the home of the famous Bow bells, which define a true cockney – you have to be born within earshot. The original bells were destroyed in the war, but new ones were recast from the fragments. The church interior after restoration is rather vulgar, but the Norman crypt, now a restaurant called The Place Below, is worth a visit. Wren was able to leave his significant mark on London because so much of it had been destroyed in the Great Fire, but some churches survived the conflagration, including **St Katherine Cree** ⓴, a mix of Classical and Gothic, in Leadenhall Street. Henry Purcell played its fine 17th-century organ, and the painter Hans Holbein, a plague victim, was buried here in 1543.

Tower of London ㉑

Tower Hill; www.hrp.org.uk/tower
0870 756 6060 Mar–Oct Tue–Sat 9am–6pm, Sun–Mon 10am–6pm; Nov–Feb Tue–Sat 9am–5pm, Sun–Mon 10am–5pm
charge Tower Hill

East of the Monument, across the river from the oval-shaped City Hall, from which the Greater London Authority's power is exercised, is the City's oldest structure. At first sight the **Tower of London** can look like a cardboard model rather than a former seat of power, but closer inspection reveals an awesome solidity which encompasses much of Britain's history. The Tower has contained at various times a treasury, public-record office, observatory, royal mint and zoo, and was so frequently remodelled for these purposes that its interiors look less ancient than one expects.

For full coverage of the Tower of London, see pages 178–181. ❑

DRINK

Visits to the Tower of London are exhausting, but refreshment is within easy walking distance. The Ship pub in Talbot Court off Eastcheap and The Samuel Pepys down Stew Lane, off Upper Thames Street on the river have real character and real ale.

BELOW LEFT: the Swiss Reinsurance Building, aka the Gherkin. **BELOW RIGHT:** the Tower of London.

BEST RESTAURANTS, BARS AND CAFÉS

Restaurants

Prices for a three-course dinner per person with a half-bottle of house wine:

£ = under £20
££ = £20–30
£££ = £30–50
££££ = over £50

British

Clerkenwell Dining Rooms

69–73 St, EC1 ☎ 7253 9000 ⌚ L & D Mon–Fri, D only Sat **££££** [p 332, B1]
An inviting smell of wine welcomes you into this small but well-presented restaurant. Predictable modern British mains like corn-fed chicken and rib-eye of beef are on offer alongside more adventurous combinations.

St John

26 St John St, EC1 ☎ 7251 0848 ⌚ L & D Mon–Fri, D only Sat. **££££** [p 332, C1]
This little restaurant a stone's throw from Smithfield's meat market, is a Clerkenwell favourite. It offers simple but curious dishes such as Middle-white belly and dandelion or pigeon and rabbit.

Fish

Rudland & Stubbs Fish Restaurant

35–37 Greenhill Rents, Cowcross St, EC1 ☎ 7253 0148 ⌚ L & D Mon–Fri. **£££** [p 332, B2]
With its cool lemon-and-lime tiled interior and ceiling fans, this attractive restaurant offers a relaxed environment. The menu is traditional (including fish and chips).

Sweetings

39 Queen Victoria Street, EC4 ☎ 7248 3062 ⌚ L only Mon–Fri. **££** [p 333, C3]
First-rate fish restaurant with bags of traditional City atmosphere, and well-prepared dishes such as grilled skate, turbot in mustard sauce or dressed crab, and old-fashioned puddings such as treacle tart.

French

Café du Marché

22 Charterhouse Square, Charterhouse Mews, EC1 ☎ 7608 1609 ⌚ L & D Mon–Fri, D only Sat. **£££** [p 332, C1]
Rustic ambience, including a countrified courtyard, and traditional French menu. The food can seem to some a little on the rich side. Ideal for a romantic meal or lunchtime treat.

Club Gascon

57 West Smithfield, EC1 ☎ 7796 0600 ⌚ L & D Mon–Sat. **£££** [p 332, C2]
Though tradition is not totally dispensed with, there's more to this Michelin-starred restaurant than the foie gras, cassoulet and *magret de canard* standards. Dishes and ingredients of southwestern France are prepared with an inventive touch and served tapas style, with a fine selection of regional wines to match. Booking essential.

Italian

Carravagio

107 Leadenhall St, EC3 ☎ 7626 6206 ⌚ L & D Mon–Fri. **£££** (set menu) **££££** [p 333, E3]
Grand and rather showy Italian restaurant in a converted bank. Fish is a good option and the fillet steak with aubergine and gorgonzola is a carnivore's dream. But the bill is likely to he high.

Modern European

Bonds

5 Threadneedle St, EC2. ☎ 7657 8088 ⌚ L & D Mon–Fri. **£££** (set lunch) **££££** [p 333, D3]
Set in the classy Threadneedles boutique hotel, overlooking the Bank of England, this top-class restaurant draws clients of the silk-lined wallet variety; the meat-dominated mains – venison or roast saddle of lamb for instance – start at £20.

LEFT: Café du Marché on Charterhouse Square.
RIGHT: St John on St John Street, near Smithfield.

Spanish

Moro

34–36 Exmouth Market, EC1 ☎ 7833 8336 ⏲ L & D Mon–Fri, D only Sat. **£££** [p 332, B1]
Laid-back restaurant with a Spanish–North-African menu. Lamb is charcoal grilled, tuna is wind-dried, monkfish wood roasted, manzanilla sherry partners prawns and garlic.

Vegetarian

The Place Below

St Mary-le-Bow, Cheapside, EC2 ☎ 7329 0789 ⏲ B & L Mon–Fri. **££** [p 333, C3]
A godsend for vegetarians is this café in the crypt of St Mary-le-Bow, with seats in the churchyard in summer. Dishes are simple: quiches and salads, and always a hot dish of the day

The Don

20, St Swithin's Lane, EC4. ☎ 7626 2606 ⏲ L & D Mon–Fri. **£££** [p 333, D3]
Hidden in a courtyard off St Swithin's Lane, this is a cosy and welcoming brick-walled bistro. The food is a flavour-packed melange of influences, with a French bias.

Eagle

159 Farringdon Rd, EC1. ☎ 7837 1353 ⏲ L & D Mon–Sat, L only Sun. **££** [p 332, B1]
This was the pub that launched a thousand gastropubs with its pioneering menu of inventive dishes. The food has a Mediterranean bias. A good choice of European beers is also available.

Little Bay

171 Farringdon Rd, EC1. ☎ 7278 1234 ⏲ daily, all day. **£** [p 332, B1]
For honest food, keenly priced, this bizarre little bistro, lit by hand-crafted copper sculptures, is hard to beat. Dishes include Barbary duck breast, red cabbage, honey and ginger.

Searcy's

Level 2, Barbican, Silk St, EC2 ☎ 7588 3008 ⏲ L & D Mon–Fri, D only Sat. **£££** (set menu), **££££** [p 333, C2]
A classy place that serves up well-executed dishes for an arts-centre restaurant. Ring first: it doesn't open if there's no performance.

Pan-Asian

Cicada

132–136 St John St, EC1 ☎ 7608 1550 ⏲ L & D Mon–Fri, D only Sun **£££** [p 332, B1]
Cicada's menu offers a range of well-executed pan-Asian dishes such as black cod with sweet miso and prawns with coconut and betel leaf. Kick off with an enticing cocktail mixed at the bar and finish with a sumptuous sorbet for dessert.

Pubs, Bars and Cafés

Given that some of London't oldest streets as well as its newest buildings are here, the mix of watering holes is diverse, ranging from hip bars and contemporary cafés to quaint pubs full of character and history. Fewer and farther between are the no-nonsense Victorian pubs, but with a bit of effort, traditionalists or anyone craving a quiet pint and a packet of peanuts can root them out. Fashionable cocktail bars include **Fluid** *(40 Charterhouse Lane, near Smithfield)*, **1 Lombard Street** *(that's the address too)*, the sleek Harvey Nichols-run **Prism** *(147 Leadenhall Street)* and the capacious **Smiths of Smithfield** *(67–77 Charterhouse Street)*.

For a more low-key atmosphere, **Match** *(45–47 Clerkenwell Road)* is a dimly lit 1990s bar with great cocktails. **Vertigo 42** *(Tower 42, Old Broad Street)* lives up to its name by serving Champagne to accompany great views from on high in the 42-storey skyscraper. The down-to-earth **Vinoteca** *(7 St John Street)* has an excellent wine list, good, unpretentious food and reasonable prices. **Royal Exchange Grand Café and Bar** *(The Courtyard, Royal Exchange, Bank)* offers breakfast, lunch dinner and drinks in opulent surroundings with prices to match. **Jerusalem Tavern** *(55 Britton Street)* is an intimate little pub dating from 1720, with cubicles, Georgian-style furniture and a selection of real ales and fruit beers. **The Counting House** *(50 Cornhill)* is a bank- turned pub, with high ceilings and chandeliers.

St Paul's Cathedral

Sir Christopher Wren built more than 50 churches in London after the Great Fire of 1666, but this is the one that remains his masterpiece

Historians believe that the first church on the St Paul's site was built in the 7th century, although it only really came into its own as Old St Paul's in the 14th century, and by the 16th century it was the tallest cathedral in England. Much of the building was destroyed in the Great Fire of 1666. Construction on the new St Paul's Cathedral began in 1675, when its architect, Sir Christopher Wren (pictured), was 43 years old.

The architect was an old man of 78 when his son Christopher finally laid the highest stone of the lantern on the central cupola in 1710. In total, the cathedral cost £747,954 to build, and most of the money was raised through taxing coal imports. Now, in preparation for the 300th anniversary, centuries of soot and grime have been scrubbed away as part of a £40 million restoration project.

The essentials

www.stpauls.co.uk

7246 8350

Mon–Fri 8.30am–4pm, tours at 11am, 11.30am, 1.30pm, 2pm

charge

St Paul's

Above: Just below the 24 windows in the dome is the Whispering Gallery, more than 100 ft (30 metres) of perfect acoustic. A whisper can be heard across the gallery, 107 ft (33 metres) away.

Above: the superb craftsmanship was supervised during the 35-year construction by one master builder, Thomas Strong, and by Wren (top left) himself.

THE HIGHLIGHTS

Features: marble steps (**A**); oak pulpit (**Q**); High Altar (**R**); Dean's pulpit and stairs to crypt (**U**); stairs to dome (**V**). **Chapels**: St Dunstan's (**B**); All Souls' (**C**); St Michael & St George's (**D**); American Chapel of Remembrance (**S**). **Tombs & Monuments**: Lord Leighton (**E**); General Gordon (**F**); Viscount Melbourne (**G**); Duke of Wellington (**H**); Joshua Reynolds (**I**); Dr Samuel Johnson (**J**); Admiral Earl Howe (**K**); Admiral Collingwood (**L**); JMW Turner (**M**); Sir John Moore (**N**); General Abercromby (**O**); Lord Nelson (**P**); John Donne (**T**)

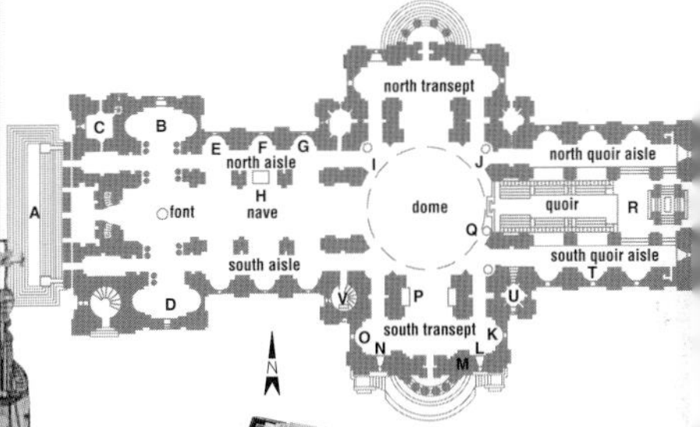

ABOVE: Admiral Lord Nelson (1758–1805) is entombed in the crypt.

RIGHT: the cathedral's appearance is deceptive. The famous dome viewed from afar would look over large if seen from inside the building. The dome you look up at from within is in fact a much smaller dome, on top of which is built a brick cone. The cone's purpose is to support the massive weight of the external Portland stone dome, which weighs more than 50,000 tons.

ABOVE: a chapel behind the High Altar, damaged during the Blitz, was restored as the American Chapel, with a book of remembrance paying tribute to the 28,000 American citizens based in the UK who died in World War II.

THE TOWER OF LONDON

Queens were beheaded here, princes murdered and traitors tortured. Once a place to be avoided, it is now one of London's top visitor attractions

Encircled by a moat (now dry), with 22 towers, the Tower, begun by William the Conqueror in 1078, is Britain's top military monument and a reminder of how power was once exercised in the nation.

Two of Henry VIII's wives, Anne Boleyn and Catherine Howard, were beheaded here, in 1536 and 1542. So were Sir Thomas More, Henry's principled Lord Chancellor (1535), and Sir Walter Raleigh, the last of the great Elizabethan adventurers (1618). The uncrowned Edward V, aged 12, and his 10-year-old brother Richard were murdered here in 1483, allegedly on the orders of Richard III. William Penn, the future founder of Pennsylvania, was imprisoned here in 1669, and the diarist Samuel Pepys in 1679. As recently as 1941, Rudolph Hess, Germany's deputy führer, was locked in the Tower.

Given that the Tower's 18 acres (7.3 hectares) contain enough buildings and collections to occupy three hours, you may prefer to skip the one-hour Beefeater-led tour and strike out on your own. An audio guide can be hired.

In summer, it's best to arrive early to beat the queues, giving priority to the Crown Jewels and the Bloody Tower. Note that the spiral staircases in some of the towers require a degree of agility. Within the Tower walls, picnics are permitted on any of the seats. There are also snack kiosks and a restaurant in the New Armouries.

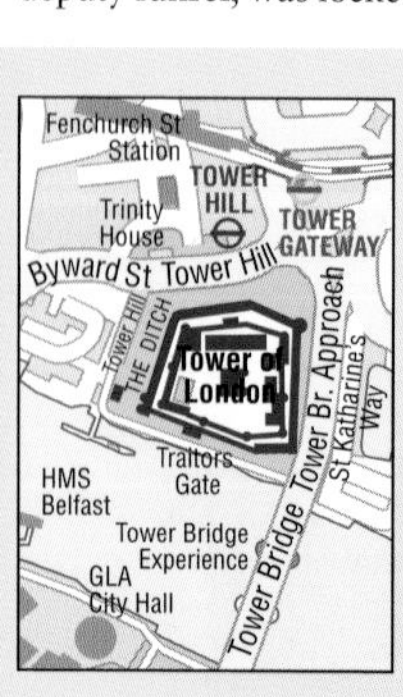

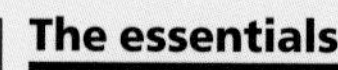

The essentials

Tower Hill; www.hrp.org.uk/tower
0870 756 6060
Mar–Oct Tue–Sat 9am–6pm, Sun–Mon 10am–6pm; Nov–Feb Tue–Sat 9am–5pm, Sun–Mon 10am–5pm
charge
Tower Hill

ABOVE: the meticulously restored interior of the Medieval Royal Residence uses replica furniture and textiles, rich colours, scents, sound and lighting effects to create an impression of 13th-century life in the palace. Edward I probably slept here, in the King's Bed Chamber, when he stayed at the Tower in 1294.

ABOVE: at the centre of the fortress is the imposing White Tower with its four weathervane-topped turrets, each of a different style. The name followed Henry III's order to whitewash the exterior.

ABOVE: Tower Green is the grassy area, west of the White Tower, that gives access (but only for guided tours) to the much rebuilt Chapel Royal of St Peter ad Vincula. In front of the chapel is the Scaffold Site where nobles were beheaded (the less illustrious were executed in public on Tower Hill, outside the castle walls).

THE SIGHTS WORTH SEEING

The Medieval Palace

Just before Traitor's Gate is the entrance to the residential part of the Tower, used by monarchs when they lived here. St Thomas's Tower, built in 1275–79 but much altered, displays archaeological evidence of its many uses. Parts of the Wakefield Tower (1220–40), such as the King's Bed Chamber, are furnished in 13th-century style and a torture exhibition has been added. A spiral staircase leads to a walkway on top of the south wall, which provides a good view of the riverside defences. The wall runs to the Lanthorn Tower (1883) containing 13th-century artefacts.

The White Tower

The oldest part of the fortress, the White Tower was probably designed in 1078 by a Norman monk, Gandulf, a prolific builder of castles and churches. It has walls 15 ft (5 metres) thick. Its original form remains, but nearly every part has been refurbished or rebuilt: the door surrounds and most windows were replaced in the 17th and 18th centuries, and much of the Normandy stone was replaced with more durable Portland stone from Dorset. The first floor gives access to the austere Chapel of St John the Evangelist, a fine example of early Norman architecture. Much of the remaining space is devoted to displays of armour, swords and muskets, taken from the Royal Armouries.

More Modern Than Medieval

Given that so much of the country's turbulent history was played out within these walls, the Tower conspicuously lacks the romantic aura that many visitors expect. The reason is that, until comparatively recently, its buildings were functional – as well as serving as a fort, arsenal, palace and prison, it also contained at various times a treasury, public record office, observatory, royal mint and zoo. As a result, it was frequently remodelled and renovated, especially in the 19th century, so that many floors and staircases, for example, look more modern than medieval. But then, how could the boards that Henry VIII trod hope to survive the footfalls of 2½ million tourists a year?

Any sense of awe is also undermined by the brightly uniformed "Beefeaters" *(see right)*. Although all have served in the armed forces for at least 22 years, some have enthusiastically embraced showbiz, apparently auditioning for the role of pantomime villain by alternating jocular banter with visitors and melodramatically delivered descriptions of torture and beheadings. In contrast, pike and musket drills by the English Civil War Society are conducted with the masterful lethargy of confirmed pacifists.

Above: the upper chamber of Wakefield Tower was used as a throne room by Henry III and later converted into an ante-room of the KIng's private chambers by his son, Edward I. Wakefield Tower also housed the state archives from 1360 to 1856 and, for a time, served as the Jewel House.

Right: attired in Tudor uniforms, Yeoman warders first took up their posts under Edward VI and have been guarding the Tower for more than 500 years. Their nickname "Beefeaters" may derive from the French word *buffetier*, meaning servant, although an "eater" was also used in English to describe a servant. In 2007 the first female Beefeater, Moira Cameron, was appointed. Like her fellow male Beefeaters she has a military background. Among the perks of the job of a Beefeater is the use of a subsidised apartment within the Tower of London.

ABOVE: in 2006 a new memorial was erected to commemorate the 10 prisoners beheaded on Tower Green, including Ann Boleyn and Catherine Howard, the unfortunate wives of Henry VIII. A glass pillow rests on two discs of glass and granite.

RIGHT: a carving in the Beauchamp Tower (1281), which held high-ranking prisoners. The inscriptions they carved on the walls can be seen.

BELOW RIGHT: Sir Walter Raleigh's room in the Bloody Tower (1603–16).

THE HIGHLIGHTS

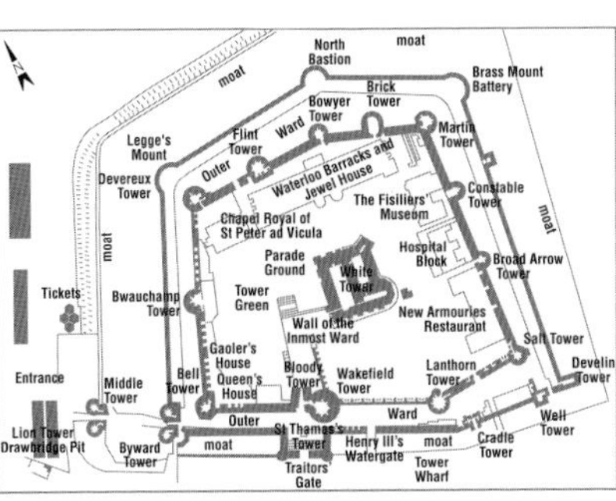

The Wall Walk

The walk along this defensive outer wall takes in the eastern towers. Access is through the Salt Tower, often used as a prison. Next are the Broad Arrow Tower, also once a lock-up, the Constable Tower, which contains a model depicting the Tower in the 14th century, and the Martin Tower, which houses an exhibition on the Crown Jewels.

The Royal Fusiliers Museum

In the centre of the Tower is the modest but elegantly housed Royal Fusiliers Museum. Opened in 1962, it follows the regiment's campaigns from its first battle for William of Orange against the French in Walcourt up to its more recent peacekeeping involvement in the Balkans and Northern Ireland. The regiment was almost destroyed in the American War of Independence.

The Crown Jewels

These are displayed in the neo-Gothic Waterloo Barracks, built in 1845. The queues here can be long, with airport-style barriers. At the centre of the display are a dozen crowns and a glittering array of swords, sceptres and orbs used on royal occasions. A moving walkway ensures that visitors cannot linger over the principal exhibits, but many other glass cases contain gold dishes, chalices and altar dishes that can be viewed at leisure. The eye is caught by a massive wine cistern weighing a quarter of a ton (250 kg).

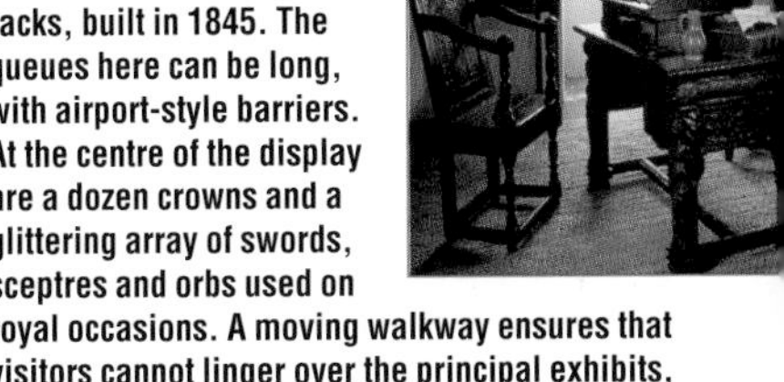

WHARF
A U R A N T

Recommended Restaurants, Bars & Cafés on pages 196–7

SOUTHWARK AND THE SOUTH BANK

The historic area south of the Thames has been transformed into a vibrant entertainment centre. Its multiple attractions, ranging from the London Eye and Tate Modern to Tower Bridge, are linked by an attractive riverside walk

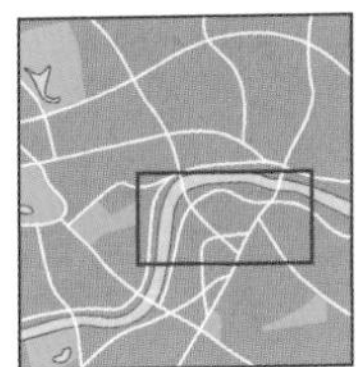

Southwark is one of the oldest parts of the capital. The first bridge across the Thames was built by the Romans near London Bridge, and the community around it developed separately from the City, as it lay in the county of Surrey, beyond the City's jurisdiction. In Shakespeare's day it was the place for putting on unlicensed plays and for setting up brothels, and it retained its reputation as an area of vice well into the 19th century. The Underground's Jubilee Line extension and the regeneration of the area around Tate Modern, Borough Market and Butler's Wharf have transformed the area.

AROUND LAMBETH BRIDGE

Opposite the Houses of Parliament, beside Lambeth Bridge, is the red-brick **Lambeth Palace ❶**, which has been the London residence of the Archbishops of Canterbury since the 12th century. The fine Tudor brickwork of the entrance tower dates from 1485, but much of the rest is Victorian. The rare occasions on which the palace is open to the public include the annual Open House weekend *(see page 57)*.

Adjacent, by Lambeth Bridge on Lambeth Palace Road, the garden and deconsecrated church of **St Mary** contains the **Museum of Garden History** (daily 10.30am–5pm; tel: 7401 8865; charge; www.museumgardenhistory.org), based on the work of two 17th-century royal gardeners, the elder and younger John Tradescant, father and son, who introduced exotic fruits such as pineapples to Britain. The old-fashioned roses and herbaceous perennials are delightful, and the church's rich history is evident in its memorials, including one

Main attractions

- IMPERIAL WAR MUSEUM
- LONDON AQUARIUM
- LONDON EYE
- ROYAL FESTIVAL HALL
- NATIONAL THEATRE
- BFI SOUTHBANK
- HAYWARD GALLERY
- TATE MODERN
- SHAKESPEARE'S GLOBE
- SOUTHWARK CATHEDRAL
- BOROUGH MARKET
- TOWER BRIDGE
- DESIGN MUSEUM

LEFT: Gabriel's Wharf.
RIGHT: the London Eye and County Hall.

FOOD

The Garden Café, within the Museum of Garden History, is a great option for a bite to eat in the Lambeth Bridge area. The café serves homecooked, vegetarian food, from panini packed with grilled vegetables to delicately spiced soups and good cakes.

ABOVE RIGHT: recalling the Crimea at the Florence Nightingale Museum. **BELOW:** works by the master of surrealism can be seen at the Dalí Universe.

remembering HMS *Bounty*'s Captain William Bligh, who lived locally.

Imperial War Museum ❷

✉ Lambeth Road; www.iwm.org.uk
☎ 7416 5320 ⏲ daily 10am–6pm; free except some special exhibitions
🚇 Elephant & Castle, Lambeth North

A 15-minute walk south from Lambeth Bridge, along Lambeth Road, leads to the **Imperial War Museum.** This impressive building, opened in 1815 to house the Bethlehem hospital for the insane (popularly known as Bedlam), was an inspired choice for a museum that chronicles the horrors of modern warfare. *For full details, see pages 200–1.*

St Thomas's Hospital

Back by the river, close to Westminster Bridge, **St Thomas's Hospital** includes a reminder of warfare's nobler side: the **Florence Nightingale Museum** ❸ (Mon–Fri 10am–5pm, Sat, Sun

10am–4.30pm; 2 Lambeth Palace Road; tel: 7620 0374; charge; www.florence-nightingale.co.uk). Don't be deterred by the walk down Lambeth Palace Road, which is unattractive at this point; this small museum is worth the detour. It has a rich collection of memorabilia, and there's an engaging 20-minute audio-visual presentation on the life and achievements of the woman whose work in the Crimean War of 1854–6 helped transform nursing.

COUNTY HALL ❹

Just downstream from Westminster Bridge and facing the Houses of Parliament is the majestic **County Hall,** designed in 1908 by architect Ralph

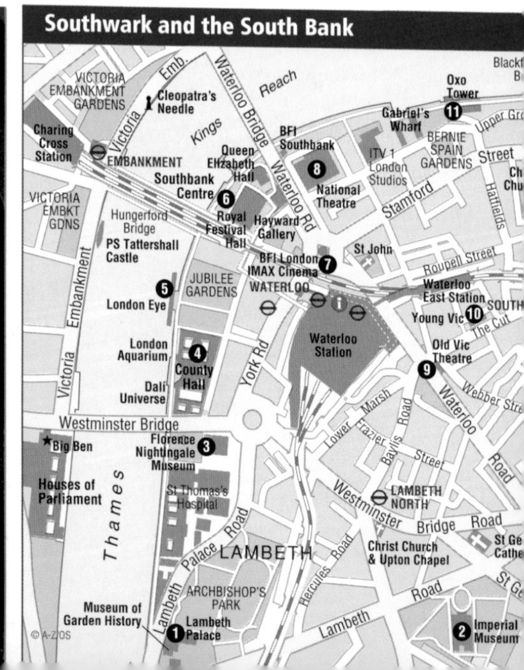

Recommended Restaurants, Bars & Cafés on pages 196–7

Knott and for years the seat of the Greater London Council, which ran London until the unsympathetic government of Margaret Thatcher abolished it in 1986. Now owned by Japan's Shirayama Shokusan Corporation, it incorporates an up-market hotel (the five-star Marriott), a budget hotel (a Travel Inn), the London Aquarium, an art gallery, a games arcade and several restaurants.

The first attraction as you walk eastwards along the river is **Namco Station** (10am–midnight; www.namcostation.co.uk), home to bumper cars video games and a bowling alley.

Next is the **Dalí Universe** (10am–5.30pm; late opening in summer; tel: 0870 744 7485; charge), displaying around 500 works by the Catalan artist, Salvador Dalí (1904–89). The three themed areas are "Sensuality and Femininity" (which includes the well-known Mae West Lips Sofa), "Religion and Mythology" (including the epic illustration of Dante's *Divine Comedy*), and "Dreams and Fantasy" (which includes *Persistence of Memory* and *Profile of Time*).

The top attraction in County Hall, especially for children is the **London Aquarium** (daily 10am–6pm, last admission 5pm; till 7pm in summer; tel: 7967 8000; www.londonaquarium.co.uk; charge). Thousands of specimens represent some 350 species of fish, and atmospheric sounds, smells and lighting are all employed to great effect. Highlights include the sharks and touch pool.

KIDS

At the London Aquarium, it's worth catching the feeding times. Fish are delivered a mix of mackerel and squid during diving displays on Monday, Wednesday and Friday from noon–12.30pm in the main Atlantic Tank, while shark feeding is on Tuesday, Thursday and Saturday at 2.30pm. Times do sometimes change, so check when you enter the aquarium.

LEFT: fish at the London Aquarium.

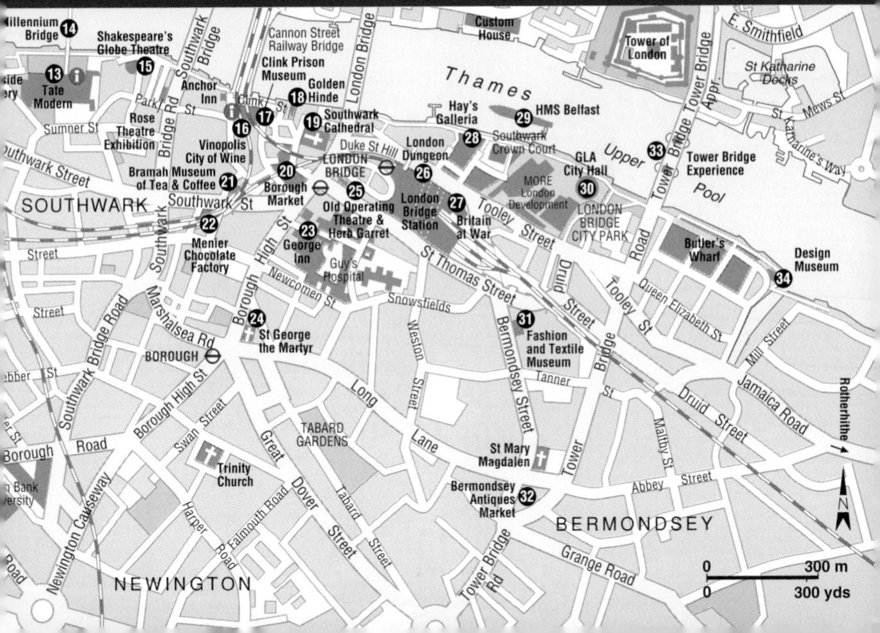

Millennium Bridge 14
Shakespeare's Globe Theatre 15
Tate Modern 13
Southwark Bridge
Cannon Street Railway Bridge
Clink Prison Museum
Golden Hinde 18
London Bridge
Custom House
Tower of London
Tower Bridge Appr.
E. Smithfield
St Katharine Docks
Thames
Anchor Inn
Rose Theatre Exhibition
Park St
Clink St
17
16
Southwark Cathedral 19
Hay's Galleria
HMS Belfast 29
Mews St
St Katharine's Way
Sumner St
Vinopolis City of Wine
Duke St Hill
London Dungeon 26
28 Southwark Crown Court
GLA City Hall
Upper Pool
33 Tower Bridge Experience
Southwark Street
Bramah Museum of Tea & Coffee 21
Bridge Rd
20 Borough Market
LONDON BRIDGE
25 Old Operating Theatre & Herb Garret
London Bridge Station 27
MORE London Development
30
LONDON BRIDGE CITY PARK
SOUTHWARK
Southwark St
22 Menier Chocolate Factory
23 George Inn
Britain at War
Tooley Street
Butler's Wharf
Design Museum 34
Street
Southwark
Borough High St
Guy's Hospital
Newcomen St
St Thomas Street
Druid Street
Tooley St
Queen Elizabeth St
Mill Street
Marshalsea Rd
24 St George the Martyr
Snowsfields
Weston Street
31 Fashion and Textile Museum
Bermondsey Street
Tanner St
Bridge
Jamaica Road
Druid Street
Rotherhithe
Southwark Bridge Road
BOROUGH
Borough High St
Long Lane
TABARD GARDENS
Tower Bridge Road
Maltby St
Swan Street
Great Dover Street
Borough Road
Trinity Church
St Mary Magdalen
Abbey Street
Falmouth Road
Tabard Street
Bermondsey Antiques Market 32
BERMONDSEY
Harper Road
Newington Causeway
Tower Bridge Rd
Grange Road
NEWINGTON
0 300 m
0 300 yds
N

At 450 ft (135 metres), the London Eye is the fourth highest structure in London. The hub and spindle weigh 330 tonnes – more than 40 double-decker buses. On average, a whopping 10,000 people take a "flight" on it every day – that's around 3.5 million people per year.

London Eye ❺

County Hall; www.londoneye.com
0870 5000 600 daily Oct–May 10am–8pm, Jun–Sep 10am–9pm
charge Waterloo

Towering over County Hall is the **London Eye**, the world's largest observation wheel, designed by architects David Marks and Julia Barfield for the turn of the millennium.

The 32 enclosed capsules take 30 minutes to make a full rotation – a speed slow enough to allow passengers to step in and out of the capsules while the wheel keeps moving. On a clear day, you can see for 25 miles (40 km). Book ahead (by phone or online) if you hope to ride the Eye at busy periods, although check the weather forecast first, if you can.

SOUTHBANK CENTRE ❻

The **Southbank Centre** (bookings tel: 0871 663 2500; www.southbankcentre.co.uk) is Europe's largest arts complex. Its policy of maintaining an "open foyer" means that its cafés, bars, book and record shops are open throughout the day.

Concert halls

The 2,900-seat **Royal Festival Hall** (RFH), the oldest and largest of the three concert halls on the South Bank, was constructed on the site of the Lion Brewery, destroyed by bombing during World War II. The building was opened in 1951 as part of the Festival of Britain, intended to improve the country's morale after years of post-war austerity. Reopened in 2007 after extensive renovation, the hall now has improved acoustics, better facilities in the foyer and a renovated restaurant, Skylon.

There are two other concerts halls within the complex, the 917-seater **Queen Elizabeth Hall**, opened in 1967 for music theatre and opera, and the 372-seater **Purcell Room**, intended for solo recitals and chamber music.

Hayward Gallery

Set on the upper level of the South Bank Centre complex is the **Hayward Gallery** (Mon, Thur, Sat, Sun 10am–6pm, Tue, Wed 10am–9pm, Fri 10am–9pm; tel: 0870 169 1000; www.haywardgallery.org.uk; charge), which

BELOW: spectacular views from the top of the London Eye. Each pod holds up to 25 people.

has changing exhibitions. Its cutting-edge programme focuses on four areas: single artists; artistic movements; other cultures; and contemporary themes. Recent exhibitions have focused on William Eggleston, Dan Flavin, Antony Gormley, Ray Lichtenstein and Sam Taylor Wood.

The Hayward's ambient, mirrored **Waterloo Sunset Pavilion**, designed by Dan Graham as part of the regeneration of the Southbank, remains open in between main exhibitions.

The **Neon Tower** on the roof of the gallery was commissioned in 1970 from Philip Vaughan and Roger Dainton for a kinetics exhibition. This Southbank landmark is composed of yellow, magenta, red, green and blue neon strips, which change according to the direction and velocity of the wind.

BFI Southbank

Next door is **BFI Southbank** (the former National Film Theatre, renovated and rebranded in March 2007), Britain's leading art house cinema since 1952. With three auditoria and an intimate studio cinema, it holds over 2,400 screenings and events each year, from restored silent movies (with live piano accompaniment) to world-cinema productions.

In 2007, following extensive renovation work, new areas of the building were opened, including a "Mediathèque", where visitors can browse the British Film Institute's archive for free; a studio cinema, for the screening of archive and contemporary film and talks; a research area; and a shop. The Film Café in front of the building, with trestle tables sheltering under Waterloo Bridge, is complemented by the chic Benugo Bar & Kitchen.

The revitalised Royal Festival Hall, a post-war addition to London, is one of the capital's finest concert halls. It is connected to the north bank of the Thames by the Hungerford Footbridge.

BELOW LEFT: the web of the London Eye. **BELOW:** second-hand bookstalls outside BFI Southbank.

The area around the Southbank Centre is great for free entertainment, from lunchtime concerts and "Commuter Jazz" (Friday 5.45–7pm) at the concert halls to talks at the National Theatre. Further along the river, there are often free concerts and talks at Tate Modern.

ABOVE RIGHT: the National Theatre.
BELOW RIGHT: the Oxo Tower.

The BFI also runs the **BFI London IMAX Cinema ❼**, which rises from the roundabout at the south end of Waterloo Bridge. Large-format film is projected onto a screen 66 ft high by 85 ft wide (20 by 26 metres), the biggest in the UK. It also specialises in screening films in 3-D.

THE NATIONAL THEATRE ❽

On the other side of **Waterloo Road**, still by the river, is the concrete **National Theatre** *(see page 299)*. Built largely by women during World War II and opened in 1976, it houses three theatres: the large 1,200-seater **Olivier**; the 900-seater **Lyttelton**, a two-tier proscenium theatre; and the **Cottesloe**, a more intimate space, accessed at the side of the building.

For a peek behind the scenes, book a one-hour backstage tour (Mon–Sat at 10.15am, 12.30pm – or 12.15pm on Olivier matinee days – and 5.15pm; tel: 7452 3400; charge).

At this point, a detour down Waterloo Road, past the IMAX cienema *(see above)*, leads to The Cut and the elegant **Old Vic Theatre ❾**, erected in 1811. A music hall in its early days, it became the first home of the National Theatre and is now a repertory theatre with Hollywood star Kevin Spacey as artistic director and musician Elton John as chairman.

Located a little further along The Cut is the **Young Vic ❿**, a theatre especially known for nurturing the talent of young theatre directors.

GABRIEL'S WHARF TO BANKSIDE

Back on the riverfront, to the east of the National Theatre, is **Gabriel's Wharf**, a cluster of shops and restaurants. East again is the Art Deco **Oxo**

The National Theatre

The idea of a National Theatre was suggested in 1848, but it wasn't until 1912, when Lilian Baylis became manager of the Old Vic Theatre that the basis for a National Theatre was established. Baylis turned the old Victorian music hall into "the home of Shakespeare and opera in English", but finding a site for a permanent theatre proved difficult. During World War II, the government introduced funding for the arts as part of the war effort, the London County Council made land available on the South Bank, and in 1949 the National Theatre Bill was passed through Parliament. In 1962 Laurence Olivier was named artistic director.

The Old Vic remained the company's home while the new theatre was being built, by architect Denys Lasdun. In 1976, after more than a century of controversy, the National Theatre was opened by the Queen, by which time Peter Hall was the director. He was succeeded by Richard Eyre in 1988 and Trevor Nunn in 1997. The current director, Nicholas Hytner, has had some success in broadening the theatre's appeal by offering some cheaper seats.

Recommended Restaurants, Bars & Cafés on pages 196–7

Tower ⓫. Architect Albert Moore had grand ideas for this project: as well as erecting what was to become London's second highest commercial building, he wanted to use electric lights to spell out the product's name. When planning permission was refused, due to an advertising ban, Moore came up with the idea of using three letters – O, X and O – as 10-ft (3-metre) high windows looking out north, south, east and west. Inside the tower are several smart restaurants.

Beyond Blackfriars Bridge, the riverside walk leads past the **Bankside Gallery** ⓬, home of the Royal Watercolour Society and the Royal Society of Painter-Printmakers.

Tate Modern ⓭

✉ Bankside; www.tate.org.uk
☎ 7887 8888 ⏲ Sun–Thur 10am–6pm, Fri–Sat 10am–10pm
£ free except special exhibitions
🚇 Southwark

Easily identifiable by its tall brick chimney, **Tate Modern** occupies the former Bankside Power Station and

houses the Tate's international modern art collection and part of its contemporary collection. The main entrance, to the west of the building, takes you onto the ground floor through a broad sweep of glass doors, then down a massive concrete ramp. The space in front of you is the Turbine Hall, the old boiler room, which is now used to house sculptural works. *(For full coverage, see pages 198–9.)*

TIP

A novel way to travel between Tate Modern and Tate Britain *(see page 78)* is to take the Tate Boat, It runs every 40 minutes during gallery hours and also stops at the London Eye.

Bankside Power Station – which, like Battersea Power Station, was designed by Sir Giles Gilbert Scott – opened in 1963 but generated electricity for only 30 years before being declared redundant.

ABOVE LEFT: Tate Modern. **BELOW:** the BFI London IMAX.

KIDS

On the third weekend in December, Bankside holds a Frost Fair (with an ice slide, stalls and free events at the Globe), inspired by the Frost Fairs of centuries past, held on the frozen Thames.

> *We wanted a platform, a flying carpet that is as thin as possible.*
>
> Roger Risdill-Smith, of Ove Arup and Partners, engineers of the Millennium Bridge

ABOVE RIGHT: *The Frozen Thames* (1677) by Abraham Hondius. **BELOW:** the Millennium Bridge.

Millennium Bridge ⓮

Giving easy access to Tate Modern from St Paul's Cathedral, the Millennium Bridge was the first new river crossing in central London since Tower Bridge opened in 1894.

Designing the footbridge was tricky: it had to be slender enough so as not to spoil the view of St Paul's from Bankside, yet it also had to make an impact as a significant millennial sculpture. The solution, a sort of stainless-steel scalpel, was provided by architect Norman Foster, sculptor Anthony Caro and engineers Ove Arup and Partners. However, opening-day crowds caused the bridge to sway excessively, and it had to be closed for two years of adjustments.

Shakespeare's Globe ⓯

✉ New Globe Walk; www.shakespeares-globe.org; ☎ box office: 7401 9918, tours: 7902 1500 ⏲ tours every 15–30 minutes £ charge for tours 🚇 London Bridge or Southwark

Bankside and Southwark are the most historic areas of the South Bank. They grew up in competition with the City opposite, but by the 16th century had become vice dens. Bankside was famous for brothels, bear- and bull-baiting, prize fights and the first playhouses, including the Globe.

The replica of the 1599 building opened in 1996 and is worth a visit even if you're not seeing a play. It has been painstakingly re-created using the original methods of construction. The season of the open-air galleried theatre runs from May to early October. It can accommodate around 1,500 people – 600 standing (and liable to get wet if it

Recommended Restaurants, Bars & Cafés on pages 196–7

rains) and the rest seated. The wooden benches feel rather hard by Act III, but you can bring or rent cushions.

Shakespeare's Globe Exhibition, to the right of the theatre, is well worth a visit. There are traditional displays, but touch screens and hands-on exhibits provide the fun element.

The Rose Theatre

Shakespeare also acted at the Rose Theatre, whose foundations were discovered close to the Globe in 1989. Turn down New Globe Walk (by the Globe's box office) and then left into Park Street. At No. 56, the **Rose Exhibition**, a sound-and-light show, tells the story of Bankside's first theatre, built in 1587.

BANKEND

Back on the riverside walk, past Southwark Bridge, on the stretch known as Bankend, is the **Anchor Inn**. The present building (1770–5) is the sole survivor of the 22 busy inns that once lined Bankside. Dr Samuel Johnson, of dictionary fame, drank here.

Vinopolis, City of Wine 16

1 Bank End; www.vinopolis.co.uk; 0870 444 4777 Mon, Thur, Fri, Sat noon–9pm, Wed and Sun noon–6pm; last tour 2 hours before closing charge London Bridge

Opposite the eastern side of the pub, occupying 2½ acres (1 hectare) of cathedral-like space under railway arches, the sprawling Vinopolis, City of Wine offers a visual wine tour through exhibits of the world's wine regions. Individual audio units give access to four hours of recorded commentary in six languages, and the admission charge to the wine tour includes tickets for five wine tastings.

Recent additions to the complex include an area on gin, courtesy of Bombay Sapphire, and a section on whisky. A branch of Southwark's tourist information office is also housed at Vinopolis.

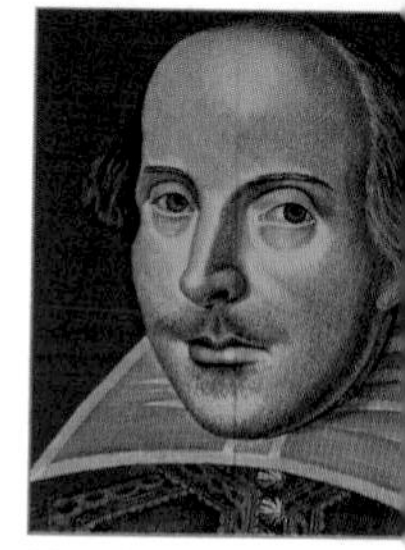

Note that there are no tours of Shakespeare's Globe theatre during performances. If you are visiting when a matinee is on, you will be given a tour of the Rose, Bankside's first playhouse, instead.

LEFT: signs at Vinopolis. **BELOW:** Shakespeare's Globe.

The Bishops of Winchester were the first authority in England to lock up miscreants. "In the clink", now a euphemism for being in jail, is thought to stem from the sound made by the clanking of the prisoners' chains. The bishops' prison operated from 1151 to 1780.

ABOVE RIGHT: remnant of Winchester Palace on Clink Street. **BELOW:** Southwark Cathedral. **BELOW RIGHT:** the *Golden Hinde.*

Clink Street

Like most country bishops, the bishops of the powerful see of Winchester had a London base. A single gable wall remains of **Winchester Palace**, their former London residence. They had their own laws, regulated the many local brothels and were the first authority in England to lock up miscreants. The prison they founded, in what is now Clink Street, remained a lock-up until the 18th century. The **Clink Prison Museum** ⓱ (Mon–Fri 10am–6pm, Sat–Sun until 9pm; tel: 7403 0900; www.clink.co.uk; charge) recalls the area's seedy past.

Clink Street leads on to Pickfords Wharf, built in 1864 for storing hops, flour and seeds, and now an apartment block. At the end of the street, in the **St Mary Overie Dock**, is a replica of Sir Francis Drake's splendid galleon, the ***Golden Hinde*** ⓲ (daily 10am–6pm; tel: 0870 011 8700; www.goldenhinde.org; charge).

Launched in 1973, the ship is the only replica to have completed a circumnavigation of the globe, thus

clocking up more nautical miles than the original, in which Drake set sail on his voyage of discovery in 1577.

Southwark Cathedral ⓳

London Bridge; www.southwark.anglican.org/cathedral 7367 6700 Mon–Fri 7.30am–6pm, Sat, Sun 8.30am–6pm free London Bridge

Southwest of London Bridge and hemmed in by the railway, Southwark Cathedral is a rich fund of local history. A memorial to Shakespeare in the south aisle, paid for by public subscription in 1912, shows

Recommended Restaurants, Bars & Cafés on pages 196–7

the bard reclining in front of a frieze of 16th-century Bankside. Above it is a modern (1954) stained-glass window depicting characters from his plays. Shakespeare was a parishioner for several years. John Harvard, who gave his name to the American university, was baptised here, and is commemorated in the Harvard Chapel.

The cathedral holds free organ recitals every Monday (1.10–1.50pm) and free classical concerts on Tuesday (3.15–4pm).

BOROUGH

The area around London Bridge is in the throes of a regeneration programme. Much of its Dickensian character lingers, adding greatly to its appeal. In addition to Borough Market, there are several quirky museums and many restaurants, cafés and specialist shops.

Borough Market ⑳

Southwark Street; www.boroughmarket.org.uk 7407 1002 Thur 11am–5pm, Fri noon–6pm, Sat 9am–4pm London Bridge

The highlight of the area is Borough Market, a wholesale food market dating from the 13th century. On Thursday, Friday and Saturday (the last two are the busiest days) a popular retail market offers gourmet and organic products. Apart from basics such as fruit and vegetables, bread and cheese, you will find stalls specialising in seafood, game, dried fruits and nuts, oils and vinegars, cakes, preserves, fresh pasta, juices, ecologically sound goods, wines and beers.

Southwark Street

A brief diversion down Southwark Street, past the splendid Victorian **Hop Exchange** (now offices), is the **Bramah Tea and Coffee Museum** ㉑ (daily 10am–6pm; 40 Southwark Street; tel: 7403 5650; www.teaandcoffeemuseum.co.uk; charge), which gives a history of the long-established trade in London. You can sample tea and coffee in the café at the front.

Opposite is the **Menier Chocolate Factory** ㉒ (51–3 Southwark Street; www.menierchocolatefactory.com; box office: 7907 7060), a theatre, gallery and restaurant housed within an 1870s chocolate factory.

Borough High Street

Situated on Borough High Street, the main road south from London Bridge, is the 17th-century **George Inn** ㉓ (No. 77), the only remaining galleried coaching inn in London and mentioned in Dickens's *Little Dorrit*. Further down the street is the renovated **Church of St George the Martyr** ㉔ (www.stgeorgethemartyr.com), also known as "Little Dorrit's Church", because Dickens's heroine was baptised and married there. There are free recitals at 1pm on Thursdays.

LONDON BRIDGE AREA

Back towards London Bridge, at 9a St Thomas Street, is the **Old Operating Theatre Museum & Herb Garret** ㉕ (daily 10.30am–5pm; tel: 7188

FOOD

There are lots of opportunities to sample the produce for free at Borough Market. Many stalls also do takeaway food, from venison burgers to scallops that are pan-fried while you wait. For a posh sit-down meal, try Roast *(see page 196)*, on the first floor; breakfast (Mon–Fri till 9.30am, later at weekends) is a great way to enjoy the up-market dining experience at a fraction of the cost of lunch or dinner.

RIGHT: *Golden Hinde* figurehead. **BELOW:** Borough Market.

KIDS

The tour of the **London Dungeon** begins with an obligatory photo opportunity – head in the stocks, a blackened chopper at your neck. It's lots of fun for kids who are keen on the macabre, but it is pretty scary and the entire visit is spent in darkened corridors (often made more atmospheric by bloodcurdling shrieks), so it's not recommended for children under eight. Even under-15s must be accompanied by an adult. Queues tend to be long, so book in advance.

RIGHT: asking for information at the London Dungeon.
BELOW: HMS *Belfast*.

2679; www.thegarret.org.uk), the only surviving 19th-century operating theatre in Britain. It offers insights into the fearsome medical techniques of the day. The Herb Garret displays herbs and equipment used in the preparation of medicines.

Tooley Street attractions

Parallel to the river, on Tooley Street, is the **London Dungeon** ㉖ (daily Sep–Jun 10am–5.30pm, July, Aug 9.30am–6.30pm; 28–34 Tooley St; tel: 7403 7221; www.thedungeons.com). Lasting about 1½ hours, the actor-led tour features ghoulish exhibits of the Black Death, the Great Fire of 1666, Jack the Ripper's exploits, Sweeney Todd the barber's gruesome deeds, a boat ride to hell, in which visitors pass through Traitors' Gate before being condemned at court, and Extremis, a fairly hair-raising ride.

Nearby **Winston Churchill's Britain at War Museum** ㉗ (Oct–Mar 10am–5pm, Apr–Sep 10am–6pm, last entry 1 hour before closing; www.britainatwar.co.uk; charge) recreates the sounds and smells of the Blitz.

Opposite is **Hay's Galleria** ㉘, a setting for shops, craft stalls and restaurants. The 60-ft (18-metre) kinetic sculpture in the centre is David Kemp's *The Navigators*.

HMS *Belfast* ㉙

Downstream from Hay's Galleria is HMS *Belfast*, the last of the warships to have seen action in World War II (Mar–Oct 10am–6pm, Nov–Feb 10am–5pm; tel: 7940 6300; charge; http://hmsbelfast.iwm.org.uk). Its tour ranges from the bridge to the engine rooms, capturing the cramped facilities of its 950-man crew.

To its east, the oval-shaped glass building is **City Hall** ㉚, seat of the Greater London Authority, the body that governs London. In front is **The**

London Bridge

The present London Bridge, dating from 1967–72, is the latest of many on this site. Until Westminster Bridge was opened in 1750, the crossing here was the only bridge across the Thames in London. A wooden bridge had existed here since the Romans, but the first stone bridge, later lined with houses, shops and a chapel, was erected in 1176. In 1823–31 a new bridge of five stone arches was built, but in 1972, having been sold to American businessman Robert P. McCulloch for US$2.46 million, it was dismantled and re-erected at Lake Havasu in Arizona. Some claimed that McCulloch bought London Bridge in error, thinking that it was the much grander Tower Bridge. He denied this.

Recommended Restaurants, Bars & Cafés on pages 196–7

Scoop, a sunken amphitheatre staging free theatre in spring and summer.

Bermondsey Street

A 10-minute detour southeast leads to hip Bermondsey Street, where, at No. 83, you can't miss the pink-and-orange **Fashion and Textile Museum** ㉛ (www.ftmlondon.org; tel: 7407 8664), the creation of British designer Zandra Rhodes. It celebrates fashion via exhibitions and its own academy.

At the other end of the street, on Friday morning only, is **Bermondsey Antiques Market** ㉜. Arrive early (ie by 9am) if you want a bargain.

TOWER BRIDGE ㉝

Dating from 1894 the Victorian Gothic **Tower Bridge** is one of London's most iconic structures. Despite its mock-medieval cladding, it contains 11,000 tons of steel, and sophisticated engineering raises its middle portion to allow tall ships through. When the capital was a flourishing port, it opened several times a day. In 1954 a bus driver was awarded a medal for putting his foot on the accelerator when, to his horror, he saw the bridge yawn open before him. The bus leapt over a 3-ft (1-metre) gap. These days the bridge opens around 500 times a year, with its bascules taking 90 seconds to lift fully.

The structure contains **Tower Bridge Experience** (Apr–Sep 10am–6.30pm, Nov–Mar 9.30am–6pm; tel: 7403 3761; www.towerbridge.org.uk; charge), an exhibition detailing the history of the bridge and explaining how the mechanism works. The view from Tower Bridge's high walkways on the Catwalk is magnificent.

Around Butlers Wharf

The old warehouses east of Tower Bridge contain a gourmet's delight. The gourmet in question is Habitat founder Sir Terence Conran, who has opened up several restaurants in the biscuit-coloured **Butlers Wharf**.

The adjacent **Design Museum** ㉞ (daily 10am–5.45pm; tel: 0870 833 9955; www.designmuseum.org; charge), inspired by Conran, showcases influential (mainly 20th-century) design through its permanent collection and excellent changing exhibitions. ❑

Further east along the south bank from Tower Bridge and the Design Museum is Rotherhithe, which has several good traditional pubs, including the Mayflower, where the Pilgrim Fathers moored their ship before sailing to Plymouth and America in 1620. The Anglo-American spirit remains: the pub sells US as well as English stamps.

BELOW: Tower Bridge raised to let through a large vessel.

BEST RESTAURANTS, BARS AND CAFÉS

Restaurants

Prices for a three-course dinner per person with a half-bottle of house wine:

£ = under £20
££ = £20–30
£££ = £30–50
££££ = over £50

British

Chop House
Butlers Wharf Building, 36e Shad Thames, SE1 ☎ 7403 3403 ◷ L & D daily **£££**, (set menu) **££££** [p 333, E4]
Carnivores should go straight for the roast sucking pig with tangy apple sauce and lots of crackling. For non-meat eaters there are fish dishes too. Other attractions include great river views and a pleasant terrace.

Roast
Floral Hall, Stoney St, SE1 ☎ 7940 1300 ◷ B & L daily, D Mon–Sat. **£££/££££** set meal (L Mon–Fri) **££** [p 333, D4]
Spectacularly set on the upper floor of Borough Market, with gorgeous views through vast windows. Sourced from the market, the excellent food is resolutely British. Enticing breakfasts.

Fish

fish!
Cathedral St, SE1 ☎ 7407 3803 ◷ L & D daily. **£££** [p 333, D4]
Specialises in tasty GM-free fish in the shadow of Southwark Cathedral. Bar seats are fun but noisy.

Livebait
43 The Cut, SE1 ☎ 7928 7211 ◷ L & D Mon–Sat. **£££** [p 332, B4 off map]
Luvvies from the Old and Young Vic theatres cram into the cool, all-over tiled rooms for good fish prepared in creative ways. The best choices, however, are the simplest ones – the grilled dishes.

Masters Super Fish
191 Waterloo Rd, SE1 ☎ 7928 6924 ◷ L & D Tue–Sat, D only Mon. **£** [p 329, E4 off map]
Need a taxi? You'll find cabbies galore tucking into huge portions of fish and chips in this old-fashioned eatery.

French

RSJ
33a Coin St, SE1 ☎ 7928 4554 ◷ L & D Mon–Fri; D only Sat **££–£££** [p 329, E3]
This pretty restaurant offers pleasant dishes such as Gressingham duck with beetroot salad, but the real attraction is the excellent selection of wines from the Loire.

Modern European

The Anchor and Hope
36 The Cut, SE1 ☎ 7928 9898 ◷ L & D daily. **££** [p 332, B4 off map]
Meat and offal feature strongly on the gastro-pub menu. Reasonable prices, hefty portions and friendly staff. The no-booking policy can mean long queues.

Cantina Vinopolis
1 Bank End, SE1 ☎ 7940 8333 ◷ L & D Mon–Sat. **£££** [p 333, C4]
Full marks to the wine (over 150 choices) at the restaurant in London's only wine museum. Then comes the decor – soaring cathedral-style arches. Appealing menu, too.

Delfina
50 Bermondsey St, SE1 ☎ 7357 0244 ◷ L Mon–Fri, D Fri. **££–£££** [p 333, D4, off map]
Lunchtime creatives flock to this light, airy restaurant for well-prepared dishes and the calm atmosphere. Upstairs are artists' studios, and artworks adorn the restaurant's walls.

Oxo Tower
Oxo Tower Wharf, Barge House St, SE1 ☎ 7803 3888. ◷ L & D daily. **££££** [p 332, B4]
Some find it overpriced, but this iconic spot is still hugely popular. The biggest draw is the fabulous view of the Thames through huge windows.

LEFT: Roast. **ABOVE RIGHT:** Cantina Vinopolis.

Le Pont de la Tour

Butlers Wharf Building, 36d Shad Thames, SE1 7403 8403 L & D daily. **££££** [p 333, E4]

Prime ministers and presidents have enjoyed the splendid view of Tower Bridge from this upmarket Conran restaurant, where the stress is on seafood. Impeccable but very expensive.

Southwark Cathedral Refectory

Southwark Cathedral, London Bridge, SE1 7407 5740 L daily. **£–££** [p 333, D4]

The restaurant at the back of the cathedral does hearty, well-priced soups and main dishes. The terrace is a bonus in summer. Also open for morning coffee and afternoon tea (10am–5pm).

Tate Modern, Café 7

Bankside, SE1 7401 5018 L daily, D Fri–Sat (last order 9.30pm). **£££** [p 332, C4]

Great views, a buzz and an arty crowd are the attractions here. Level 2 Café is nice for lunch, too, but lacks the views.

Others

Baltic

74 Blackfriars Rd, SE1 7928 1111 L & D daily. **£££** [p 332, B4 off map]

A cool bar filled with media types leads to the skylit dining room. The menu features dishes such as roast pork and spiced meatballs. Alternatively, try vodka and blinis at the bar.

Mesón Don Felipe

53 The Cut, SE1 7928 3237 L & D Mon–Sat, D only Sun. **££** [p 332, B4 off map]

Londoners in the know flock to this excellent tapas bar. Tables fill up fast, but there's often room at the bar. The juicy fresh anchovies are particularly scrumptious.

Tapas Brindisa

18–20 Southwark St, SE1 7357 8880 B Fri, Sat, L & D Mon–Sat. **£££** [p 333, D4]

The sleek restaurant connected to one of the most popular stalls in the market is usually packed. Authentic tapas and a buzzing ambience. The only downside is that you can't reserve, so expect a wait at the bar.

Tas

33 The Cut, SE1 7928 2111 L & D daily. **££** [p 332, B4 off map]

A local favourite and good for vegetarians. It's easy to go overboard on the *meze*, so save room for the equally tasty mains. Branches at 72 Borough High St (7403 7200) and 20–2 New Globe Walk (7633 9777).

Cafés and Bars

In Chaucer's *Canterbury Tales*, the Miller states, "And if the words get muddled in my tale, just put it down to too much Southwark ale." Sobriety has never been a characteristic of this area, which still has many pubs. The **George Inn** *(77 Borough High St)*, owned by the National Trust, is London's only galleried coaching inn. The **Market Porter** *(9 Stoney St)* is famous for opening its doors 6–8.30am for Borough Market workers.

For a traditional wine bar, try the **Boot and Flogger** *(10–20 Redcross Way; closes 8pm)*, named after a corking device. Reminiscent of a gentleman's club, it trades as a Free Vintner, meaning that it does not have to have a licence.

Other good places to drink include the Old Vic theatre's **Pit Bar** *(The Cut; closed Sun)*, which opens late. The **Wine Wharf** *(Stoney St; closed Sun)*, part of the Vinopolis, offers great wines and light meals, while next door the **Brew Wharf** has a micro-brewery and does gastropub-style food.

For cafés, try **Monmouth Coffee Co.** *(Stoney St)*, **Konditor & Cook** *(22 Cornwall Rd and 10 Stoney St)* or the café in **Bramah Tea and Coffee Musum** on Southwark Street *(see picture above)*.

Tate Modern

Once it generated electricity. Now it is is a powerhouse of modern and contemporary art

Tate Modern has caught the public's imagination in a quite unprecedented way, both for its displays and its building, a magnificent presence on the South Bank. In 1998 the decision was taken to transform the redundant Bankside Power Station, a massive horizontal block with a huge central tower, into a gallery showcasing the Tate's collection of modern and contemporary art.

Machinery from within the power station was removed to create an entrance the height of the building; three gallery floors, shops and cafés, a restaurant and an auditorium were piled into a compact bank on one side. Visitors pour into the museum down a huge ramp, which is part of the towering Turbine Hall, used to accommodate large-scale installations.

On the way round visitors can enjoy views into the Turbine Hall from the mezzanine bridge on level 2 and various gallery levels. Between the two suites on each of the gallery floors is seating where one can rest, read, and watch the boats go by on the Thames.

Above: *Whaam!* by Roy Lichtenstein (1923–97), on show at Tate Modern. Lichtenstein's interest in Americana dated from the early 1950s, but his involvement in pop art received a crucial boost from one of his young sons, who showed him a Mickey Mouse comic book and said: "I bet you can't paint as good as that."

Left: *Lobster Telephone* by Salvador Dalí (1904–89). Fans of Dalí's can view a lot more of his work, as well as information about the artist himself, at the Dalí Universe exhibition, close by in County Hall *(see page 185)*.

Above: the Turbine Hall is used to display large-scale, specially commissioned works that are financed by Unilever. Past projects include Carsten Holler's crowd-pleasing *Test Site* (2006), a series of large-scale, covered slides.

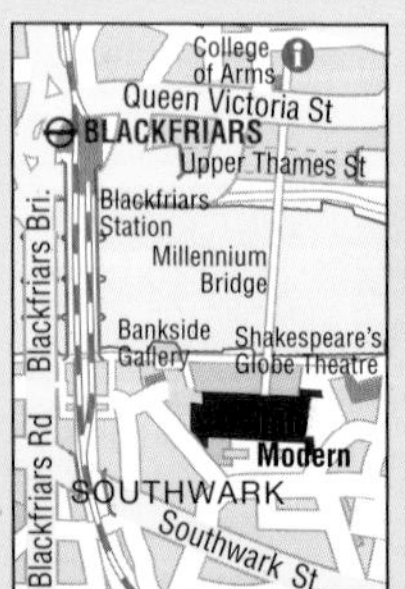

The essentials

Bankside; www.tate.org.uk
7887 8888
Sun–Thur 10am–6pm, Fri–Sat 10am–10pm
free except special exhibitions
Southwark or London Bridge

ABOVE: Kandinsky's *Swinging* (1925), in Ideas and Objects on Level 5. Kandinsky began his artistic career as a figurative landscape painter in Russia, but moved towards abstraction through the influence of German Expressionism. He used colour for emotional effect. Also in Tate Modern's permanent collection is Kandinsky's *Cossacks* (1910–11).

THE COLLECTION

In order to make the permanent collection more accessible to, and more popular with, the general public, the works are ordered by theme. Note that the displays change from time to time, so the examples picked out here may not all be on show when you visit.

The permanent collection is hung in four suites, over two floors. On level 3 are "Material Gestures" and " Poetry and Dream". The former covers post-war European and American painting and sculpture, and includes work by Anish Kapoor, Barnett Newman, Claude Monet and Tacita Dean, while "Poetry and Dream" focuses on Surrealism, thus embracing the work of artists from Juan Miró, Max Ernst and Salvador Dalí to Francis Bacon, Joseph Beuys and Gillian Wearing. On level 5 are "Idea and Object" and "States of Flux", with the former showcasing minimalist or conceptual art works by such artists as Martin Creed, Sol LeWitt, Dan Flavin and Gary Hill. "States of Flux" is devoted to Cubism, Futurism and Vorticism, with work by Georges Braque, Paul Cézanne, Fernand Léger, Roy Lichtenstein, Martin Parr, Tomoko Takahashi and Richard Hamilton.

ABOVE: *Little Dancer Aged Fourteen* by Edgar Degas (1834–1917). The original wax version outraged propriety when first exhibited in Paris in 1881.

BELOW: power station turned art gallery.

The Imperial War Museum

It vividly chronicles a century of conflict around the world

The building that now houses the Imperial War Museum opened in 1815 as Bethlem Royal Hospital for the insane, popularly known as Bedlam. After the hospital moved out of London in the 1930s, the central block of the building was turned over to the Great War collection of the Imperial War Museum, previously housed in South Kensington. The former psychiatric hospital was an inspired choice for a museum chronicling the horrors of modern warfare.

After World War II the museum began to gather material from this and later conflicts, and three smaller sites, including the warship HMS *Belfast* *(see page 194)*, were acquired.

Over the past 10 years, the museum has expanded its remit from the purely military to include a rolling programme of exhibitions covering many aspects of modern history, some only loosely connected with conflict – from code breaking and refugees to fashion and sport.

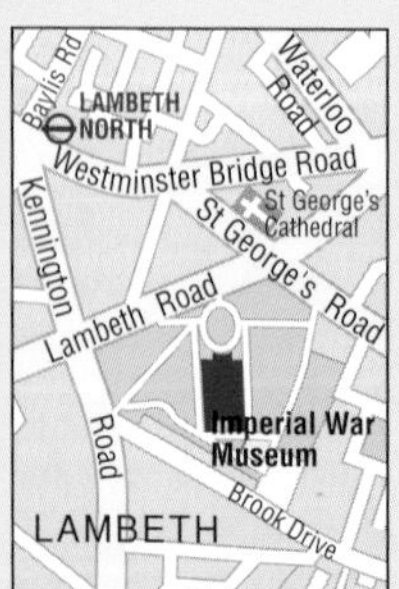

The essentials

Lambeth Road; www.iwm.org.uk
7416 5320
daily 10am–6pm
free except for some special exhibitions
Elephant & Castle, Lambeth North

Above: the Imperial War Museum, formerly Bethlem Royal Hospital.

Left: Some parts of the museum are harrowing and not recommended for young children. The **Holocaust Exhibition**, built around the testimonies of survivors and with many poignant exhibits, has a lower age limit of 13.

Below: the details of the trench warfare of World War I are imaginatively conveyed in the "Trench Experience".

MUSEUM LAYOUT

Imperial War Museum

This floor plan will help you find your way around the Museum. You will find further information on your ticket and there are direction signs on all floors to temporary as well as permanent exhibitions.

4 Crimes against humanity

3 Holocaust exhibition

2 Art galleries
John Singer Sargent room
Temporary exhibition

1 Large exhibits
Secret War
Victoria Cross and George Cross

G Large exhibits
Temporary exhibitions
Information and ticket desk
Shop and café

Main entrance

LG Historical displays
Trench Experience
Blitz Experience

West entranc

As you enter the main hall, your direction will depend on where your interest lies. The stairs at the back of the **Large Exhibits Gallery** lead down to exhibitions on the two world wars. Here artefacts, art, photography, film and sound recordings weave an atmosphere as close as possible to the mood of the time, while interactive screens give access to further information. Upstairs is an extension of the Large Exhibits Gallery. The fascinating **Secret War** exhibit on counter-intelligence is also on this floor.

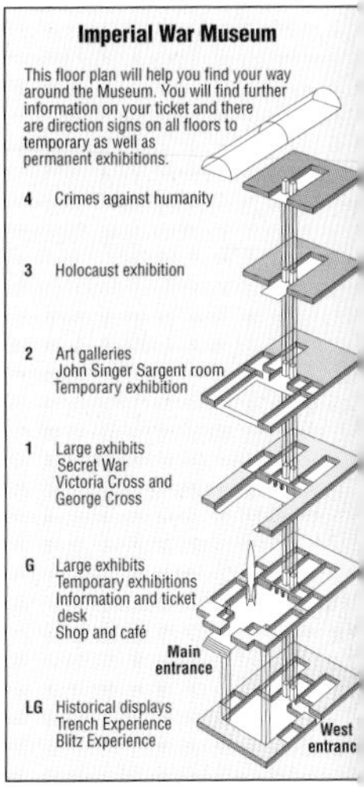

The second floor holds one of Britain's leading collections of **20th-century art** – the World War I gallery is to the right; World War II to the left. Many of the works were officially commissioned for propaganda purposes, including the famous painting *Gassed* in the **John Singer Sargent** room. The top floors house the **Holocaust Exhibition** and the room entitled **Crimes against humanity**.

ABOVE weapons and vehicles are displayed in the Large Exhibits Gallery.
LEFT: the museum runs an interesting programme of temporary exhibitions. The Children's War, running for three years to mark the 60th anniversary of the end of World War II, documents the plight of youngsters during the war. On the left is four-year-old Jeannie Lebby celebrating VE Day on 8 May 1945.

BRITISH
ISLANDS
LITTLE SECRETS
www.caribbean.co.uk
WiFi Zone

Recommended Restaurants, Bars & Cafés on pages 212–13

KNIGHTSBRIDGE, KENSINGTON AND NOTTING HILL

Wealthy and elegant, Knightsbridge and Kensington have long been the London home of the British upper classes, and the areas' cultural attractions reflect their dilettantish interests. Neighbouring Notting Hill Gate is more diverse and younger, with more edge

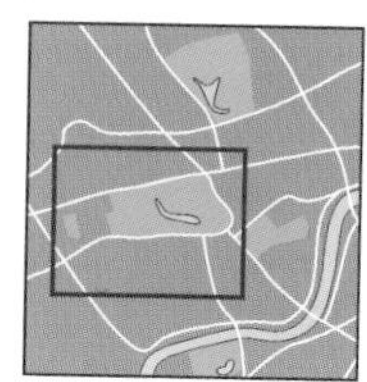

Main attractions

- APSLEY HOUSE
- HARRODS
- VICTORIA AND ALBERT MUSEUM
- NATURAL HISTORY MUSEUM
- SCIENCE MUSEUM
- ROYAL ALBERT HALL
- ALBERT MEMORIAL
- KENSINGTON SQUARE
- HOLLAND PARK
- NOTTING HILL
- PORTOBELLO ROAD MARKET
- KENSINGTON PALACE
- KENSINGTON GARDENS
- HYDE PARK

These three areas of London encompass many of its best features; Knightsbridge has grand architecture, designer shops and two of London's top department stores; Kensington is home to three world-class museums and Queen Victoria's monuments to her husband Prince Albert; while Notting Hill Gate, the stamping ground of the young, hip and famous, has Portobello Road, one of London's funkiest street markets.

In the heart of all this is a huge area of parkland, where you can skate, jog, hire a boat or just stroll around and forget you're in the city, and throughout the area are pretty cobbled mews and squares lined with elegant town houses that make venturing off the main streets rewarding.

This chapter begins at Hyde Park Corner, proceeds via Knightsbridge to Kensington and Notting Hill Gate, and then dips into Kensington Gardens and Hyde Park.

HYDE PARK CORNER

At the junction of Piccadilly, Park Lane and Knightsbridge, **Hyde Park Corner** is a major hub of traffic now, but it used to stand on the outskirts of London.

LEFT: Harvey Nichols in Knightsbridge is renowned for its window displays.
RIGHT: Apsley House at Hyde Park Corner.

Apsley House ❶

149 Piccadilly, Hyde Park Corner; www.english-heritage.org.uk 7499 5676 Tue–Sun 10am–5pm, Nov–Mar till 4pm charge Hyde Park Corner

The mansion on the northern side of Hyde Park Corner is known colloquially as No. 1, London, as it was the first house you came to after passing through the tollgates at the top of Knightsbridge. Built in 1770 by Robert Adam, and bought by

You can take a lift inside Wellington Arch up to the galleried balconies, from where there are good views all around, including into the gardens of Buckingham Palace.

Arthur Wellesley, the first Duke of Wellington, in 1816, just after he had defeated Napoleon at Waterloo, it is still lived in by the Wellington family. Inside are collections of furniture, silver and porcelain, and paintings by Velázquez, Rubens, Van Dyck and Goya. Among its sculptures is a huge nude of Napoleon by Canova.

Wellington Arch ❷ (Wed–Sun 10am–5pm, until 4pm Nov–Mar; may close for functions so ring ahead, tel: 7930 2726; charge), in the middle of Hyde Park Corner, was designed in 1828 as part of a grand approach to London. The huge bronze statue of a charioteer and four horses (the *Quadriga*) depicts the angel of peace descending on the chariot of war.

KNIGHTSBRIDGE

Running west of Hyde Park Corner is Knightsbridge, where you'll find two of London's most famous stores: Harrods and Harvey Nichols.

Harvey Nichols ❸, well known for its innovative window displays, opened on the corner of Knightsbridge and Sloane Street in the 1880s; with eight floors of fashion, beauty and home collections, it caters to a discerning – and affluent – clientele. The Fifth Floor is a very smart place to eat *(see page 213)*.

Harrods ❹

✉ 87–135 Brompton Road; www.harrods.com ☎ 7730 1234 ◷ Mon–Sat 10am–8pm, Sun noon–6pm Ⓤ Knightsbridge

Nearby in Brompton Road, **Harrods** is hard to miss, especially at night when it is brightly illuminated. The food hall is ornately decorated and sells a wide range of gourmet items; it's worth looking, even if you only come out with a tin of speciality tea. The store's January sales are famous events, when the English lose their dignity in the scramble to save hundreds of pounds.

Knightsbridge, Kensington and Notting Hill

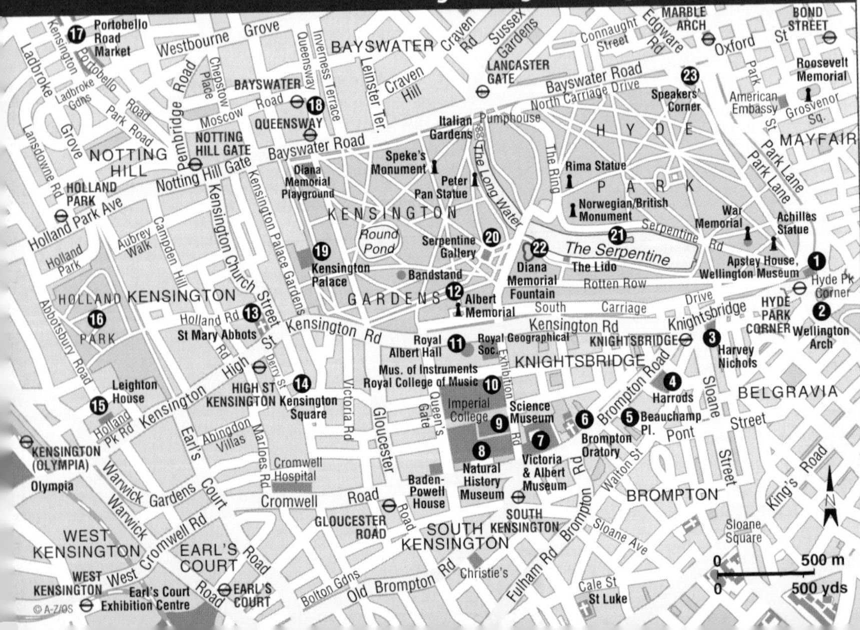

The store was started by Henry Charles Harrod when his grocery business opened in 1849, although the present building was opened in 1905. The Egyptian Al-Fayed brothers bought the store and other House of Fraser outlets for £615 million in 1983, and the flamboyant Mohamed Al-Fayed (whose son Dodi died with Princess Diana in the 1997 Paris car crash) still owns the store.

Beauchamp Place ❺ (pronounced *Beecham*), a stylish street west of Harrods lined with designer stores and expensive restaurants, is the stamping ground of the well-heeled, including sundry royals.

Beyond Harrods, at the point where Brompton Road branches left, is the **Brompton Oratory** ❻ (daily 6.30am–8pm), a flamboyant Italian baroque building designed by a 29-year-old country-dwelling architect, Herbert Gribble. Opened in 1884, its wide nave, huge dome, extravagant decor and lavishly gilded mosaics are seldom seen in British churches.

SOUTH KENSINGTON

South Kensington exudes affluence; Christie's has an auction house here, in Old Brompton Road, and there are designer shops and up-market restaurants.

It's also very cosmopolitan: the Lycée Français is at 35 Cromwell Road, teaching the children of the many French people who live in the area, and the German Goethe Institute is in Princes Gate.

Three Victorian museums

At the heart of South Kensington are three world-class museums: The Victoria and Albert Museum, The Natural History Museum and the Science Museum, which owe their existence to the spirit and enterprise of the Victorian age. In 1851, the Great Exhibition, held in Hyde Park, was an astonishing success. For the first time elements of the far-flung Victorian Empire were brought under the curious gaze of the public. The idea for the exhibition had come from Henry Cole (1808–82), chairman of the Society of Arts, and it had been taken up enthusiastically by Prince Albert.

More than 6 million visitors came to the park to see the Crystal Palace, and after it moved to Sydenham, south London, the following year, the profits were used to purchase

A cabmen's shelter in front of the V&A Museum, one of 13 still dotted around London. Now Grade II-listed, they provide shelter and refreshment to cab drivers.

LEFT: Harrods fashion. **BELOW:** Harrods lights up at night.

Figures in the Cast Court at the V&A.

87 acres (35 hectares) of land in adjoining South Kensington to build a more permanent home for the arts and sciences.

Greatest of them all is undoubtedly the **Victoria and Albert Museum ❼**, popularly known as the V&A, which Henry Cole began assembling the year after the Great Exhibition, though Queen Victoria did not lay the foundation stone of the current building until 1899, 38 years after Albert was dead. It was the first museum to be gas-lit, allowing working people to visit in the evening after finishing their jobs. *For a detailed guide to its collections, see pages 216–17.*

On the other side of Exhibition Road is the neo-Gothic pile of the **Natural History Museum ❽**, built between 1873 and 1880. With its collection of 75 million plants, animals, fossils, rocks and minerals and, of course, its dinosaurs, it is justly celebrated and a big hit with children. *For details, see pages 218–19.*

The **Science Museum ❾**, round the corner in Exhibition Road, traces the history of inventions from the first steam train – Stephenson's Rocket – to the battered command module from the Apollo 10 space mission, and is a particular favourite of children. The Wellcome Wing focuses on contemporary science and technology. *See pages 214–15 for more details.*

On the corner of Queen's Gate Terrace, opposite the Natural History Museum, is **Baden-Powell House,** with a statue of the Boy Scouts' founder standing on watch outside. It is now a budget hostel, but there is a small exhibition area dedicated to Lord Baden-Powell (1857–1941).

RIGHT: detail on the intricately carved stonework of the Natural History Museum.
BELOW LEFT: courtyard of the Victoria and Albert Museum.
BELOW RIGHT: Natural History Museum.

Recommended Restaurants, Bars & Cafés on pages 212–13

Music and geography

Further up Exhibition Road, on Prince Consort Road, is the **Royal College of Music**, containing the **Museum of Instruments** ❿ (Tue–Fri 2–4.30pm in term time and summer holidays only; tel: 7591 4346, www. cph.rcm.ac.uk), a collection of over 800 instruments from 1480 to the present.

On the corner of Exhibition Road and Kensington Gore is the **Royal Geographical Society** (Mon–Fri 10am–5pm; tel: 7591 3000; www. rgs.org). Exhibitions are held in the new extension, and for a small fee you can visit the library, which holds many antiquarian maps.

Royal Albert Hall ⓫

Kensington Gore; www.royal alberthall.com 7589 8212 (tickets and tours) South Kensington

The **Royal Albert Hall**, an ornate building with a capacity of 8,000, was built in 1871 in honour of Prince Albert. The frieze around the outside illustrates "The Triumph of Arts and Sciences". Events here range from boxing to rock concerts, but the hall is best known for the Proms, a series of BBC-sponsored classical concerts. Named after the promenading audience, who have the option of standing or sitting on the floor, they provide a rich diet of affordable music.

Queen Victoria's most expressive tribute to her husband is the **Albert Memorial** ⓬ in Kensington Gardens, opposite the Albert Hall. Designed by Sir George Gilbert Scott, it depicts the prince as a god or philosopher, clutching in his right hand the catalogue of the Great Exhibition which he masterminded. Marking the corners of the monument are symbols for the spread of the British Empire: a camel for Africa, a bull bison for America, an elephant for Asia and a cow for Europe (Australia, then the Empire's dumping ground for convicts, failed to merit a mention).

In a 1960s building next door to the Albert Hall is the **Royal College of Art**, where annual graduation exhibitions allow the public to buy the works of future greats. David Hockney and Henry Moore studied here.

The Albert Memorial has been restored to its former gilded – some say gaudy – glory.

BELOW LEFT: Prince Albert. **BELOW:** frieze running around the Albert Hall.

Prince Albert

Albert of Saxe-Coburg-Gotha, born in Germany in 1819, was Queen Victoria's first cousin. When they married in 1839, both aged 20, his English was limited, but he worked to improve it. He enjoyed hunting and winter sports, and was a family man, siring nine children. His great interest in the sciences and the natural world made him a typical Victorian and he was largely responsible for establishing the museums in South Kensington. Victoria was shattered when he died in 1861, and she spent the next 40 years in mourning.

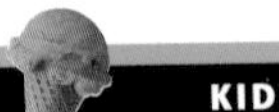

KIDS

Holland Park is great for kids. As well as the wildlife – rabbits, squirrels and peacocks – there is an adventure playground (for ages 6–15 approximately), and a smaller sand pit play area for children under 8. After they've let off steam, take them to the Japanese garden, which has a waterfall and stepping stones.

Kensington High Street

Kensington Gore runs into Kensington High Street, a useful shopping area, more compact and stylish than Oxford Street but with most of the big-name stores and fewer people. **Kensington Church Street**, branching off to the right towards Notting Hill Gate, is the place for antiques. On the corner behind the flower stall stands **St Mary Abbots Church** ⓭, designed by Victorian architect Sir George Gilbert Scott, and a fine example of Victorian Gothic Revival. Walk through the cloisters to reach St Mary Abbots Gardens, a quiet spot away from the crowds. To the right, Kensington Church Walk is lined with exclusive boutiques. At the top, Holland Street, running off Kensington Church Street, has designer shops and a pretty pub, the Elephant and Castle.

Back on Kensington High Street, go down Derry Street to the entrance to the **Roof Gardens** (tel: 7937 7994; Mon–Fri, tel: 7368 3993 Sat–Sun), a members' club and restaurant (Babylon, *see page 213*), six storeys above street level. With 1½ acres of ornamental gardens and views over west London, this is one of the most original places to eat in the city. The gardens are open every day if there is not a function on – call ahead to check.

Further down Derry Street is **Kensington Square** ⓮, one of the oldest in London, and an elegant mix of architectural styles dating from the late 17th century. The Pre-Raphaelite painter Edward Burne-Jones lived at No. 41, and the philosopher John Stuart Mill, another eminent Victorian, at No. 18.

RIGHT: detail of an Islamic tile in Leighton House Museum.
BELOW: Edward Burne-Jones's house in Kensington Square.

At the other end of Kensington High Street is **Leighton House Museum** ⓯ (Wed–Mon 11am–5.30pm; 12 Holland Park Road; tel: 7602 3316; charge). The red-brick exterior conceals one of the most extraordinary interiors in the city. The home of the Victorian artist Lord Leighton (1830–96), president of the Royal Academy, it is a mix of lavish Orientalism and conventional Victorian comforts. It contains his highly romanticised works, as well as many by fellow Pre-Raphaelites, but the centrepiece of the house is the grand Arab Hall, displaying Leighton's collection of Islamic tiles.

South of here is cosmopolitan **Earl's Court**, named after the earls of Oxford who owned the land in the 12th century. It is famous for its massive exhibition centre, built in 1937.

Recommended Restaurants, Bars & Cafés on pages 212–13

To the west is **Olympia**, another exhibition centre. To the north is **Holland Park** ⓰, the grounds of the Jacobean Holland House, mostly destroyed in World War II. Peacocks preen among the formal gardens, and the ruins provide an appealing set for open-air concerts. For refreshments, try the restaurant in the Orangery, or the more informal café nearby.

NOTTING HILL

The northeastern exit of Holland Park leads down a steep path to Holland Park Avenue, at the top of which is Notting Hill Gate, the heart of hip London.

Portobello Road Market ⓱

Portobello Road; www.portobelloroad.co.uk Mon–Wed and Fri–Sat 8am–6pm, Thur 8am–1pm; antiques market Sat 8am–6pm Ladbroke Grove or Notting Hill Gate

On Saturdays Notting Hill's Portobello Road is home to a vast antiques market; people come here from all over the world to enjoy the buzz and browse amongst the stalls. The antiques are concentrated in the more genteel southern end of the street, while further north, under the Westway flyover, a flea market mixes junk, cutting-edge fashion and arts and crafts (Fri–Sun). Between these two, the traditional fruit, veg and flower stalls have been joined by traders selling foodstuffs from around the world.

As a backdrop to the stalls, the refurbished **Electric Cinema** is London's oldest surviving cinema, (1905).

Just off Portobello Road, on Blenheim Crescent, is the **Travel Bookshop**, the setting for the 1999 romantic comedy *Notting Hill*, in which Hugh Grant improbably wooed Julia Roberts. What the film didn't convey is that Notting Hill is a melting pot in which several races and just about every social class rub shoulders.

Ladbroke Grove

Notting Hill's main north–south artery, **Ladbroke Grove**, is the parade route for the **Notting Hill Carnival**, a three-day Caribbean festival which takes over the area on the last weekend of August.

Turquoise Island in Westbourne Grove is home to Notting Hill's funkiest public toilets and a florist's.

BELOW LEFT: Farm Place, Notting Hill Gate. **BELOW:** colourful Portobello Road.

Dating from 1912, Peter Pan's statue in Kensington Gardens was erected secretly one night so it might seem as if it had appeared by magic.

QUEENSWAY AND KENSINGTON GARDENS

Westbourne Grove heads eastwards to **Queensway** ⓲, home to Whiteleys Shopping Centre, which has cafés, restaurants and a cinema on the second floor. At the top of Queensway, past the ice rink, is Kensington Gardens.

London's great green lung is **Hyde Park** and **Kensington Gardens**, which cover 1 sq. mile (2.5 sq km) – the same area as the City of London. Although they are a single open space, they are two distinct parks, divided by West Carriage Drive.

Kensington Palace ⓳

Kensington Gardens; www.hrp.org.uk 0870-751 5170 Mar–Oct 10am–5pm, Nov–Feb till 4pm charge Notting Hill Gate or Queensway

BELOW: Horse Guards near Kensington Palace. **ABOVE RIGHT:** the State Apartments, Kensington Palace.

On the west side of Kensington Gardens, overlooking the Round Pond, is **Kensington Palace**, the former home of Diana, Princess of Wales.

The palace was given its present appearance by Sir Christopher Wren and Nicholas Hawksmoor, and was the centre of the Court after William III bought the mansion in 1689. Several monarchs were born here, the last of them Victoria in 1819, who 18 years later was called from her bed to be told she had become Queen.

On first entering the palace you see the **Royal Dress Collection**, a presentation of royal, court and ceremonial dress dating from the 18th century to the present day, including some of Princess Diana's gowns. On the first floor are the **State Apartments**, displaying paintings from the Royal Collection.

Around the grounds of the palace are an attractive sunken garden and an **Orangery**, designed by Nicholas Hawksmoor in 1704 and modified by Sir John Vanbrugh. It has wood carvings by Grinling Gibbons and is now a café *(see page 212)*.

A path east of the gilded main gates of Kensington Palace leads to **Kensington Palace Gardens**. The lake on the eastern side (called The Long Water here, and the Serpentine in Hyde Park) has, at its northern edge, the delightful **Italian Garden**, commissioned by Prince Albert, with energetic fountains, stone urns and a statue of Edward Jenner, who developed the vaccination against smallpox. The loggia in Italian

Renaissance-style was originally the pumphouse for the fountains.

Along the path by the water is a statue, by George Frampton, of J.M. Barrie's **Peter Pan** – the full title of this classic children's story is *Peter Pan in Kensington Gardens*.

The **Serpentine Gallery** ⑳ (daily 10am–6pm; tel: 7298 1515; www.serpentinegallery.org.uk; free) by the road bridge is a dynamic exhibition space for contemporary art.

HYDE PARK

Across the road is **Hyde Park** which, as the *Domesday Book* of 1086 records, was inhabited by wild bulls and boars. First owned by the monks of Westminster Abbey, it was turned into a royal hunting ground by Henry VIII and then opened to the public in the 17th century. The **Serpentine** ㉑ was created in the 1730s as a royal boating lake, and boats can still be hired from the north bank. **Rotten Row**, William III's Route du Roi, running along the southern edge, is where the Household Cavalry, based in the barracks on Knightsbridge, exercise their horses.

The **Princess Diana Memorial Fountain** ㉒, a circular ring of flowing water surrounding a landscaped area, was designed by Seattle-based landscape architect Kathryn Gustafson. Some find the rock 'n' rolling water a little underwhelming.

At the northeast corner, near Marble Arch, is **Speakers' Corner** ㉓, where anyone can pull up a soap box and sound off, especially on Sunday afternoons. This tradition goes back to when the Tyburn gallows stood here (1388–1783) and condemned felons were allowed to make a final unexpurgated speech to the crowds before being hanged. ❑

In the northwestern corner of Kensington Gardens is the popular Diana Memorial Playground, perhaps a more fitting tribute to the princess than the Princess Diana Memorial Fountain.

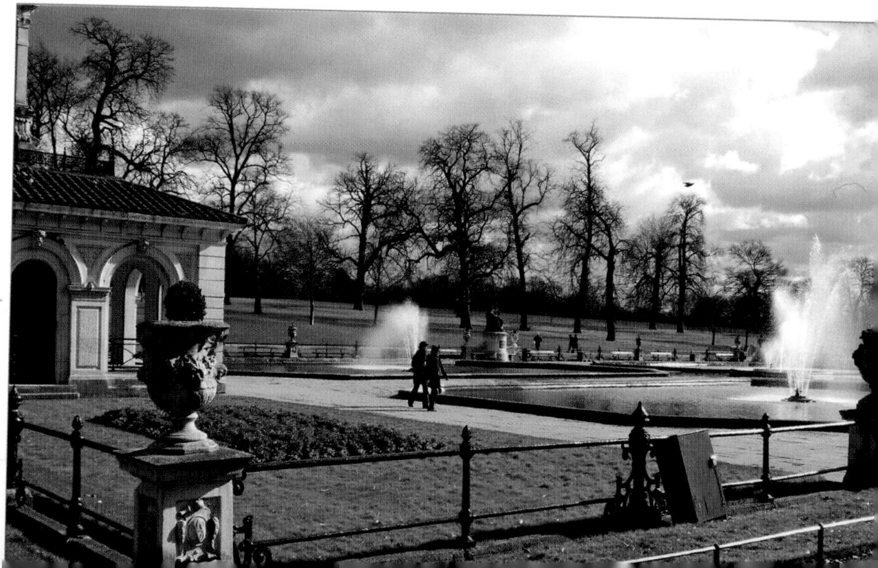

LEFT: a swan-out-of-water in Hyde Park. **BELOW:** the Italian Gardens, Hyde Park.

BEST RESTAURANTS, BARS AND CAFÉS

Restaurants

Prices for a three-course dinner per person with a half bottle of house wine:

£ = under £20
££ = £20–30
£££ = £30–50
££££ = over £50

British

Geales
2 Farmer Street, Notting Hill Gate, W8 ☎ 7727 7528 ⏲ L & D Mon–Sat, D only Sun. **££** [p 337, B3]
An up-market fish and chip restaurant which has been keeping locals happy for years.

Maggie Jones's
6 Old Court Place, Kensington Church St, W8 ☎ 7937 6462 ⏲ L & D daily. **£££** [p 337, C4]
This cosy restaurant, with its paraphernalia-filled nooks and crannies, is a fun place to eat with friends. The food is of the comfort variety.

The Orangery
Kensington Gardens, W8 ☎ 7938 1406 ⏲ Mar–Oct daily 10–6pm, Nov–Feb 10am–5pm. **££** [p 337, C3]
In a magnificent building designed for Queen Anne in 1704, this is the place to come for traditional afternoon tea. Light lunches also served.

French

Bibendum
Michelin House, 81 Fulham Road, SW3 ☎ Restaurant: 7581 5817; Oyster Bar: 7589 1480 ⏲ L & D daily. **£££** (set lunch) **££££** [p 336, C3]
Opened by Sir Terence Conran and Paul Hamlyn in 1987, Bibendum continues to thrive; there's an oyster bar on the ground floor and a restaurant on the first floor of this individual Art Deco-style building.

La Bouchée
56 Old Brompton Rd, South Kensington, SW7 ☎ 7589 1929 ⏲ L & D daily. **££** (set meal noon–3pm, 4.30–5.30pm) **£££** [p 336, B3]
Across the threshold of this bistro lies a corner of France. The dark wooden interior has a romantic feel and the menu offers many traditional dishes, such as coq au vin and snails in garlic butter.

Brasserie St Quentin
243 Brompton Road, SW3 ☎ 7589 8005 ⏲ L & D daily. **££** (set meal served until 7pm) **£££** [p 336, C3]
Small suppliers provide seasonal produce, so depending on the time of year you'll find smoked Irish eel, English asparagus, oysters and partridge alongside snails and seared foie gras.

Racine
239 Brompton Road, Knightsbridge, SW3. ☎ 7584 4477 ⏲ L & D daily. **££** (set menu until 7.30pm) **£££** [336, C3]
Come here for traditional French staples: snails, foie gras, steak, rabbit and *tarte tatin*. Good value for this part of town.

Indian

Bombay Brasserie
Courtfield Rd, SW7 ☎ 7370 4040 ⏲ L & D daily, last orders midnight. **££** (set lunch) **£££** [p 336, A3]
This up-market Indian has rejuvenated its classic menu and deserves its reputation for good, if expensive, food. Try to book a table in the conservatory.

Malabar
27 Uxbridge Street, Notting Hill Gate, W8 ☎ 7727 8800 ⏲ L & D daily. **££** (set lunch) **£££** [p 337, B3]
Uses fresh herbs, whole spices and gives an innovative twist to traditional dishes. Good value buffet lunch on Sundays.

Zaika
1 Kensington High St, W8 ☎ 7795 6533 ⏲ L & D daily. **£££** (set menu) **££££** [p 337, C4]
The name translates as

LEFT: the Orangery, Kensington Gardens. **ABOVE RIGHT:** salads in Ottolenghi. **RIGHT:** Elbow Room, Notting Hill.

sophisticated flavours and this is what you get – the menu incorporates traditional favourites with "new" Eastern dishes. The Indian home smoked salmon is terrific.

Italian

Osteria Basilico

29 Kensington Park Road, Notting Hill, W11 7727 9372 L & D daily. **£££** [p 337, A1]
Established in 1992, this place buzzes with a Notting Hill crowd, Friendly staff serve classic Italian home cooking and pizzas,

Pizza on the Park

11 Knightsbridge, SW1 7235 7825 L & D daily. **££** [p 334, B2]
This flagship restaurant of the Pizza Express chain offers live jazz on Wednesday to Saturday evenings, plenty of space and very good pizzas.

San Lorenzo

22 Beauchamp Place, SW3 7584 1074 L & D Mon–Sat. **££££** [p 336, C2]
Swanky Knightsbridge venue patronised by fashion, music and media moguls, as well as royals. The food is not as noteworthy as the clientele.

Modern European

Babylon

The Roof Gardens, 7th Floor, 99 Kensington High St, W8 7368 3993 L & D Mon–Sat, L only Sun. **££££** [p 337, C4]
Situated on the seventh floor, this Richard Branson-owned modern restaurant overlooks 1½ acres of gardens and offers great views of London. The food lives up to the spectacular setting.

Clarke's

122–4 Kensington Church Street, W8 7221 9225 D Tue–Sat. L Mon–Fri, Br Sat. **££££** [p 337, C3]
Colchester crab with Irish smoked salmon, dill flatbread and pea leaves is a classic Sally Clarke dish. High-quality ingredients treated simply is the key to the restaurant's success, and it's been working since the 1980s. A bakery supplies divine fresh bread.

Fifth Floor

Harvey Nichols, 109–125 Knightsbridge, SW1 7235 5250 L & D Mon–Sat, L only Sun. **£££** [p 334, A2]
A postmodern space popular with media types and models offering an effective combination of big flavours and light dishes.

Kensington Place

201–9 Kensington Church St, W8 7727 3184 L & D daily. **£££** [p 337, B3]
A trailblazer of the Modern European scene, it still serves simple yet inventive good food. Noise levels are high.

Ottolenghi

63 Ledbury Road, Notting Hill W11 7727 1121. Also at 1 Holland Street, Kensington W8 7937 0003 Mon–Sat 8am–7pm, Sun 9am–6pm. **££** [p 337, B1]
Fabulous fresh food made on the premises – sit at the communal table or take away. The Kensington branch is take away only – ideal for a picnic in Kensington Gardens.

Bars and Pubs

The best bars are found in the area's many grand hotels where extravagant cocktails are mixed in the elegant and refined spaces of sumptuous living – places such as the **Library Bar** in the Lanesborough Hotel on Hyde Park Corner, the **Blue Bar** in the Berkeley Hotel in Wilton Place, and the **Mandarin Bar** in the Mandarin Oriental in Knightsbridge. Those looking for something a bit more funky can try the **Townhouse** *(31 Beauchamp Place)*, **Montgomery Place** *(31 Kensington Park Road)* or **The Elbow Room** *(103 Westbourne Grove)*.

Good food is to be found in pubs these days, especiallly in "gastropubs", where the quality of the food is high on the agenda.

Here are a few of the best: **Anglesea Arms** *(15 Selwood Terrace, South Kensington)*, the **Cross Keys** *(1 Lawrence St, Chelsea)*, **The Abingdon** *(54 Abingdon Rd)*, **Churchill Arms** *(119 Kensington Church Street)*, **Windsor Castle** *(114 Campden Hill Road)*, **The Cow** *(89 Westbourne Park Road*, **The Fat Badger** *(310 Portobello Road)*.

The Science Museum

This museum is an astounding tribute to the ingenuity of human beings over the centuries

With more than 10,000 exhibits, plus additional attractions such as an IMAX theatre and "Launch Pad", an interactive play area for children, this museum could take days to explore, so it is best to assign priorities before you start.

An important point to note is the distinction between the main wing, dating to 1928 and containing the classic steam engines and planes, and the Wellcome Wing, opened in 2000, concentrating on information technology. You can walk between the two wings at five of the museum's seven levels, but the ambience of the wings is quite different and it is more satisfying to explore one wing at a time.

Above: The Making the Modern World gallery brings together many of the museum's most exciting exhibits. "Modern" is defined as post-1750 and the stars include the world's oldest surviving steam locomotive, the coal-hauling Puffing Billy (circa 1815), Stephenson's Rocket passenger locomotive (1829), a Ford Model T (1916), a Lockheed Electra airliner hanging in silvery splendour from the ceiling (1935), a copy of Crick and Watson's DNA spiral model (1953) and the battered Apollo 10 command module (left, 1969).

Below: the first gallery you enter is the Energy Hall, dominated by a 1903 mill engine.

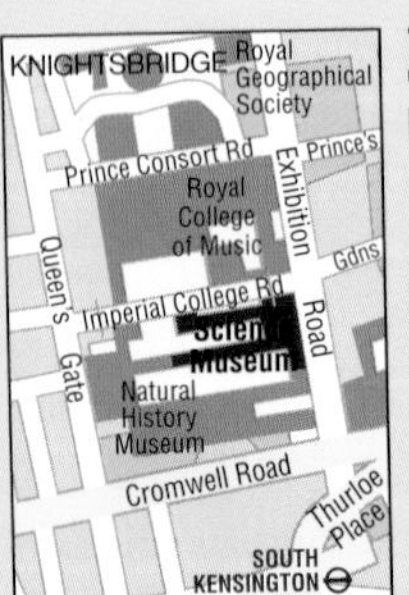

The essentials

Exhibition Road, SW7; www.sciencemuseum.org.uk

0870 870 4868

daily 10am–6pm

free except for some special exhibitions

South Kensington

OTHER HIGHLIGHTS

The Wellcome Wing *(above)* looks to the future rather than the past. On the ground floor, Antenna is a series of changing exhibits based around current science news, while an IMAX film theatre conjures up dinosaurs or outer space. The theme of the first floor is "Who am I?", asking such questions as "How does your brain make you so special?" and "Do we all come from Africa?" In Future, on the third floor, is a series of large digital board games on which contestants are invited to vote on health, communications and lifestyle topics – for example, "Should men be allowed to give birth?"

The Flight Gallery (third floor) is a favourite with all ages; exhibits range from a seaplane to a Spitfire, from hot-air balloons to helicopters. The 1919 Vickers Vimy in which Alcock and Brown made the first non-stop transatlantic flight is here, as is Amy Johnson's *Gipsy Moth Jason*, and there's a replica of the Wright Flyer in which Wilbur and Orville Wright pioneered powered flight in 1903.

The Garden (basement) is a hands-on play area where 3–6 year-olds have fun with water, sand and weights. The Launch Pad (basement) for older kids is packed with experiments they can try out; "explainers" help them understand what's going on.

The Secret Life of the Home (basement) displays domestic appliances and gadgets, with lots of buttons to press and levers to pull, one of which shows the internal workings of a flushing lavatory.

ABOVE: the ever-popular Exploring Space gallery has been revamped to include a range of new exhibits, including the huge Spacelab 2 x-ray telescope – the actual instrument that was flown on the Space Shuttle – and full-size models of the Huygens Titan probe and Beagle 2 Mars Lander. The replica of the Apollo 11 lunar excursion module has been reconfigured to a new level of accuracy.

RIGHT: The Rocket, George Stephenson's 1829 locomotive, is on display in the Making of the Modern World gallery.

Victoria and Albert Museum

The world's largest collection of decorative and applied arts covers everything from massive sculptures to knitting

With 5 million objects and almost 8 miles (13 km) of galleries, the Victoria and Albert Museum (founded in 1852) is colossal. Its exhibits range from exquisite Persian miniatures to a whole room designed by Frank Lloyd Wright. One minute one can be admiring Raphael's cartoons for the tapestries in the Sistine Chapel, and the next examining E.H. Shepard's illustrations for *Winnie-the-Pooh* or admiring a plaster cast of Michelangelo's *David* (left).

The museum is undergoing a 10-year refurbishment. So far, the British Galleries have received a major overhaul and the Islamic Galleries have been redesigned with the superb Ardabil carpet, the oldest carpet in the world, as a centrepiece. At the end of 2006 the stunning Morris, Gamble and Poynter refreshment rooms were reopened. Serving their original purpose once again, they open out onto the remodelled John Madejski Courtyard.

ABOVE: an immense glass sculpture by the American glass artist Dale Chihuly hangs in the foyer of the Cromwell Road entrance.

RIGHT: a British Empire builder is savaged in *Tipoo's Tiger* (Mysore, 1790), in the South Asia Gallery.

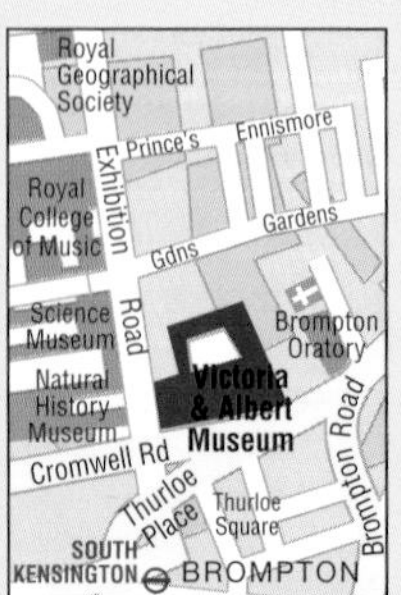

The essentials

Cromwell Road, SW7; *www.vam.ac.uk*

7942 2000

daily 10am–5.45pm, selected galleries until 10pm Fri

free except for some special exhibitions

South Kensington

TOP: the British Galleries document British taste, exploring "what was hot and what was new from the time of Henry VIII and the Tudors to William Morris." The exhibits relate to four key themes: Style, Who Led Taste?, Fashionable Living, and What Was New.

Above: the Iranian Ardabil carpet (1539–40) in the newly refurbished Jameel Gallery of Islamic arts.

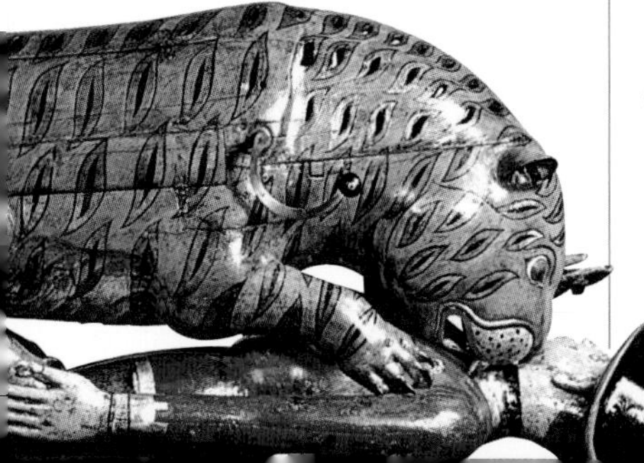

OTHER HIGHLIGHTS

The Sculpture Courts. British and neoclassical works from the late 18th and early 19th centuries.
Plaster Casts and Fakes & Forgeries. Fine copies, from Trajan's Column to Michelangelo's *David.*
Raphael Cartoons (1515–6). Templates for a series of tapestries in the Sistine Chapel.
The Italian Collection. Renaissance pieces include Andrea Briosco's 16th-century *Shouting Horseman.*
The Fashion Galleries. Fashions through the ages from the 17th century to the present day.
The Ceramic Staircase. Completed in 1869, it symbolises the relationship between art and science.
The Hereford Screen. An intricate choir screen (1862) studded with semi-precious stones.
Henry Cole Wing. Prints, drawings, paintings and photographs ranging from John Constable's paintings to Beatrix Potter's watercolours. Don't miss the Frank Lloyd Wright Gallery.
Refreshment Rooms. Three fabulously ornate café interiors from the 19th century, interlinked and opening onto the courtyard garden.
The Museum Shop. Quite simply irresistible.

ABOVE: platform shoes in stamped leather by Vivienne Westwood (1993) in the Fashion Galleries. This section of the museum frequently has special exhibitions.

The Natural History Museum

This colossal collection has 75 million plants, animals, fossils, rocks and minerals – and it's growing by 50,000 new specimens a year

If any of London's museums encapsulates the Victorians' quest for knowledge and passion for sifting and cataloguing data, it's this one. Yet, in spite of its vast size, the layout is easy to master. It divides between the "Life" galleries, starting from Cromwell Road, and the "Earth" galleries, beginning from Exhibition Road.

One of the museum's greatest delights is the way it presents superb high-tech exhibits alongside beautifully kept Victorian-style galleries filled with meticulously labelled cabinets. Many of the latter are found in quiet by-ways of the museum, but one vintage member of the collection appreciated both by children and adults alike is the wood and plaster model of a blue whale, which has been the centrepiece of the Mammals section since it was built in 1938.

Above: the Central Hall of the museum. The extravagant Gothic Romanesque building, by architect Alfred Waterhouse, was the first in Britain to be faced entirely in terracotta. Its soaring arches and rich ornamental detail bring to mind a cathedral, an effect intended by Sir Richard Owen, the superintendent of the collection. Owen wanted the building to be a temple of nature.

Above: the skeleton and dramatic full-size model of a blue whale is a big attraction. Many families also make a bee-line for the Dinosaurs section (Life Galleries), the highlight of which is a full-scale animatronic T-Rex that roars and twists convincingly, impressing most children.

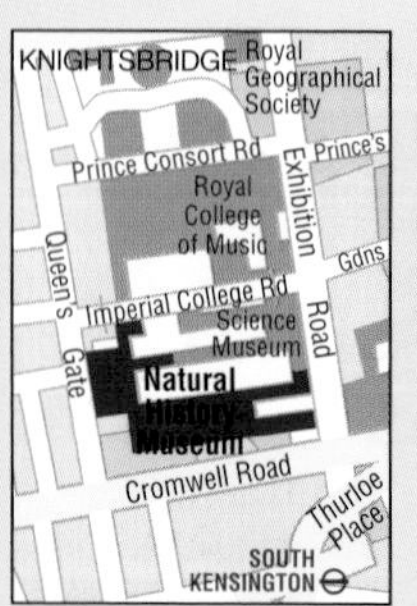

The essentials

Cromwell Road, SW7; www.nhm.ac.uk
7942 5000
daily 10am–5.50pm
free except for some special exhibitions
South Kensington

OTHER HIGHLIGHTS

LEFT: a cross-section of a giant redwood. **BELOW:** An escalator transports visitors into a vast globe, the entrance to the Earth Galleries, where. Restless Surface covers earthquakes and volcanoes. The tremors of an earthquake are simulated in a mock-up of a Japanese mini-market.

Investigate (basement). Here *(above)* children can touch, weigh, measure and examine under a microscope a range of specimens. A team of explainers is on hand to help. There is also an outdoor section where children can inspect pond life close up.

Human Biology. This section is packed with interactive exhibits: you can test your memory and senses or be tricked by optical illusions.

Mammals. As well as displaying an astonishing array of taxidermy, these galleries contain sobering statistics on the rapid rate at which species are becoming extinct.

Creepy Crawlies. Wander through a house and learn about the many uninvited housemates in an average home; sit in a life-size model of a termite mound; and watch a colony of leaf-cutter ants.

Earth's Treasury. This conveys the planet's beauty, displaying rocks, gems and minerals glittering in the gallery's semi-darkness.

The Jerwood Gallery. This houses a superb collection of watercolours, oils, prints and drawings, some of which are the original illustrations to books by famous 19th-century explorers.

The Darwin Centre. This a top-class centre for scientific study and a repository for millions of specimens, with guided tours and "meet-the-scientists" sessions.

The Wildlife Garden *(the West Lawn)*. There's a tour twice daily in spring and summer. This lush spot is a refreshing way to end a visit.

CHELSEA

Backing on to a secluded stretch of the Thames, Chelsea has tranquil gardens, royal connections and a village feel. It also has a strong bohemian side. Running through it is the King's Road, the centre of Swinging London in the 1960s and later of punk

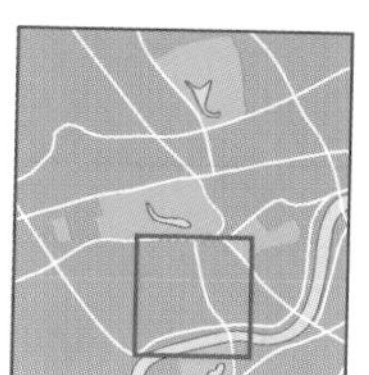

Sandwiched between Kensington and the Thames, Chelsea's tranquil enclaves still hint at the riverside hamlet it was until the late 18th century. Despite a modest character, by the 16th century Chelsea had become known as a "Village of Palaces", with strong royal links – King Henry VIII among them – and was destined to be the site of Wren's Royal Hospital in 1682.

A reputation for art took root with the Chelsea Porcelain Works and the illustrations generated by the Chelsea Physic Garden's botanical publications. By the 19th century, a bohemian set had moved in wholesale, including the painters Rossetti, Whistler and Sargent and writers such as George Eliot (and later, T.S. Eliot).

BELGRAVIA TO SLOANE SQUARE

When the squares and terraces of **Belgravia** were built around 1824, these streets west of Hyde Park Corner were intended to rival Mayfair. From Knightsbridge, the best entrance to Belgravia is via **Wilton Place**. The stucco terraces were developed by architect Thomas Cubitt, who gave his name to the modern construction company known for its motorway bridges. Like much of Mayfair, **Belgrave Square** is largely occupied by embassies and various societies and associations. The square usually has a heavy police presence.

Eaton Square, to the south, is more residential. However, many of its supposed residents live in other parts of the world and the houses are dark and obviously under-used. Chopin gave his first London recital here at No. 88.

In 1895 the playwright Oscar Wilde was arrested in the Cadogan Hotel in Sloane Street, tried and sent

Main attractions

- ROYAL COURT THEATRE
- SLOANE SQUARE
- KING'S ROAD
- DUKE OF YORK SQUARE
- CHELSEA TOWN HALL
- ANTIQUES MARKETS
- ST LUKE'S CHURCH
- ROYAL HOSPITAL
- NATIONAL ARMY MUSEUM
- CHELSEA PHYSIC GARDEN
- CHEYNE WALK
- THE EMBANKMENT
- CHELSEA OLD CHURCH

LEFT: decorative ironwork on Albert Bridge.
RIGHT: the King's Road.

to prison for his homosexual conduct. Sloane Street leads from Knightsbridge to **Sloane Square** ❶, where **Chelsea** proper begins. On the east side of the square is the **Royal Court Theatre**, where John Osborne's mould-breaking anti-establishment play *Look Back in Anger* was first staged in 1956. The company still has a robust reputation for shaping the classics of the future.

Sloane Square was named after a physician, Sir Hans Sloane (1660–1753), whose personal collection formed the basis of what is now the British Museum. He laid out much of this area and his name crops up often on street plans. He also unwittingly gave his name to a typical young upper-class urbanite living in Chelsea in the 1980s: the Sloane Ranger, a lady in flat shoes, pearls, gathered skirt and a quilted jacket.

Along the King's Road

Until 1829 the **King's Road** ❷, leading west from Sloane Square, was a private royal road leading from Hampton Court to the court of King James. It rose to fame during the 1960s, and was later linked to punk fashions, after Vivienne Westwood

Chelsea

and Malcolm McLaren opened their designer shop, Sex, at No. 430 in 1972. Westwood still sells her designs from these premises, renamed World's End, which is what this part of Chelsea is called. Other long-established stores include Sloane Square's GTC (General Trading Company), and Peter Jones department store.

Duke of York Square ❸

Lately, the biggest innovation on the King's Road's retail front has been the redevelopment of the Duke of York's Headquarters, formerly a military campus. The main building with its Tuscan portico (1801), designed as a school for the orphans of soldiers, now houses the **Saatchi Gallery**, which moved here in November 2007 (www.saatchi-gallery.co.uk). It contains the work of contemporary British artists assembled by former advertising mogul Charles Saatchi. In recent years the collection's bias has shifted towards paintings and away from works such as Damien Hirst's celebrated sheep in formaldehyde solution.

Old Chelsea Town Hall ❹

Prettily painted 18th- and 19th-century terraces leading off the King's Road have a tradition of housing artists and intellectuals. On the left-hand side of the road opposite Sydney Street stands the Old Chelsea Town Hall. The old borough of Royal Kensington, given its royal appellation by Queen Victoria in 1901, was merged much against its wishes with Chelsea in 1965, and took over the administration of both. The Old Chelsea Town Hall continues to provide a cultural and social focus for residents. The Register Office next door is well-known for society and celebrity weddings.

Duke of York Square includes a pedestrian enclave of up-market homeware and fashion units (Zara, Joseph, Space.nk, etc), cafés and a seasonal ice rink. Partridges the grocers organises a regular Saturday food market outside their shop

FAR LEFT: the Royal Court Theatre.
LEFT: home furnishings on the King's Road.
BELOW LEFT AND RIGHT: a wedding at Chelsea Register Office.

The Chelsea Pensioners, who live in the Royal Hospital, are world war veterans. They are given board and lodging, nursing care and a small allowance, including a pint of beer a day.

SYDNEY STREET

In 1836, Charles Dickens was married more conventionally – in **St Luke's**, a stunning Gothic church halfway up Sydney Street, running north of the King's Road. Eagle-eyed Disney fans may recognise it from the 1996 film version of *101 Dalmatians*. If the weather is fine its gardens are a lovely spot to unwind.

Sydney Street is also home to the popular Chelsea Gardener nursery; as well as the **Chelsea Farmers Market**, a small shopping enclave with a boho feel thanks to its organic supermarket and one-storey clapboard units where the emphasis is on natural remedies and ingredients.

BELOW: enjoying a drink at Chelsea Farmers Market.

At the top of Sydney Street is **Brompton Cross**, a network of streets containing up-market shops and restaurants, including Bibendum *(see page 212)*, in the Art Deco-style former headquarters of the Michelin Tyre Company on Fulham Road.

HOSPITAL ROAD

Among the leggy would-be models gliding along the King's Road are uniformed old gents with the initials RH on their caps. These are Chelsea Pensioners, retired war veterans who live in the **Royal Hospital**, built by Christopher Wren in 1692 on Royal Hospital Road. From the King's Road, a practically uninterrupted vista is afforded down the length of **Royal Avenue**, the hospital perfectly framed in the distance. The gravelled boulevard now lined with 19th-century houses was laid out by Wren with the purpose of providing a direct route from the hospital to Kensington Palace. The scheme failed to materialise when Charles II, the sponsor, died, and this first and only section now stands as testimony to Wren's grand vision. Royal Avenue was the fictional home of James Bond.

Royal Hospital ❺

Royal Hospital Road; www.chelsea-pensioners.org.uk 7881 5246 daily 10am–noon, 2–4pm; closed Sun Oct–Mar; grounds year round 10am–sunset, Sun from 2pm free Sloane Square

The idea behind this magnificent building housing the Chelsea Pensioners was inspired by the Hôtel des Invalides in Paris. The main buildings, two residential wings linked by the Great Hall and Chapel, were designed in English baroque style.

The wood-panelled Great Hall, the dining room, features a vast mural with Charles II on horseback, painted by Verrio. It was in this hall in 1852 that Wellington lay in state. Decorated with regimental colours, the adjoining Chapel features *Christ Rising from the Tomb*, a fresco by Sebastiano Ricci. A huge painting of the Battle of Waterloo by George Jones hangs in the entrance to a small museum. It overlooks a 1:300 scale model that, with an audio presentation, illustrates the hospital and its massive grounds in the 18th century.

National Army Museum ❻

Royal Hospital Road; www.national-army-museum.ac.uk 7730 0717 daily 10am–5.30pm free Sloane Square

The permanent exhibition follows the history of the British Army from the defeat of the French at Agincourt in 1415 to the present day, although with much less emphasis on the latter. Massive flamboyant paintings, some as long as 20 ft (6 metres), celebrate soldiers' greatest and worst moments, while portraits by Gainsborough, Reynolds and lesser artists

KIDS

The National Army Museum's Kid Zone is a free interactive learning and play space designed to unleash children's imaginations. There's a medieval castle to explore, life in a forest army camp to negotiate, and a variety of activity areas to challenge and entertain the under-10s. A soft play area for babies is also included. Entry is by timed ticket.

ABOVE LEFT: the Great Hall, Royal Hospital.
BELOW: produce market on Duke of York Square, off the King's Road.

The Chelsea Flower Show

The Chelsea Flower Show (www.rhs.org.uk.chelsea), one of the largest of its kind in the world, is a great social event held in the Royal Hospital's spacious gardens during May. First held in 1862, the Royal Horticultural Society show has grown to encompass an impressive number of show gardens, hastily but immaculately assembled in the days running up to the show, plus an astonishing variety of plants and flowers.

The show lasts for five days. The first two are open only to members of the RHS, but the last two days are open to all.

Chelsea Physic Garden can lay claim to the oldest rock garden in England, if not Europe. Dating back to 1771, it is made of salvaged building stone from the Tower of London as well as basaltic lava from Iceland.

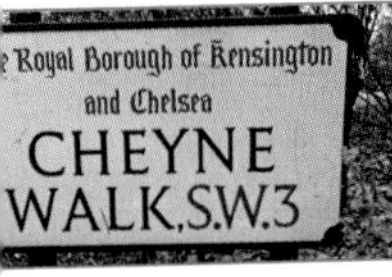

TOP RIGHT: The Artists of Leonard Fuchs, from *De Historia Stirpium*, 1542. **ABOVE AND BELOW:** Cheyne Walk.

crowd other walls. There is the skeleton of Napoleon's favourite horse, Marengo; and you can feel the weight of a Tudor cannonball or try on a soldier's helmet, while the replica World War I trench is a place for quiet reflection. Three sections of the Berlin Wall stand outside the museum.

Chelsea Physic Garden ❼

66 Royal Hospital Road; www.chelseaphysicgarden.co.uk 7352 5646 Apr–Oct Wed noon–sunset/9pm latest, Thur–Fri noon–5pm, Sun noon–6pm; closed Nov–Mar charge Sloane Square

Behind a high wall is the Chelsea Physic Garden, founded in 1676 for the study of medicinal plants. The 3½-acre (1.5-hectare) garden is divided into four contrasting sections: a Garden of World Medicine, a Pharmaceutical Garden, and systematic order beds in the two southern quadrants. The Pharmaceutical Garden displays plants according to their medical uses while the Garden of World Medicine details the use of specific plants in different parts of the world.

You will also find a pond rockery, History of Medicine beds, perfumery and aromatherapy borders, glasshouses and herb and vegetable gardens. A woodland area has birds' nesting boxes, and there are themed trails for adults and children.

CHELSEA EMBANKMENT

At the foot of **Royal Hospital Road**, a fine row of Queen Anne houses make up **Cheyne Walk** *(see box below)*. Cheyne Walk sits back from the flagstoned, windblown sweep of **Chelsea Embankment**, roaring with traffic in the shadows of old plane trees but beautiful nonetheless.

The Ultimate Des Res

Cheyne Walk has long been one of London's most exclusive streets. A host of famous people have lived in its fine mainly 18th-century properties, ranging from writers George Eliot and Hilaire Belloc and the artist J.M.W. Turner to the engineer Isambard Kingdom Brunel. It is still a choice address today. Paul Getty, Mick Jagger and Keith Richards have all been residents.

The pre-Raphaelite artist Dante Gabriel Rossetti lived with the poet Swinburne in No. 16, and they kept peacocks in their back garden. The birds so disturbed the neighbours that nowadays every lease on the row prohibits tenants from keeping them.

Recommended Restaurants, Bars & Cafés on pages 228–9

Flanked by greenery it is also known as Chelsea Gardens and opened to great fanfare in 1874. It retains its sculptural lampposts with their fat, milky globes, and its cast-iron benches with end supports shaped like sphinxes. The views stretch out across the Thames to the Battersea Park Peace Pagoda on the opposite bank, built by Japanese monks and nuns in 1985; east to the iconic chimneys of the Battersea Power Station; and west to the pink and cream confection of the **Albert Bridge** (1873).

Carlyle's House 8

24 Cheyne Row; www.nationaltrust.org.uk 7352 7087 mid-Mar–Oct Wed–Fri 2–5pm, Sat–Sun 11am–5pm charge Sloane Square

A statue of the Scottish essayist Thomas Carlyle (1795–1881) watches the traffic grind by further down the Embankment. The dour essayist lived here between 1834 and 1881. The house is preserved exactly as it was – to the point of not having electricity – and it is easy to imagine Mr and Mrs Carlyle sitting in their kitchen, although it may not have been a cosy scene. It was fortunate the Carlyles married each other, it was said; otherwise there would have been four miserable people in the world instead of two. Yet leading intellectuals, including Charles Dickens, John Ruskin and Alfred, Lord Tennyson, used to visit Carlyle here.

Sir Hans Sloane's tomb is outside **Chelsea Old Church** (All Saints) on Cheyne Walk. The church has several fine Tudor monuments and was painstakingly rebuilt after being destroyed by a landmine in 1941.

The site was formerly occupied by a 12th-century Norman church. Henry VIII, who had a large house on the river where Cheyne Walk now is, supposedly married Jane Seymour in secrecy here, several days before the official ceremony. Thomas More (1478–1535), author of *Utopia*, which sketched out an ideal commonwealth, had a farm here. His stormy relationship with Henry VIII, which resulted in his execution, was the subject of Robert Bolt's 1960 play *A Man For All Seasons.* ❑

The telltale enormous windows looking out onto Tite Street (off Royal Hospital Road) betray the origins of these houses: in the 1870s, this street was crammed with artists' studios, including The Studios, at No. 33. The American painter John Singer Sargent (1856–1925) died at No. 31, while Oscar Wilde once occupied No. 34.

BELOW: a statue of Sir Thomas More in front of Chelsea Old Church.

BEST RESTAURANTS, BARS AND CAFÉS

Restaurants

Prices for a three-course dinner per person with a half-bottle of house wine:

£ = under £20
££ = £20–30
£££ = £30–50
££££ = over £50

Chinese

Eight Over Eight
392 King's Rd SW3 ☎ 7349 9934 ⌚ L & D Mon–Sat, D only Sun. **£££** [p 338, C3]
This stylish restaurant in a former pub offers Asian dishes with a modern twist. Salad of rare salmon, green mango and palm, duck and foie gras shu mai, and chocolate pudding with green tea ice cream are just some of the delights on offer.

Ken Lo's Memories of China
65–9 Ebury St, SW1 ☎ 7730 7734 ⌚ L & D Mon–Sat, D only Sun. **£££** (set lunch avail) [p 334, B3]
Ken Lo's menus skewed towards western tastes have stood the test of time, though the final bill invariably comes as a costly surprise.

Fish

Poissonnerie de L'Avenue
82 Sloane Avenue, SW3 ☎ 7589 2457 ⌚ L & D Mon–Sat. **££–£££** (set menu) **£££** [p 336, C3]
Run by the same family for over 40 years, it serves fresh fish and seafood from the adjoining fishmonger's. Dishes are old-school French, although some come with an Italian flourish.

French

Cheyne Walk Brasserie
50 Cheyne Walk, SW3 ☎ 7376 8787 ⌚ L & D Tue–Sat, L only Sun, D only Mon. **££** (weekday lunch menu) **£££** [p 338, C3]
The flavours of Provence are cooked up over the central grill of this Belle Époque dining room. Also offers views of the Albert Bridge and a sumptuous cocktail lounge.

La Poule au Pot
231 Ebury St, SW1 ☎ 7730 7763 ⌚ L & D daily. **££** (set lunch) **£££** [p 334, B4]
The £16 fixed-price lunch menu features dishes such as escargots or soupe de poisson with *bifteck et frites* to follow. In the evening candle-light and romantic nooks make it a hit with couples.

Indian

Chutney Mary
535 King's Rd, SW10 ☎ 7351 3113 ⌚ D only Mon–Fri, L & D Sat/Sun. **££** (set lunch) **£££** [p 338, B4]
At the sister restaurant to Veeraswamy – the UK's oldest Indian eatery – you can take your pick of regional dishes from Goa to Delhi and Kerala to Bombay. The Sunday jazz brunch is popular.

Quilon
41 Buckingham Gate, SW1 ☎ 7821 1899 ⌚ L & D Mon–Fri, Sun, D only Sat. **££** (set lunch) **£££** [p 335, C2]
The lunch menu is good value, though an evening meal of, say, pepper shrimps followed by Manglorean chicken or pistachio lamb curry, is pricier.

Rasoi
10 Lincoln St, Sloane Sq, SW1 ☎ 7225 1881 ⌚ L Mon–Fri, D only Sat. **££** (set lunch) **£££** [p 338, C3, off map]
Run by celebrated chef Vineet Rasoi and awarded a Michelin star in 2006, this restaurant offers the ultimate Indian dining experience. It serves superb food in a traditional Chelsea townhouse. Good-value set lunches available.

Italian

Buona Sera at the Jam
289A King's Rd, SW3 ☎ 7352 8827 ⌚ L & D Tue–Sun, D only Mon; all day Sat–Sun. **££** [p 338, C3]
The Jam has occupied a blink-and-you'll-miss-it sliver of the King's Road frontage for aeons. It is

LEFT: Ken Lo's Memories of China. **TOP RIGHT:** Itsu.

now part of the Buona Sera chain, but remains fun. Its narrow dining room has two levels of booths, each of the raised ones with its own ladder.

Elistano
25–27 Elystan St, SW3 ☎ 7584 5248 ⌚ L & D daily. £££ [p 336, C4]
Unfussy but good. Dishes include homemade gnocchi with walnuts and cream and calves' liver in a butter and sage sauce.

Japanese

Itsu
118 Draycott Avenue, SW3 ☎ 7590 2400 ⌚ Mon–Sat noon–11pm, Sun noon–10pm. £ [p 336, C3]
If the offerings on the conveyor-belt plates don't appeal, try a dish from the hot grill such as chicken teriyaki. Bookings not accepted.

Modern European

Gordon Ramsay
68 Royal Hospital Rd, SW3 ☎ 7352 4441 ⌚ L & D Mon–Fri. £££ (lunch menu) ££££ [off map]
The celebrity chef's gastronomic offerings – such as roasted sea scallops with octopus, black pudding tempura, cauliflower purée and parmesan velouté – are exquisite. The lunchtime set menu costs £40 for 3 courses.

Others

Blue Kangaroo
555 King's Road, SW6. ☎ 7371 7622 ⌚ 9.30am–7.30pm daily. ££ [p 338, A4]
While tucking into pasta, risotto and the like on the ground floor, adults can watch via TV screens their kids enjoying the basement playzone. A café alongside the playzone serves the same menu and breakfast too. Non-junk children's menu.

Ed's Easy Diner
362 King's Rd, SW3 ☎ 7352 1956 ⌚ Mon–Thur 10am–10.30pm, Fri–Sat until 11.30pm, Sun until 10pm. £ [p 338, C3]
Mock-1950s American diner for juicy hamburgers and thick milkshakes.

Patara
181 Fulham Road, SW3 ☎ 7351 5692 ⌚ L & D daily. ££ [p 336, C4]
Good Thai food at low prices for the area. Try the DIY fresh spring rolls for starters, duck breast for main, sorbet for dessert and green tea to finish.

The Stockpot
273 King's Rd, SW3. ☎ 7823 3175 ⌚ L & D daily. £ [p 338, C3]
Simple but filling dishes Good for late meals (last orders 11.30pm).

Bars and Cafés

The King's Road has several good watering holes. There is the **Chelsea Potter** *(119 King's Rd)* or **Henry J Beans** *(195–7)*, an American bar and grill with the lure of a beer garden. But head off its well-trodden track to unearth some of the area's best pubs. These include the **Pig's Ear** *(35 Old Church St)*, lacking in authenticity after a continental-style refit, but with a fine real ale to its name; the **Surprise** *(6 Christchurch Terrace)*, a small local with stained glass and bar billiards; the **Cooper's Arms** *(87 Flood St)*, upholding the Campaign for Real Food; the **Cross Keys** *(1 Lawrence St)*, dating from 1765 and worth a visit for its gorgeous rooms; and the **Lots Road Pub and Dining Room** *(114 Lots Rd)*, a good gastropub.

Closer to Belgravia, the **Orange Brewery** *(37–9 Pimlico Rd)* retains remnants of its former brewery and the tiny **Fox and Hounds** *(29 Passmore St)* has armchairs and classic tomes aplenty. There's also the historic **Grenadier** *(18 Wilton Row)*, and **Thomas Cubitt** *(44 Elizabeth St)*, a fine gastropub.

If cocktails are your thing, the **Blue Bar** at The Berkeley Hotel *(Wilton Place)* does it in great style. Also try **Bardo** *(196–8 Fulham Rd)*, **Apartment 195** *(195 King's Road)* with the feel of a private club, New-Age Indian **Mokssh** *(222 Fulham Rd)* and the **606 Club** *(90 Lots Rd)* for live jazz.

Brompton Cross is the preserve of a more select class of bar, among them **Eclipse** *(111–3 Walton St)* serving the original Watermelon Martini, **Art Bar** *(87–9 Walton St)* and **The Collection** *(264 Brompton Rd)*. Pub-wise the **Admiral Codrington** *(17 Mossop St)* attracts a smart-casual set.

Village London

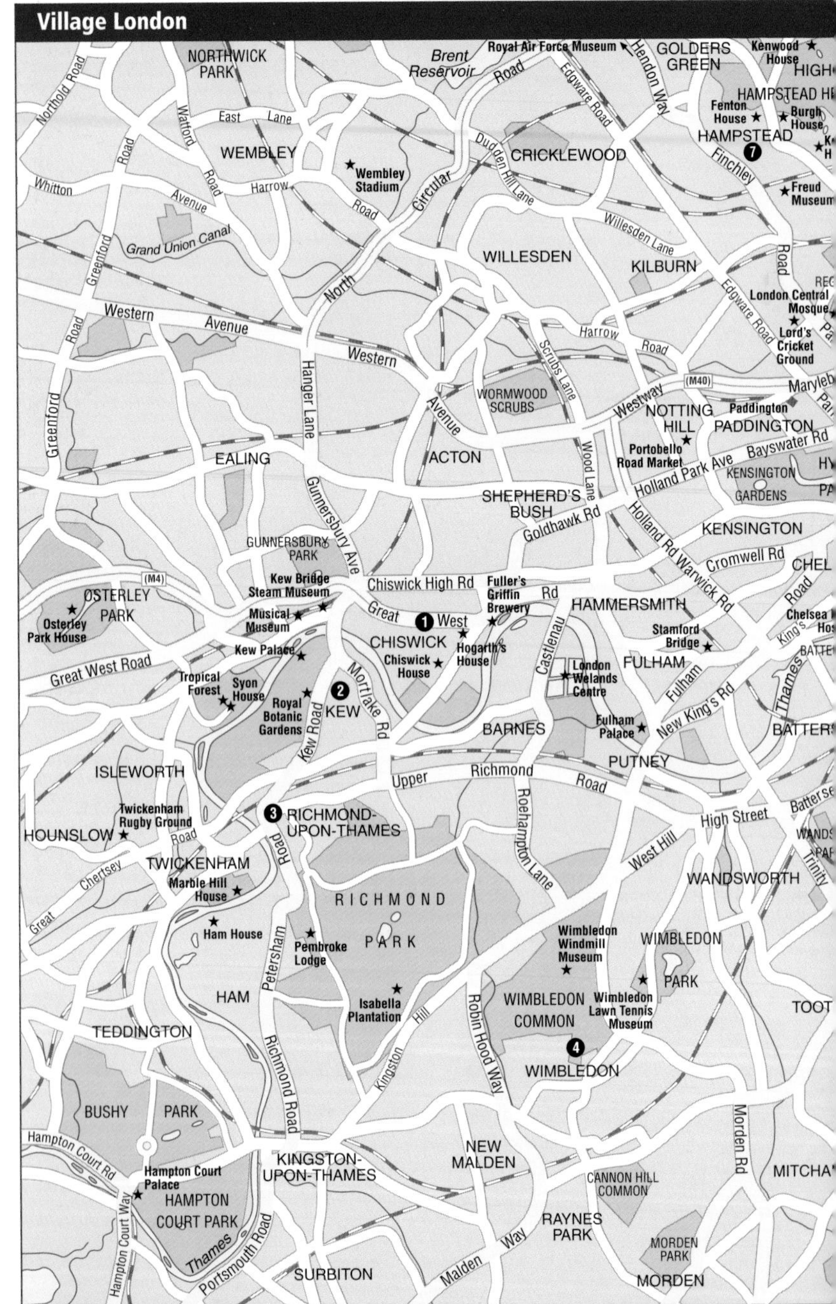

Village London

D. French Milliner 42
OYSTERS PIES SAUSAGES
WELSH CAKES SUGAR MICE
REAL FARM EGGS KIPPERS
SAFFRON CAKES TOFFEE SHOP FUDGE
OPEN
nal Foods of Britain

VILLAGE LONDON

London grew by swallowing up surrounding villages. But many are still there in spirit, each with its own distinctive character. Here we explore them by the four points of the compass

At its widest point, from South Croydon to Potter's Bar, the metropolis is nearly 60 miles (100 km) across and, though the overall population has been in decline since World War II, London remains one of the world's most populous cities. Perhaps because it is so big, many of those who live within its confines hardly think of it as a unified city at all, but as a collection of largely independent villages or communities. While Londoners may commute many miles to work, they are likely to do their shopping in their local high streets and build their social lives on their home patch.

The River Thames cuts through London, forming an effective physical and psychological block to free movement. While south Londoners stream across London Bridge to work in the City every day, they are more likely to go shopping in Croydon or Bromley than in the West End, and north Londoners will head further north to such shopping citadels as Brent Cross. Many people born within the metropolis rarely move more than a few miles from their home, and would not dream of "transponting" to the other side of the river.

Where to go

While most visitors are busy with the tourist haunts of the West End and the City, those who go further afield are rewarded with a glimpse of what the locals call "real London". Head west to Kew for Kew Gardens and river walks at Chiswick and Richmond, and north to Islington and Camden for good shopping, nightlife, restaurants and Regent's Canal, or to Highgate and Hampstead for historic pubs and Hampstead Heath. Travel east of the centre to see high-rise Docklands, historic Spitalfields and Hoxton. In the southern suburbs are Greenwich, famous for its observatory and naval museum, Blackheath, Dulwich and Brixton.

All can be reached by public transport, either the Tube, Docklands Light Railway, buses or, in the case of the southern suburbs, overground railway from London Bridge or Charing Cross stations. ❑

LEFT: a slice of old London in Spitalfields.

WEST LONDON

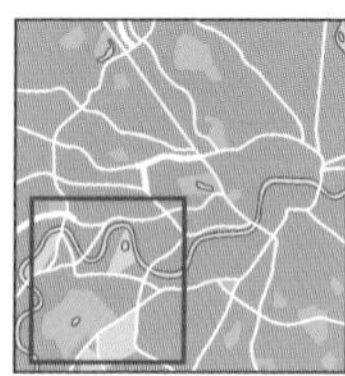

West London offers 18th-century mansions, magnificent parks and walks along the River Thames. To the southwest is Henry VIII's great palace, Hampton Court, and Wimbledon, home of the famous tennis championship

Main attractions

- CHISWICK HOUSE
- HOGARTH'S HOUSE
- ROYAL BOTANIC GARDENS, KEW
- KEW BRIDGE STEAM MUSEUM
- SYON HOUSE AND PARK
- OSTERLEY PARK HOUSE
- RICHMOND PARK
- HAM HOUSE
- HAMPTON COURT PALACE
- WIMBLEDON LAWN TENNIS MUSEUM
- WIMBLEDON WINDMILL MUSEUM

Heading west out of London you can choose between grand riverside mansions, built as country retreats for royals and landed gentry, and wide-open spaces such as Richmond Park and Kew Gardens, the world-renowned botanic gardens.

CHISWICK ❶

Although it accommodates the main artery to the M4 and Heathrow Airport, Chiswick has the feel of a small town, with its independent shops, flower stalls, fashionable restaurants and pretty terraces. Near the fragrant Fuller's Brewery *(see margin note, opposite page)*, off Hogarth roundabout, stands a hidden gem, much loved by locals and at last being given the attention it deserves.

Chiswick House

Burlington Lane; www.english-heritage.org.uk 8995 0508 Apr–Oct Wed–Sun 10am–5pm, Nov–Mar pre-booked appointments for groups only charge train Waterloo to Chiswick 190

This romantic 18th-century villa was designed by Lord Burlington (1694–1753), a renowned architect and patron of the arts, who was inspired by classical Rome. Burlington's Palladian house launched a new taste in architecture which was to spread throughout Britain and North America.

The gardens are historically important too, for it was here that the idea of the "natural style" of gardening – one of England's main contributions to European culture – was conceived. Burlington brought in his friend William Kent to redesign the grounds; Kent broke from the rigid formality which had characterised gardens of the early 18th century and created a more natural landscape. Thus the English landscape movement was

Recommended Restaurants, Bars & Cafés on page 241

born. A £12-million project is underway to restore the gardens, which include an abundance of statuary, a classical bridge, an Ionic temple, and a large conservatory.

Inside the house, the grand rooms are reserved for the first floor, which has a very unusual structure: in the centre is an octagonal room with a lavish domed ceiling – the tribune or saloon. This was the heart of the building and the setting for gatherings and *conversazioni*.

Amongst the celebrated guests welcomed here were Alexander Pope, Jonathan Swift, Handel and several crowned heads of state. The small scale and rounded edges of the rooms in the northern part of the house are intimate and sensual, with the overall symmetry heightened by framed views of the gardens through the doorways of the interconnected rooms. The most sumptuous of the Green, Red and Blue Velvet rooms, so-called because of their vivid wallpaper, is Lord Burlington's study, elegantly adorned in blue. The room's tiny dimensions and rich colours convey an impression of standing inside a jewel box, or inside a Fabergé egg.

Hogarth's House

Hogarth Lane, Great West Road; 8994 6757 Apr–Oct Tue–Fri 1–5pm, Sat & Sun 1–6pm, Nov–Dec and Feb–Mar Tue–Fri 1–4pm free train Waterloo to Chiswick 190

Not far from Chiswick House, sitting incongruously on the six-lane Great West Road, is Hogarth House, the modest residence of the father of political cartoons, William Hogarth (1697–1764). Hogarth highlighted the ills of society in a series of witty, engravings that became bestsellers. Although the house is now looking rather neglected, the collection of drawings, including *The Rake's Progress* and *Marriage à la Mode*, is worth seeking out. (Free parking for Chiswick House and Hogarth's house can be found a short distance from the Hogarth roundabout along the A4.)

William Hogarth moved with his family to this three-storey house from busy Leicester Fields (now Leicester Square) in 1749. In a monstrous bit of irony that would not be lost on the satirist, this "little country box by the Thames" now lies by the A4 to

To see how a pint of fine English ale is made, take a tour around Fuller's Griffin Brewery on the Hogarth roundabout. Pre-booking is essential (tel: 8996 2063).

LEFT: Chiswick House. **BELOW LEFT:** azaleas in the grounds of Chiswick House. **BELOW:** Chiswick House and gardens in a 1742 painting by George Lambert.

William Hogarth's grand tomb is in the cemetery of Chiswick parish church; take the underpass near Hogarth's house, then go down Church Street towards the river.

Heathrow, its owner immortalised in the thundering Hogarth roundabout. The traffic noise is muted in the house though, and a small garden at the back attempts a pastoral charm. The mulberry tree here is said to date from Hogarth's day, one of the few to survive from a time when the trees were brought to England in a vain attempt to get silkworms to breed.

KEW ❷

Downriver from Chiswick is Kew, home to the Royal Botanic Gardens, known as Kew Gardens. The village green gives the place a rural feel, particularly when cricket matches are played here. On the green is St Anne's Church, where the painter Thomas Gainsborough is buried.

Royal Botanic Garden

Kew, Richmond, Surrey; www.kew.org 8332 5655
Feb–Oct daily 9.30am–5.30pm, Nov–Jan 9.30am–4.15pm charge
Tube from Waterloo to Kew bridge

Kew Gardens, with 300 acres (120 hectares) of plants from all over the world, were first established in 1759 under the direction of Princess Augusta. In 1772, George III put Kew in the hands of the botanist Sir Joseph Banks, who had just returned from a round-the-world expedition to collect plant specimens with Captain Cook. Other explorers and amateur enthusiasts added to the collection over the centuries, so that today Kew is not only a vast botanical garden but also a formidable repository and research centre. In 2003 Kew was added to UNESCO's list of World Heritage Sites.

The gardens present a mix of landscaped lawns, wooded areas, formal gardens and glasshouses. Make the most of the map you will be given on entering; it features seasonal highlights and where to find them.

The most famous of Kew's nursery buildings is the Grade-I-listed **Palm House**, built in 1844–8. The steamy warmth hits you as you enter this verdant tropical world, in which coconuts, bananas and coffee beans grow. Nearby, the **Waterlily House** (closed Nov–April) houses tropical aquatic plants. The **Temperate House** is the world's largest surviving Victorian glass structure.

BELOW: Kew's 19th-century glasshouses are spectacular. **BELOW RIGHT:** Kew's Chinese Pagoda.

Recommended Restaurants, Bars & Cafés on page 241

In addition to the glasshouses there are various temples and other follies dating back to the period of royal ownership of the gardens in the 18th and early 19th centuries. The **Chinese pagoda**, built in 1762, reflects the fashion for chinoiserie in English garden design in the mid 18th century. The classically-styled Orangery dating from 1761, too dark to house citrus trees as was intended, is now a pleasant café-restaurant.

Kew Palace

Built in 1631 for a Dutch merchant, **Kew Palace** (end Mar–end Oct Tue–Sun 10am–5pm; tel: 0870-751 5179; charge) was the country retreat of George III, Queen Charlotte and some of their children from 1801; the king came here during his bouts of supposed madness. The palace has been meticulously restored and brought back to life, revealing aspects of the original Georgian decor and architecture, and many of the family's treasures.

SYON PARK AND MUSEUMS

Across Kew Bridge is the **Kew Bridge Steam Museum** (Tue–Sun 11am– 5pm; Green Dragon Lane; tel: 8568 4757; www.kbsm.org), whose original purpose was to supply London's water in the 19th century. It now houses the world's largest collection of steam-pumping engines and a steam railway, which you can ride (Sundays only Mar–Nov).

Further west along the high street is the **Musical Museum** (399 High Street, Brentford, tel: 8560 8108; www.musicalmuseum.co.uk; charge), which displays a large collection of automatic instruments, from clockwork music boxes to self-playing Wurlitzer organs.

Syon House

Syon Park, Isleworth; www.syonpark.co.uk 8560 0881
Syon House: end Mar–end Oct Wed, Thur, Sun and bank holiday Mon 11am–5pm; gardens: Mar–Oct daily 10.30am–5pm; Nov–Feb Sat & Sun 10.30am–4pm charge

Syon House and its 200-acre (80-hectare) park is the London home of the Duke of Northumberland, whose family have lived here for over 400 years. Its 18th-century interior by Robert Adam is unsurpassed, celebrated as the architect's early English masterpiece. From the Long Gallery is a spectacular view over the last tidal water meadow on the Thames. The gardens were created by the great English landscape gardener Capability Brown in the mid-18th century.

Children are well catered for at

In Evolution House at Kew Gardens you can take a walk through 3,500 million years of the history of plants.

ABOVE LEFT: the Waterlily House at Kew. **BELOW:** 17th-century Kew Palace.

At the **Tropical Forest** (daily 10am– 5.30pm) in Syon Park, children can have a "close encounter" with a variety of exotic animals (snakes, toads, tarantulas, caiman). Feeding time is at 1pm at weekends and during school holidays, and other wildlife includes marmosets, parrots and a raccoon.

BELOW: Robert Adam's drawing room at Osterley Park.
BELOW RIGHT: close encounter at Tropical Forest at Syon Park

Syon Park with the **Tropical Forest** *(see margin)* and Snakes and Ladders, a huge indoor play centre.

Further west is another grand house built as a country retreat; **Osterley Park House** (house: Apr–Oct Wed–Sun and bank hols 1–4.30pm, garden: Apr–Oct Wed–Sun and bank hols 11am–5pm; Jersey Road, Isleworth; tel: 8232 5050; www.nationaltrust.org.uk; charge) is a neoclassical mansion, with fine interiors by Robert Adam, 18th-century gardens, and a large landscaped park.

RICHMOND UPON THAMES ❸

Richmond makes for a pleasant day out, easily reached by District Line Underground or by overground trains from Waterloo. Richmond Green is lined with 17th- and 18th-century buildings, while the town centre is good for shopping. Richmond Bridge is the oldest on the river, and the waterfront is always lively, with boats available for hire.

The walk up Richmond Hill to the park leads past views over the Thames and London; in the foreground you may see cows grazing on Petersham Meadows. This view is the only one in England to be protected by an Act of Parliament, passed in 1902.

Richmond Park

✉ Richmond; www.royalparks.gov.uk/parks/richmond_park ☎ 8948 3209 ⏰ daily 7.30am–dusk ⓔ free 🚇 District Line to Richmond, then No. 371 or 65 bus to Petersham Gate

At 2,500 acres (1,000 hectares), Richmond Park is the largest of the royal parks. The pastoral landscape of hills, ponds, gardens and grasslands is popular with walkers, cyclists and horse-riders. Since 1625, when Charles I brought his court to Richmond Palace (now demolished) to escape the plague, there have been herds of red and fallow deer in the park.

The **Isabella Plantation**, an ornamental woodland garden in the southwest corner, has been designed to be interesting all year round, though a favourite time to visit is from April, when the azaleas and rhododendrons bloom. At Pembroke Lodge, a Georgian man-

Recommended Restaurants, Bars & Cafés on page 241

sion on the western edge of the park, are fabulous views over west London. There's a car park here, and refreshments.

Ham House

Ham Street, Ham, Richmond; www.nationaltrust.org.uk 8940 1950 house: Apr–Oct Sat–Wed 1–5pm; garden: all year Sat–Wed 11am–6pm charge District Line to Richmond, then No. 371 bus

About a mile along the Thames Path from Richmond Hill is Ham House, built in 1610 with a sumptuous interior and important collections of textiles, furnishings and paintings. The formal garden is being restored to its former splendour.

Across the river is **Marble Hill House** (Apr–Oct Sat 10am–2pm, Sun and bank hols 10am–5pm; tel: 8892 5115; www.english-heritage.org.uk), an elegant Palladian villa set in riverside parkland.

Intended as an Arcadian retreat, the house was built in 1724 for Henrietta Howard, mistress to King George II when he was Prince of Wales. There is a fine collection of early Georgian paintings.

Hampton Court Palace

East Molesey, Surrey; http://hrp.org.uk/hampton 0870-752 7777 late Mar–late Oct daily 10am–6pm, late Oct–mid Mar daily 10am–4.30pm charge mainline train from Waterloo to Hampton Court

Surrounded by 60 acres (24 hectares) of magnificent gardens on the banks of the Thames, this vast palace, built to rival Versailles in France, dates

TIP

To visit Marble Hill House from the Richmond side of the river, take the Hammertons ferry, which runs between the riverbank outside Ham House in Richmond and Marble Hill Park in Twickenham (tel: 8892 9620; Feb–Oct daily 10–6pm or dusk if earlier; Nov–Jan weekends only. 10am–dusk).

LEFT: Ham House. **BELOW:** the Thames Path at Richmond.

The Thames Path

Starting at the Thames Barrier in the east and ending at the river's source in the Cotswolds 180 miles (290 km) away, the Thames path provides some of the best views of the city and beyond. From Putney the path takes on a rural aspect, passing Barnes Wetland Centre, the grand riverside houses of Chiswick and the pretty cottages of Strand on the Green. After Kew Bridge, the path skirts round Kew Gardens, with Syon Park across the river. At Richmond, with Petersham meadows on your left and a great sweep of the river ahead of you, it's hard to believe the city is in spitting distance. Along this stretch you'll see Marble Hill House and, a little further, Ham House.

The King's Staircase in the State Apartments of William III, Hampton Court Palace.

from the reign of Henry VIII (reigned 1509–47). In the late 1600s many of the Tudor apartments were rebuilt by Sir Christopher Wren, but the Great Hall and Chapel Royal – the most striking rooms – survive.

Start at the introductory exhibition behind the colonnade in Clock Court; here you can decide on your route and find out about activities for children. Costumed guides give entertaining tours of some parts of the palace, including Henry VIII's **State Apartments**.

These you enter through the **Great Hall**, the last of its kind to be built, and the largest room in the palace. The hammer-beam roof and richly carved decoration are original. In the **Tudor Kitchens**, you can feel the heat of the massive kitchen fires and smell the meat simmering in the boiling pot, as if in preparation for a feast in Henry VIII's time.

Allow time to visit the riverside gardens, and the famous maze, planted in 1702 and recently been given sound effects such as whispers of conversation and a dog barking.

WIMBLEDON ❹

This southwest suburb hosts one of the world's top tennis tournaments in June/July and its history is brought to life in the **Wimbledon Lawn Tennis Museum** (daily 10.30am–5pm; Church Road, Wimbledon, tel: 8946 6131; www.wimbledon.org.uk; charge).

On the edge of Wimbledon Common, a partly wooded expanse with nature trails, is the **Wimbledon Windmill Museum** (Apr–Oct Sat 2–5pm, Sun and public hols 11am–5pm; tel: 8947 2825; www.wimbledonwindmillmuseum.org.uk), in a disused windmill. Displays illustrate the milling process, with hands-on milling for children. ❑

RIGHT: the famous Wimbledon trophies.
BELOW: Hampton Court Palace Gardens.

BEST RESTAURANTS AND PUBS

Restaurants

Prices for a three-course dinner per person with a half-bottle of house wine:

£ = under £20
££ = £20–30
£££ = £30–50
££££ = over £50

Chiswick

Giraffe
270 Chiswick High Road, W4 8995 2100 B, L & D daily. £
Bright decor, varied dishes – burgers, stir fries, enchiladas – make this chain member a popular choice for families.

High Road Brasserie
162–4 Chiswick High Road, W4 8742 7474 B, L & D daily. £££
A new location for Chiswick's boho-chic crowd, serving platters of *fruits de mer*, salads, grilled meats and other classic brasserie fare.

Sam's
Barley Mow Centre, 11 Barley Mow Passage, W4 8987 0555 B, L & D daily. £££
Excellent local restaurant which will suit all moods and appetites.

La Trompette
5–7 Devonshire Road, W4 8747 1836 L daily, D Mon–Sat. ££££
Award-winning French country menu with mix of simple classics such as côte de boeuf and more sophisticated offerings.

Kew

The Glasshouse
14 Station Parade, Kew, TW9 8940 6777 L & D daily. ££ (set lunch), ££££
In a pleasant spot, this is one of southwest London's culinary hotspots, Modern French-inspired cuisine.

The Orangery
Kew Gardens, TW9 8332 5655 10am till 1 hour before Gardens close. £
Enjoy coffee, lunch or afternoon tea in this elegant Grade-I listed building.

Richmond

Chez Lindsay
11 Hill Rise, TW10 8948 7473 L & D daily. £ (set lunch), ££
Breton fishing village atmosphere, with superb fish, shellfish, *galettes*, *crêpes* and *steak-frites*.

H20
Floating Restaurant, Richmond Riverside, TW10 8948 0220 L & D daily. ££
The roof of this old barge moored by Richmond Bridge is a great spot for lunch. The Italian food doesn't quite match up to the location.

RIGHT: H20, a floating restaurant in Richmond.

Petersham Nurseries
Off Petersham Road, TW10 8605 3627 seasonal – call for details. £££
This is an enchanting café with tables arranged around the greenhouse of a nursery.

Tootsies
Hotham House, Riverside Richmond, TW9 8948 3436 L & D daily. £
Good burgers and steaks and a great location.

The Richmond Café
58 Hill Rise, TW10 8940 9561 L & D daily. £ (set lunch), ££
Good-value Thai café.

Pubs

Chiswick
Have a drink on the river at Strand on the Green; pubs include **City Barge** (at No. 27) and the **Bell and Crown** *(11 Thames Road)*.

Hammersmith
Riverside pubs include **The Old Ship** *(25 Upper Mall)* and **The Dove** (19 Upper Mall), a pretty 17th-century pub.

Kew
The pubs around the green are appealing, especially when there's a cricket match. The **Inn at Kew Gardens** *(292 Sandycombe Road)* serves imaginative food.

Richmond
Pubs include **The White Swan** *(25–6 Old Palace Lane)*, in a lane off Richmond Green.

Wimbledon
The **Fox and Grapes** *(9 Camp Road)* offers a rural experience, with the Common on three sides, and serves hearty food.

NORTH LONDON

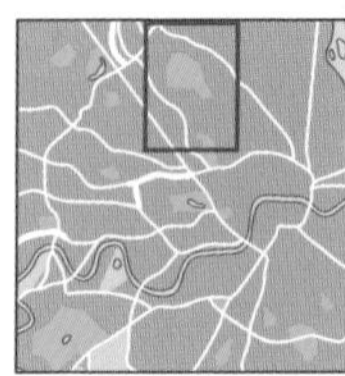

For centuries north Londoners did their best to consign brothels, jails and polluting industries to the south side of the river. The well-to-do preferred to live in areas such as Islington, Hampstead and Highgate, which still retain a distinct and often resented air of superiority

Main attractions
ARSENAL EMIRATES STADIUM
CAMDEN LOCK MARKET
REGENT'S CANAL
HAMPSTEAD HEATH
KEATS MUSEUM
FREUD MUSEUM
HIGHGATE CEMETERY

BELOW: Camden Passage in Islington, a hunting ground for bric-a-brac and antiques.

If you have time, there are several interesting areas to visit in north London, all of them most animated at weekends when they are a magnet for Londoners themselves. Choose between Islington with its vibrant eating and shopping scene, Camden with its canal and market, Hampstead with its famous heath, handsome period properties and museums, or Highgate with its overgrown Victorian cemetery containing the remains of many famous figures. They can all be reached on the Northern Line.

ISLINGTON 5

North of the City of London, City Road rises to the Angel, named after a long-gone coaching inn, marking the start of Islington. In the first half of the 20th century this was a poor and even dangerous area of London. Its once handsome properties were in deep decline, their buddleia-sprouting facades hiding slum conditions and multi-family occupancy.

But as London's Georgian and Victorian dwellings were refurbished in the 1970s, Islington rose phoenix-like from the ashes. It came to to epitomise gentrification, and by the 1980s a popular stereotype portrayed it as the happy hunting ground of liberal-minded *bien pensants*. This is where Tony and Cherie Blair lived before moving to 10 Downing Street.

Place of entertainment

In the 18th and 19th centuries Islington was a place of entertainment. It remains a lively area, thronged with visitors both day and night. There are more than 100 restaurants and café-bars on Upper Street alone, a mile-long corridor of consumerism linking the Angel and Highbury and Islington Tube stations.

The area also has several theatres, most notably the **Almeida Theatre** in Almeida Street, one of London's most innovative small theatres, and,

Recommended Restaurants, Bars & Cafés on pages 248–9

just around the corner, the **King's Head**, the best of several pub-theatres. At the southern end of Islington, on Rosebery Avenue **Sadler's Wells** is one of London's principal dance venues.

Shopping

Near the **Angel**, the crossroads at the top of Islington, the Angel Centre is a small mall of mainstream chain stores. More interesting for visitors is **Chapel Market**, a traditional London streeet market that retains its working-class character, and **Camden Passage** (off the other side of Islington High Street), whose elegant buildings and arcades have become a treasure trove of antiques shops, ranging from simple stalls to grand shops.

For offbeat individual shops, seek out Cross Street and environs, near the Almeida Theatre halfway along Upper Street.

Islington's classic terraces

Prime examples of these can be found in **Gibson Square** and also **Canonbury Square**, where authors George Orwell and Evelyn Waugh

once lived. At 39A Canonbury Square is the **Estorick Collection** (Mon–Sat 11am–6pm, Sun 2–5pm; tel: 7704 9522; charge), a collection of Italian Futurist and figurative art in an elegant Georgian house.

Last, but to many minds by no means least, Islington is also the home of **Arsenal Football Club**, which in 2006 moved to the new Emirates stadium (the team's old stadium is being turned into luxury

Tickets for the better Arsenal fixtures are virtually impossible to obtain unless you are a club member. Tickets can occasionally be secured for minor matches (www.arsenal.com; tel: 7704 4040, recorded info: 7704 4242). But anyone can take a stadium tour (which includes a visit to the musueum) or a "Legends Tour" in which you can meet one of five Arsenal "legends", including Charlie George and John Radford. For further information about these, consult the website.

BELOW: Islington's Upper Street.

KIDS

You can take a 50-minute narrowboat trip from Camden (on the *Jenny Wren*, tel: 7485 4433) or Little Venice (Jason's Narrowboats, tel: 7286 3428)

apartments). Although it is pretty difficult for non-members to obtain tickets for a game *(see margin note, page 246)*, you can take a tour of the stadium and visit the museum.

CAMDEN ❻

It's **Camden Market** that attracts the crowds to Camden, though like Islington it also has many fine period terraces and squares, and a hip pub and club scene. The main market (Camden High Street, Thur–Sun 9am–5.30pm) has cheap clothes. **Camden Lock Market** (off Chalk Farm Road, outdoor stalls Sat–Sun 10am– 6pm, indoor stalls daily except Mon) focuses on crafts *(also see pages 54–5)*. The quality of goods has fallen in recent years, even if the size of the crowds haven't.

One of the delights of Camden is Camden Lock. A sequence of two locks and a bridge in quick succession, it is one of the most attractive stretches of the **Regent's Canal**. From here the towpath, busy with cyclists (including bicycling commuters during the weekday rush hours), walkers and fishermen, heads west to Little Venice and east to Hackney *(see box below)* and beyond. The last horse-drawn cargo passed along the canal in 1956.

BELOW: Camden Lock.
RIGHT: narrowboats on Regent's Canal.

The Jewish Museum

✉ 128–129 Albert Street;
www.jewmusm.ort.org ☎ 7284 1997
🕒 Mon–Thur 10am–4pm (Sun 5pm)
£ charge 🚇 Camden Town

The Camden branch of the Jewish Museum (there is another one at 80 East End Road, Finchley, tel: 8349 1143) occupies an elegant early Victorian building but the interior is modern with sophisticated displays, including an interactive map

Regent's Canal

This 8½-mile (14-km) stretch of water running from Little Venice near Paddington in west London to Limehouse in Docklands was dug between 1812 and 1820 and drops 86 ft (25 metres) through 12 locks beneath 57 bridges. The canal has some delightfully rural stretches and also passes through London Zoo. The stretch between Camden and Victoria Park in Hackney takes around a morning to complete (the towpath is interrupted in Islington, where the canal passes through a ¾ mile (1.5 km) tunnel, but can be picked up again close to the Angel). To learn more about the history of the canal visit the Canal Museum at Battlebridge Basin, King's Cross *(see page 140)*.

Recommended Restaurants, Bars & Cafés on pages 248–9

showing centres of Jewish population in different periods, and there is a gallery devoted to Judaica illustrating religious rituals as passed down the centuries. The Finchley branch depicts the migrations of Jews to London and has a Holocaust gallery.

HAMPSTEAD 7

Hampstead has long been a desirable address and attracts a literary set. Open spaces predominate. The 3-sq-mile (8-sq-km) **Heath** leads down to **Parliament Hill** which gives splendid views across London, as does the 112-acre (45-hectare) **Primrose Hill** overlooking Regent's Park. These are all welcome acres over which locals stride, walk dogs, fly kites, skate and swim in the bathing ponds. History-laden pubs near the heath include **Jack Straw's Castle**, the **Spaniards Inn** and the **Old Bull and Bush.**

Keats House

Keats Grove, NW3; www.keatshouse.gov.uk 7435 2062 May–Oct Tue–Sun noon–5pm charge Hampstead

The poet John Keats (1795–1821) wrote much of his work, including *Ode to a Nightingale*, during the two years he lived in Hampstead. It was here that he met and fell in love with Fanny Brawne, the daughter of his next door neighbour. His house-museum contains memorabilia such as facsimiles of his letters, a lock of his hair and Fanny Brawne's engagement ring.

The Freud Museum

20 Maresfield Gardens, NW3; www.freud.org.uk 7435 2002 Wed–Sun noon–5pm charge Finchley Road

Sigmund Freud, fleeing the Nazis in 1938, moved from Vienna to this house in Hampstead. He died just a year later, but his daughter Anna, also a psychoanalyst, looked after it until her own death in 1982.

The museum preserves the house as they left it, and includes many pieces of furniture and other possessions brought over from Vienna. Freud's study on the ground floor includes the couch on which his Viennese patients free-associated, oriental rugs, books and pictures, plus his prize collection of antiquities, including framed Roman frescoes and Greek vases.

Keats lived in Hampstead between 1818 and 1820. In the winter of 1820 he was advised by his physician to leave England for the warmer climate of Italy. He never returned, dying in Rome in 1821, aged 25.

LEFT: Freud's famous couch at the Freud Museum in Hampstead. **BELOW:** views over London from Hampstead Heath.

Hampstead's elevation gave it a sense of safety. When a great flood that would wipe out London was forecast for 1 February 1524, crowds climbed the hill to observe it. In 1736, the end of the world was predicted and many came here to await their doom.

Kenwood House

Hampstead Lane; www.english-heritage.org.uk
8348 1286 daily 10am–6pm, Oct–Mar until 4pm free
Archway or Highgate

Looking like a great wedding cake, Kenwood House was remodelled in 1764–79 by Robert Adam and overlooks Hampstead Heath. Its beautifully maintained rooms showcase the **Iveagh Bequest**, a major collection with works by Rembrandt, Vermeer, Reynolds, Turner and Gainsborough. Upstairs rooms are usually reserved for exhibitions, but the one small public gallery contains an exquisite collection of cameos, intaglios (incised brooches and seals) and belt buckles. Poetry readings and chamber music recitals take place in the Orangery.

Other grand houses

Hampstead has several other notable houses open to the public. On Windmill Hill, parallel to Heath Street, Fenton House (Apr–Nov Wed–Fri 2–5pm, Sat–Sun 11am–5pm; tel: 7435 3471; www.nationaltrust. org.uk; charge) is a 17th-century mansion containing notable collections of harpsichords and ceramics.

Tucked away among the lanes is **Burgh House** (Wed–Sun noon–5pm; New End Square, tel: 7431 0144) which has a fine music room and library and an award-winning garden. One of London's finest Queen Anne-style houses, it doubles as **Hampstead Museum**, which has a display on the landscape painter John Constable (1776–1837), a one-time local.

HIGHGATE 8

Neighbouring Highgate, a hill-top suburb built round a pretty square, contains London's grandest cemetery. Highgate Cemetery (www.highgate-cemetery.org; tel: 8340 1834; charge) comprises two sections (see box). The eastern cemetery (Mon–Fri 10am–5pm, weekends 11am–5pm, until 4pm Nov–Mar) can be visited independently, though guided tours are available. The western section, across Swain's Lane, is more atmospheric but it can only be visited on one of the one-hour guided tours (at weekends tours are conducted every hour

BELOW RIGHT: the memorial to Karl Marx. **BELOW FAR RIGHT:** Highgate Cemetery is full of elaborate memorials and staues, including plenty of weeping angels.

Highgate Cemetery

As London expanded in the early 19th century, the matter of where to bury the dead became a pressing problem. A number of new cemeteries were therefore built on the city's outskirts, including, in 1839, the western section of Highgate Cemetery. In 1854 the cemetery was expanded when another section was opened on the eastern side of Swain's Lane.

These quintessentially Victorian cemeteries are noted for their grandiose mausoleums (many listed structures) and statues, artfully covered in creepers and set amidst wild flowers. One of the chief attractions is the rather grim bust of Karl Marx, who was buried in the eastern section in 1883. There are some 850 notable people buried in the two cemeteries, among them the novelist George Eliot, members of the Rosetti family, and the scientist Michael Faraday. It is well worth taking one of the guided tours *(see contact details in the main text).*

between 11am and 4pm or 3pm Nov–Mar; on weekdays tours should be booked). The cemetery is administered as a museum, with charges for taking photographs.

NORTHERN OUTPOSTS

Also worth highlighting are a couple of attractions in suburbs further north. Hendon is reached by the Northern Line and Walthamstow by the Victoria Line.

Hendon

The main reason to visit this northern suburb is the **Royal Air Force Museum** (daily 10am–6pm; Grahame Park Way; tel: 8205 2266; www.rafmuseum.org.uk; free). It has a large array of bombers and fighter jets, plus flight simulators and a Battle of Britain Hall with tableaux of scenes from World War II. You can wander among some of the most famous aeoplanes in history.

Walthamstow

An outpost at the far end of the Tube's Victoria line, Walthamstow is not an obvious tourist attraction, but

admirers of the British Arts and Crafts movement may like to visit the **William Morris Gallery** (Lloyd Park, Forest Rd, Walthamstow, E17; www.lbwf.gov/wmg/home.htm; tel: 8527 3782; Tue–Sat and first Sun of the month 10am–1pm and 2–5pm; charge). It contains an outstanding collection of fabrics, rugs, wallpapers, furniture, glass and tiles, designed by Morris and members of his circle. ❑

KIDS

Though rather a long trek by Tube to Colindale, plus a 15-minute walk from there, the Royal Air Force Museum is a huge hit with most children, especially boys. It is also free, as is the Tube journey for children under the age of 11.

ABOVE LEFT: characteristic William Morris fabric at the William Morris Gallery.
BELOW: the Royal Air Force Museum, Hendon.

BEST RESTAURANTS, BARS AND CAFÉS

Restaurants

Prices for a three-course dinner per person with a half-bottle of house wine:

£ = under £20
££ = £20–30
£££ = £30–50
££££ = over £50

Islington

Afghan Kitchen
35 Islington Green, N1. 7359 8019 L & D Tue–Sat. £
A favourite of many Islingtonians, this tiny restaurant offers a small choice of delicately spiced, melt-in-the-mouth dishes such as chicken in yoghurt and lamb with spinach. One large table downstairs. Best to book. Cash only.

The Almeida
30 Almeida Street, N1. 7354 4777 L & D daily. £££
Conran restaurant specialising in regional French cuisine, with old favourites such as frogs' legs and *coquilles St Jacques*. Bang opposite the Almeida Theatre. Also offers a tapas menu in summer.

Casale Franco
Rear of 134–7 Upper Street, N1 7226 8994 L & D daily. £££
Stylish Italian with a mellow buzz tucked up an alleyway just off Upper Street. The menu includes plenty of fish as well as pasta and wheel-sized pizzas.

The Draper's Arms
44 Barnsbury Street, N1 7619 0348 L & D Mon–Sat, D only Sun. £££
In a leafy residential street, this is one of the area's top gastropubs. Robust flavours include lamb shank with butter beans and chorizo.

The Fish Shop on St John Street
360–2 St John Street, EC1. 7837 1199 L & D Tue–Sat. £££
Handy for visitors to Sadler's Wells, this modern fish restaurant features char-grilled whole sea bass, lobster, and cod or plaice fried in batter or with a traditional Jewish coating of egg and matzo meal. Child portions available.

Isarn
119 Upper St, N1 7424 5153 L & D daily. ££
Long and slender Thai restaurant with a few tables on the deck at the back. Well-prepared dishes range from simple green curries and stir-fries to lobster in tamarind sauce.

Ottolenghi
287 Upper S, N1 7288 1454 L & D daily. £–££
Stylish, with one long white table stretching down the centre of the restaurant. Great for breakfasts, light lunches (including inventive salads), savoury pastries, and divine cakes and tarts. They sell items on a takeaway basis too.

Pasha
301 Upper St, N1 7226 1454 L & D daily. ££
Upper Street has several inexpensive Turkish restaurants, but this one is a cut above the rest. It offers a plush and sophisticated interior, good service and modern European food with a Turkish twist. The good-value meze is a great option for lunch.

Camden

Camden Brasserie
9 Jamestown Road, NW1 7482 2114 L & D daily. £££
Long established and perennially popular. The space is elegantly decorated and dishes, particularly the grills, are satisfyingly tasty.

Cottons
55 Chalk Farm Road, NW1 7485 8388 D only Mon–Fri (until 1am on Fri) L & D Sat and Sun. ££
Inspiring Caribbean

LEFT: the Almeida restaurant, Islington.
ABOVE RIGHT: sweet treats at Ottolenghi, Islington.

restaurant with inventive options as well as firm favourites such as jerk chicken and roasted goat. A party atmosphere prevails on Friday and Saturday evenings.

Lemonia

89 Regents Park Road, NW1
7586 7454 L & D Mon–Fri, D only Sat, L only Sun. **££**
Long-established local serving tasty meze and Greek char-grills. A bona fide family restaurant.

Sardo Canale

42 Gloucester Ave, NW1
7722 2800 L & D daily. **££**
Sardinian restaurant with a bustling Mediterranean atmosphere, superb fish and seafood.The canal-side patio is a great spot for a summer lunch.

Singapore Sling

16 Inverness Street, NW1
7424 9527 L & D daily. **££**
An extensive range of Malaysian dishes served in atmospheric surroundings, close to Camden Tube station.

Odette's

130 Regent's Park Rd, NW1
7586 8569 Tue–Sat L & D, D only Sun. **£££**
Primrose Hill restaurant where Noel Gallagher famously proposed to Patsy Kensit in the 1990s. Fussy over-the-top interior – swagged curtains and fancy wallpaper – but good modern European food.

Hampstead

The Wells

30 Well Walk, NW3 7794 3785 L & D daily. **£££**
A spacious gastropub with discreet corners and pretty views from its upstairs restaurant. Dishes include grilled plaice with garlic crust, braised endive and red-wine lentils. A cheaper menu is available in the less exclusive downstairs bar.

Woodlands

102 Heath St, NW3 7794 3080 L & D daily. **£**
Sophisticated setting for authentically spiced vegetarian dishes from southern India. Part of a global chain that began in India around 70 years ago.

Zara

11 South End Road, NW3
7794 5498 L & D daily. **££**
Friendly Turkish place, with well-cooked meat dishes. Ottoman rugs and cushions abound.

Bars, Pubs and Cafés

Islington
Bars include the enjoyable, canal-facing **Babushka** *(125 Caledonian Rd, N1)*, the quirky **Bar & Dining House** *(2 Essex Rd, N1)*, the intimate, slightly louche **Embassy** *(119 Essex Rd, N1)*, the funky **Medicine Bar** *(181 Upper Street, N1)* and the music-oriented **Social** *(Arlington Square, N1)*. Traditional pubs include the ornate **Camden Head** *(2 Camden Walk, N1)* and the **King's Head** (115 Upper St, N1) which pioneered pub theatre.

Islington has a host of lively cafés, but for possibly the best almond croissants in town visit **Patisserie Bliss** at 426 St John's St, a tiny café just south of the Angel. **Ottolenghi** *(see main listings)* is also great for mid-morning or afternoon treats.

Camden
Bars include the bohemian **Monkey Chews** *(2 Queen's Crescent, NW5)*, and the hip **Bar Vinyl** *(6 Inverness Street, NW1)*. **The Engineer** *(65 Gloucester Avenue, NW1)* is a grandiose gastropub with good but pricey food.

Hampstead
Bars include the mirrored, good-value **Babushka** *(58–62 Heath Street, NW3)*, the pub conversion **Hill** *(94 Haverstock Hill, NW3)*, and the Asian-oriented **Opera** *(68 Heath Street, NW3)*. Celebrated pubs include the Victorian **Flask** *(14 Flask Walk, NW3)*, **Jack Straw's Castle** *(North End Way, NW3)*, handy for the heath, and **Spaniards Inn** *(Spaniards Road, NW3)*, a large 16th-century coaching inn with garden.

EAST LONDON

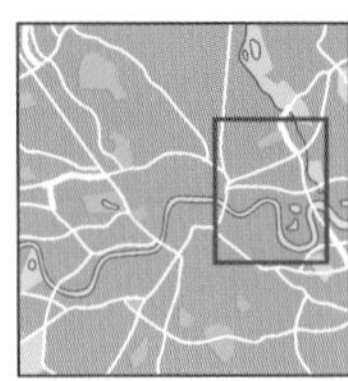

For centuries, waves of immigrants settled in areas such as Bethnal Green and Spitalfields, often in slum conditions. Today museums recall their struggles to succeed, and the docklands which once provided them with jobs have given way to canyons of office blocks

Main attractions

- COLUMBIA ROAD FLOWER MARKET
- MUSEUM OF CHILDHOOD
- BRICK LANE CURRY HOUSES
- TRUMAN BREWERY
- SUNDAY UPMARKET
- CHRIST CHURCH
- SPITALFIELDS MARKET
- WHITECHAPEL ART GALLERY
- MUSEUM IN DOCKLANDS

East London was the first stop for many of the immigrants whose labour helped fuel the Industrial Revolution and build the docks through which much of the British Empire's trade passed. Poverty and overcrowding were endemic.

Today, many areas remain poor, but others have been gentrified.

HOXTON

Hoxton, north of Old Street first became fashionable when young artists such as Damien Hirst and Tracey Emin moved here, creating studios in redundant warehouses. As they became successful, art dealers and web designers followed and urban desolation became urban chic.

Commercial galleries radiate from **Hoxton Square**, the location of Jay Jopling's White Cube2 gallery. Café-bars and clothes shops line the streets around Curtain Road, and the area is one of London's most popular places for a night out. On Sundays Hoxton's **Columbia Road market** (8am–2pm) specialises in flowers, plants and garden accessories *(see pages 56–7)*.

BELOW: Columbia Road Market.

The Geffrye Museum Ⓐ

136 Kingsland Rd, E2; www.geffrye-museum.org.uk 7739 9893 Tue–Sat 10am–5pm, Sun noon–5pm free Old Street

This museum charts the interior decorating tastes of the urban middle classes from 1600 to the present day. Housed in a square of former almshouses, built in 1714, it was intended to inspire workers in the East End furniture trade. The rooms – all of which are "sitting" or "living" rooms – are arranged chronologically from 1620 to 1990. Behind the buildings, the museum's gardens (Apr–Oct) display period gardens, overlooked by a pleasant restaurant.

Recommended Restaurants, Bars & Cafés on page 255

BETHNAL GREEN

This is one of the poorest areas of London. Nonetheless, it has two excellent museums, both focusing on childhood.

Museum of Childhood B

Cambridge Heath Rd, E2; www. vam. ac.uk/moc 8980 2415
daily 10am–5.45pm free
Bethnal Green

Displays in this outpost of the V&A Museum *(see pages 216–7)* range from classic children's toys to the development of nappies and the root of adolescent rebellion. There's much to appeal to children. A magnificent rocking horse can be ridden, the model railways can be activated, a dressing-up box can be rifled through, an activity corner encourages learning through play. There are also some sobering facts to be learnt about childcare and health.

Less than a mile away, the **Ragged School Museum C** (Wed–Thur 10am–5pm, first Sun of month 2–5pm; 46–50 Copperfield Road; tel: 8980 6405; www.ragged schoolmuseum.org.uk; free) has a reconstructed kitchen and classroom to

A Regency period room, 1800–30, at the Geffrye Museum.

East London

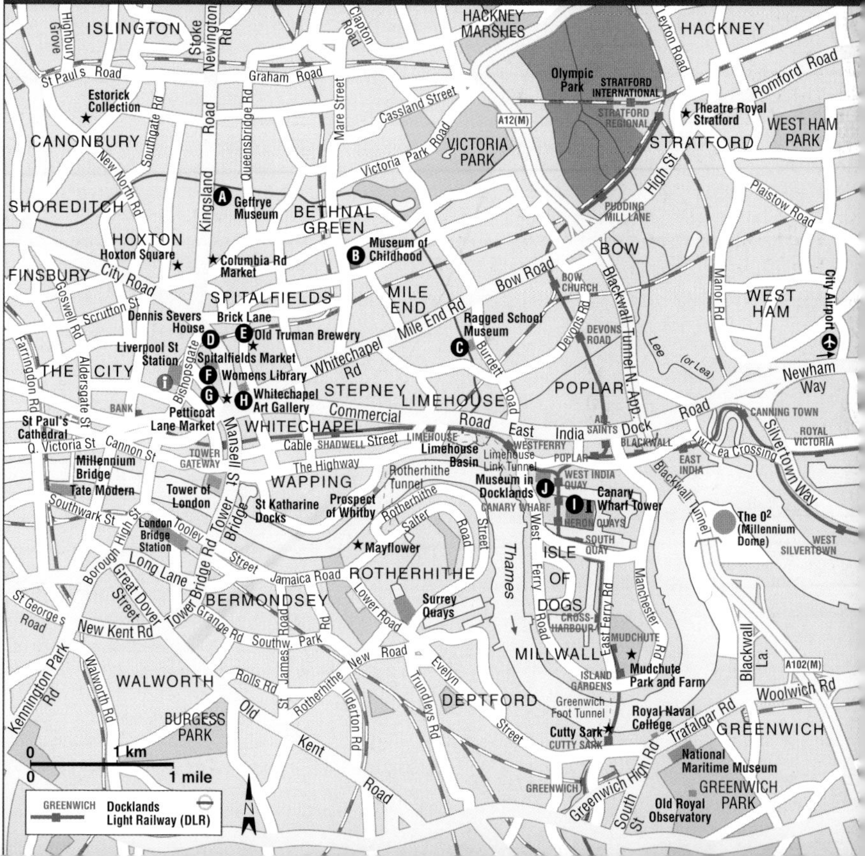

The 2012 Olympics

With London set to host the Olympic Games for a third time in 2012, a huge regeneration project is underway in east London, where most of the events will take place.

Following a closely fought contest between London and Paris in 2005, the International Olympic Committee announced that London would host the 2012 Olympics and Paralympics. One of the strengths of the London bid, which was led by former Olympic gold medalist Sebastian Coe, was the opportunity for urban development in east London.

The construction of a new Olympic Park in Stratford has brought much needed investment to the area. Situated in the Lower Lea Valley, the 500-acre (200-hectare)-site will house nine purpose-built sporting venues, a media centre and an Olympic Village providing accommodation for all of the athletes. The centrepiece of the park will be an 80,000-seat athletics stadium which will also be the setting for the opening and closing ceremonies. A state-of-the-art aquatics centre is planned, as well as a hockey centre, a velopark and four multi-sports arenas for fencing, volleyball, basketball and handball.

Existing sports venues in other parts of London will also be used for the games, with football matches at the new Wembley Stadium, tennis at Wimbledon and archery at Lord's Cricket Ground. Some of London's many parks have been incorporated into the extensive network of venues. Greenwich Park will provide a picturesque backdrop for equestrian events, while the Triathlon will take place in Hyde Park and a road-cycling course will be created in Regent's Park. Horse Guards Parade, a parade ground usually reserved for royal occasions, will be transformed into a beach volleyball pitch.

London's ailing transport network is being extended and improved in order to accommodate the 500,000 spectators expected to travel to the Olympic Park each day. Many of these visitors are expected to travel on the Javelin, a high-speed shuttle which will whizz passengers from central London to the Olympic Park in just 7 minutes. Extensions to the East London line and the Docklands Light Railway are under construction, as is a Channel Tunnel rail link from Stratford.

The redevelopment has not been without controversy, however. Budgets have rocketed and the total bill is expected to be more than £7 billion, far exceeding original estimates.

Perhaps with this in mind, much emphasis has been placed on the legacy of the games. The Olympic Park itself will become the largest urban public park in Europe, complete with waterways and wildlife areas, while the Olympic Village will be converted into apartments. Most of the sports venues in the park will remain and become available for public use, while some will offer training facilities for potential future Olympians.

ABOVE AND LEFT: computer-generated impressions of the main stadium.

show how life was once lived by London's indomitable East Enders. An exhibition entitled "Tower Hamlets: A Journey Through Time" testifies to the solidarity shown by East Enders during hard times such as the Blitz.

SPITALFIELDS

Spitalfields contains several streets of fine 18th-century houses that were originally the homes of Huguenot silk weavers.

Dennis Severs' House D

18 Folgate St; www.dennissevershouse.co.uk 7247 4013 first and third Sun of month 2–5pm, first and third Mon of month noon–2pm charge Liverpool St

Among the fine 18th-century properties is this four-storey town house still lit only by gaslight. The late Dennis Severs, an American, laid out the 10 rooms as if they were still occupied by an 18th-century family.

Markets

Successive waves of immigrants have left their mark on **Brick Lane** E. French Huguenots sought refuge here at the end of the 17th century, Jews fleeing the Russian pogroms arrived in the late-19th century and today the area has a large Bangladeshi community. Famous for its curry houses, it also has some of East London's best bars and nightclubs, most of which are within the Old Truman Brewery, the self-styled "creative hub" of the East End. Also here is the Sunday UpMarket (Ely's Yard, Sun 10am–5pm), selling clothes from independent designers and gastronomic treats.

Spitalfields Market F (Commercial Street; Mon–Fri 10am–4pm, Sun 9am–5pm), once a wholesale fruit and vegetable market, now sells mainly clothes and crafts, as well as records and books on Tuesdays, and antiques on Thursdays. To the south, centring on Middlesex Street is **Petticoat Lane** G market, packed on Sundays with dozens of stalls specialising in cheap clothes.

WHITECHAPEL

On Old Castle Street, parallel to Middlesex Street, a Victorian bathhouse has been converted into The Women's Library (tel: 7320 2222; www.thewomenslibrary.ac.uk), a collection of suffragette memorabilia, plus publications produced over the years by the women's movement. Proof of

At the end of Fournier Street, one of Spitalfields finest streets, is Christ Church (1729), the greatest of Nicholas Hawksmoor's churches.

LEFT: Spitalfields Market. **BELOW:** the Museum of Childhood in Bethnal Green.

KIDS

An incongruous attraction in this over-concreted part of Docklands (known as the Isle of Dogs) is the 35-acre (14-hectare) **Mudchute Park and Farm** (daily 9am–5pm; tel: 7515 5901; www.mudchute.org; free) on Pier Street. As well as farm animals, it has llamas, a pets' corner and a riding centre.

identification is required to access the library. A space on the ground floor hosts exhibitions exploring all aspects of women's lives.

A local vicar and his wife founded the **Whitechapel Art Gallery** H (80–82 Whitechapel High Street, tel: 7522 7861; www.whitechapel.org; Wed–Sun 11am–6pm, Thur until 9pm; free) in 1897. Lacking a permanent collection, it mounts high-profile exhibitions in a spectacular space. Picasso's *Guernica* was here in 1939.

DOCKLANDS

London's docks, made derelict by heavy World War II bombing and rendered obsolete by new container ports to the east, were transformed in the 1990s. Their proximity to the financial institutions of the City made them an attractive location for buildings such as **Canary Wharf** I, whose main tower, One Canada Square, is Britain's highest building, at 800 ft (244 metres). Several national newspapers are based here.

It's worth taking a ride through the area on the **Docklands Light Railway** (from Bank to Greenwich) to see how property developers turned the place into an architect's adventure playground.

The **Museum in Docklands** J (daily 10am–6pm; No 1 Warehouse, West India Quay; tel: 0870 444 3857; www.museumindocklands.org.uk; charge) recounts 2,000 years of history. It includes a 20-ft (6-metre) model of Old London Bridge, a re-creation of the Rhinebeck Panorama, portraying a teeming Pool of London at the end of the 18th century, and an evocative reconstruction of the 19th-century Sailortown district. ❑

RIGHT: ground level in Docklands.
BELOW: llamas at Mudchute Farm *(see margin tip above).*

BEST RESTAURANTS, BARS AND CAFÉS

Restaurants

Prices for a three-course dinner per person with a half-bottle of house wine:

£ = under £20
££ = £20–30
£££ = £30–50
££££ = over £50

Spitalfields

Eyre Brothers Restaurant
70 Leonard St, EC2 7613 5346 L & D Mon–Fri, D only Sat. ££££]
Adventurous fusion of European-influenced meat and vegetable dishes. Simple, distinct flavours.

Great Eastern Dining Room
54–56 Great Eastern St, EC2 7613 4545 L & D Mon–Fri, D only Sat. £££
Contemporary pan-Asian food, from dim sum to prawn *pad thai*. Chic but cramped interior. Attracts a young crowd.

Les Trois Garçons
1 Club Row, E1 7613 1924 D only Mon–Sat. ££££
Extravagantly decorated (stuffed tigers, etc) ex-pub with French food. The nearby Loungelover cocktail bar run by the same people is the perfect place for a pre- or post-dinner drink.

Canteen
2 Crispin Place, E1
0845 686 1122
L & D daily. ££
Modern British food made with seasonal ingredients. Down-to-earth restaurant.

Hoxton

The Real Greek
14–15 Hoxton Market, N1
7739 8212 L & D Mon–Sun. ££
Authentic and award-winning taverna, serving delicious meze platters, plus *souvlaki* and meat dishes cooked on a charcoal grill.

Docklands

Bar Spice
145 Three Colt Street, Limehouse, E14 7093 0111 L Mon–Fri, D only Sat. £££
Traditional Bengali and tandoori dishes, plus more unusual Indian takes on dishes such as John Dory. Elegant.

Browns Restaurant & Bar
Hertsmere Road, E14.
7987 9777 L & D daily.
£££
Traditional British atmosphere and popular classics such as salmon fishcakes.

ABOVE RIGHT: Favela Chic on Great Eastern Street.
RIGHT: coffee stop, Spiltalfieds.

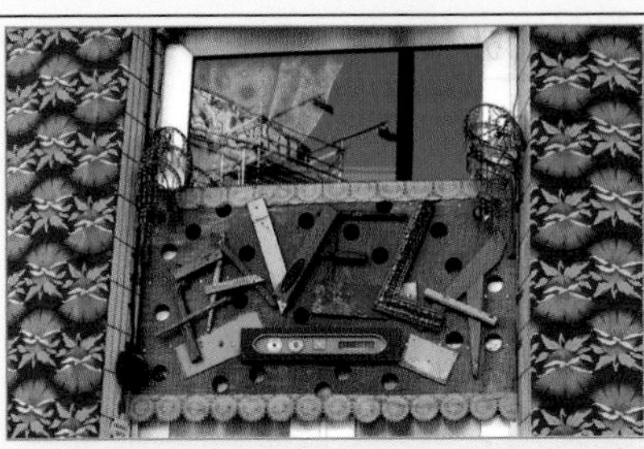

Bars, Pubs and Cafés

From classic East End pubs to trendy bars, there is no shortage of places to go drinking in east London. With its "shantytown" interior, **Favela Chic** *(Great Eastern Street)* offers good food and even better music. At **Hoxton Square Bar and Kitchen** you can catch live music, sip cocktails or enjoy a tasty steak from their flame grill. Just the other side of Old Street, Curtain Road is lined with bars, including **The Elbow Room Pool Lounge and Bar**, a lively bar-cum-pool-hall. Around the corner on Shoreditch High Street, **Bar Kick** is a laid-back place with a good food and drinks menu and table football. Just off Brick Lane, the Old Truman Brewery houses **Café 1001**, a coffee shop and DJ bar, and **The Big Chill Bar** which lives up to its name with comfy sofas and groovy tunes. The **Vibe Bar** is a buzzing venue with DJs every night of the week. Another Brick lane institution, **93 Feet East** has two bars, a large courtyard area and a main hall which plays host to a variety of gigs, DJs and film screenings. There are plenty of East End pubs around Spitalfields Market, including the **Ten Bells**, where one of Jack the Ripper's victims was allegedly last sighted.

SOUTH LONDON

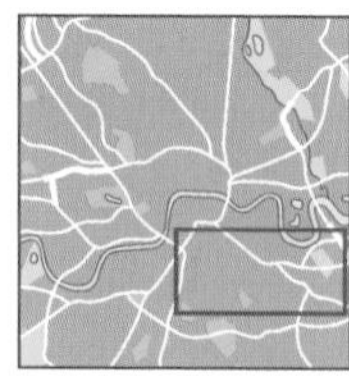

South London's suburban "villages"include Greenwich and Woolwich, with their distinguished naval and military heritage, historic Blackheath, leafy Dulwich and, in the southwest, vibrant Brixton

Main attractions
- NATIONAL MARITIME MUSEUM
- ROYAL OBSERVATORY
- GREENWICH PARK
- GREENWICH MARKET
- ROYAL NAVAL COLLEGE
- CUTTY SARK
- THAMES BARRIER
- HORNIMAN MUSEUM
- DULWICH PICTURE GALLERY
- BRIXTON MARKET

BELOW: the Docklands from Greenwich.

Neighbourhoods and communities on the southern bank of the Thames offer parkland, museums, art galleries and great places to eat out. They are connected by a spaghetti of overground railway lines emanatine from London Bridge and Charing Cross railway stations.

GREENWICH ❾

A good way of getting to Greenwich is the time-honoured tradition of arriving at this maritime centre by water. Boats leave Westminster Pier daily from 10am (10.40am in winter) and take about 60 minutes. The best alternative is via the Docklands Light Railway.

Cutty Sark

✉ King William Walk, SE10; www.cuttysark.org.uk ⏲ temporary exhibition 11am–5pm ☎ 8858 3445 🚉 DLR

On the waterfront at Greenwich the *Cutty Sark* usually stands proudly in dry dock. However, the sailing ship from the great days of the 19th-

Recommended Restaurants, Cafés & Bars on page 2

century tea clippers, now a museum, has been undergoing a £25 million restoration, a process that has been considerably lengthened by a serious fire at the site in 2007 *(see below)*.

Built at a Dumbarton shipyard in 1869 the vessel was only expected to last about 30 years. But it has outlived its builders and crews. It opened as a museum in 1957 and was a popular London icon until old age began to show. While the conservation work is underway the Master's Saloon, removed from the ship, forms part of an exhibition in a pavilion next to the museum site.

National Maritime Museum

Park Row, SE10; www.nmm.ac.uk
daily 10am–5pm, summer til 6pm;
8858 4422 free DLR

Located in Greenwich Royal Park, the **National Maritime Museum** displays an unrivalled collection of maritime art and artefacts. Its 16 galleries are set around the Neptune Courtyard, a spectacular space spanned by a glass roof.

Ground Floor

Two of the six ground-floor galleries cover great explorers, from Vikings to 19th-century polar pioneers. In addition, the Passengers Gallery focuses on the mass migrations from Europe to America in the 19th and early 20th centuries; the Cargoes Gallery covers post-war maritime trade and the evolution of the cargo ship; the Maritime London Gallery explores the city's naval heritage; and the Rank and Style Gallery displays practical and ceremonial clothing worn at sea.

First Floor

Here Trade and Empire covers the expansion of the British Empire, focusing on slavery, the tea trade and opium wars, and Cook's Pacific voyages; the Art and the Sea Gallery displays European marine art from the past 400 years; and the Sea Power Gallery covers the history of the Navy.

A giant sphere in the courtyard area projects images of the sea onto 32 screens, showing both the beauty of the oceans and the modern world's careless destruction of them.

A statue of the explorer Captain James Cook (1728–79) looks out to the Royal Observatory.

BELOW LEFT: Greenwich Park. **BELOW:** the *Cutty Sark* will eventually be returned to its former glory.

Restoration and Devastation

The *Cutty Sark* is the last ship of its kind in the world and for that reason the old tea clipper was made the subject of a £25-million restoration project in 2006. It was temporarily dismantled so that the hull and other valuable parts could be restored by a specialist team.

Then, in May 2007, midway through the project, there was a devastating early-morning fire at the site. The flames took two hours to contain. Although many sections of the ship were in safe storage at the time, including the masts, the stern, considered too fragile to move, suffered acute damage, and about 50 percent of the hull's ironwork and timber were destroyed.

However, the blaze was a set-back rather than a death blow, and restoration was resumed. When the ship eventually reopens, it will be suspended 3 metres (10 ft) above ground, with elevators transporting visitors from the dry berth to all decks.

An alternative way to reach central London from Greenwich is to walk through a foot tunnel under the Thames and board a Docklands Light Railway train at Island Gardens. The 1,217-ft (365-metre) tunnel, built in 1897–1902, enabled local workers to reach the West India Docks on the north bank of the river.

ABOVE RIGHT: entrance to the foot tunnel under the Thames. **BELOW LEFT:** the Royal Observatory and Flamsteed House. **BELOW RIGHT:** the Queen's House.

Third Floor

Here, a whole gallery is dedicated to Admiral Horatio Nelson (1758–1805). The museum's most prized possession is the uniform coat he wore on board the *Victory* during the Battle of Trafalgar. The fatal bullet hole at the shoulder is clearly visible.

There are two interactive galleries on this floor: the All Hands Gallery, where visitors can send a Morse code message, have a go at gunnery target practice or try out a diver's suit; and the Bridge, where you can take the helm of a Viking longship or try to steer a virtual paddle steamer on the Thames.

The Queen's House

Completed in 1637, the Queen's House, showcasing the museum's art collections, was designed as a summer palace for Queen Anne of Denmark, the wife of James I (reigned 1603–25). Designed by Inigo Jones, it was England's first classical Renaissance building.

Royal Observatory

Greenwich Park, Blackheath Avenue, SE10; www.rog.nmm.ac.uk
8858 4422 daily 10am–5pm
free DLR Greenwich

It's a steep climb through the park – but worth it – to the **Royal Observatory**. Greenwich Mean Time was established here in 1884, and the observatory has Britain's largest refracting telescope. A brass rule on the ground marks the line between the Eastern and Western hemispheres.

Flamsteed House, designed by Sir Christopher Wren (himself a keen astronomer), contains exhibits tracing the history of astronomy from its earliest origins in the ancient civilisations of Sumeria and Egypt. A £15-

Map on pages 230–1
Recommended Restaurants, Cafés & Bars on page 263

million expansion has added gallery space to showcase the valuable items on display, including a Chinese sundial and a lodestone, an ore used for magnetising compass needles.

The *pièce de résistance* is a complete collection of John Harrison's ornate sea clocks, designed to remain accurate through the heat and cold, humidity and constant motion experienced on a ship at sea. They allowed mariners to determine their position east or west – an achievement chronicled in Dava Sobel's 1995 bestseller *Longitude*. John Harrison's story is retold by costumed actors daily at noon, 1.05pm, 2pm and 3pm.

A short distance from the main complex is the South Building, housing the state-of-the-art **Peter Harrison Planetarium** (10am–5pm, until 6pm July–Aug; shows Mon–Fri 2.30pm; weekends various times, tel: 8312 6608; charge). It includes interactive exhibits and an education centre.

Royal Naval College

2 Cutty Sark Gardens, SE10; www.oldroyalnavalcollege.org
8269 4747 daily 10am–5pm
free DLR Greenwich

The **Royal Naval College** begun by Christopher Wren in 1696 was built in two halves to preserve the view from Queen's House to the river. Originally a royal palace, it was given over to the training of naval officers in 1873. The chapel, where regular Sunday services are held, is full of decorative touches, and the ceiling of the Painted Hall, originally a sailors' dining room, displays a celebrated painting of William and Mary (who reigned 1689–1702) handing Liberty and Peace to Europe.

In 2006, during routine maintenance, Tudor brickwork was unearthed in the grounds. Subsequent

The Royal Observatory's Octagonal Room, whose tall windows were used to observe comets and eclipses.

LEFT: the magnetic clock outside the Royal Observatory.
BELOW: the Royal Naval College.

Greenwich Market (Thur–Sun) spreads out from Greenwich Church Street. Here clothes, crafts created by local artisans, books and antiques are on sale, and there are numerous stalls selling tasty snacks and produce.

excavations revealed the remains of the palace chapel and vestry.

Greenwich centre

The heart of Greenwich lies just to the west of the park. The town centre has interesting restaurants and shops, as well as Greenwich Market around Greenwich Church Street *(see margin tip)*. On the same street is **St Alfege's Church**, built in 1712–18 by Nicholas Hawksmoor to replace an earlier church in which Henry VIII had been baptised. It was restored in 1952 after being badly bombed during World War II.

In an elegant period house is the **Fan Museum** (Tues–Sat 11am–5pm, Sun noon–5pm; 12 Croom's Hill, tel: 8305 1441; www.fan-museum.org; charge) displaying an unusual collection of hand-held fans from fashion and the stage.

WOOLWICH ⑩

River trips continue downriver from Greenwich, sweeping back up the eastern side of the Isle of Dogs to **Blackwall Reach**, around the **Millennium Dome**, an expensive exhibition arena built for the year 2000 and now in search of a role.

Access to Woolwich is by overground train from Waterloo East, Charing Cross, London Bridge and Cannon Street, or river boat, the Woolwich ferry, and the Docklands Light Railway from 2009.

Thames Barrier

1 Unit Way, SE18 8305 4188 Apr–Sep daily 10.30am–4pm, Oct–Mar 11am–3.30pm charge for information centre

Beyond the Dome is the massive **Thames Barrier**, which protects 45 sq. miles (117 sq. km) of London, including the Houses of Parliament, from the very real danger of flooding. In 1953, 300 people died in disastrous floods and the threat remains. The giant gates of the £435-million barrier, finished in 1982, can rise to 15 ft (4.6 metres) higher than the highest Thames tide, forming a wall of steel against the river's flow.

You can reach the visitor centre on the south side by boat or bus from Greenwich. The barrier is raised once a month for tests; phone 8305 4188 for times.

RIGHT and BELOW: interesting places to eat and shop at Greenwich Market.

Recommended Restaurants, Cafés & Bars on page 263

Beyond is **Woolwich,** once the Royal Navy's dockyards and arsenal. The main attraction at the Royal Arsenal is **Firepower** (10.30am–5pm, Wed–Sun in summer, Fri–Sun in winter; tel: 8855 7755; www.firepower.org.uk; admission charge), also known as the Royal Artillery Museum.

The centrepiece of this military museum is the ground-shaking "Field of Fire", which puts viewers in the midst of battle. Bombs and shells whizz overhead, guns roar and smoke fills the room. There is also a large two-level gunnery gallery which has an impressive display of artillery and "have a go" simulator.

BLACKHEATH ⓫

A few miles south of Greenwich is **Blackheath**, one of London's neat middle-class villages. The windy heath is where Henry V was welcomed home after beating the French at Agincourt in 1415. Overlooking the heath is the Paragon, a crescent of colonnaded houses. **St Michael's Church** (1829) has a severely tapering spire known as "the needle of Kent".

DULWICH ⓬

With leafy streets, elegant houses and a spacious park, Dulwich is an oasis of calm. It is largely the creation of one man, Edward Alleyn, an Elizabethan actor-manager who bought land in the area in 1605 and established an estate to administer a chapel, almshouses and a school for the sons of the poor.

Today, the estate has more than 15,000 homes, Dulwich College, Alleyn's School and James Allen's Girls' School.

Dulwich Picture Gallery

Gallery Road, SE21; www.dulwichpicturegallery.org.uk 8693 5254 Tue–Fri 10am–5pm, Sat–Sun 11am–5pm charge

Dulwich College, which schooled the writers P. G. Wodehouse and Raymond Chandler, spawned the **Dulwich Picture Gallery** by combining Edward Alleyn's collection with a bequest of paintings intended for a Polish National Gallery but diverted when the King of Poland was forced to abdicate.

TIP

There are excellent views of the Thames Barrier from a small urban park on the northern bank of the river. Thames Barrier Park on North Woolwich Road has a café, visitor centre, a children's playground and paths lined with shrubs and flowers. Transport: Pontoon Dock DLR.

BELOW: view from the Thames Barrier to the Dome and Docklands.

An 18th-century toll road still operates alongside Dulwich College boys' school. Just up the road from the school is Dulwich Park with a dense wooded area. It was created in 1890 and Queen Mary visited the park regularly.

KIDS

The Horniman is a veritable treasure trove for children. Special events and activities are frequently held. Check the website for details.

RIGHT: Raphael's *St Francis of Assisi*, Dulwich Picture Gallery **BELOW:** Brixton Market.

The magnificent building, designed by Sir John Soane, opened in 1814 as the country's first major public art gallery. It contains 300 works by Rembrandt, Rubens, Van Dyck, Gainsborough and Murillo. A highlight is seven paintings by Poussin, including *The Roman Road*.

Horniman Museum

100 London Road, SE23; www.horniman.ac.uk 8699 1872 10.30am–5.30pm; free train to Forest Hill from London Bridge.

A mile to the east of the gallery, the **Horniman Museum** is one of south London's unsung treasures. Combining rich collections of ethnography and natural history, it was founded in 1901 by a wealthy tea merchant, Frederick Horniman and is set in 16 acres (6.5 hectares) of parkland.

Highlights include a spectacular collection of African masks, bronze plaques from Benin, stuffed mammals and birds, a large aquarium and a reptiles area. You can play some of the unusual and historical musical instruments from a vast collection.

BRIXTON 13

It's not the architecture but the people who give **Brixton** its character. The population is around 60 percent white, and the balance includes Cypriots, Vietnamese, Chinese, Africans and Caribbeans. Its laid-back attitude to recreational drugs gets it a bad press, but the area also attracts affluent young professionals keen to own their own homes.

Brixton Market (Mon–Sat 8am–6pm, Wed until 3pm), running from Electric Avenue to shabby Brixton Station Road, mixes Caribbean produce with traditional fruit, vegetables and fish, plus stalls of second-hand clothes, music and junk. There's a community buzz here, but keep valuables out of sight.

Nightlife is lively here. The five-screen **Ritzy** cinema in Coldharbour Lane is popular, as are edgy dance clubs such as the **Fridge** (1 Town Hall Parade), and bar/clubs such as **Dogstar** (389 Coldharbour Lane).

Good restaurants and bars line the high street of nearby Clapham. ❑

BEST RESTAURANTS, BARS AND CAFÉS

Restaurants

Prices for a three-course dinner per person with a half-bottle of house wine:

£ = under £20
££ = £20–30
£££ = £30–50
££££ = over £50

Blackheath

Chapter Two
43–45 Montpelier Vale, SE3 8333 2666 L & D daily. ££ (set menu), £££
Eclectic menu (pan-fried nuggets of foie gras and carmelised endives; ham hock *boudin* and creamed turnips) and a range of excellent desserts.

Laicram
1 Blackheath Grove, SE3. 8852 4710 L & D Tues–Sun. ££
Friendly low-key Thai restaurant offering the standard satay, *pad thai* and green curry formula, but well executed.

Brixton

Asmara
386 Coldharbour Lane, SW9 7737 4144 D daily. ££
This quirky little Eritrean place offers a traditional Messob dinner, a "royal feast" of pancakes topped with various stews and vegetable concoctions, placed in the centre of the wicker table for everyone to share.

The Gallery
256a Brixton Hill, SW2. 8671 8311 D Thur–Sat, L & D Sun. ££
No-frills Portuguese restaurant tucked behind a takeaway. Hearty fish and meat dishes.

The Satay Bar
447–455 Coldharbour Lane, SW9 7326 5001 L & D daily. £
Round the corner from the Ritzy cinema. Offers cheap Indonesian rice and noodle dishes.

Dulwich

Dulwich Gallery Café
College Road, SE21 8693 5244 daily 10am–5pm. £
Enjoy lunch or afternoon tea in a pastoral setting. Outdoor space too.

Franklins
157 Lordship Lane, SE22 8299 9598 L & D Tue–Sun, D only Mon. £££
A little off the beaten track, this local eatery has unfussy modern British dishes.

Greenwich

Greenwich Park Bar & Grill
King William Walk, SE10 8853 7860 L & D daily. £££
The eclectic menu ranges from Manhattan clam chowder to roast loin of lamb.

Inside
19 Greenwich South Street, SE10 8265 5060 L & D Tue–Sat, Br Sat, L only Sun. £££
Reliable local serving Modern European dishes, such as pan-fried sea bass and barbary duck.

SE10 Restaurant & Bar
62 Thames Street, SE10. 8858 9764 L & D Mon–Sat, L only Sun. £££
Popular place specialising in good quality fish and shellfish.

Davy's Wine Vaults
159–161 Greenwich High Road, SE10 8858 7204 L & D Mon-Sat, L only Sun ££
Informed wine list,and good food. Sunday's two-course lunch is served until 5pm.

The Spread Eagle
1–2 Stockwell Street, SE10 8853 2333, L & D daily. £££ French restaurant occupying a 17th-century coaching inn. Excellent wine list.

Pubs, Bars and Cafés

Blackheath
Traditional pubs in Blackheath include the **Hare & Billet** *(1a Eliot Cottages, SE3)* by the heath, and the **Princess of Wales** *(1a Montpelier Row, SE3)*, where drinkers spill out onto the grass in summer.

Brixton
Once viewed as a black ghetto, Brixton is now buzzing with multiculturalism. **Dogstar** *(389 Coldharbour Lane, SW9)* is a legendary dance-bar. **The Fridge Bar** *(1 Town Hall Parade, Brixton Hill, SW2)* was one of the first local dance bars.

Convivial pubs in Brixton include the **Hope and Anchor** *(123 Acre Lane, SW2)* and **Trinity Arms** *(45 Trinity Gardens, SW2)*.

Clapham
An alternative to nearby Brixton, try the **Belle Vue** *(1 Clapham Common, South Side)*, a friendly pub, or **Esca** *(160 Clapham High Street)* a café/deli.

Dulwich
The **Crown and Greyhound**, a decorative Victorian pub, is handy for the Dulwich Picture Gallery and has a pleasant beer garden.

Greenwich
The **Trafalgar Tavern** *(Park Row, SE10)*, a traditional Thames-side pub. A less touristy riverside pub is the **Cutty Sark** *(Ballast Quay, off Lassell Street, SE10)*. The **Greenwich Union** (56 Royal Hill, SE10) has unusual beers such as Blonde Ale.

Recommended Restaurants, Cafes & Bars on page 273

DAY TRIPS

Within striking distance of the capital is a vast range of places to visit, from castles to country houses, from theme parks to seaside resorts. Bath, Brighton, Oxford, Cambridge and Canterbury are within reach, too

The roads around the capital are as busy as any European city's and, unless you are following a complex itinerary, it is best to travel by train or coach. For directions on how to reach places in this chapter, see the Transport section of Travel Tips, pages 276–7.

WINDSOR

JJust 25 miles (40 km) from central London is **Windsor Castle** ❶ (daily Mar–Oct 10am–5.30pm, Nov–Feb 10am–4pm; last admission one hour before closing; tel: 01753-868286; charge), still a favourite residence of the Royal Family. William the Conqueror began fortification here in 1066, immediately after defeating King Harold at the Battle of Hastings.

The present stone castle was started 100 years later by Henry II. Queen Victoria had a special love for Windsor and is buried, along with her husband, Albert, at **Frogmore** (limited opening times; wwwroyalresidences.com), a former royal residence, set among sweeping lawns and exotic trees, about a mile (2 km) away.

Though overshadowed by its vast castle, **Windsor** is a pleasant town, with lovely walks among deer and ancient trees in Windsor Great Park, which spreads south from the castle, and also along the river.

A great draw for children is **Legoland Windsor** ❷ (2 miles/3 km from town centre on the B3022 Bracknell/Ascot road; daily Mar–mid-Oct, closed selected weekdays in Apr, May, Sep, Oct, Nov; tel: 08705-040404; www.legoland.co.uk). This theme park is based on the children's building blocks – in this case, millions of them. Its 150 acres (60 hectares) of wooded

Main attractions
- WINDSOR CASTLE
- LEGOLAND WINDSOR
- BLENHEIM PALACE
- SISSINGHURST CASTLE
- CHARTWELL
- ROCHESTER
- WINCHESTER
- CANTERBURY
- BRIGHTON
- BATH
- CAMBRIDGE
- OXFORD
- STRATFORD-UPON-AVON

PRECEDING PAGES: Brighton Pavilion.
LEFT: the Roman Baths and Abbey, Bath.
RIGHT: visitors to Windsor Castle.

Blenheim Palace, one of England's finest stately homes, built in the early 18th century by John Vanbrugh and the birthplace of Winston Churchill.

landscape has rides for all age groups, ranging from white-knuckle roller-coasters for teenagers to gentle jaunts for toddlers.

More sedate, but also very popular with children, is **Bekonscot Model Village and Railway** (Apr–Oct daily 10am–5pm; tel: 01494 672919; www.bekonscot.com; charge), near Beaconsfield, a stone's throw north of the M40 (junction 2). This delightful attraction, rich in detail, has been expanding since 1929.

GREAT HOUSES AND GARDENS

The largest private house in England, **Blenheim Palace** ❸ (mid-Feb–Oct daily 10.30am–4.45pm, Nov–early Dec Wed–Sun only; tel: 08700 602080; www.blenheimpalace.com; charge) is just outside the Oxfordshire village of Woodstock (8 miles/ 13km north of Oxford on the A44 Evesham Road).

The palace was built by John Vanbrugh for the first Duke of Marlborough as a reward for his victory over the French at the Battle of Blenheim (1704). Winston Churchill was born here in 1874. He is buried in the church at nearby Bladon, on the edge of the Blenheim estate.

One of the country's most popular gardens is in Kent. **Sissinghurst Castle** ❹ (mid-Mar–Oct; tel: 01580-710700; www.nationaltrust.org.uk; charge) has the famous garden created in the

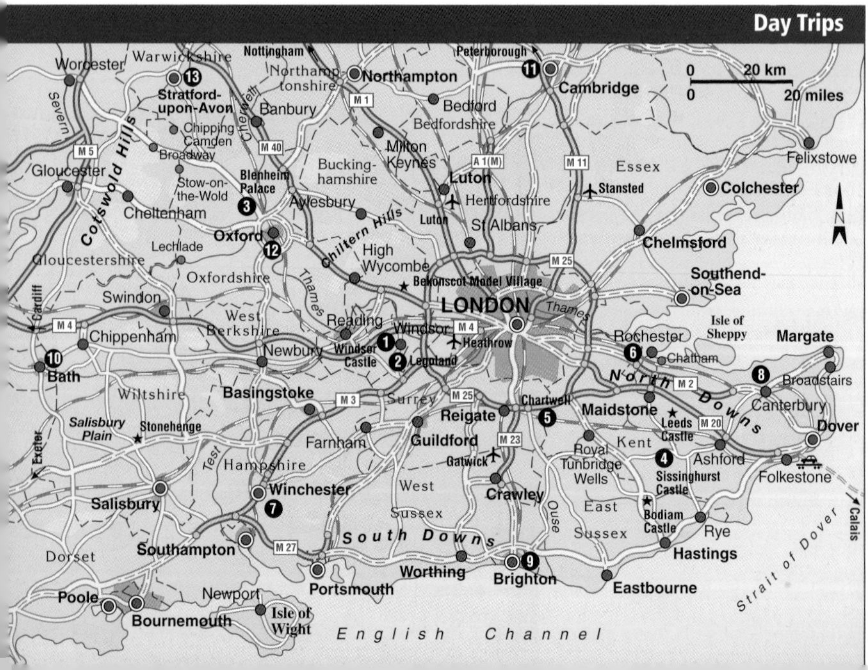

Day Trips

Recommended Restaurants, Cafes & Bars on page 273

1930s by the English aristocrats Vita Sackville-West and her husband, Harold Nicolson.

Winston Churchill's country home at **Chartwell** ❺ (end-Mar–end-Oct, Wed–Sat and Bank Hol Mon; tel: 01732-866368; www.nationaltrust.org.uk; charge) at Westerham, close to the M25, has a water garden and rose garden, and you can visit Churchill's studio.

CATHEDRALS AND DICKENS

Rochester ❻ has a lovely Norman cathedral, and its huge castle, a gaunt ruin, stands brooding over the River Medway, 30 miles (48 km) east of London. For many years it was home to Charles Dickens, and in nearby Chatham you will find **Dickens World** (daily 10am–7pm; tel: 08702 411415; www.dickensworld.co.uk; charge}, a recreation of Victorian London complete with Dickensian characters, which opened in 2007.

Winchester ❼, a refined country town 66 miles (106 km) from London, was the capital of England in Saxon times. Its cathedral has a fine English Perpendicular interior.

Canterbury ❽, 62 miles (100 km) from London, is also famous for its cathedral, where Thomas à Becket was martyred in 1170.

SEASIDE EXCURSION

Brighton ❾, 59 miles (95 km) from London, is a perennially bright spot. The old-fashioned pedestrianised streets known as The Lanes are a

KIDS

Brighton, easily accessed by train, is a great day out for families. As well as the beach and the promenade with their many attractions (sandpits, paddling pools, crazy golf and the Volks Railway to name a few), Palace Pier is packed with fairground attractions, from state-of-the-art terrifiers to a traditional helter-skelter. Also worth visiting, near the pier, is the Sea Life Centre, a modern walk-through aquarium.

FAR LEFT: Blenheim Palace. **ABOVE LEFT:** detail on Brighton Pavilion. **BELOW:** Brighton's fun-filled Palace Pier.

ABOVE: the Bridge of Sighs, Hertford College, Oxford. **BELOW:** the Circus, Bath.

maze of antiques shops, book sellers and souvenir stores, and much of enjoyment in the town is in wandering. The jewel of Brighton is the exotic **Royal Pavilion** (daily 9.30am–5pm; tel: 01273-290900; charge), built in the architectural style of Mughal India by Henry Holland and John Nash for the Prince Regent at the end of the 18th century. The brilliant oriental interiors are decorated with golden dragons, chinoiserie, burnished palms and coloured glass.

ROMAN BATH

Bath ❿, with its beautifully integrated crescents, squares and terraces, is a Georgian masterpiece and well worth making a special effort to visit. Although 116 miles (187 km) from London, it can be reached in 80 minutes by fast train from Paddington. At its elegant heart are the impressive **Roman Baths** (daily 9.30am–5.30pm, until 9pm in July and August; tel: 01225 477 743; www.romanbaths.co.uk; charge;) to which has been added a new complex utilising the hot springs *(see margin tip, page 271)*.

The adjacent **Pump Room** (Apr–Sep 9am–6pm, Oct–Mar 9.30am–5.30pm rest of year) was built in the 1790s as an elegant antechamber to the baths where visitors could sample the water, promenade and listen to musical entertainment. Today it is a restaurant and a lovely spot to have lunch or tea.

Other architectural highlights of

Recommended Restaurants, Cafes & Bars on page 273

the city include the sweeping **Royal Crescent**, **Queen Square**, the **Circus**, the **Assembly Rooms** (which contain an excellent Museum of Costume) and pretty **Pulteney Bridge**, which is lined, like the Pontevecchio in Florence, with tiny shops.

UNIVERSITY TOWNS

Within easy reach of the capital are the UK's finest university towns, each of which offers tours around the historic colleges, a pleasant city centre and that quintessentially Oxbridge pastime, punting on the river Cam or Isis.

Cambridge ⓫, 61 miles (98 km) from London is compact and best explored on foot. It gained its first college, Peterhouse, in 1281, but undoubtedly the finest of all the college buildings is **King's College Chapel**, which boasts magnificent fan vaulting, 16th-century stained-glass windows and Rubens' *Adoration of the Magi*.

The college is also famous for the King's College Choir, whose carol performance is broadcast live across the world on Christmas Eve.

Among the other historic colleges, Sidney Sussex College in Sidney Street is remarkable for being the last resting place of the head of Oliver Cromwell, leader of the Roundheads in the English Civil War (1642–49), who had briefly been a student here.

Like Cambridge, **Oxford ⓬**, 56 miles (90 km) from London, is also easily explored on foot. There's something about the light in Oxford, reflecting off the ancient stones, that gives the town a unique allure. Indeed, it was regarded by the poet John Keats as "the finest city in the world".

Coach-loads of tourists come to check, trooping respectfully round the university's three dozen colleges, a few of which have been centres of learning for up to seven centuries.

The best place to start a tour is Carfax, where the four main streets – Cornmarket, High Street, Queen Street and St Aldate's – meet. On St Aldate's is **Christ Church**, the grandest of Oxford's colleges, founded in 1525 by Cardinal Wolsey, Henry VIII's chancellor, on the site of an earlier priory.

After many aborted attempts, Bath has finally reopened its spa facilities in the form of Thermae Bath Spa, a luxurious and architecturally inspiring complex utilising two of the historic spa buildings. It offers an extensive range of pampering treatments to both men and women, and incorporates a roof-top pool with lovely views over Bath (tel: 01225 331234; www.thermaebathspa.com.

BELOW LEFT: punting on the River Cam.
BELOW: choristers walking back from King's College Chapel.

TIP

The RSC (Royal Shakespeare Company) presents a varied programme of Shakespeare and other plays at its venues in Stratford (the Royal Shakespeare Theatre, The Courtyard and the Elizabethan-style Swan Theatre). Check its website, www.rsc.org.uk for details.

For drivers, the Cotswolds to the west of Oxford beckon, their quaint showpiece villages seeming to grow out of the earth, so perfect is their relationship with the landscape. Tourism is intensive here, though it is possible to get off the beaten track with your own transport. Among the prettiest villages are Lechlade, Stow-on-the-Wold, Broadway and Chipping Camden.

SHAKESPEARE COUNTRY

Stratford-upon-Avon ⓭, birthplace of Shakespeare, is 40 miles (64 km) north of Oxford. The **Shakespeare Centre** (www.shakespeare.org.uk) in Henley Street is the headquarters of The Shakespeare Birthplace Trust which administers five properties associated with the Shakespeare family (each with its own opening times, check website for details; money-saving multi-house tickets available).

Shakespeare's Birthplace, adjacent to the centre, was the Shakespeare family home and business premises – his father was a glove maker, wool merchant and moneylender, and became mayor in 1568. Like the other period properties run by the Trust, it has been authentically restored and furnished.

Ann Hathaway's Cottage, the childhood home of Shakespeare's wife, is in Shottery, about 1 mile (2 km) west of town. It is an idyllic timber-framed thatched cottage with a pretty garden rather than the working farmyard it would have been in Shakespeare's day ❑

RIGHT: Knot Garden at Stratford-upon-Avon.
BELOW: Ann Hathaway's Cottage.

BEST RESTAURANTS, BARS AND CAFÉS

Restaurants

Prices for a three-course dinner per person with a half-bottle of house wine:

£ = under £20
££ = £20–30
£££ = £30–50
££££ = over £50

Bath

Demuths

2 North Parade Passage
01225 446 059 L & D daily. £–££
Terrific vegetarian restaurant near the Roman Baths. Sample dishes include char-grilled vegetables and lasagne stack, and smoky squash salad.

The Hole in the Wall

16 George St 01225 425242 L & D daily. ££
Long-established restaurant serving modern European food in a period property. Good-value set lunches and pre-theatre menus available. Log fires in winter.

The Moon and Sixpence

6A Broad Street 01225 460962 L & D daily. ££
A long-established restaurant in the centre of town. British favourites are given an imaginative twist. Smart but casual ambience.

LEFT: the Moon & Sixpence, Bath.

Brighton

Food for Friends

17–18 Prince Albert Street, The Lanes 01273 202310 L & D daily. £
This is a vegetarian favourite.

The Gingerman

21a Norfolk Square
01273 326688 L & D
£££
Modern European dishes incorporating best quality ingredients. Pretty dining room.

The Regency

131 King's Road 01273 325014 L & D daily.
£–££
Old-fashioned and bustling fish restaurant on the seafront. Serves everything from straightforward fish and chips to mussels, sea bass and more. Some meat choices too.

Terre à Terre

71 East Street 01273 729051 L & D daily. ££
Bustling café with innovative vegetarian menu. Just off the sea-front.

Cambridge

Midsummer House

Midsummer Common
01223 369299 L & D daily. ££
Elegant modern European cuisine in stylish surroundings besides the River Cam.

Three Horseshoes

High Street, Madingley
01954 210221 L & D daily. ££
Thatched inn in a pretty village 2 miles (3 km) from Cambridge. Modern Mediterranean food.

Oxford

Browns

5–11 Woodstock Road
01865 511995 B, L & D daily. ££
This well-established restaurant offers good food in a relaxed atmosphere.

Le Petit Blanc

71–2 Walton Street
01865 510999 B, L & D daily. ££
Member in a small chain of Raymond Blanc restaurants that pride themselves on providing real French food at reasonable prices. Open all day including breakfast.

Stratford

Bensons

4 Bard's Walk 01789 261116 B & L Mon–Fri.
£
Come here for a slap-up champagne breakfast of scrambled eggs and smoked salmon, a light lunch or a first-rate afternoon tea. Booking is advisable for tea.

Windsor

Oakley Court

Windsor Road, Water Oakley Windsor 01753 609988 B, L & D daily.
£££
An elegant, formal restaurant with wood panelling and high ceilings, set in magnificent grounds. Excellent modern European cuisine.

barbican
art/theatre/music
dance/film/education
conferences/library
restaurants/bars

INSIGHT GUIDES

LONDON

Travel Tips

TRANSPORT

GETTING THERE AND GETTING AROUND

London's size, and its knots of semi-static traffic, can make getting around slow. But things are getting better: thanks to the Congestion Charge traffic moves more freely in the city centre, bus services have improved, and even fares – so long as you make the most of Travelcards and Oystercards (*see page 278*) – are more reasonable than a few years ago. Information on all London's transport, including fares, is available from Transport for London, tel: 7222 1234, www.tfl.gov.uk.

Note: London telephone numbers are shown as 8-digit numbers. If dialling from elsewhere in the UK, precede these with the code 020. If outside the UK, dial 44-20 and then the 8 digits.

GETTING THERE

By Air

London is served by two major international airports: Heathrow, 15 miles (24 km) to the west (mainly scheduled flights); and Gatwick, 24 miles (40 km) to the south (scheduled, charter and low-cost flights). The smaller airports of Stansted and Luton, both to the north of London, are used by many European low-cost airlines, but have some long-haul flights. The tiny London City Airport in Docklands is used by small aircraft connecting London with some European cities.

Heathrow Airport

Heathrow can be a daunting place in which to arrive, and it's important to plan how you'll get into central London. For further information on all airport services, see www.heathrowairport.com.

Train The fastest route is the **Heathrow Express** to Paddington Station, which runs every 15 minutes and takes 15 minutes. Paddington connects with several Underground (Tube) lines *(see map inside back cover)*. The fare is £14.50 single (US$28.60) – perhaps the world's costliest rail ticket per mile. A cheaper option is the 25-minute **Heathrow Connect** service, which stops at several stations en route to Paddington, and costs £6.90 (US$13.60).

Underground There is also a direct Tube route on the Piccadilly Line, which reaches the West End in around 50 minutes. It goes directly to Kensington, Park Lane (Hyde Park Corner), Piccadilly, Covent Garden and King's Cross, and operates from 5am (6am on Sunday) until 11.49pm daily. A single ticket to central London will cost £4; keep your ticket, as you need it to exit the system. Heathrow terminals 1, 2 and 3 all connect to the same Tube station, but there is a separate one for Terminal 4. Heathrow is also building a Terminal 5, due to open in 2008, and while it is being built there may be short interruptions in Tube services, in

FLIGHT INFORMATION

- Heathrow Airport, tel: 0870-000 0123
- Gatwick Airport, tel: 0870- 000 2468
- Luton Airport, tel: 01582-405100
- Stansted Airport, tel: 0870-000 0303
- London City Airport, tel: 020-7646 0000

which case shuttle buses will be provided from the next station along the line, Hatton Cross.

Bus National Express runs coaches from Heathrow to Victoria Coach Station; the journey takes between 45 and 80 minutes, depending on traffic, and the single fare is £4. The bus station is at Terminals 1, 2 and 3; from Terminal 4, take the Heathrow Express train for free. Information, tel: 0870-580 8080. www.nationalexpress.com

Taxis Heathrow is well-served by taxis. A ride into town in a London "black cab" will cost from £45 plus 10 percent tip, depending on destination.

Car Hire Heathrow offices of major car rental firms:
Avis, tel: 0870-157 8700
Budget, tel: 0870-608 6313
Europcar, tel: 8897 0811
Hertz, tel: 0870-846 0006

Gatwick Airport

Gatwick airport, 28 miles (45 km) from the city centre, isn't on the Underground network, but trains and buses run to and from Victoria rail and coach stations. For further information, see www.gatwickairport.com.

The **Gatwick Express** train leaves every 15 minutes from 4.35am to 1.35am; it takes 30 minutes and costs £14.90 one-way. Children under five travel free; children aged 5–15 travel for half the adult fare. For more details see www.gatwickexpress.com or tel: 0845-850 1530.

Southern Trains also runs services from Gatwick to Victoria, with stops en route: journey time is 30–40 minutes, and the fare £8.90. First Capital Connect has trains to King's Cross in London, via Blackfriars and London Bridge. Journey time is 45 minutes; the fare, from £9.

Jetlink (tel: 08705-747777) and National Express (tel: 0870-580 8080) bus services operate the 32-mile (51-km) journey between Heathrow and Gatwick (£19 single), taking between 60 and 90 minutes.

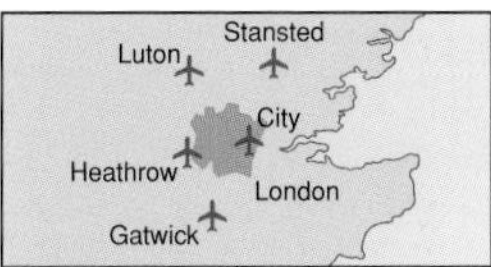

Car Hire from Gatwick:
Avis, tel: 0870 010 4068
Europcar, tel: 01293-531 062
Hertz, tel: 0870 846 0003
National, tel: 01293-567 790

Luton Airport

Luton is linked by First Capital Connect rail services with London King's Cross; some trains continue to Gatwick via Blackfriars. There is a shuttle bus between the airport and Luton train station. The journey to King's Cross takes about 40 minutes, and trains run every 20 minutes. Green Line buses route 757 run to Victoria in London, and take about 90 minutes; tel: 0870 608 7261, www.greenline.co.uk.

Stansted Airport

Stansted Express trains run to Liverpool Street Station in London every 15 minutes; journey time is 45 minutes, and a single ticket is £14.50. Buses run from Stansted to several destinations in London, notably the A50 bus direct to Victoria. It runs every 30 minutes, and tickets cost £8.

London City Airport

London City Airport is mainly used by business travellers. The airport has its own station on the Docklands Light Railway (DLR), which connects with the Underground network at Bank station. For airport and flight enquiries, tel: 7646 0088; www.londoncityairport.com.

COACH CONNECTIONS

National Express coach (long-distance bus) services connect Heathrow, Gatwick, Stansted and Luton airports with one another and with Victoria coach station. There are also direct bus services from all the main airports and destinations around Britain. For details and bookings, tel: 0870-580 8080, www.nationalexpress.com.

By Channel Tunnel

In November 2007 the London terminus for **Eurostar** passenger trains from Paris and Brussels moved from Waterloo to St Pancras/King's Cross. Journey times are about 2 hours 10 minutes from Paris, or 1 hour 50 minutes from Brussels. For information and reservations, tel: 08705 186186 (UK); 01 70 70 99 49 (France); or 00 44 1233 617 575 (from Belgium), or check www.eurostar.com.

Vehicles are also carried by **Le Shuttle** trains through the tunnel between Folkestone in Kent and Sangatte in France. There are two to five departures each hour, and the trip takes 35 minutes. Bookings are not essential, but advisable at peak times. Fares vary according to the time of travel: late at night or early morning are cheaper. Taking a car (with any number of passengers) through the tunnel costs from about £122 return, or €188. For information and reservations, tel: 08705 353535 (UK), 0810 63 03 04 (France), or see www.eurotunnel.com.

By Ferry

Ferries operate between many British and Continental ports. Calais–Dover is the shortest crossing (75–90 minutes). Some of the main companies are listed below:.

Brittany Ferries, tel: 0870 907 6103 (UK), 0825 82 88 28 (France), www.brittanyferries.com. Portsmouth to Caen, Cherbourg and St-Malo; Poole–Cherbourg; Plymouth–Roscoff.

Norfolk Line, tel: 0870 870 1020 (UK), 03 28 59 01 01 (France), www.norfolkline.com.

ABOVE: Docklands Light Railway.

Dover–Dunkerque.
P&O Ferries, tel: 08705 980333 (UK), 0825 12 01 56 (France), www.poferries.com. Dover–Calais.
SeaFrance, tel: 0870 443 1653 (UK), 0825 04 40 45 (France), www.seafrance.com. Frequent sailings from Dover to Calais.
SpeedFerries, tel: 0870 2200 570 (UK), 02 31 10 50 00 (France), www.speedferries.com. Fast ferries from Dover to Boulogne, with low-cost prices.

GETTING AROUND

Public Transport

The Tube

The Underground (known as the Tube, see map on the inside back flap) is the quickest way across town, but it badly needs more investment. In rush hours (8am–9.30am and 5–7pm) every station is packed with commuters. Trains run from 5.30am to around midnight. If you're heading for the end of a line, the last train may leave closer to 11pm.

Make sure you have a valid ticket and keep hold of it after you have passed through the electronic barrier – you will need it to exit at your destination. If you have an Oystercard *(see right)*, be sure to touch in on entry and on exit, or you may be charged the maximum fare for the line. Stations are divided into one of six zones, spreading out from the centre; the minimum adult fare for a single ticket in zones 1–2 is £4, but only £1.50 with an Oystercard. A single ticket from Heathrow to the centre will also cost £4.

It is illegal to smoke within the Tube system or on buses.

You can print out itineraries from the website www.thetube.com

Docklands Light Railway

Known as the DLR, this is a fully automated railway that runs through redeveloped areas of east London and to Greenwich, and connects with the Tube network at Bank, Tower Hill, Strat-

BELOW: taxis at the ready.

FARES & TRAVELCARDS

Single tickets on London's transport networks are very expensive, so it's best to buy one of several multi-journey passes. **Travelcards** give unlimited travel on the Tube, buses and DLR. London is divided into six fare zones, with zones 1–2 covering all of central London. A one-day Travelcard for zones 1 and 2 and off-peak (valid after 9.30am) costs £5.10 (£3.30, children aged 5–15). You can also buy three-day or seven-day cards. **Oystercards** are smart cards that you charge up with however much you wish to pay, then touch in on card readers at Tube stations and on buses, so that an amount is deducted each time you use it. They are cheaper than Travelcards if you only expect to travel a few times each day.

Cards and Oysters can be bought from Tube or DLR stations and newsagents. Visitors can order them ahead from www.visitbritaindirect.com.

Children under 16 travel for free at all times on buses, and under-11s travel free on the Tube and DLR at off-peak times provided they are with an adult. For full details of all fares, see www.tfl.gov.uk.

ford and a few other stations. Tickets and fares are the same as for the Tube.

Buses

Bus routes run throughout the city. The flat fare in central London is £2, but only £1 for Oystercard holders. On several routes, if you do not have a Travel- or Oystercard, you must buy single tickets before boarding, from machines at the bus stops. Several bus routes run 24 hours a day, and on others Night Buses (identified by an N) run about every 30 minutes from midnight to 6am. Most Night Bus routes run through Trafalgar Square. A full bus-route map is available from Travel Information Centres.

Taxis

Licensed **taxis** ("black cabs", the famous, squat London taxis, even though many are now in other colours) are licensed and display the regulated charges on a meter. If you have a complaint, note down the driver's licence number and contact the Carriage Office, tel: 0845 602 7000.

If you telephone for a taxi you will be charged for the time and miles it takes to pick you up as well. **Minicabs** are cheaper than black cabs, but can only be hired by telephoning for one, as they're not allowed to pick up passengers on the street. Use minicabs with caution, particularly if travelling alone, and do not use any of the unlicensed cabs that tout for business on the street late-night in central London. Only call for a cab from a reputable company.

PHONE CABS

To arrange for a licensed black cab by phone, call:
Radio Taxis
Tel: 7272 0272
MINICAB COMPANIES
Addison Lee
Tel: 7387 8888
Lancaster Private HIre
Tel: 7723 1184

RAILWAY STATION TERMINALS

Britain's rail services are run by a variety of private companies. These are the principal mainline stations, with the areas they serve:

Charing Cross Station. Services to south London and southeast England: Canterbury, Folkestone, Hastings, Dover Priory.

Euston Station. Services to northwest London and beyond to Birmingham and the northwest: Liverpool, Manchester, Glasgow.

King's Cross Station. Services to north London and beyond to the northeast: Leeds, York, Newcastle, Edinburgh and Aberdeen.

St Pancras Station. Points not quite so far north, such as Nottingham, Derby and Sheffield, and the new Eurostar terminal for trains from Paris and Brussels.

Liverpool Street Station and **Fenchurch Street**. To east and northeast London, Cambridge and East Anglia.

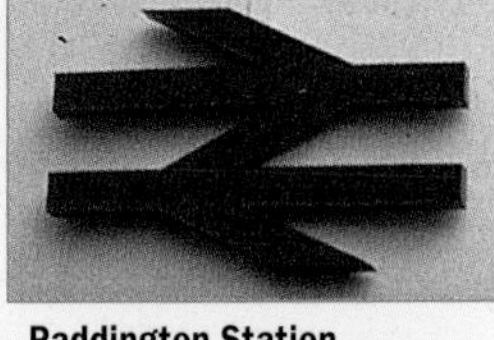

Paddington Station. Services to west London and to Oxford, Bath, Bristol, the west, and South Wales.

Victoria Station. Services to south London and southeast England, including Gatwick airport, Brighton, Newhaven and Dover.

Waterloo Station. To southwest London, Southampton, and southern England as far as Exeter, including Richmond, Windsor and Ascot.

Other termini, such as **Marylebone**, **London Bridge**, **Cannon Street** and **Blackfriars**, are mainly commuter stations, used for destinations around London.

For information on **train times**, tel: 0845 748 4950.

Coaches

Coach (long-distance bus) travel is generally cheaper than travelling by train. National Express runs services throughout the country from Victoria Coach Station, Buckingham Palace Road. Tel: 0870-580 8080, www.nationalexpress.com.

Driving

Central London is a nightmare to drive in, with its web of one-way streets, bad signposting, and impatient drivers (taxi drivers hate hesitation). Drive on the left and observe speed limits (police detection cameras proliferate). Do not drive in bus lanes at the hours signposted. There are heavy penalties for driving after drinking over the limit. Drivers and passengers (front and back) must also use seat belts.

Parking

Meters are slightly cheaper than car parks, but only allow parking for a maximum of two or four hours. Wardens are unforgiving. Most meter parking is free after 6.30pm each evening, after 1.30pm in many areas on Saturday afternoons and all day Sunday. However, always check the details given on the meter.

Congestion Charge

Cars driving into a clearly marked Congestion Zone in inner and west London between 7am and 6.30pm Mon–Fri are filmed and their owners fined if an £8 payment is not made by 10pm the same day. You can pay at many small shops (newsagents, off licences/liquor stores) or by telephoning 0845-900 1234. Cars with non-UK plates usually escape a fine.

CYCLING

Cycling in London can be intimidating, but a bike is often the quickest means of getting around the city. Extensive information on cycling in London can be found on the Transport for London website, www.tfl.gov.uk, and more is available from the London Cycle Network (www.londoncyclenetwork.org.uk) and the London Cycling Campaign (www.lcc.org.uk).

CYCLE HIRE
Banana Rent
tel: 0845 644 2868
www.bananarent.com
Tube stations in west London.
London Bicycle Tour Company
tel: 7928 6838
www.londonbicycle.com
On the South Bank.
OY Bike
tel: 0845 226 5571
www.oybike.com
Various locations.

Car Rental

To rent a car you must be over 21 years old and have held a full driving licence for more than a year. The cost usually includes insurance and unlimited mileage.
Europcar, tel: 0870 607 5000
Alamo, tel: 0870 600 4004
Hertz, tel: 0870 599 6699
Avis, tel: 0870 606 0100

Trips Out of London

This section details how to reach the day-trip destinations described on pages 267–72.

Windsor
Trains from Paddington, journey time 30–50 minutes; also from Waterloo; journey time about 45 minutes.
Green Line coaches (tel: 0870 608 7261; www.greenline.co.uk) from Victoria approx. every hour, journey time approx. 1 hour.

Blenheim Palace
Trains from Paddington to Oxford, journey time 1 hour *(see also under Oxford)*. Bus no. 20 from Oxford to Woodstock at approx. 30-minute intervals.

Sissinghurst Castle
Trains from Charing Cross to Staplehurst Station, journey time 1 hour. A bus link from Staplehurst to the castle runs Tues & Sun only from May (tel: 01580 200226); or Arriva bus no. 4/5 Maidstone–Hastings alighting at Sissinghurst.
By road, it is 2 miles/3 km NE of Cranbrook, 1 mile/1.6 km E of Sissinghurst village.

Chartwell
Trains from London Bridge or Charing Cross to Sevenoaks, journey 30 minutes; or from Victoria or London Bridge to Oxted, journey time approx. 35 minutes.
By road, it is 2 miles/3 km S of Westerham, fork left off B2026.

Rochester
Trains from Victoria, journey time 40 minutes–1 hour.

Winchester
Trains from Waterloo, journey time 1 hour.
National Express coaches from Victoria, journey approx. 2 hours.

Canterbury
Trains from Victoria and Charing Cross, journey time 90–105 minutes.
National Express coaches from Victoria, journey time 110 minutes.

Brighton
Trains from Victoria or London Bridge, journey time 50 minutes–1 hour.
National Express coaches from Victoria stopping at Gatwick and elsewhere, journey time 2 hours.

Bath
Trains from Paddington, journey time 80 minutes.
National Express coaches from Victoria; direct-service journey time 3¼–3¾ hours.

Cambridge
Trains from King's Cross, journey time 45–80 minutes; a slower service runs from Liverpool Street Station.
National Express coaches from Victoria, journey time 2 hours.

Oxford
Trains from Paddington, journey time 1 hour.
Two competing bus lines, Oxford Tube and Oxford Bus Company, run from Victoria bus station; they have services every 12 or 20 minutes .

Stratford-upon-Avon
Trains from Marylebone station, direct-service journey time 2¼ hours.
National Express coaches from Victoria: three services a day.

BELOW: beating the traffic

ACCOMMODATION

SOME THINGS TO CONSIDER BEFORE YOU BOOK THE ROOM

London's hotels are famously expensive, and foreign visitors can be disappointed by the standard provided for the high rates charged. But fortunately, this is less true than it used to be. New hotels offering affordable accommodation in a central location, many belonging to mid-range chains, have sprung up in areas such as the South Bank and the City, and even top-end hotels offer special deals. And in addition to hotels, you will find family-run guesthouses, self-catering flats and youth hostels.

Insight's Service

The website, www.hotelclub.com, lists hundreds of hotels in London. All listings give detailed descriptions and many include photographs of the establishments.

Choosing a Hotel

London has everything from grand hotels of international renown to family-run hotels, guest houses, self-catering flats and youth hostels. The choice of accommodation can make or break a visit to the capital; this is especially true from a budget point of view. The flip-side of the massive choice is the equally massive prices often charged.

However, there are bargains to be had. As with most things, you need to shop around. If a clean room and a hot breakfast are all you ask, a small hotel may offer them for about a sixth of the price of a top hotel. The smaller hotels are often more friendly, making up in the welcome what they may lack in facilities. Just don't expect a lot of space – the cheaper rooms really are cell-like.

Hotel Areas

There are hotels everywhere in London, but some areas have more than others. Don't necessarily expect to find a bargain two minutes walk from Piccadilly Circus, though the main concentrations tend to be around Victoria, Earls Court/Kensington, the West End and Bayswater. SW1 is London's traditional hotel district. There are some delightfully old-fashioned hotels in Victoria, in most price brackets, and the streets close to Victoria Station are full of terraced bed-and-breakfast accommodation. There are also streets full of terraced (or rather town houses, for this is Kensington) hotels in the second big hotel area of SW5 and SW7. This zone, around Kensington High Street, Earls Court and Gloucester Road, is another major centre for medium-range hotels of dependable comfort.

The West End is the third area and the best-known zone. You'll pay more for budget or moderate accommodation here than you will in SW1 or SW5. W1 hotels at the bottom end of the price range can be very humble. WC1 is a clever choice: it's central and has reasonable prices, and there is still some dignity, even romance, in Bloomsbury (don't expect to find either quality in Oxford Street).

Bayswater, or at least the area between Edgware Road, Bayswater Road, Paddington and Queensway, is full of hotels. It does have a few large expensive hotels on its fringes but has a greater concentration of moderate and budget accommodation. Quality and prices vary enormously but the area is convenient for the West End.

Budget Chains

Premier Travel Inn is Britain's biggest budget hotel chain, with several outposts in central London, including County Hall (by Westminster Bridge), Euston, Kensington, Southwark and Tower Bridge. There are also branches close to Gatwick and Heathrow. They are clean and modern and between £80 and £99 per night. Central reservations: 0870-242 8000. www.premiertravelinn.com

The expanding **Travelodge** chain does a similar job at similar prices; book early for good deals: www.travelodge.co.uk

Prices and Booking

The following listings are organised according to price brackets. The categories are based on one night's accommodation in a double room, exclusive of breakfast. Generally you can get whatever your heart desires in expensive hotels. In budget accommodation, you're not buying a view; if you get one it's a bonus. Almost all hotels offer special deals that are cheaper than the published "rack rate", particularly at weekends, so it is always worth checking.

Book ahead. London fills up in the summer months (May and September are also crowded because of conference traffic), but if you arrive without a reservation, you can call **Visit London**'s telephone accommodation booking service on 08456-443 010 and book by credit card.

Hotel bills usually include service and no extra tip is needed, but if you wish to repay good service, 10 percent split between the deserving is the custom. Equally, you can insist that service be deducted if you feel you've been treated poorly.

Check when booking that the price quoted is inclusive of VAT, whether it includes breakfast and if the price is per room or per person. If you reserve in advance, you may be asked for a deposit. Reservations made, whether in writing or by phone, can be regarded as binding contracts, and you could be prosecuted for breaching that contract by not turning up on the day. Rooms must usually be vacated by midday on the day of departure.

Youth Hostels

English Youth Hostels tend to be extremely basic. You get a single bed in a dormitory with basic washing and cooking facilities. Most hostels also have restaurants. The price is low, especially if you book reasonably far in advance or for several nights; it will often include breakfast.

The **Youth Hostelling Association** (YHA) has six London locations, including St Pauls (36 Carter Lane, EC4V 5AB. Tel: 7236 4965), Oxford Street (14 Noel Street, W1F 8GJ. Tel: 7734 1618) and Kensington (Holland Walk, W8 7QU. Tel: 7937 0748).

Prices for members are about £20–25; non-members pay slightly more. To join, write to the YHA: Trevelyan House, Matlock, Derbyshire, DE4 3YH. www.yha.org.uk.

Another popular choice is **Piccadilly Backpackers Hostel** (12 Sherwood Street, W1F 7BR. Tel: 7434 9009, www.piccadillyhotel.net), which has 700 beds, online booking prices starting from £12–15 per night, and a lively location just off Piccadilly Circus.

Details of other student and budget accommodation are free from the **Tourist Information Centre** (TIC) at 1 Regent Street, Piccadilly Circus, SW1, or online at www.visitlondon.com.

Bed and Breakfasts

Staying in a private home ensures that you meet at least one London family. The **London Bed & Breakfast Agency** specialises in such accommodation, with prices from £25–47 per person per night double occupancy, or £27–60 single occupancy, depending on the area. Tel: 7586 2768. www.londonbb.com

A Place of Your Own

There's no shortage of agents and private companies offering London apartments, many of them luxurious, others basic and frankly overpriced. Many holiday letting agencies ask for a deposit which is also to cover against cancellation. Avoid agents who charge a fee for finding you accommodation (such a fee is chargeable only when you have agreed to take a property).

Rental in the following apartments includes all bills excluding the telephone:

Allen House, 8 Allen Street, W8. Tel: 7938 1346. 42 Kensington flats, 1–3 beds. From £650–2,090 a week.

Apartment Services, 2 Sandwich Street, WC1H 9PL. Tel: 7388 3558. 60 flats in central London, particularly Bloomsbury. From £200–500 a week.

Holiday Flats, 1 Princess Mews, Belsize Crescent, NW3 5AP. Tel: 7794 1186. Studio flats to 3-bed flats in Hampstead, St John's Wood and Swiss Cottage. From £425–800 a week.

Holiday Serviced Apartments, P.O.Box 226, Northwood, HA6 2ZJ, tel: 0845-060 4477. Have a large number of serviced flats in Greater London from £630–1,400. Brochure available.

Kensgate House, 38 Emperor's Gate, SW7 4HJ. Tel: 7370 1040. Three Victorian houses split into studios and 1-bed apartments in Kensington and Victoria. From £180–450 a week.

Halls of Residence

University halls of residence offer some of the best value for money accommodation in central London during the summer (mid-June to the end of September). The **London School of Economics** (LSE) for example, has a number of residences that are centrally situated. Tel: 0870 067 5713 www.lsevacations.co.uk.

ACCOMMODATION LISTINGS

WESTMINSTER & VICTORIA

Luxury

41
41 Buckingham Palace Road, SW1W 0PS
Tel: 7300 0041
[p 334, C2]
www.41hotel.com
You can't sleep closer to Buckingham Palace than in this posh 30-room boutique hotel with full amenities and club-like atmosphere.

Berkeley Hotel
Wilton Place, SW1X 7RL
Tel: 7235 6000
[p 334, A2]
www.the-berkeley.co.uk
Many regular guest consider the Berkeley to be the best hotel in London. It's low-key, seldom advertised, with a comfortable country-house atmosphere. Facilities include a pool. Attracts a lot of British customers.

Goring Hotel
15 Beeston Place, Grosvenor Gardens, SW1W 0JW
Tel: 7396 9000
[p 334, B2]
www.goringhotel.co.uk
This is a family-owned (the present manager, George Goring, is last in a long line of Goring managers), traditional hotel not far from Buckingham Palace. Relaxed atmosphere.

Halkin Hotel
5–6 Halkin St, SW1X 7DJ
Tel: 7333 1000
www.halkin.como.bz
[p 334, B2]
The style is very contemporary and there's a first-class restaurant.

The Rubens
39–41 Buckingham Palace Road, SW1W 0PS
Tel: 7834 6600
[p 334, C2]
www.rubenshotel.com
Traditional hotel with a smart location near the Royal Mews, but also conveniently close to Victoria station. 173 rooms, including eight "royal" rooms named (and themed) after British monarchs.

Moderate

Sanctuary House Hotel
33 Tothill Street, SW1H 9LA
Tel: 7799 4044
[p 335, D2]
www.fullershotels.co.uk
Handy for St James's Park; even handier for the Fullers pub beneath the hotel's 34 rooms.

Inexpensive

Elizabeth Hotel
37 Eccleston Square
SW1V 1PB
Tel: 7828 6812
[p 334, C4]
www.elizabethhotel.com

Friendly hotel set in an elegant period square, only two minutes' walk from Victoria Station. 40 rooms, 22 with bath.

Georgian House Hotel
35 St George's Drive, SW1V 4DG
Tel: 7834 1438
[p 334, B4]
www.georgianhousehotel.co.uk
Friendly and well-run bed and breakfast hotel close to Victoria station. 53 rooms.

Royal Westminster Thistle Hotel
49 Buckingham Palace Road, SW1W 0QT
Tel: 0870 333 9121
[p 334, C2]
www.thistlehotels.com
Close to Buckingham Palace and St James's Park, with 134 rooms.

Victoria Park Plaza
239 Vauxhall Bridge Road, SW1V 1EQ
Tel: 7769 9999
[p 334, C3]
www.parkplaza.com
Four-star hotel close to Victoria station, with full amenities. 300 rooms.

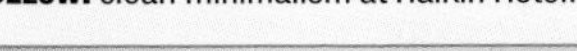

BELOW: clean minimalism at Halkin Hotel.

PRICE CATEGORIES

Price categories are for a double room without breakfast:
Budget: under £100
Inexpensive: £100–150
Moderate: £150–200
Luxury: more than £200

Budget

Airways Hotel
29–31 St George's Drive, SW1V 4DG
Tel: 7834 0205
[p 334, B4]
www.airways-hotel.com
This is a pleasant hotel close to Buckingham Place and Westminster Abbey. 40 en-suite rooms.

Blair Victoria Hotel
78–84 Warwick Way, SW1V 1RZ
Tel: 7828 8603
[p 334, C4]
www.blairvictoria.com
Attractive period hotel close to the train and bus stations. 48 rooms.

Dover Hotel
44 Belgrave Road, SW1V 1RG
Tel: 7821 9085
[p 334, C3]
www.dover-hotel.co.uk
Friendly B&B hotel three minutes' walk from Victoria Station. 13 rooms.

Grapevine Hotel
117 Warwick Way, SWIV 4HT
Tel: 7834 0134
[p 334, C4]
www.grapevinehotel.com
Friendly family-run B&B in Victoria. English breakfast.

Hanover
32 St George's Drive, SW1V 4BN
Tel: 7834 0367
[p 334, C4]
www.hanoverhotel.co.uk
Good hotel hotel close to Victoria Station. Situated between two garden squares. 42 compact rooms.

New England Hotel
20 St George's Drive, SWIV 4BN
Tel: 7834 8351
[p 334, C4]
www.newenglandhotel.com
Friendly, privately-owned hotel in Victoria. English breakfast is included. 27 rooms.

Sidney Hotel
68–76 Belgrave Road, SWIV 2BP
Tel: 7834 2738
[p 335, C4]
www.sidneyhotel.com
Informal no-smoking hotel situated near Victoria station. 82 rooms.

Victoria Inn
65 Belgrave Road, SWIV 2BG
Tel: 7834 6721
[p 335, C4]
www.victoriainn.co.uk
Popular and brightly furnished no-smoking hotel with 43 rooms conveniently situated. Breakfast is included.

SOHO AND COVENT GARDEN

Luxury

One Aldwych
1 Aldwych, WC2B 4RH
tel: 7300 1000
[p 329 , D2]
www.onealdwych.com
Smart and stylish, One Aldwych has an excellent location a stone's throw from theatreland and Covent Garden. This recently built hotel is a showcase of modernity throughout with high-profile guests to match. 105 rooms, each with a minimum 6-ft (2-metre) wide bed and television in the bathroom.

St Martin's Lane
45 St Martin's Lane, WC2N 4HX
Tel: 7300 5500
[p 328, C2]
www.stmartinslane.com
Designed by Phillipe Starck, and still the most fashionable hotel in London. Outlandish lighting, good if expensive food and 204 blindingly white bedrooms. Very well placed for West End theatres and Trafalgar Square.

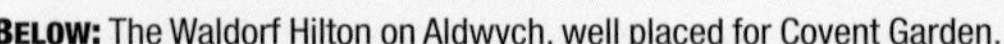

BELOW: The Waldorf Hilton on Aldwych, well placed for Covent Garden.

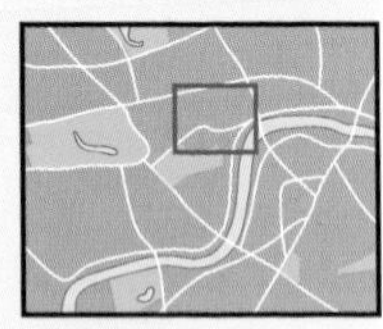

The Savoy
Strand, WC2R 0EU
Tel: 7836 4343
[p 329, D2]
www.fairmont.com/savoy
This classic London hotel has a reputation for comfort and personal service. A massive and long-awaited refurbishment in 2007 should restore its reputation as one of London's very top hotels.

The Waldorf Hilton
Aldwych, WC2B 4DD
Tel: 7836 2400
[p 329, D1]

PRICE CATEGORIES

Price categories are for a double room without breakfast:
Budget: under £100
Inexpensive: £100–150
Moderate: £150–200
Luxury: more than £200

www.hilton.co.uk/waldorf
Renowned Edwardian hotel (292 rooms). Modernised and with a superb location, close to Covent Garden and theatreland.

Hazlitt's
6 Frith Street, W1D 3JA
Tel: 7434 1771
www.hazlittshotel.com
[p 328, B1]
Named after the great English literary critic, Hazlitt's occupies one of London's oldest houses (1718), in the heart of Soho. 23 rooms, all furnished with antiques.

Moderate

Charing Cross Hotel Strand
The Strand, WC2N 5HX
Tel: 0870-333 9105
www.thistlehotels.com
[p 329, C3]
Comfortable and reliable, in a busy location close to Covent Garden.

Inexpensive

Holiday Inn
57–59 Welbeck Street, W1G 9BL
Tel: 7935 4442
[p 330, B3]
www.ichotelsgroup.com
Very central but also a quiet hotel, modern behind its Edwardian facade. 164 rooms.

Thistle Marble Arch
Bryanston Street, W1H 7EH
Tel: 0870-333 9116
www.thistlehotels.com
[p 330, A3]
A very central hotel, overlooking Oxford Street. 692 rooms.

Budget

Edward Lear Hotel
30 Seymour Street, W1H 7JB
Tel: 7402 5401
www.edlear.com
[p 330, A3]
The former home of the Victorian painter and versifier, one minute from Oxford Circus. 31 rooms.

Royal Adelphi Hotel
21 Villiers Street, WC2N 6ND
Tel: 7930 8764
[p 329, C2]
www.royaladelphihotel.co.uk
In a busy little street behind Charing Cross station, and close to the river. A short walk from Covent Garden and theatreland. 47 rooms, 37 with bath.

St James's & Mayfair

Luxury

Brown's Hotel
30 Albemarle Street, W1S 4BP
Tel: 7493 6020
[p 328, A2]
www.brownshotel.com
A distinguished, very British hotel. Smart Mayfair location. 118 rooms.

Claridge's
Brook Street, W1K 4HR
Tel: 7629 8860
[p 330, C4]
www.claridges.co.uk
Has long had a reputation for dignity and graciousness, and the film stars' favourite.

The Connaught
16 Carlos Place, W1K 2AL
Tel: 7499 7070
www.savoygroup.com
[p 330, C4]
One of the best hotels in London, and very popular with British visitors. Renovation in 2007 has refreshed the decor and facilities. Discreet but immaculate service, and a restaurant with one Michelin star. Only 90 rooms.

The Dorchester
Park Lane, W1K 1QA
Tel: 7629 8888
[p 334, B1]
www.dorchesterhotel.com
This is one of the most expensive hotels in London, owned by the Sultan of Brunei. Lovely views over Hyde Park.

Duke's Hotel
35 St James's Place, SW1A 1NY
Tel: 7491 4840
[p 328, A3]
www.dukeshotel.com
Small (89 rooms) traditional hotel in smart St James's. The courtyard is lit by gaslamps, and each of the suites is named after a duke.

The Four Seasons
Hamilton Place, Park Lane, W1A 1AZ
Tel: 7499 0888
[p 334, B1]
www.fourseasons.com/london
This is a temple of modern opulence overlooking Hyde park. Friendly and efficient service.

Lanesborough Hotel
1 Lanesborough Place, SW1X 7TA
Tel: 020 7259 5599
[p 334, B1]
www.lanesborough.com
Deluxe hotel overlooking Hyde Park Corner. The stately neo-classical facade of the former St George's hospital complements the opulent Regency-style interior. Despite being a relative newcomer this is one of London's finest hotels.

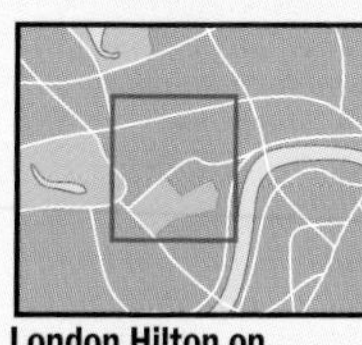

London Hilton on Park Lane
22 Park Lane, W1K 1BE
Tel: 7493 8000
[p 334, B1]
www.hilton.co.uk
Like many other Hiltons across the world, it has its devotees. Of its 446

BELOW: Brown's Hotel is sophisticated and discreet.

ABOVE: the Dorchester on exclusive Park Lane.

rooms, double rooms are classed as "executive", "deluxe" or plain "superior".

London Inter-continental Hotel
1 Hamilton Place, Hyde Park Corner, W1J 7QY
Tel: 7409 3131
[p 334, B1]
www.ichotelsgroup.com
This is perhaps the most opulent hotel on Park Lane's "millionaire's row". Modern and well equipped, courtesy of a £76-million refurbishment in 2007. Superb park views.

Metropolitan
19 Old Park Lane, W1K 1LB
Tel: 7447 1000
[p 334, B1]
www.metropolitan.como.bz
Christina Ong's attempt to create a New York ambience. In the exclusive and achingly trendy bar the staff are known as "mixologists".

No. 5 Maddox Street
5 Maddox Street, W1S 2QD
Tel: 7647 0200
[p 328, A1]
www.living-rooms.co.uk
A stylish range of suites with minimalist decor and full facilities including kitchen and work stations.

The Ritz
150 Piccadilly, W1J 9BR
Tel: 7493 8181
www.theritzlondon.com
[p 328, A3]
This is one of the most famous hotel names in the world. Not quite what it was, despite refurbishment, but it endeavours to keep up standards. Jackets and ties must be worn. Tea at the Ritz is an institution. 130 rooms.

Stafford Hotel
16 St James's Place, SW1A 1NJ
Tel: 7493 0111
[p 334, C1]
www.thestaffordhotel.co.uk
Beautifully located just minutes away from Piccadilly near Green Park. Good choice for those who like small hotels (80 rooms); old-fashioned service.

PRICE CATEGORIES

Price categories are for a double room without breakfast:
Budget: under £100
Inexpensive: £100–150
Moderate: £150–200
Luxury: more than £200

Moderate

Durrants Hotel
George Street, W1H 5BJ
Tel: 7935 8131
[p 330, B3]
www.durrantshotel.co.uk
Period hotel in Georgian terrace, 200 years old and oozing graciousness.

Montcalm Hotel
34–40 Great Cumberland Place, W1H 7TW
Tel: 7402 4288
[p 330, A3]
www.montcalm.co.uk
Quiet and rather plush hotel integrated into an elegant Georgian crescent. 120 rooms.

Inexpensive

Cumberland Hotel
Gt Cumberland Place, W1A 4RF
Tel: 0870 333 9280
[p 330, A3]
www.guoman.com
Over 1,000 hi-tech designer rooms, each with individual works of art. Near Marble Arch.

Montagu House Hotel
3 Montagu Place, W1H 2ER
Tel: 7935 4632
[p 330, A3]
Well-equipped bed and breakfast hotel. All rooms have TV, phones and tea-making facilities. 16 rooms (three with bath).

Sherlock Holmes Hotel
108 Baker Street, W1U 6LJ
Tel: 7486 6161
[p 330, B2]
www.sherlockholmeshotel.com
Handy for Oxford Street shopping, close to Regents Park. Contemporary furnishings strive for a boutique feel. 119 rooms.

St George's Hotel
Langham Place, Regent Street, W1B 2QS
Tel: 7580 0111
[p 331, C3]
www.saintgeorgeshotel.com
Close to the BBC and Oxford Street. Impressive views from its public rooms and restaurant. Only 87 rooms.

BELOW: the Lanesborough *(see previous page)*.

Budget

Beverley House Hotel
142 Sussex Gardens, W2 1UB
Tel: 7723 3380
[p 330, A3]
www.beverleyhousehotel.com
Well-equipped hotel in victorian building between Oxford Street and Hyde Park. 23 rooms.

Lincoln House Hotel
33 Gloucester Place, W1U 8HY
Tel: 7486 7630
[p 330, A3]
www.lincoln-house-hotel.co.uk
Georgian-style bed-and-breakfast hotel, with well-equipped rooms.

Marble Arch Inn
49–50 Upper Berkeley Street, W1H 5QR
Tel: 7723 7888
[p 330, A3]
www.marblearch-inn.co.uk
Convenient for Oxford Street and Hyde Park. 29 rooms.

The Regency Hotel
19 Nottingham Place, W1U 5LQ
Tel: 7486 5347
[p 330, B2]
www.regencyhotelwestend.co.uk
An elegantly converted mansion in the heart of the West End close to Regent, Oxford and Harley streets. Just 20 comfortable rooms.

Wyndham Hotel
20 Wyndham Street, W1H 1DD
Tel: 7723 7204
[p 330, A2]
www.wyndhamhotel.co.uk
Simple family-run hotel in a period property on quiet street, 11 rooms.

Marylebone, Bloomsbury & Holborn

Luxury

Landmark London
222 Marylebone Road, NW1 6JQ
Tel: 7631 8000
[p 330, A2]
www.landmarklondon.co.uk
Modern eight-storey building with a glass domed atrium has good-sized rooms and all facilities.

Langham
1 Portland Place, Regent Street, W1B 1JA
Tel: 7636 1000
[p 330, C3]
london.langhamhotels.com
Elegant and efficient hotel renovated to a high standard in 2006–7. Two bars and a good restaurant. The attractive fountain room is a good place for taking afternoon tea. A short walk from Oxford Circus. 379 rooms.

Sanderson Hotel
50 Berners Street, W1T 3NG
Tel: 7300 1400
[p 331, D1]
www.sandersonlondon.com
A surrealist ultra-chic hotel, restaurant and bar just north of Soho. A hotel with modern sex appeal and good retreat from the bustle of the city. 150 rooms.

Moderate

Montague on the Gardens
15 Montague Street
WC1 5BJ
Tel: 7958 7731
[p 331, E2]
www.montaguehotel.com
A pretty period property with a garden at the rear. Flamboyant decor.

Hotel Russell
Russell Square, WC1B 5BE
Tel: 7837 6470
[p 331, E2]
www.principal-hotels.com
Landmark building in the heart of Bloomsbury. 373 rooms, all with bath.

Thistle Euston
43 Cardington Street, NW1 2LP
Tel: 7387 4400
[p 331, D1]
www.thistlehotels.com
Modern air-conditioned hotel located next to Euston station. 362 rooms with private bath.

Inexpensive

Academy Hotel
21 Gower Street, WC1E 6HG
Tel: 7631 4115
[p 331, D2]
www.theetoncollection.com
A small and welcoming Bloomsbury hotel. Licensed bar; evening meal available. There are 48 rooms, five with private bath.

Holiday Inn Bloomsbury
Coram Street, WC1N 1HT
Tel: 0870 400 9222
[p 331, E1]
www.ichotelsgroup.com
Modern, pleasant hotel. Small indoor pool and leisure club. 284 rooms with private bath.

Budget

Crescent Hotel
49–50 Cartwright Gardens, WC1H 9EL
Tel: 7387 1515
[p 331, D1]
www.CrescentHotelofLondon.com
Situated in a quiet Bloomsbury crescent, with private gardens and tennis courts. 27 rooms.

Euro Hotel
53 Cartwright Gardens, WC1H 9EL
Tel: 7387 4321
[p 331, E1]
www.eurohotel.co.uk
Handy for British Museum. Child-friendly. 34 rooms.

Euston Square Hotel
152–6 North Gower Street, NW1 2LU
Tel: 7388 0099
[p 331, D1]
www.euston-square-hotel.com
Close to Tottenham Court Road. 75 rooms.

George Hotel
58–60 Cartwright Gardens, WC1H 9EL
Tel: 7387 8777
[p 331, E1]
www.georgehotel.com
Traditional B&B hotel in quiet street. 40 rooms.

Gower House Hotel
57 Gower Street, WC1E 6HJ
[p 331 D2,]
www.gowerhousehotel.co.uk
Pleasant bed-and-breakfast hotel near the British Museum.

Lonsdale Hotel
9–10 Bedford Place, WC1B 5JA
Tel: 7636 1812
[p 331, E2]
Long-established bed and breakfast hotel with real character. 39 rooms.

Norfolk Towers Hotel
34 Norfolk Place, W2 1QW
Tel: 7262 3123
[p 330, A3]
www.starcrown.com
Elegant hotel with cocktail bar and restaurant, convenient for the West End. 85 rooms.

THE CITY

Luxury

Grange City
8–14 Cooper's Row, EC3N 2BO
Tel: 7863 3700
[p 333, E3]
www.grangehotels.com
This new 5-star hotel is a member of a small well-run chain. Close to the Tower of London with views of the City. Excellent business facilities plus a pool.

Novotel Tower Bridge
10 Pepys Street, EC3N 2NR
Tel: 7265 6000
[p 333, E3]
www.novotel.com
Overlooks the Tower of London and London Bridge. 203 light, bright well-equipped rooms. Full range of business facilities. Good rates at weekends.

The Tower
St Katharine's Way, E1W 1LD
Tel: 0870-3339106
[p 333, E4]
www.guoman.com
Member of the luxury branch of Thistle Hotels. Modern and extremely comfortable with wonderful views of London.

Moderate

Apex City of London
1 Seething Lane, EC3 4AX
Tel: 7702 2020
[p 333, E3]
Modern medium-size hotel near the Tower of London. Rooms have good views of the City, walk-in power showers and widescreen TVs. 130 rooms.

St Gregory
100 Shoreditch High Street E1 6JO
Tel: 7613 9800
[p 333, E1]
www.saintgregoryhotel.co.uk
Situated in the heart of the City, a few minutes' walk from Liverpool Street Station and Spitalfields Market. Roof-top restaurant. Like many City hotels, weekend rates are considerably cheaper than weekday rates. 200 rooms.

West India Quay Marriott
22 Hartsmere Road
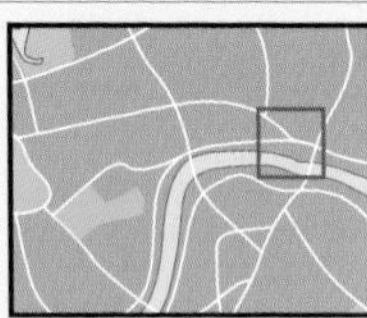
Canary Wharf, E14 46D
Tel: 7093 1000
marriott.com
This branch of the Marriott offers particularly good weekend rates. Good facilities.

BELOW: St Katharine's Dock, Tower Bridge.

SOUTHWARK & THE SOUTH BANK

Luxury

Marriott London County Hall
County Hall, SE1 7PB
Tel: 7928 5200
www.marriott.com
[p 329, D4]
Luxurious setting, with many rooms facing the river at Westminster Bridge. Full-size indoor pool plus health centre. 200 rooms.

Moderate

London Bridge Hotel
8–18 London Bridge Street, SE1 9SG
Tel: 7855 2200
www.londonbridgehotel.co.uk
[p 333 D4]
Efficient location for Bankside's attractions.

Mercure London City Bankside
75–79 Southwark Street, SE1 0JA
Tel: 7902 0800
www.mercure.com
[p 332, C4]
French chain hotel close to Tate Modern and the Globe Theatre.

Park Plaza County Hall
County Hall, SE1
[p 329, D4]
www.parkplaza.com
Brand-new hotel with grand atrium due to open in 2008. Good for families, as rooms will include a small kitchenette equipped with fridge and microwave.

Riverbank Park Plaza
18 Albert Embankment, SE1
Tel: 7269 2400
[p 335, E3]
www.parkplaza.com
Large new hotel (394 rooms) awarded a bronze award for best large hotel by Visit London.Views over the Houses of Parliament and the London Eye.

Inexpensive

Mad Hatter
3–7 Stamford Street, SE1 9NY
Tel: 7401 9222
www.fullershotels.com
[p 332, B4]
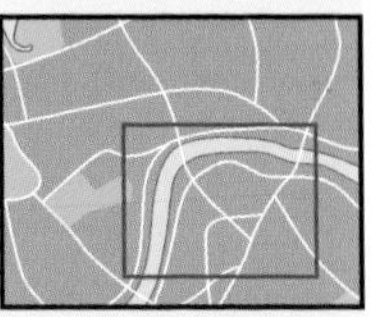
30 rooms above a Fullers pub, just a short stroll from Tate Modern and other attractions on the South Bank.

Novotel City South
53–61 Southwark Bridge Road SE1 9HH
Tel: 7089 0400
[p 333, C4]
www.novotel.com
Close the Shakespeare's Globe and Tate Modern. Clean modern rooms.

KNIGHTSBRIDGE, KENSINGTON & CHELSEA

Luxury

Blakes Hotel
33 Roland Gardens, SW7 3PF
Tel: 7370 6701
www.blakeshotel.com
[p 338, B2]
Very trendy and up-to-the-minute hotel which is popular with theatrical and media folk. Cosmopolitan, tolerant, laid-back in style. 51 rooms.

Cadogan Hotel
75 Sloane Street, SW1X 9SG
Tel: 7235 7141
www.cadogan.com
[p 334, A3]
Another 19th-century style hotel, owned by Historic House Hotels. 65 rooms. Interesting position between Knightsbridge and Chelsea. Lily Langtry once lived in what is now the bar.

Capital Hotel
22 Basil Street, SW3 1AT
Tel: 7589 5171
www.capitalhotel.co.uk
[p 334, A2]
Luxurious little hotel (48 rooms) in the heart of Knightsbridge. Restrained in style, with tasteful decor, and rooms in the Laura Ashley style of interior design. Friendly service. Restaurant has Michelin star.

Conrad London
Chelsea Harbour,
Off Lots Road, SW10 0XG
Tel: 7823 3000
www.conradhotels.com
[p 338, B4]
Luxury hotel (160 rooms) within the exclusive Chelsea Harbour complex by the Thames.

The Gore
190 Queen's Gate, SW7 5EX
Tel: 7584 6601
www.gorehotel.co.uk
[p 336, B2]
This idiosyncratic Kensington hotel is close to the Royal Albert Hall. Every inch of the walls is covered in paintings and prints, and it attracts a lively, fashionable crowd. There are 54 individually themed rooms, some with four-poster beds.

Mandarin Oriental Hyde Park
66 Knightsbridge, SW1X 7LA
Tel: 7235 2000
www.mandarinoriental.com
[p 334, A2]
A hotel of character (185 rooms), right on Knightsbridge, close to Harrods. Sumptuous in a Victorian marble-and-chandeliers style.

Royal Garden Hotel
2–24 Kensington High Street
W8 4PT
Tel: 7937 8000
www.royalgardenhotel.co.uk
[p 336, A2]
Refurbished from top to bottom, this is now Kensington's only 5-star hotel. Decorated throughout in a luxurious contemporary style, it has a health club and one of London's finest views over Kensington Gardens from the top-floor Tenth Restaurant. 396 rooms.

BELOW: a fashionable choice in South Kensington.

Moderate

Knightsbridge Green Hotel
159 Knightsbridge, SW1X 7PD
Tel: 7584 6274
www.thekghotel.co.uk
[p 334, A2]
This family-run hotel is very good value for the location and is unusual in that it consists mostly of suites, double and family-sized rooms. 28 rooms, all non smoking.

The Willett
32 Sloane Gardens, SW1W 8DJ
Tel: 7824 8415
www.willett@eeh.co.uk
[p 334, A4]
Excellent small hotel with 19 rooms in a fashionable neighbourhood – it's on a quiet street just yards from Sloane Square. In view of this, it represents exceptionally good value for money.

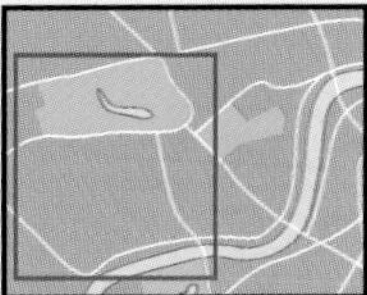

Inexpensive

Abbey Court
20 Pembridge Gardens,
W2 4DU
Tel: 7221 7518
www.abbeycourthotel.com
[p 337, B2]
Beautifully restored Notting Hill town house, with the atmosphere of a private home. 22 rooms, with Italian marble bathrooms with whirlpool baths.

Abbey House
11 Vicarage Gate, W8 4AG
Tel: 7727 2594
www.abbeyhousekensington.com
[p 337, C3]
Grand Victorian house overlooking a pleasant garden square in the heart of Kensington. The rooms are basically furnished, but well maintained. The Abbey is frequently cited as the "Best B&B in London" in surveys. 15 rooms, none en suite.

Abcone Hotel
10 Ashburn Gardens, SW7 4DG
Tel: 7460 3400
www.abcone.co.uk
[p 338, A1]

PRICE CATEGORIES

Price categories are for a double room without breakfast:
Budget: under £100
Inexpensive: £100–150
Moderate: £150–200
Luxury: more than £200

Located not far from Kensington High Street in a pleasant, rather old-fashioned hotel district. 35 rooms, 26 with bath.

Barkston Gardens Hotel
34–48 Barkston Gardens, SW5 0EW
Tel: 7373 7851
www.barkstongardens.com
[p 338, B2]
Set in a quiet tree-lined street, but close to the bustle of Earls Court. Meals available. 93 rooms, all with private bath.

Bayswater Inn
8–16 Princes Square, W2 4NT
Tel: 7727 8621
www.bayswaterinn.co.uk
[p 337, C2]
Situated in a quiet residential square, close to Portobello Road Market, and handy for the Tube. 139 rooms, all with private bath.

My Place Hotel
1–3 Trebovir Road SW5 9LS
Tel: 7373 0833
www.myplacehotel.co.uk
[p 338, A2]
Modern amenities with Victorian ambience in Earls Court area. 50 rooms. Recently refurbished.

Budget

Curzon House Hotel
58 Courtfield Gardens, SW5 0NF
Tel: 7581 2116
www.curzonhousehotel.co.uk
[p 338, A2]
Economical but comfortable small hotel close to Gloucester Road tube. 18 rooms including dormitories at £16 per person.

Eden Plaza Hotel
68–9 Queen's Gate, SW7 5JT
Tel: 7370 6111
www.edenplazahotel.co.uk
[p 338, B1]
Small but brightly furnished rooms. Bistro and bar.

Enterprise Hotel
15–25 Hogarth Road, SW5 0QJ
Tel: 7373 4974
www.woodleygroup.co.uk/enterprise
[p 338, A2]
Good location close to Kensington High Street and Earls Court Underground station. 100 small, but functional en-suite rooms.

Kenwood House Hotel
114 Gloucester Place, W1H 3DB
Tel: 7935 3473
[p 330, B3]
This is a friendly family-run hotel with bed and breakfast accommodation in a central location. 16 rooms, with 2 family rooms also available.

Oliver Plaza Hotel
33 Trebovir Road, SW5 9NF
Tel: 7373 7183
www.capricornhotels.co.uk
[p 338, A2]
Bed-and-breakfast hotel providing good, friendly service and comfortable rooms, all 32 of which have private baths. Good value option.

Vicarage Private Hotel
10 Vicarage Gate, W8 4AG
Tel: 7229 4030
www.londonvicaragehotel.com
[p 337, C3]
Clean rooms and full English breakfast provided, but shared facilities. Handy for Notting Hill Gate.

OUTSIDE THE CENTRE

Luxury

Cannizaro House
Wimbledon Common, SW19
Tel: 8879 1464
www.cannizarohouse.com
Named after a Sicilian Duke this grand 18th-century country house hotel on the edge of Wimbledon Common is in as rural a setting as London can offer. The more interesting of the 46 rooms lie in the original building.

BELOW: Cannizaro House, Wimbledon.

Moderate

Hendon Hall
Ashley Lane, Hendon, NW4 1HF
Tel: 8203 3341
www.hendonhall.com
An 18th-century Georgian mansion with its own grounds, giving a country atmosphere in the middle of north London. Fully modernised kitchen and opulent dining room. Meals available. 52 rooms.

The Petersham Hotel
Nightingale Lane, Richmond, Surrey, TW10 6UZ
Tel: 8940 7471
www.petershamhotel.co.uk
Unspoilt views over parkland and the river Thames. Richmond BR or Tube for easy ride into London (20 mins). 60 rooms.

Inexpensive

Hampstead Britannia Hotel
Primrose Hill Road, Hampstead, NW3 3NA
Tel: 7586 2233
www.britanniahotels.com
Near affluent and fashionable Primrose Hill. Relaxed atmosphere. Restaurant and bar. 100 rooms.

Hotel Orlando
83 Shepherd's Bush Road, W6 7LR
www.hotelorlando.co.uk
Family-run hotel in Hammersmith, near Tube. 14 rooms.

Kingston Lodge Hotel,
94 Kingston Hill, Kingston upon Thames, KT2 7NP
Tel: 8541 4481
www.corushotels.com
Country house hotel in a pretty location to the

west of London. Close to Richmond Park and Hampton Court Palace, and Kingston shopping centre. 63 rooms, restaurant and bar.

Notting Hill Guest House
72 Holland Park Avenue, W11 3QZ
Tel: 7229 9233
www.nottinghillbedandbreakfast.co.uk
Guesthouse with cable TV and cooking facilities in all 6 rooms.

Richmond Hill Hotel
146-150 Richmond Hill, Richmond, Surrey, TW10 6RW
Tel: 8940 2247
www.foliohotels.com/richmondhill
Traditional English hotel has a friendly atmosphere and spectacular views over the Thames. Close to Kew Gardens and Richmond Park. 138 rooms.

Budget

Andrews House Hotel
12 Westbourne Street, W2 2TZ
Tel: 7723 5365
www.andrewshousehotel.co.uk
Family-run, in a busy area close to Paddington and Marble Arch. 17 rooms, 10 with bath.

Benvenuti
217 Court Road, SE9 4TG
Tel: 8857 4855
www.benvenuti.cwc.net
Family-run B&B in Eltham, near Greenwich and Blackheath. 3 rooms.

Buckland Hotel
6 Buckland Crescent Swiss Cottage, NW3 5DX
Tel: 7722 5574
www.bucklandhotel.co.uk
Victorian bed and breakfast hotel in a smart, bustling area. 15 rooms, 12 of them with private baths.

Dillons Hotel
21 Belsize Park, Hampstead, NW3 4DU
Tel: 7794 3360
www.dillonshotel.com
Small family-style guesthouse in charming area close to public transport. 13 rooms, 9 with bathrooms.

Foubert's Hotel
162–8 High Road Chiswick, W4 1PR
Tel: 8995 6743
Family-run hotel with restaurant and wine cellar-bar. Music on weekends. 31 rooms.

EXCURSIONS

ABOVE: the Royal Crescent Hotel, Bath

Brighton

The Grand
(Luxury)
Kings Road, BN1 2FW
Tel: (01273) 224300
www.grandbrighton.co.uk
Victorian grandeur and friendly service. Overlooks beach, indoor pool, gym.

Hotel Pelirocco
(Budget)
10 Regency Square
Tel: (01273) 327055
Cheap but Chic hotel in the best preserved regency square in town.

Bath

The Royal Crescent
(Luxury)
16 Royal Crescent, BA1 2LS
Tel: (01225) 8333333
www.royalcrescent.co.uk
Exclusive hotel in the centre of the splendid Royal Crescent. Traditional furnishings, every comfort.

Holly Lodge
(Inexpensive)
8 Upper Oldfield Park, BA2 3JZ
Tel: (01225) 424042
www.hollylodge.co.uk
Large Victorian house on south side of Bath. Emphasis on service and comfort. Excellent breakfasts.

Cambridge

Cambridge Garden House
(Luxury)
Granta Place, Mill Lane CB2 1RT
Tel: (01223) 259988
www.moathousehotels.com
Modern Moat House by river, with own punts and rowing boats. Convenient central location.

Arundel House Hotel
(Budget)
53 Chesterton Road CB4 3AN
Tel: (01233) 367701
www.arundelhousehotels.co.uk
Privately owned terraced hotel overlooking the River Cam near the centre of town.

Oxford

Bath Place Hotel
(Moderate)
4-5 Bath Place OX1 3SU
Tel: (01865) 791 812
www.bathplace.co.uk
Family-run 12-room hotel in the heart of Oxford occupying a group of restored 17th-century cottages.

River Hotel
(Budget)
17 Botley Road OX2 0AA
Tel: (01865) 243475
www.riverhotel.co.uk
Excellent riverside location. Friendly, small and comfortable hotel within easy reach of the centre.

Stratford

Mercure Shakespeare
(Moderate)
Chapel Street CV37 6ER
Tel: (01789) 293636
www.accor.co.uk
17th-century, half-timbered hotel next to the town hall.

PRICE CATEGORIES

Price categories are for a double room without breakfast:
Budget: under £100
Inexpensive: £100–150
Moderate: £150–200
Luxury: more than £200

SHOPPING

BEST BUYS

London is a great place to shop. Whether you prefer to spend hours roaming around one of its grand department stores – Harrods, Liberty's, Selfridges and Harvey Nichols are four of the best – or to rummage among the bargains of its many and diverse markets, there are retail opportunities to suit all budgets and tastes. The city is also known for its terrific end-of-season sales, especially after Christmas until the end of January and throughout July.

WHERE TO BUY

Antiques

London has an enormous selection of antiques shops and markets. Over 400 of the most elite dealers are in Mayfair, centring around Old Bond Street, many at **Grays Antique Market** at 58 Davies Street, W1, with valuable collections of silver, fine art, jewellery, porcelain, carpets, furniture and antiquities.

Chelsea and **Knightsbridge** have a large share of fine dealers. **Fulham Road** is excellent for period furniture and decorative items, as is the **King's Road**, with indoor markets such as **Antiquarius** housing a wide variety of artefacts.

Westbourne Grove in W11 has many interesting dealers. The whole area comes to life on Friday and Saturday mornings when hordes of tourists descend on the antique arcades and stalls of Portobello Road market. **Kensington Church Street** in W8 is filled with a great variety of expensive antiques shops dealing in everything from fine art to porcelain. **Alfie's Antique Market** in Church Street, NW8, is London's largest indoor antiques bazaar and has a lively atmosphere. Many former dealers have now set up shops along the same road.

BELOW: ready to shop.

Bermondsey's early-morning Friday antiques market at Bermondsey Square, SE1, is a major trading event. The best items change hands by 10am. **Islington**, N1, is also a popular but more expensive area with more then 100 dealers. Of particular interest is the **Mall Antiques Arcade** at 359 Upper Street and the adjacent **Camden Passage**.

Further advice and information on buying antiques in Britain as a whole can be obtained from: **London and Provincial Antique Dealers' Association (LAPADA)**, 535 King's Road, SW10. Tel: 7823 3511. They run an up-to-date online information service on auctions, specific items and antiques offerings throughout the country.

Art

Commercial galleries are subject to the dictates of rent and market prospects, and their geographic centres shift accordingly. Bond Street and Cork Street in London's West End are as upmarket as E.57th Street in New York and have been the high streets of the art trade since the late 19th century. Leases expire, though, and the galleries there are being replaced by fashion outlets; the presence, nearby, of the Sotheby's and Christie's auction houses is reason enough for some to remain, however. They include **Agnews** and **Colnaghi's**, specialising in the traditional, which includes the Old Masters.

Gallery-going technique is a matter of nonchalance and confidence. You are not expected to buy: galleries are shop windows and the selling takes place behind the scenes, usually before an exhibition opens: nothing is expected of you beyond your willingness to take a look.

A stroll from Oxford Circus to Green Park should be by way of Dering Street (**Annely Juda**, **Anthony d'Offay**), Bond Street (the **Fine Art Society**), Cork Street (**Bernard Jacobson**, **Flowers Central**, **Waddington**, **Mayor**, **Browse** and **Darby**) and, in adjacent streets, **Sadie Coles HQ**, **Stephen Friedman** and **Marlborough Fine Art**. The **Frith Street Gallery** has recently moved to Golden Square in Soho.

Flowers East at 82 Kingsland Road, E2 is worth the trek to see young British talent in a vast white space.

Many of the "Young British Artists" who leapt to fame in the 1990s rented studios in Hoxton, north of Old Street, N1. Commercial galleries followed them. In Hoxton Square, the dealer Jay Jopling has **White Cube²**, a larger and more conventional version of his original premises in Duke Street. Others to note include **Lux** in Hoxton Square, **Maureen Paley/Interim Art** in Herald Street, E2, **Matt's Gallery** (for large installations) in Copperfield Road, E2, **Modern Art** in Redchurch Street, E2, **Victoria Miro** in Wharf Road, N1, **The Agency** in Cremer Street, EC2, and **The Approach** in Approach Road, E2.

ABOVE: The Travel Bookshop in Notting Hill.

Books

Charing Cross Road is traditionally the home of book selling. Cecil Court is its old-fashioned heart, selling second-hand and rare books of all kinds. **Foyles** on Charing Cross Road is still among the largest, and its traditional eccentricities have given way to greater efficiency.

Waterstone's, **Borders** and **Books Etc** are well-stocked chains with good travel sections. Borders (203 Oxford Street) and Waterstone's (311 Oxford Street and 203 Piccadilly) are both superstores with the usual coffee bars, sofas and events. **Blackwell's** (100 Charing Cross Road) is the London flagship of the Oxford book seller. The **W.H. Smith** chain has a smaller, more general selection.

Book shops in W1 project an up-market image: **Hatchard's** on Piccadilly, London's oldest book shop, features a huge variety of biographies and fiction. Of the second-hand and rare book sellers in W1, **Quaritch** in Lower John Street is the best known.

Specialist book shops abound. **Bertram Rota** at 31 Long Acre, Covent Garden, is good for modern first editions. **Stanfords** on Long Acre is the best map and travel book shop. **Daunt Books**, at 83 Marylebone High Street, has a great mix of travel-oriented books and guidebooks. **French's**, the theatre book shop, is at Fitzroy Street, W1. **Grant & Cutler** on Great Marlborough Street, W1 is the place to go for foreign-language books. Close to Portobello market is **The Travel Bookshop** at 13 Blenheim Crescent, W11, made famous by Hugh Grant in the 1999 film *Notting Hill*.

China and Glass

All of the big department stores have excellent china and glass departments. For more upmarket English goods, try **Thomas Goode** at 19 South Audley Street, W1. **Wedgwood** is at 158 Regent Street; not everything here is dazzlingly expensive. Their other shop, **Waterford**

BELOW: the finishing touches.

ABOVE: designer footwear.

Wedgwood, is at 173 Piccadilly. The **Reject China Shop** at 183 Brompton Road is good for discount china and kitchenware with a few imperfections.

Clothing and Footwear

Agent Provocateur, 6 Broadwick Street, W1. The place to go for decadently sexy lingerie.
Alexander McQueen, 4–5 Old Bond Street, W1. Once the "bad boy" of the industry, McQueen is now one of Britain's most famous designers, known for his imaginative, cutting-edge fashions.
Anya Hindmarch, 15–17 Pont Street, SW1. London's bag queen sells lines ranging from the classic and bespoke leather to totes with pictures or environmental slogans printed on.
Aquascutum, 100 Regent Street, W1. This venerable British luxe label has recently had a contemporary overhaul, but you can still find their classic traditional pieces and smart raincoats.
Austin Reed, 103–113 Regent Street, W1. Good-quality gentlemen's suits, casual menswear and women's separates, aimed at professionals.
Browns, 25 South Molton Street, W1. With over 100 leading labels stocked in Browns' five interconnecting shops, this is a very popular one-stop fashion boutique. Browns Labels for Less and the directional Browns Focus are alternatives on the same street.
Burberry, 21–23 New Bond Street, W1. Traditional trenchcoats and accessories in the famous plaid are sold alongside the stylish Prorsum range, which offers a fresh, contemporary take on a classic British aesthetic.
The Cross, 141 Portland Road, W11. An eclectic mix of designers, both home-grown and imported, alongside own-brand cashmere at this trendy shop.
Dover Street Market, 17–18 Dover Street, W1. At the height of cutting-edge cool is this fashion baazar, with lines by directional designers displayed in conceptual spaces.
Harvey Nichols, Brompton Road. London's leading fashion department store, with an excellent range of women's designer fashions and footwear under one roof, while men and children are also well catered for.
Jaeger, 204 Regent Street, W1. Tailored classic English clothes for men and women with formal, business and casual ranges.
Jimmy Choo, 27 New Bond Street, W1. Footwear of choice for many celebrities and girls-about-town. Glamorous, vertiginous stilettos abound.
Joseph, 77–9 Fulham Road, SW3. Sexy trousers and sleek classics make up the basis of this label's success; stores also stock a smattering of other designers such as Gucci and Diane von Furstenberg.
Koh Samui, 65 Monmouth Street, WC2. A cornucopia of the hottest British and European designers. Chic clothes in a wide variety of styles, arranged by colour with coordinating shoes.
Kurt Geiger, 198 Regent Street, W1. Incorporates a number of lines, ranging from affordable diffusion to luxe lines, providing a huge variety of footwear choices.
Lulu Guinness, 3 Ellis Street, SW1. Fun, retro bags and other pieces, stylistically positioned between ladylike and kitsch.
Matthew Williamson, 28 Bruton Street, W1. Brightly coloured and patterned womenswear, often intricately embellished and ethnic-inspired.
Mulberry, 41 New Bond Street. Modern clothes along classic British lines, but most renowned for the leather pieces. Their range of handbags is enormously fashionable and the men's accessories are interesting too.
Myla, 77 Lonsdale Road, W11. Sensual, gorgeous lingerie boutique. Also sells swimwear.
Nicole Farhi, 158 New Bond Street, W1. Smart, yet comfortably casual, classic separates in soft fabrics.
Paul Smith, 40 Floral Street, W1. Designer famous for his quirky take on classic tailoring and use of colourful patterns. Men's and women's clothing is found here.
Rellik, 8 Golbourne Road, W10. Probably the most fashionable of London's many vintage emporiums, specialising in retro pieces from the 1920s to 1980s, including by many iconic designers.
Size?, 33–4 Carnaby Street, W1. Trainers specialist, stocking a good range of technical sports shoes as well as classic and old-school trainers.

BELOW: vital accessories.

ABOVE: Paul Smith's store in Covent Garden.

Stella McCartney, 30 Bruton Street, W1. Femininity with an edge and "vegetarian" (non-leather) shoes is the house style of this high-profile British designer.
Ted Baker, 9–10 Floral Street, WC2. Trendy casual and sophisticated clothing, often with a quirky edge, for men and women.
Temperley, 6–10 Colville Mews, W11. Romantic, slightly bohemian dresses and daywear, popular with fashionistas.
Topshop, 216 Oxford Street, W1. No shopping trip in London would be complete without scouring for a bang-on-trend bargain. The largest fashion store in the world, this flagship branch is fast becoming iconic.
Urban Outfitters, 36–38 Kensington High Street, W8. A boutique featuring many hot young designers. Not only clothes, but all a stylish young person's lifestyle needs from jewellery to curtains.
Vivienne Westwood, 6 Davies Street, W1. This is formal compared to Westwood's eccentric World's End boutique on the King's Road, and is the outlet for her more tailored collections. Her menswear collection is available at 44 Conduit Street, W1.
Whistles, 20 The Market, Covent Garden. One of the best places to shop for good clothing with an individualistic take on trends.

Men's Clothes

London is well served for men's clothes shops. Covent Garden is full of them: the fashion-conscious man is catered to with quality designers such as **Paul Smith** and **Michiko Koshino**, as well as the reasonably priced **Reiss**, **All Saints** and **Ted Baker**.

What really distinguishes London's menswear from any other is its traditional gentlemen's outfitters. Savile Row is the best-known street for tailor-made suits. **Gieves & Hawkes** at No. 1 is synonymous with hand-made and off-the-peg classic English tailoring and has a long and noble history. As does the prestigious **Anderson and Sheppard** at the other end of the street, who have discreetly tailored suits for Marlene Dietrich and Prince Charles, amongst other notables. **Tommy Nutter**, across the road, was the young upstart of the Row. Popular with pop and film stars, Nutter had a reputation for flamboyant and eccentric tailored suits. **Huntsman & Sons**, like many tailors in the Row, has been established since the 18th century.

The St James's area, which is littered with gentlemen's clubs, is full of shops selling expensive well-made clothes, toiletries and shoes. In St James's Street is **John Lobb**, considered to make some of the finest hand-made shoes in the world, and the fine hat maker **James Lock**. In Jermyn Street are **Turnbull & Asser**, famed for their made-to-measure and striped shirts. **Bates** hat shop and **Geo Trumpers** traditional toiletry shop are here too. Dover Street and Burlington Gardens are also worth a visit.

If you want the look without paying the price, second-hand and period clothes shops are an option and can yield up great finds; for instance, vintage tailoring and second-hand Savile Row suits can be found at **Bertie Wooster** at 284 Fulham Road, SW10.

Department Stores

Conran Shop, Michelin Building, 81 Fulham Road, SW3. Tel: 0844-561 6161. Sir Terence Conran's unique and stylish shop sells

BELOW: almost anything you ever wanted can be bought in Harrods.

ABOVE: mapping out the options.

designer furniture and household accessories, and in many ways resembles a design museum. Set within the beautiful Art Nouveau tiled Michelin Building, it is worth a visit just to browse.

Fortnum & Mason, 181 Piccadilly, W1. Tel: 7734 8040. Fortnum and Mason opened their store in the 18th century with the grocery needs of the Palace in mind. They began importing exotic and unusual foodstuffs which have long been the basis of the shop's success. The Queen's grocer also stocks fine clothes and household goods. At Christmas the window displays are a joy to behold and many hanker after one of their famous hampers. Pop in for a browse and to see very proper English folk buying their expensive groceries. A fashionable place to have tea.

Harrods, Knightsbridge, SW1. Tel: 7730 1234. One of the world's largest and most famous department stores, now owned by Egypt's Al-Fayed family. Since the 19th century Harrods has maintained a reputation for quality and service, priding itself on stocking the best of everything. No one should miss the fabulous displays in the Edwardian tiled food halls. Harrods sales are major events with those hungry for bargains and prepared to queue a long time to be first through the door.

Liberty, Regent Street, W1. Tel: 7734 1234. The goods on sale in this distinctive and characterful store are still largely based along the same lines as the Oriental, Art Nouveau and Arts and Crafts furniture, wallpaper, silver, jewellery and fabrics Liberty began selling in the late 19th century. There are particularly fine furniture and fashion-accessory departments and an exotic bazaar in the basement.

Marks & Spencer, 458 Oxford Street, W1. Tel: 7935 7954. The venerable chain has triumphantly revitalised over the past few years, with strong advertising and a big push to update its clothes collections. Its food department, with its gourmet ready-cooked meals, remains fantastic, as does the underwear range.

Peter Jones, Sloane Square, SW1. Tel: 7730 3434. This King's Road branch of John Lewis promises customers that its prices cannot be beaten and assures to refund the difference if you can prove otherwise. Stocks a variety of quality goods, most notably household furnishings and appliances.

Selfridges, 400 Oxford Street, W1. Tel: 0870-837 7377. For sheer variety of quality goods, this 100-year-old institution has cornered the market, in a massive one-stop shop. Home furnishings, china, stationery, beauty products, food and a vast selection of fashions are just some of what's on offer. Selfridges is also the most fashionable of the department stores, managing to combine a sense of its history with contemporary style.

BELOW: fine cheese at Paxton & Whitfield on Jermyn Street.

Food & Drink

Degustibus, 4 Southwark Street, SE1. Artisan bakers.

Fresh & Wild, 69–75 Brewer Street, W1. Organic, healthy food store that also comprises a juice bar, deli and café.

Justerini & Brooks, 61 St James's Street, SW1. Top range of fine wines and whiskies.

Konditor & Cook, 10 Stoney Street, SE1. Delicious cakes; also hot and cold lunches.

Paxton & Whitfield, 93 Jermyn Street, SW1. Traditional cheesemongers; they also sell chutneys, preserves, wines and real ales.

Rococo, 321 King's Road, SW3. Gourmet chocolates for connoisseurs.

Vinopolis, 1 Bank End, SE1. A large branch of Majestic Wines and the well-stocked Whiskey Exchange, attached to the wine-tasting and dining complex.

Gifts & Souvenirs

Asprey & Garrard, 167 New Bond Street, W1. Seriously expensive sterling silver and jewellery. Favourite for wedding gifts.

Cath Kidston, 51 Marylebone High Street, W1. Homeware, bags and gifts all in Kidston's unmistakeable patterns: flowers, strawberries and stars.

Octopus, 28 Carnaby Street, W1. Bright, often witty designs in bags, watches, jewellery, umbrellas, ties and much more.

ABOVE: Butler and Wilson in South Molton Street.

Oliver Bonas, 801 Fulham Road, SW6. Small chain of lifestyle shops selling pieces for the home, fashion and beauty accessories, stationery and novelty items.
Smythson, 40 New Bond Street, W1. Luxurious, expensive stationery, as well as diaries and gifts in vibrantly coloured or classic leather.

Jewellery

For innovative modern jewellery, head for Fulham Road and check out **Theo Fennell** at No. 169. For period or Art Deco jewellery try **Cobra & Bellamy** at 149 Sloane Street while at the other end is **Boodle & Dunthorne** for classic and modern designs at No. 1. Stylish and innovative pieces in gold and silver can be found at **Links of London**, at 16 Sloane Square. This is also a good place to find gifts. The finest costume jewellery can be found at **Butler & Wilson**, 20 South Molton Street or **Agatha**, at No. 4.

If you want to spend serious money on serious rocks or simply gawp at the gems, then head for Bond Street (**Asprey & Garrard**) and New Bond Street (**Cartier**, **Bulgari** and **Graff**).

The other main centre is Hatton Garden EC1, a street of nothing but jewellery retailers and wholesalers. A lively area and home to the London Diamond Bourse.

Specialist Shops

The Button Queen, 19 Marylebone Lane, W1. Lots of antique and modern buttons.
Ellis Brigham, 30–32 Southampton Street, WC2. The ideal store for stocking up on outdoor equipment, for camping, climbing and sports. They also sell a good range of backpacks and their staff are very knowledgable.
Legends Boardriders, 119–21 Oxford Street, W1. Heaven for skaters and surfboarders.
Neal's Yard Remedies, 15 Neal's Yard, WC2. Alternative health shop which also sells aromatherapy blends, shampoos, skin protection and gift boxes.
Vintage Magazine Shop, 39–43 Brewer Street, Soho, W1. A cardboard cutout of Harrison Ford or Marilyn Monroe? They've got it, as well as a huge collection of vintage mags.

Markets

Camden Market, NW1. Hugely popular at the weekends, this sprawling market near Camden Lock sells clothes, jewellery, arts and crafts, food and antiques amongst other things.
Columbia Road Flower Market, E2. All kinds of cut flowers and houseplants are sold here at wholesale prices on Sundays, 8am–2pm. Other specialist shops on Columbia Road open to coincide with the market.
Petticoat Lane, Middlesex Street, E1. London's oldest market is so-named for the undergarmets and lace once sold here by French Huguenots. Cheap clothes, fabrics and leather goods are still sold here, among many other things, on some of the 1,000 stalls.
Portobello Road, W11. Renowned for its antiques, this is also a good place to pick up fashionable and vintage clothing, art and general bric-a-brac. It gets very crowded on Saturdays, but has a buzzing atmosphere.
Spitalfields, Commercial Street, E1. This historic covered market has been gentrified with cafés and boutiques, but remains a great place to spot new talent, as many young fashion and jewellery designers sell their wares here. Music, vintage clothing, organic food and childrenswear can also be found here.

BELOW: Legends Boardriders.

ACTIVITIES

THE ARTS, NIGHTLIFE, FESTIVALS, SHOPPING AND SPORTS

In the famous words of Samuel Johnson, "If a man is tired of London he is tired of life." The city has long offered a wealth of activities and entertainments to choose from, but never more than in the 21st century. The ever-expanding range of options caters to all manner of passions and tastes, and although the cost of a great day (or night) out can be expensive, there are many great museums, festivals and spectacles that are free.

ABOVE: performance at the Globe.

THE ARTS

Museums & Art Galleries

A public lottery funded the British Museum's foundation in 1759 and fittingly it was lottery money released in the late 1990s to celebrate the new millennium that helped finance its spectacular Great Court. The same millennial largesse aided many of London's museums and galleries and the government decreed that the great national collections should abolish entrance fees.

Alongside the rejuvenation of the star attractions came a rash of specialist new museums. There are more than 130 museums and galleries worth a visit.

Money-saving Passes

Although national museums and galleries are free, most others have entrance charges. Energetic visitors will benefit from the London Pass, which allows free entry to several dozen attractions. Free travel on the Tube and buses is also included. At press time, prices ranged from £39 for a one-day pass to £112 for a six-day pass (children £22–£70). Details: tel: 01664-485020 or check www.londonpass.com

Joining the Art Fund costs £40 a year and provides free admission to more than 200 museums, galleries and historic houses around the country, plus discounts on some exhibitions. Details on 0870-848 2003 or from www.artfund.org

Theatre

The only way to get a ticket at face value is to buy it from the theatre box office. Most open 10am–mid-evening. You can pay by credit card over the phone for most theatres, or reserve seats three days in advance before paying. A ticket booth (TKTS) on the south side of Leicester Square offers unsold seats at half price or three-quarter price (plus booking fee) on the day of performance (open Mon–Sat 10am–7pm, Sun noon–3pm). A second TKTS booth is at Canary Wharf (platform 4/5 of Docklands Light Railway, Mon–Sat 10am–3.30pm). There are booking agents throughout London (and quite a few unofficial kiosks around Leicester Square), but beware: some charge high fees. It's sensible to ask what the face value of a ticket is before parting with your money. Two reputable 24-hour agents are **Keith Prowse** at 0870-840 1111 and **Ticketmaster** at www.ticketmaster.co.uk.

Ignore ticket touts unless you're prepared to pay several times a ticket's face value for sell-outs.

● *For further information see Theatreland chapter, page 42. For West End theatre locations, see the map on page 353.*

ABOVE: theatre's showcase.

Holland Park Open Air Theatre, Holland Park, W8. www.operahollandpark.com
During the warm summer months opera, dance and theatre performances are staged here in the semi-open air. Tube: Holland Park/High Street Kensington.

National Theatre, South Bank, SE1. Tel: 7452 3000.
Three repertory theatres are housed within the National's concrete mass. They always provide a good and varied selection of plays. Tube: Waterloo/ Embankment.

Open Air Theatre, Regent's Park Tel: 08700-601811; http:// openairtheatre.org
With a 15-week summer season, this not-for-profit charity hosts a variety of plays, including Shakespeare. Tube: Baker Street.

Shakespeare's Globe Theatre, Bankside, SE1. Tel: 7401 9919.
May–Sept season in a recreation of the Tudor original. Tube: Southwark/London Bridge.

Ballet

Coliseum, St Martin's Lane, WC2. Tel: 7632 8300.
Hosts performances of ballet in the summer months by the Royal Festival Ballet and visiting companies. Is particularly popular with visiting Russian ballets. Tube: Leicester Square.

Sadlers Wells Theatre, Rosebery Avenue EC1. Tel: 7863 8000.
A flexible, state-of-the-art performance space that offers an exciting and innovative programme of dance and opera. London's leading venue for contemporary and classical dance. Tube: Angel.

Royal Opera House, 48 Floral Street, WC2. Tel: 7304 4000.
Home to the Royal Ballet and the Royal Opera. Was extensively refurbished for the millennium. Backstage tours are available. Tube: Covent Garden.

Opera

Coliseum, St Martin's Lane, WC2. Tel: 7632 8300.
This elegant Edwardian theatre is easily distinguished on London's skyline by the illuminated golden globe on its roof. Home to the English National Opera (ENO), this is where English-language operas are performed. Productions tend to be more theatrical than those of the Royal Opera. Tube: Leicester Square.

Royal Opera House, 48 Floral Street, WC2. Tel: 7304 4000.
More traditional than the Coliseum, this theatre attracts the crème de la crème of the opera world. Operas are performed in their original language and tickets are very expensive. Dressy affair. Tube: Covent Garden.

Classical Music

Barbican Arts Centre, Silk Street, EC2. Tel: 7638 8891.
Home to the London Symphony Orchestra and the English Chamber Orchestra. This huge concrete complex built for the arts is one of London's major classical-concert venues. Tube: Barbican.

The Royal Albert Hall, Kensington Gore, SW7. Tel: 7589 8212.
This circular hall comes alive every summer for the Henry Wood Promenade Concerts, known simply as The Proms. Tubes: Kensington High Street/ South Kensington.

Royal Festival Hall, South Bank, Belvedere Road, SE1. Tel: 0871-663 2500.

BELOW: the annual proms at the Royal Albert Hall.

ABOVE: the Royal Festival Hall on the South Bank.

London's premier classical music venue was built as part of the Festival of Britain of 1951. The exterior of this hall appears somewhat dated and arouses mixed public comment on its appearance. However, it is an excellent concert hall with space for large-scale performances. Next door is the Queen Elizabeth Hall where chamber concerts and solos are performed. Also the small Purcell Room for more intimate music. Tube: Waterloo/Embankment.
Wigmore Hall, 36 Wigmore Street, W1. Tel: 7935 2141. Delightful intimate hall with seating for 550. It has a pleasant atmosphere and excellent acoustics and is most renowned for chamber recitals. Also Sunday-morning coffee concerts. Tube: Bond Street.

Churches

Many of London's historic churches also offer superb music, and in some cases for free. Three of the best are:
St John's, Smith Square, Westminster, SW1. Tel: 7222 1061. This church has been converted into a concert hall hosting chamber music and BBC lunch-time concerts. Tube: Westminster.
St Martin-in-the-Fields, Trafalgar Square, WC2. Tel: 7839 8362. Concerts are held at lunch times and evenings in this church designed by James Gibbs. Tube: Charing Cross.
St Mary-le-Bow, Cheapside, EC2. Tel: 7248 5139.
Lunch-time recitals most Thursdays (www.stmarylebow.co.uk has details). Home to the famous Bow bells. Tube: St Paul's/ Mansion House/Bank.

NIGHTLIFE

Late Spots

If you're under 30 and believe the hype, London is one of the best places to party in the world. It certainly has built a solid reputation as one of the great international clubbing centres. But not all nightlife is dance-till-dawn. Older swingers in town can enjoy dinner dances, drinking bars, casinos and smart nightclubs.

Despite its reputation, and despite a relaxation of licensing laws in recent years,London is not an especially late city. Most restaurants, pubs and even bars have wound down by 1am, leaving just a few determined establishments to stagger on until the city awakes.

Jazz Clubs

Jazz Café, 5 Parkway, Camden NW1. Tel: 0870-060 3777 (tickets). Tel: 7534 6955 (table). Intimate jazz club in Camden Town that attracts some top names. Tube: Camden.
Jazz@Pizza Express, 10 Dean Street, W1. Tel: 7439 8722. This Soho branch of the pizza chain has a high standard of performers. Tube: Leicester Square/Piccadilly Circus/ Tottenham Court Road.
Ronnie Scott's, 47 Frith Street, W1. Tel: 7439 0747.
Scott, who died in 1996, had eclectic taste, and this is still reflected in this legendary Soho venue, which has hosted some of the biggest names in jazz since 1959. Very relaxed. Tube: Leicester Square/Piccadilly Circus/ Tottenham Court Road.

Dance Clubs

Café de Paris, 3–4 Coventry Street, SW1. Tel: 7734 7700. Posh old dancehall attracts an older sophisticated crowd. Trendy/smart. Tube: Piccadilly Circus/Leicester Square.
Cargo, 83 Rivington Street, EC2. Tel: 7739 3440.
This venue under the railway arches offers a variety of live line-ups. Tube: Old Street.
EGG
5–13 Vale Royal, N7. Tel: 7609 8364.
Spacious venue with three dance floors. Fashionable gay nights. Tube: Caledonian Road.
Electric Ballroom, 184 Camden High Street, NW1. Tel: 7485 9006.
This old dancehall has a huge main dance floor where on Saturday nights Shake attracts a mixed crowd playing hits of the 1970s, '80s and '90s. Upstairs

ABOVE: for reliably good jazz visit Ronnie Scott's on Frith Street.

it's R&B and hip-hop. Casual. Tube: Camden.
The End, 18 West Central Street, WC1. Tel: 7419 9199.
Stunning sound system. Known for its cutting-edge acts and DJs. Tube: Tottenham Court Road/Holborn.
Fabric, 77A Charterhouse Street, EC1. Tel: 7336 8898.
Celebrated club that mixes big names (generally on Fridays), with top DJs (Saturdays) and new talent. Bars open until 3am. Tube: Farringdon.
The Fridge, Town Hall Parade, Brixton Hill, SW2. Tel: 7326 5100.
Spectacular one-nighters. Worth seeking out. Tube: Brixton.
Heaven, The Arches, Villiers Street, WC2. Tel: 7930 2020.
Submerged beneath the Charing Cross development is one of the best dance clubs in town. Gay nights are Tuesday, Wednesday, Friday and Saturday. Very casual dress code. Tube: Charing Cross/Embankment.
Mass, St Matthew's Peace Garden, SW2. Tel: 7738 7875.
Atmospheric Brixton venue in the bowels of a converted church. Wide range of music, with great R&B in the Friday Nite Mass. Tube: Brixton.
Ministry of Sound, 103 Gaunt Street, SE1. Tel: 0870 060 0010.
This renowned dance club is London's top house-music venue. Tube: Elephant & Castle/ Borough.
Neighbourhood, 12 Acklam Road, W10. Tel: 7524 7979.
West London's main club with its well-designed modern interior hewn out of the concrete structure of the Westway. Trendy/hip. Tube: Westbourne Park.
Salsa
96 Charing Cross Road, WC2. Tel: 7379 3277.
A good Latin venue in the heart of the West End. Lots of fun, very busy and a good place to practise your moves with regular dance classes. Casual. Tube: Charing Cross/Leicester Square.
Soho Lounge, 69–70 Dean Street, W1. Tel: 7734 1231 (10am–6pm). Tel: 7734 4895 (night line).
West End basement club with a variety of one-nighters – a favourite with Soho regulars – caters for all musical tastes, from reggae to heavy metal. Trendy. Tube: Leicester Square/Piccadilly Circus/ Tottenham Court Road.
The Telegraph, 228 Brixton Hill, SW2. Tel: 8678 0777.
A former home of punk, this long-established venue combines a club and a Thai restaurant, has fair bar prices and a cheerful atmosphere. Tube: Brixton.
333, 333 Old Street, EC1. Tel: 7739 5949.
Hipp club with a good drinking lounge upstairs and pounding dance music in the basement. Tube: Old Street.

BELOW: the cocktail hour can last a lot longer.

Gay Venues

Candy Bar, 4 Carlisle Street, Soho, W1. Tel: 7494 4041. www.candybarsoho.com
Claiming to be the most prolific lesbian bar in the world Candy offers everything from hip-hop and R&B to acoustic sets and poetry, striptease in the basement and its very own pole-dancing candy girls all set in retro pink. Tube: Tottenham Court Road.

Heaven, Villiers Street, WC2. Tel: 7930 2020. www.heaven-london.com
Considered London's premier gay club, Heaven saves its best for the weekend. Its flagship night on Saturday holds five rooms of music, DJs and performance, It also has early-week fun with Popcorn on Mondays. Tube: Charing Cross/Embankment.

Ghetto, 5–6 Falconberg Court, W1. Tel: 7287 3726. www.ghetto-london.co.uk
With its aim "to squeeze some sense in to Soho" Ghetto promises a nitty-gritty alternative experience with weekday indie, electro and pop nights. Drinks from £2. Tube: Tottenham Court Road.

Crash, 66 Albert Embankment, SE1. Tel: 7793 9262. www.crashlondon.co.uk
Shirts are an extra at Crash: most men go without as they spread themselves across its two dance floors. Top DJ sets are supplied every Friday and Saturday. The club also has rock, indie and pop nights. Tube: Vauxhall.

G.A.Y.
157 Charing Cross Road, WC2. Tel: 7374 9592. www.g-a-y.co.uk
G.A.Y. regularly rocks the creaking joints of the Astoria to breaking point with its PA systems and camp pop fun. London and possibly Europe's biggest gay club has played host to Bjork and can boast regulars such as Kylie Minogue and Sophie Ellis-Bextor. Tube: Tottenham Court Road.

Turnmills, 63 Clerkenwell Road, EC1. Tel: 7250 3409.
Great sound system, mixed crowd and wide variety of dance styles. Two good restaurants and regular gay techno nights. Tube: Farringdon.

Comedy/Cabaret

Comedy Store, 1a, Oxendon Street, SW1. Tel: 0870-060 2340.
A night at this well-established venue for stand-up comedians will remind you that comedy need not always be accompanied by canned laughter. On a good night, the comedians in the audience are as famous as those on stage. Avoid sitting in the front row unless you want to become part of the show. Tube: Piccadilly Circus/Leicester Square.

Jongleurs, Middle Yard (Camden Lock), Chalk Farm Road, NW1. Also at Battersea and Bow. Tel: 0870-787 0707.
Leading stand-up comedy club. Camden attracts the best acts. Tube: Chalk Farm/Camden.

Madame Jo Jo's, 8 Brewer Street, W1. Tel: 7734 3040.
Ultra-camp transvestite revue bar popular for hen or stag nights. Lacking in the sleaze and daring associated with Soho's sometimes unsavoury past, Madame Jo Jo's still offers one of the best late-night outings in London with captivating cabaret shows from Kitsch Cabaret with Teri Pace and her male leggy lovelies in their amazing costumes. Closes 3am. Tube: Piccadilly Circus.

Stringfellow's, 16 Upper St Martin's Lane, WC2. Tel: 7240 5534.
This slightly tongue-in-cheek lap-dancing joint is strong on tacky glamour, so dress accordingly. Tube: Covent Garden/Leicester Square.

Dinner Dance

Some of the best and most romantic dine and dance places are at the luxury hotels. Or you could try:

Concordia Notte, 29 Craven Road, W2. Tel: 7723 3725.
Set within a tastefully luxurious cavern is this sophisticated restaurant which courts the rich and famous. The superb classic Italian cuisine is accompanied by an impressive wine list, charming service and gentle dance music with which to while away the night. Last orders 1am. Tube: Lancaster Gate.

Round the Clock

Takeaways

Beigel Bake, 159 Brick Lane, E1. Tel: 7729 0616.
Join Londoners who ritually pile across to Brick Lane after a night out to stock up on freshly baked bagels filled with smoked salmon and cream or hot salt beef with lashings of mustard and gherkin. Open 24 hours. Tube: Shoreditch.

Dionysius, 3–5 Oxford Street, W1. Tel: 7434 4204. Popular fast-food joint serving kebabs, hummous, and fish and chips to eat in or takeaway. Sun–Thurs until 4am, Fri/Sat until 6am. Tube: Tottenham Court Road.

Mr Bagel's (2000), 13 Ridley Road, E8. Tel: 7923 4331.
Grab a black cab and take a detour to Ridley Road on your way home for the fashionable late-night snack. This bagel hot spot in Dalston is as much of an institution as its Brick Lane rival *(see above)*. Open 24 hours.

Coffee/Breakfast

Bar Italia, 22 Frith Street, W1. Tel: 7437 4520.
A piece of real Italy located in the centre of Soho. No matter what the hour this family-run bar is always buzzing. Can be expensive but reputed to have the best coffee in London. Open 24 hours

Mon–Sat, until 4am Sun (Mon morning). Tube: Leicester Square.
Chelsea Bridge Snack Kiosk. A kiosk is reputed to have been doing hot food and teas at this location since the 1920s. Ever popular with early-morning truck drivers, cabbies and their passengers. Open all night.

ABOVE: for fantastic fireworks head to the Thames on New Year's Eve.

CALENDAR OF EVENTS

January

New Year's Day Parade from Parliament Square to Berkeley Square.
London International Boat Show, ExCel, Docklands. This is the world's largest exhibition of its kind. DLR: Custom House.
Charles I Commemoration (last Sunday). English Civil War Society dress up as Royalists from the King's army and make their way from Charles I's statue in Whitehall to his place of execution outside Banqueting House.

February

Chinese New Year. Colourful Chinese celebrations centring around Gerrard Street in Chinatown, Soho. Tube: Leicester Square.
Great Spitalfields Pancake Day Race (Shrove Tuesday). Old Truman Brewery, Brick Lane, E1. Teams run along Dray Walk tossing pancakes which must be caught in the pan. Musicians and jesters accompany them. Tube: Aldgate East/Shoreditch.

March

Ideal Home Exhibition. Earl's Court. Tel: 7385 1200. Exhibition of new ideas and products for the home. Tube: West Brompton/ Earl's Court.
Easter Parade, Battersea Park. Carnival with floats and fancy-dress costumes.

BELOW: the Chelsea Flower Show in late May.

April

London Marathon. One of the world's biggest runs, starting at Greenwich Park and ending at Westminster.
Queen's Birthday (21st). The Queen's real birthday (as opposed to her official one in June) is celebrated with a gun salute in Hyde Park and at the Tower of London.

May

Chelsea Flower Show, Royal Hospital, SW3. Tel: 7834 4333. Major horticultural show, featuring spectacular displays, and social event in the fine grounds of the Chelsea Royal Hospital. Tube: Sloane Square.
FA Cup Final, Wembley. The final of the nation's main football competition. Tube: Wembley Park/Wembley Central.
Oak Apple Day, Chelsea Royal Hospital. Parade of the Chelsea Pensioners in memory of their founder, Charles II. Tube: Sloane Square.
Coin Street Festival, South Bank. Starts on Spring Bank Holiday (last Monday in May) and continues most weekends until September. Music and street performances from around the world. Tube: Blackfriars/Waterloo.

ABOVE: the Proms, an occasion for flag-waving in July.

June

Beating Retreat, Horse Guards Parade, Whitehall. Annual ceremonial display of military bands. Tube: Charing Cross/ Westminster.
Derby Day, Epsom Racecourse. Tel: 01372-470047. Famous flat race for 3-year-old colts and fillies. Train: Vauxhall/Victoria to Epsom or Victoria to Tattenham Corner.
Royal Academy Summer Exhibition, Burlington House, Piccadilly. Tel: 7300 5760. Large exhibition of work by professional and amateur artists running until August. All works for sale. Tube: Piccadilly/Green Park.
Trooping the Colour. Tel: 7414 2479. The Queen's official birthday celebrations, with a royal procession along the Mall to Horse Guards Parade for the ceremonial parade of regimental colours. Followed by the presence of the royal family on the balcony of Buckingham Palace. Tube: Green Park/St James's Park.
Royal Ascot, Ascot Racecourse. Tel: 0870 727 1234. Elegant and dressy race meeting attended by royalty. Train: Vauxhall to Ascot.
Grosvenor House Antiques Fair, Grosvenor House Hotel, Park Lane. Tel: 7499 6363. A large and prestigious event. Tube: Marble Arch.
Wimbledon Lawn Tennis Championships, All England Club. Tel: 8946 2244. World-famous fortnight of tennis on grass courts. Tube: Southfields.
Flower Festival. Last week. Exhibition on the history of Covent Garden's fruit and vegetable market, and demonstrations on garden design and flower arranging. Tube: Covent Garden.
Greenwich & Docklands International Festival. Three-week festival beginning at the end of June, with music, dance, theatre and spectacular firework displays. Various venues.

July

Henry Wood Promenade Concerts, Royal Albert Hall. Tel: 7589 8212. Series of classical concerts known as The Proms, culminating in the rumbustious Last Night which spills out into Hyde Park. Tube: South Kensington/High Street Kensington.
Royal Tournament, Earl's Court. Tel: 7385 1200. Spectacular military displays from the Royal Army, Navy and Air Force.
Swan Upping on the Thames. All the swans on the Thames belong to the Queen, the Vintners and the Dyers and for five days every year officials can be seen rowing on the river registering them.
Doggett's Coat and Badge Race. Race for single-scull boats between London Bridge and Chelsea that has been a tradition since 1715.
Motor Show, Excel, Docklands. Tel: 7654 0600. Major international car show held every two years; next one end July/early August 2008. DLR: Custom House.

August

Notting Hill Carnival, Ladbroke Grove (bank holiday weekend). Colourful and lively West Indian street carnival (Europe's largest) with exciting and imaginative costumes, live steel bands and reggae music. The streets can get extremely crowded. Tube: Notting Hill Gate.
London Riding Horse Parade, Rotten Row, Hyde Park. Elegant competition for best turned-out horse and rider. Tube: Hyde Park Corner/Knightsbridge/Lancaster Gate/Marble Arch.
International Street Performers' Festival, Covent Garden Piazza. Free street entertainment. Tube: Covent Garden.

September

Chelsea Antiques Fair, Old Town Hall, King's Road, SW3. Tel: 0870 350 2442. Wide range of antiques on sale. Tube: Sloane Square.
Horseman's Sunday, St John's Church Hyde Park, W2. Morning service dedicated to the horse with mounted vicar and congregation. Followed by procession through Hyde Park. Tube: Paddington/Edgeware Road.
Thames Festival, between Waterloo Bridge and Blackfriars Bridge. Fanfare, river displays, face painting, craft and food stalls.

October

Judges' Service marks the beginning of the legal year in Britain with a procession of judges in full attire from Westminster Abbey to the Houses of Parliament. Tube: Westminster.
Costermongers' Pearly Harvest Festival (1st Sunday), St Martin-

in-the-Fields, Trafalgar Square. Pearly Kings and Queens (street traders) attend a service in their traditional attire, which is elaborately adorned with pearl buttons. Tube: Charing Cross.

Trafalgar Day Parade commemorates Nelson's victory over the French and Spanish at Trafalgar on 21 October. Tube: Charing Cross.

November

London to Brighton Veteran Car Run (1st Sunday). Hundreds of immaculately preserved veteran cars and their proud owners start out from Hyde Park and make their way sedately to Brighton. Tube: Hyde Park Corner.

Lord Mayor's Show. Grand procession from the Guildhall in the City to the Royal Courts of Justice, celebrating the annual election of the Lord Mayor. Tube: Bank.

Remembrance Sunday (nearest the 11th). Commemorates those lost at war. Main wreath-laying service at the Cenotaph. Tube: Westminster.

State Opening of Parliament, House of Lords, Westminster. Official re-opening of Parliament (following the summer recess) by the Queen, who travels down the Mall in a state coach. Tube: Westminster.

Guy Fawkes Day (5 November). Traditional firework celebration of the failure to blow up the Houses of Parliament by Guy Fawkes in 1605. Bonfires and organised firework displays all over London.

Christmas Lights switched on in Oxford and Regent streets. Tube: Oxford Circus/Piccadilly Circus.

December

London International Horse Show, Olympia. Tel: 01753-847900. Major international show-jumping championships. Tube: Kensington (Olympia).

Christmas Carol Services, Trafalgar Square: carols (Christmas hymns) in the evenings beneath the giant tree which is presented each year by Norway. Tube: Charing Cross. Carol services are also held in many churches all over London.

New Year's Eve, Trafalgar Square. Thousands of people congregate around the fountains to drink, hold hands and sing *Auld Lang Syne* at midnight. Tube: Charing Cross.

SPORT

Spectator Sports

Football (Soccer)

The football season runs from August to May, with matches usually held Saturday 3pm, sometimes on Sundays, and Tuesday evenings. The top football clubs in London are Arsenal (Emirates Stadium, Highbury, tel: 7704 4242), Chelsea (Stamford Bridge, Fulham Road, SW6, tel: 0870-300 1212) and Tottenham Hotspur (White Hart Lane, 748 High Road, N17, tel: 8365 5000).

Rugby

This is played Sept–April/May. Top Rugby Union games are played at Twickenham Rugby Football Ground (Whitton Road, Twickenham, Middlesex, tel: 8831 6666). The Rugby League holds its cup final matches at Wembley Stadium.

Cricket

The game is played in summer only, at the Oval, Kennington, SE11, tel: Surrey County Cricket Club: 7582 6660, or at Lord's Cricket Ground, St John's Wood, NW8, tel: 7289 1611. You should buy tickets well in advance for Test matches but there's generally less competition for seats for one-day internationals.

Tennis

Wimbledon, on the District line of the Underground (Southfields), is the venue for the famous two-week tennis championship, which starts in the last week in June. Seats for the show courts (Centre Court and courts 1 and 2) are allocated by ballot and should be applied for before mid-December the preceding year by writing to the All England Tennis Club, P.O. Box 98, Wimbledon, SW19 5AE, enclosing a self-addressed envelope (or an inter-

BELOW: a summer game of croquet.

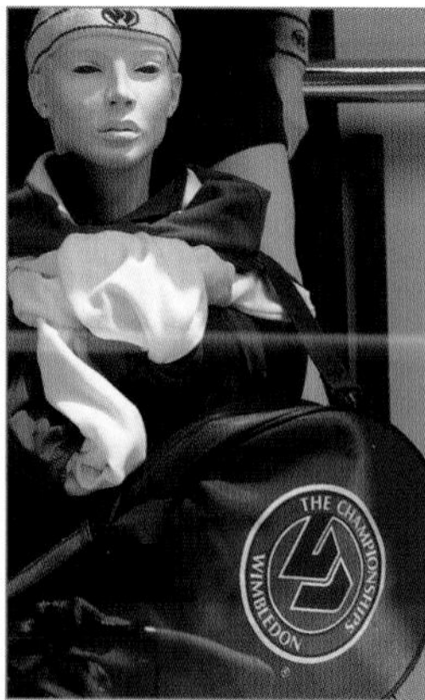

ABOVE: Wimbledon fortnight begins in the last week of June.

national reply coupon if applying from overseas). However, apart from Centre Court action on the last four days, you can queue on the day for tickets (cash only, to speed things up), though for popular games this can mean queueing all night under the watchful eye of supervisors. For information contact the ticket office on 8971 2473 or check www.wimbledon.org. Buses for the championships leave Victoria and Marble Arch every 30 minutes; trains from Waterloo are met by a shuttle bus at Wimbledon station.

Greyhound Racing

Going "down the dogs" is a popular night out in the East End of London. At most tracks you can choose between standing by the track or watching from a table in the restaurant. Most tracks hold two meetings a week; the days vary so call ahead to check. Tracks: Hackney Wick, Romford, Walthamstow, Watford, Wembley, Wimbledon. The best is Walthamstow Race Track, Chingford Road, E4. Tel: 8498 3300.

Horse Racing

The flat-racing season is March to November, while steeplechasing takes place virtually all year round. The nearest racetracks to London are: Ascot, tel: 01344-878555; Jockey Club Race Courses (Kempton Park, Epsom and Sandown Park), tel: 01372-464348 and Windsor, tel: 01753-498400.

The Boat Race

Rowers from Oxford and Cambridge universities race down the Thames from Putney to Mortlake. This annual event (since 1856) in late March/early April is watched by around 250,000 cheering spectators lining the riverbanks.

Participant Sports

Golf

Contact the English Golf Union (www.englishgolfunion.org; tel: 01526-354500) for details of courses.

Many golf courses in London's suburbs offer "pay and play" access, though booking is advisable at weekends. They include:
Beckenham Place Park, Beckenham Hill Road, Beckenham, BR3 (tel: 8650 2292), a parkland course with an imposing 18th-century mansion for a clubhouse.
Lee Valley, Lee Valley Leisure Complex, Picketts Lock Lane, Edmonton, N9 (tel: 8803 3611), an urban course built on reclaimed land.
Stockley Park, Uxbridge, UB11 (tel: 8813 5700), a championship-length course in 240 acres (97 hectares) of pleasantly undulating parkland.

Horse Riding

Hyde Park Stables (tel: 7723 2813) can arrange rides.

Tennis

Many local parks have bookable courts. The Lawn Tennis Association (www.lta.org.uk; tel: 8487 7000) has a leaflet on grass courts and you can locate a court in a park or leisure area near you by checking www.londontennis.co.uk.

SWIMMING

In spite of the UK's reputation for cold, wet weather, summers in London have been very warm in recent years. Few hotels have swimming pools and most municipal pools are indoors.
Outdoor pools include:
The Oasis, 32 Endell Street, WC2. Tel: 7831 1804
Between Covent Garden and Tottenham Court Road, this heated outdoor pool is a hidden gem and open year-round (steamy in winter). It isn't smart but it is clean and well-loved by regulars.
Brockwell Lido, Dulwich Road, SE24. Tel: 7274 3088
www.brockwelllido.com
Very popular amenity open during the summer months only. Barbecues on hot days.
Other pools include the **Serpentine** in Hyde Park and the Bathing Ponds on **Hampstead Heath**. The latter comprise three pools – a men's, a women's and a mixed one, open 7am–7pm year-round for the single-sex pools and summer only for the mixed.

TOURS

Guided Tours

A guided tour of London by bus is the best way for visitors to familiarise themselves with the city. All tours that are registered with the London Tourist Board use Blue Badge Guides, whose ranks number around 1,000.
The Big Bus Company, tel: 7233 9533. Open-top bus tours over a choice of two routes lasting 2½ to 3½ hours. You are free to hop on or hop off at any of the 80 stops. Buses run every 5–15 minutes. Tours have live commentary in English or recorded commentary in seven languages as well as

English. Tickets are valid for 24 hours; buses operate 8.30am–8pm in the summer and until 6.30pm in the winter. Cost: £22 for adults and £10 for children.
Evan Evans, tel: 7950 1777. A variety of tours giving a comprehensive introduction to the city with emphasis on historic sites. Admittance to St Paul's Cathedral, the Royal Albert Hall and the Tower of London are part of some tours. Picks up from many hotels. Cost: £72 (£62 for children under 16).
Golden Tours, tel: 7837 3111. Various tours of the city in air-conditioned coaches accompanied by guides who hold the coveted Blue Badge. The London Experience full-day tour takes in major sights such as the Tower with optional stops at Westminster Abbey and the London Eye. Cost: £78 (£68 for children).
The Original London Sightseeing Tour, tel: 8877 1722. A choice of three different tours in traditional red double-decker buses, some of which are open-top. The Original tour features live commentary in English; the other two have recorded commentary in a choice of seven languages. A unique feature is the recorded children's commentary – by kids for kids. Tours run from 9am approximately every 12 minutes and passengers can hop on and off at any of the 90 stops. Tickets cost £19 for adults and £12 for children under 16 and are valid for 24 hours. Departure points throughout central London; Marble Arch, Baker Street, Strand, Haymarket, Victoria, and others. A free river cruise from Embankment is included in the price.
Jack the Ripper Tours, tel: 8530 8443, www.rippertour.com. As the title suggests, a two-hour after-dark tour which explores London's more murky past and shady courtyards. Cost: £6.50.
Ghost Walk, tel: 8530 8443, www.london-ghost-walk.co.uk. Explores the graveyards, nooks and crannies of the City of London.

River Tours

Bateaux London, tel: 7695 1800. Romantic dinner cruises along the Thames with cabaret and dancing. From £39.50–£46.50 for a Sunday-lunch jazz cruise, £69–£105 per person for a dinner cruise (including wine).
Thames Cruises, tel: 7928 9009. Evening disco cruises and private hire.
Thames River Services, tel: 7930 4097. Trips between Westminster and Greenwich piers every 30 minutes (£8.60 return, child £4.30). Tours go beyond Greenwich to the Millennium Dome and the Thames Flood Barrier.
Catamaran Cruisers, tel: 7695 1800. Fifty-minute circular cruises with commentary in nine languages departing hourly from Westminster Pier (11am–6pm). Point-to-point cruises allow passengers to hop on and hop off throughout the day, with boats leaving from Embankment, Waterloo (London Eye), Bankside, Tower and Greenwich piers. (£9 for adults, £5 for children).

Walking Tours

Some walking tour operators use London Tourist Board-trained Blue Badge Guides – a guarantee of quality. Walks generally last one or two hours. *Time Out* magazine lists a selection of weekly walks in its Visitors section.
Original London Walks, tel: 7624 3978. More than 200 walks, including Along the Thames Pub Walk, Historic City, Hidden London, Hampstead, Historic Westminster, Little Venice and Ghost walks. Adults £6, under 15s free with an adult. www.walks.com

Theatrical Tours

Royal National Theatre, tel: 7452 3400. Daily tours and workshops. Up to five times a day (Mon–Sat), with each tour lasting 1¼ hours. £5.
Theatre Royal Drury Lane, tel: 7087 7599. Tours (Mon–Sat) lasting about 1 hour. £12.
Shakespeare's Globe Theatre, tel: 7902 1500. Daily (10am–5pm) 40-minute tours. Adults £9, children £6.50.
Theatreland Walking Tour, tel: 7557 6700. Two-hour tours on last Sunday of month, year-round. Book in advance. £6.
BBC Television Tours, tel: 0870-603 0304. The BBC runs tours of its Television Centre at Wood Lane, W12 (Tube: White City). Pre-booking essential. Adults £9.50, children over nine £7. www.bbc.co.uk/tours

BELOW: cruise Old Father Thames in a catamaran.

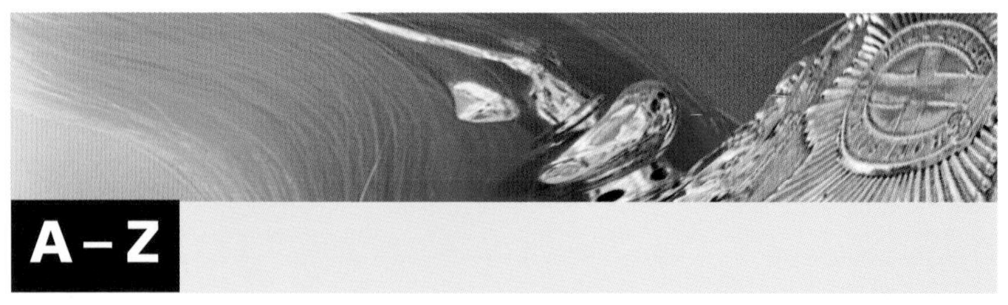

A–Z

AN ALPHABETICAL SUMMARY OF PRACTICAL INFORMATION

Accidents

In the event of a serious accident or emergency, dial 999. In the case of minor accidents, your hotel will know where to find the nearest hospital with a casualty department. If you're outside, hail a taxi – cabbies know even more than hotel receptionists.

Budgeting for a Visit

London is a very expensive city. You'll be lucky to find a conveniently located double room for less than £70 a night and prices soar to well over £300. Breakfast is often included in the price, but if not, a full English will start at £6 and a Continental breakfast at £3. Expect to pay from £25 to £40 each for a three-course dinner, including a modest wine, at a reasonable restaurant. Most cinema tickets cost £6–12, and a good seat for a West End musical is about £40. Taxis aren't cheap, especially at night, but neither is the Underground, with a short Tube journey costing from £4 – check out the special passes listed on page 278.

Car Breakdown

The following organisations operate 24-hour breakdown assistance. Phone calls to these numbers are free, but the service is free only to members:
AA, tel: 0800-887 766
RAC, tel: 0800-828 282
Green Flag, tel: 0800-051 0636

Children

For ideas on museums and other attractions suitable for children of various ages, *see Best of London, page 10.*
Accommodation. Some hotels do not accept children under a certain age, so be sure to check when you book. Most restaurants accept well-behaved children, but only those that want to encourage families have children's menus and nappy-changing facilities. Only pubs with a Children's Certificate can admit children, and even these will usually restrict the hours and areas open to them. Publicans, like restaurateurs, reserve the right to refuse entry.
Public transport. Up to four chil-

dren aged 11 or under can travel free on the Tube if accompanied by a ticket-holding adult. Eleven–13-year-olds can get unlimited off-peak travel for £1 per day or "Kids for a Quid" single fares if travelling with an Oyster or Travelcard-holding adult, as can 14–15-year-olds providing they have a photo Oyster card (this can take up to two weeks to obtain).

Buses are free for all children under 16, but 14–15-year-olds will need a 14–15 Oyster photocard. Buses can take up to two unfolded pushchairs (buggies) at one time (they must be parked in a special area halfway down the bus). Any further pushchairs must be folded.

Supplies. Infant formula and nappies (diapers) can be found in chemists (pharmacies) and supermarkets.

Hospitals. In a medical emergency, take your child to the Accident & Emergency department of the nearest hospital. If you require over-the-counter medications such as Calpol (liquid paracetamol) late at night, Bliss Pharmacy (5 Marble Arch; tel: 7723 6116) is open until midnight every day.

ABOVE: keeping a watchful eye.

Climate & Clothing

The climate in London is mild, with the warming effects of the city itself keeping off the worst of the cold in winter. Snow and temperatures below freezing are unusual, with January temperatures averaging 43°F/6°C. Consequently, if it does snow hard, London is unprepared. Temperatures in the summer months average 64°F/18°C, but they can soar, causing the city to become airlessly hot (air conditioning is not universal). Rainfall is unpredictable, and it's wise, even in summer, to keep a fold-up umbrella close by.

What to Wear

Between the stuffy Tube and often damp weather, it's best to dress in layers. A cool, rainy day can turn beautiful unexpectedly and vice versa. In general, short sleeves and a jacket are recommended for summer and a warm coat and woollens for winter.

While a few of the traditional restaurants retain a dress code, smart-casual is generally the norm for restaurants and theatres. In general, Londoners are quite style-conscious but also practical; most getting around will be on foot or via public transport, so wearing comfortable shoes is wise.

Crime

Serious crime is low for a city of this size, but the Dickensian tradition of pickpocketing is alive and well. Hold on tightly to purses, do not put wallets in back pockets, and do not place handbags on the ground in busy restaurants. Gangs of professional thieves target the Tube.

In a genuine emergency, dial 999 from any telephone (no cash required). Report routine thefts to a police station (address under Police in a telephone directory). The threat of terrorism has led to an increase in police patrols, so don't hesitate to report any suspicious packages.

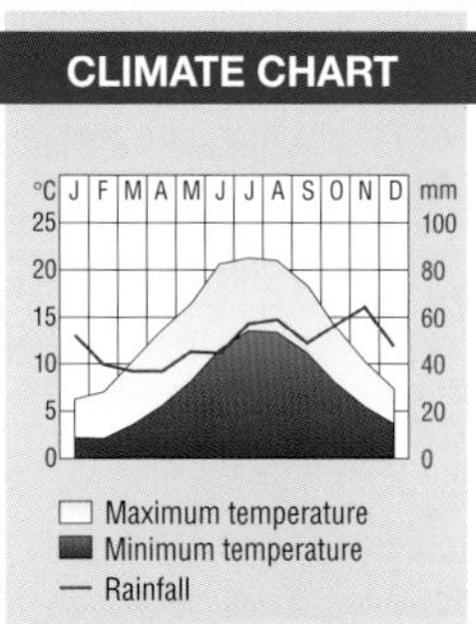

Customs Regulations

There are no official restrictions on the movement of goods within the European Union, provided those goods were purchased within the EU. However, British Customs have set the following personal-use "guide levels".

Tobacco 3,200 cigarettes or 400 cigarillos or 200 cigars or 3kg tobacco. (Limits are 200 cigarettes or 250gm of smoking tobacco if coming from Bulgaria, Czech Republic, Estonia, Hungary, Latvia, Lithuania, Poland, Romania, Slovakia and Slovenia.)

Alcohol 10 litres spirits, 20 litres fortified wines, 90 litres wine, 110 litres beer.

Those entering from a non-EU

state are subject to these limits:
Tobacco 200 cigarettes or 100 cigarillos or 50 cigars or 250g of tobacco.
Alcohol 1 litre of spirits, or 2 litres of fortified or sparkling wine, or 2 litres of table wine (an additional 2 litres of still wine if no spirits are bought).
Perfume 60cc perfume, 250cc toilet water.
Animals Cats and dogs may enter Britain from EU countries providing they have the appropriate documentation. All other pets are placed in quarantine for six months at the owner's expense. For further details, log on to www.defra.gov.uk.
The following are prohibited entry into the United Kingdon:
Plants and **perishable foods** such as meats and meat products, eggs, fruit; some drugs (check with your doctor if you need to carry strong medication).
Firearms and ammunition (without special arrangement).
Obscene film or written material.

There are no restrictions on the amount of currency you can bring into the country.

Disabled Access

Venues. Artsline, London's information and advice service on access to the arts and entertainment for disabled people, provides detailed access information for venues across London, including theatres, cinemas, museums, arts centres, tourist attractions, comedy and music venues, and selected restaurants. Tel: 7388 2227, www.artslineonline.com
Advice. William Forrester is a museum lecturer, co-author of *Access in London*, a trained guide and wheelchair user. He offers tailor-made tours of the city for chair users utilising accessible taxis, and arranges special visits to the Houses of Parliament, Westminster Abbey and the British Museum. He operates a telephone advice service for anyone planning to visit the UK in a wheelchair.
Tel: +44 (0)1483 575401.
Toilets. Britain has a system of keys to open many of the public toilets available for disabled people. To obtain a key, contact RADAR on 7250 3222. There is a charge of £3.50 (plus value-added tax – VAT) for the key and £10.25 (including post and packing) for the guidebook detailing their locations.
Public transport. Wheelchair-friendly buses have been progressively introduced across the network; almost all are accessible via low-floor vehicles or retractable ramps. Tubes are difficult as entry is mainly by steps; the exception is the Jubilee Line, which has lifts. Ticket offices can provide a free leaflet on *Access to the Underground* or alternatively call 7222 1234 for help planning an accessible route.
River cruises. Step-free access is available from most major piers and newer boats have designated wheelchair spaces. Mobility-impaired groups can obtain information by telephoning London River Services on 7941 2400.

ABOVE: entry requirements depend on where you are coming from.

Electricity

230 volts. Square, three-in plugs are used, and virtually all visitors will need adaptors if planning to plug in their own equipment.

Embassies

Australia Australia House, Strand, WC2B 4LA. Tel: 7379 4334
Canada Macdonald House, 1 Grosvenor Square, W1X 4AB. Tel: 7258 6600
India India House, Aldwych, WC2B 4NA. Tel: 7836 8484
Ireland 17 Grosvenor Place SW1X 7HR. Tel: 7235 2171
Jamaica 1–2 Prince Consort Road, SW7 2BZ. Tel: 7823 9911
New Zealand 80 Haymarket, SW1Y 4TQ. Tel: 7930 8422
South Africa South Africa House, Trafalgar Square, WC2N 5DP. Tel: 7451 7299
United States 24 Grosvenor Square, W1A 1AE. Tel: 7499 9000.

Entry Requirements

To enter Britain you need a valid passport (or any form of official identification if you are an EU citizen). Visas are not needed if you are from the USA, a Commonwealth citizen or an EU national (or from most other European or South American countries). Health certificates are not required unless you have arrived from Asia, Africa or South America. If you wish to stay for a protracted period or apply to work, contact the Border and Immigration Agency. First look at the website www.ind.homeoffice.gov.uk. London's nearest Public Enquiry Office (PEO) is Lunar House, 40 Wellesley Road, Croydon, CR9 2BY, tel: 0870-606 7766.

Gay and Lesbian

With Europe's largest gay and lesbian population, London has an abundance of bars, restaurants and clubs to cater for most tastes. Many of them will make space for one or more of London's free gay weekly magazines, *Boyz*, the *Pink Paper*, and *QX*. Monthly magazines on sale at newsstands include *Gay Times*, *Diva* and *Attitude*.

Two established websites for meeting other gay people in London are www.gaydar.co.uk and the female version, www.gaydargirls.com. Other websites reflecting the gay scene include www.rainbownetwork.com and www.outuk.com.

Useful telephone contacts for advice and counselling include **London Lesbian and Gay Switchboard** (tel: 7837 7324) and **London Friend** (7.30–10pm, tel: 7837 3337). Support and advice about legal issues concerning HIV and Aids is available from the **National Aids Helpline** (tel: 0800-567 123).

Government

When people refer to London, they mean the county of Greater London. When they speak of the City of London, they generally mean the financial district, the historic square mile between St Paul's Cathedral and the Tower of London, governed by the Corporation of London and headed by the Lord Mayor, which even has its own police force. The rest of the metropolis is run by 12 inner boroughs and 20 outer boroughs, each of which is responsible for local services.

In 1986 Margaret Thatcher's Conservative government, tiring of the left-wing policies of the Greater London Council and its leader, Ken Livingstone, abolished it. This draconian action left London's government balkanised between the existing 32 local boroughs. The most conspicuous victim of this lack of central planning was transport: traffic congestion slowed down bus services and the Underground's infrastructure and rolling stock deteriorated because of lack of investment.

Tony Blair's first Labour government, elected in 1997, restored a measure of local government by creating a Greater London Authority under the direction of a mayor – a new post for London and distinct from the centuries-old post of Lord Mayor who presides over the Corporation of London's administration. Four bodies eat up most of the GLA's budget: the Metropolitan Police Authority, the London Fire and Emergency Planning Authority, the London Development Agency and Transport for London.

Local services such as refuse disposal, housing grants and parking control are still run by the 32 boroughs: Barking, Barnet, Bexley, Brent, Bromley, Camden, Croydon, Ealing, Enfield, Greenwich, Hackney, Hammersmith and Fulham, Haringey, Harrow, Havering, Hillingdon, Hounslow, Islington, Kensington and Chelsea, Kingston-upon-Thames, Lambeth, Lewisham, Merton, Newham, Redbridge, Richmond-upon-Thames, Southwark, Sutton, Tower Hamlets, Waltham Forest, Wandsworth, and Westminster.

Health & Medical Care

If you fall ill and are a national of the European Union, you are entitled to free medical treatment for illnesses arising while in the UK. Many other countries also have reciprocal arrangements for free treatment. However, most visitors will be liable for medical and dental treatment and should ensure they have adequate health insurance. Emergency treatment, however, is always free, and usually very good.

Major hospitals include Charing Cross Hospital (Fulham Palace Road, W6, tel: 8846 1234), St Mary's Hospital, Praed Street, W2, tel: 7886 6666, and St Thomas's (Lambeth Palace Road, SE1, tel: 7188 7188).

Emergency dental treatment is available on weekdays 9am–5pm (queuing begins at 8am) at Guy's Hospital, St Thomas Street, SE1, tel: 7188 7188.

Chemists (pharmacists). Boots is a large chain of pharmacies with branches throughout London that will make up prescriptions. The branch at 75 Queensway, W2 is open until 10pm daily, whilst Bliss Chemist at 5 Marble Arch is open until midnight daily.

Accidents: in the case of an emergency, dial **999**.

Internet

London has many internet cafés. The most widespread is the EasyEverything chain which has mega cafés in Oxford Street, Trafalgar Square, Tottenham Court Road and Kensington High Street, all open 24 hours a day: www.easyeverything.com

You can also surf at Waterstone's bookshop in Piccadilly.

Left Luggage

Most of the main railway stations have left-luggage departments where you can leave your suitcases on a short-term basis, although all are very sensitive to potential terrorist bombs. Left-luggage offices close at 11pm with the exception of Victoria, which is open until midnight.

Lost Property

If you can't find a policeman, dial directory enquiries (118500 or 118888 or 118811) and ask for the number of the nearest police station. Don't call the emergency number 999 unless there has been a serious crime or accident. If your passport has been lost, let your embassy know as well.

For possessions lost on public transport or in taxis, contact Transport for London's central Lost Property, 200 Baker Street, NW1 5RZ (tel: 0845 330 9882) Mon–Fri 8.30am–4pm, or fill in an enquiry form, available from any London Underground station or bus garage. It can take two to four days for items left on a Tube train or bus to reach the office and more than a week for items a taxi driver has handed in at a police station. So wait for several days before visiting or phoning the office, which can search for your property while you are on the phone. It will also mail your property back to you for a fee. The office receives 600 items a day.

Maps

Insight Guides' *FlexiMap London* is laminated for durability and easy folding. For detailed exploration of the city centre and suburbs, the *London A–Z* books come in various formats. Free Tube maps are available at Underground stations. Map lovers should head for Stanford's (12–14 Long Acre, in the Covent Garden area), one of the world's top map and guidebook stores.

Money

The pound sterling (divided into 100 pence) is the currency, though many large London stores will accept euros.

Most **banks** open Mon–Fri 9.30am–5pm (or even later), with Saturday-morning banking common in shopping areas. Major British banks tend to offer similar exchange rates; it's only worth shopping around if you have large amounts of money to change. Banks charge no commission on sterling traveller's cheques. If a London bank is affiliated to your own bank, it may make no charge for cheques in other currencies either. However, there will be a charge for changing cash into another currency.

Some High Street travel agents, such as Thomas Cook, operate **bureaux de change** at comparable rates. There are also private bureaux de change (some are open 24 hours) where rates can be very low and commissions high. Chequepoint is a reputable chain with branches at Piccadilly Circus, Leicester Square, Marble Arch, Bayswater Underground and Victoria mainline station.

International **credit cards** are almost universally accepted. However, a few stores and restaurants do not accept them; check for signs at the entrance.

Tax refunds enable visitors from outside the European Union to reclaim the 17.5 percent value-added tax when spending over a certain amount. Stores can supply VAT-refund forms which should be presented to Customs when leaving the country.

Newspapers

Politically speaking, the *Daily Telegraph* and *The Times* are on the right, *The Guardian* is on the left and *The Independent* has a liberal, international slant. To appeal to commuters, some are printed in a compact (tabloid) format rather than the traditional full-size broadsheet. On Sunday *The Observer* is more liberal than the *Sunday Times, Independent on Sunday* and *Sunday Telegraph*. The *Financial Times* is renowned for the clearest, most unslanted headlines in its general news pages (plus, of course, its exhaustive financial coverage).

Among the mass-market tabloids, *The Sun* and *The Star* are traditionally on the right (and obsessed with royalty, soap operas and sex), ditto the Sunday

BELOW: newsstands abound, but free newspapers are also plentiful.

News of the World. *Daily Mirror* and *Sunday Mirror* are slightly left-ish, as is the *Sunday People*. The *Daily Mail* and *Mail on Sunday* are more up-market and right-wing equivalents of the politically eclectic *Express*.

Editions of the London-only *Evening Standard* come out Mon–Fri mid-morning and are good for London news, cinema and theatre listings. The free tabloid *Metro* can be picked up at stations in the morning; competing new kids *The London Paper* and *London Lite* are handed out from the afternoon on. All of these contain useful but not comprehensive listings sections.

Listings magazines. Supreme in this field is the long-established weekly *Time Out*.

Foreign newspapers and magazines can be found at many street newsstands, at mainline stations, and at these outlets:
Capital Newsagents: 48 Old Compton Street, W1.
A Moroni & Son: 68 Old Compton Street, W1.
Selfridges: Oxford Street, W1.
Eman's: 123 Queensway, W2.
Victoria Place Shopping Centre: Victoria Station, SW1.

Population and Size

After decades of decline, London's population has increased since the mid-1980s to its present 7.2 million and forecasts show it surging to almost 8 million by 2016. More than a quarter of residents are from a minority ethnic group, and around 300 languages are spoken (from Abem, a language of the Ivory Coast, to Zulu, from South Africa).

Officially, London's area is 610 sq. miles (1,580 sq. km), but the urban sprawl around the capital makes it hard to know where to stop measuring.

Postal Services

Post offices open Mon–Fri 9am–5pm, Sat 9am–noon. Stamps are available from post offices and selected shops, usually newsagents, and from machines outside some post offices. There is a two-tier service within the UK: first class is supposed to reach a UK destination the next day, second class will take at least a day or two longer. London's main post office is at Trafalgar Square, behind the church of St Martin-in-the-Fields. It stays open until 6.30pm Mon–Fri.

ABOVE: a familiar red post box.

The cost of sending a letter or parcel depends on weight and, since 2007, also size. Queues tend to be long over the lunch period.

Postcodes

The first half of London postcodes indicate the general area (WC = West Central, SE = South East) and the second half, used only for mail, identifies the exact block. Here is a key to some of the commoner codes:
W1 Mayfair, Marylebone, Soho; **W2** Bayswater; **W4** Chiswick; **W8** Kensington; **W11** Notting Hill; **WC1** Bloomsbury; **WC2** Covent Garden, Strand; **E1** Whitechapel; **EC1** Clerkenwell; **EC2** Bank, Barbican; **EC4** St Paul's, Blackfriars; **SW1** St James's, Belgravia; **SW3** Chelsea; **SW7** Knightsbridge, South Kensington; **SW19** Wimbledon; **SE1** Lambeth, Southwark; **SE10** Greenwich; **SE21** Dulwich; **N1** Hoxton, islington; **N6** Highgate; **NW3** Hampstead.

Public Holidays

Compared to most European countries, the UK has few public holidays:
January New Year's Day (1)
March/April Good Friday, Easter Monday
May May Day (first Monday of the month), Spring Bank Holiday (last Monday)
August Summer Bank Holiday (last Monday)
December Christmas Day (25), Boxing Day (26).

Radio Stations

You can receive national stations as well as many targeted specifically at London. A selection:

Commercial Stations

Capital FM – 95.8FM, 24-hour pop music.
Classic FM – 100.9FM, 24-hour light classical music.
Choice FM – 96.9FM, soul music.
Heart – 106.2FM, classic rock.
Kiss FM – 100FM, 24-hour dance music.
LBC – 97.3FM, 24-hour chat, showbiz, opinion, news.
Smooth FM – 102.2FM, bland playlist of jazz, soul and blues and middle-of-the-road.
Virgin – 105.8FM, adult-oriented rock.

BBC Stations

Radio 1 – 98.8FM, mainstream pop.
Radio 2 – 89.2FM, easy-listening music, chat shows.
Radio 3 – 91.3FM, 24-hour classical music, plus drama and serious talks.

Radio 4 – 93.5FM, heavyweight news, current affairs, plays.
Radio Five Live – 909MW, rolling news, sport.
BBC Radio London – 94.9FM, London-oriented music, chat and sports station.
BBC World Service – 648 kHz, international news.

Smoking

In July 2007 England imposed a ban on smoking in all enclosed public spaces, including pubs, clubs and bars (though not in outside beer gardens).

Student Travellers

International students can obtain various discounts at attractions, on travel services (including Eurostar) and in some shops by showing a valid ISIC card. www.isiccard.com

Telephones

Despite the ubiquity of mobile phones (cellphones), London still has an adequate number of public kiosks and public phones in pubs. It is cheaper to use a public phone than one in your hotel as many hotels still make an outrageous charge for calls from your room.

British Telecom (BT) is the main telephone operating company. The smallest coin accepted is 20p. Most kiosks will also accept phone cards, which are widely available from post offices and newsagents in varying amounts between £3 and £20. Credit-card phones can be found at major transport terminals and on busy streets.

Phoning Abroad

You can telephone abroad directly from any phone. Dial 00 followed by the international code for the country you want, and then the number. Some country codes:
Australia (61); **Hong Kong** (852); **Ireland** (353); **New Zealand** (64); **Singapore** (65); **South Africa** (27); **US and Canada** (1).

If you are using a US credit phone card, first dial the company's access number as follows:
Sprint, tel: 0800-890877
MCI, tel: 0800-279 5088
AT&T, tel: 0800-890011.

Useful Numbers

Emergency – police, fire, ambulance: 999
Operator (for difficulties in getting through): 100
International Operator: 155
Directory Enquiries (UK): 118500 or 118888 or 118811
International Directory Enquiries 118505 or 118866 or 118899
London Regional Transport 24-hour information: 7222 1234
Rail information for all London stations: 0845-748 4950.
Accommodation bookings: 0870-156 6366.

BELOW: telling the time at Greenwich.

Television Stations

The BBC (British Broadcasting Corporation) is financed by compulsory annual television licences and is advertising-free. The independent channels (ITV1, C4 and Five) are funded by commercials.

In recent years the choice of channels has expanded exponentially as cable, satellite and digital channels have joined the small number of terrestrial channels. The BBC has several digital channels, including the round-the-clock BBC News 24, the youth-oriented BBC3, and the arts-oriented BBC4.By 2012 the terrestrial broadcasting network will cease to exist, and even BBC1, BBC2 and the terrestrial commercial channels will only be available through digital technology.

Teletext. A vast range of information (news, business, sport and entertainment) is available on the teletext services transmitted by all the terrestrial channels. This is accessed via the TV set's remote control.

Time

British Summer Time (one hour ahead of Greenwich Mean Time)

operates from the last Sunday in March until the last Sunday in October. Greenwich Mean Time is 8 hours in front of Los Angeles, 5 hours in front of New York and Montreal, and 10 hours behind Sydney.

Tipping

Most hotels and many restaurants automatically add 10–15 percent service charge to your bill. It's your right to deduct it if you're not happy with the service. If you pay by chip and PIN, the machine will often require you to add or decline to add a tip before you insert your PIN number, which feels rather cheeky when the waitress or waiter is standing in front of you. If a service charge has already been included in the bill, you certainly shouldn't feel obliged to add anything extra.

It is not customary to tip in pubs, cinemas, theatres or elevators. You do tip hairdressers, sightseeing guides, railway porters and cab drivers. They get around 10 percent.

Tour Operators

The Original Tour is the first and biggest London sightseeing operator. Hop on and hop off at over 90 different stops. With commentary in a wide choice of languages and a Kids' Club for 5–12 year olds. Buy tickets on the bus or in advance. Operates year-round. Tel: 8877 2120; www.theoriginaltour.com

Big Bus Company operates three routes of hop-on hop-off services. Tel: 7233 9533; www.bigbustours.com.

Duck Tours use World War II amphibious vehicles which drive past famous London landmarks before taking to the water. Great for children. Departure from County Hall. Tel: 7928 3132; www.londonducktours.co.uk

Tourist Offices

The offical tourist board maintains a website at www.visitlondon.com. It contains a huge amount of information on sights and attractions, upcoming events and festivals, as well as practical information and a commercial hotel booking service.

Personal enquires can be made at **Britain and London Visitor Centre**, 1 Regent Street, Piccadilly Circus, SW1Y 4XT. The office is open: Mon 9.30am–6.30pm, Tues–Fri 9am–6.30pm, Sat & Sun 10am–4pm (June–Sept, Sat 9am–5pm). You can email to BLVCenquiry@visitbritain.org, otherwise personal callers only.

Other tourist information centres are located at:

City Information Centre, St. Paul's Churchyard, EC4M 8BX. Tel: +44 (0) 20 7332 1456.

Greenwich TIC, Pepys House, 2 Cutty Sark Gardens, Greenwich SE10 9LW. Tel: +44 (0)870 608 2000. Fax: +44 (0)20 8853 4607. Open daily 10am–5pm. Email: tic@greenwich.gov.uk

Southwark TIC, Vinopolis, 1 Bank End, SE1 9BU. Tel: +44 (0)20 7357 9168. Email: tourisminfo@southwark.gov.uk

Websites

www.insightguides.com includes comprehensive hotel listings for London.

www.visitlondon.com The official tourist board site, with lots of advice, listings, links.

www.thisislondon.com Run by the *Evening Standard*; has detailed listings of events.

www.netlondon.com Internet directory. Links to hotels,

www.london-se1.co.uk has up-to-date coverage of the South Bank and Bankside.

www.streetmap.co.uk locates the address you type in.

www.24hourmuseum.co.uk has up-to-date information of what UK museums are exhibiting.

www.bbc.co.uk is a gigantic site with lots on London.

BELOW: getting one's bearings on the Southbank.

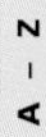

FURTHER READING

Good Companions

A Literary Companion: London by Peter Vansittart. A journey around the capital with the literary luminaries.
Secret London by Andrew Duncan. Uncovers London's hidden landscape from abandoned tube stations to the gentlemen's club.
The London Blue Plaque Guide by Nick Rennison. Details the lives of more than 700 individuals who have been commemorated with a blue plaque on their houses.
A Literary Guide to London by Ed Glinet. A very detailed, street-by-street guide to literary lives.
London on Film by Colin Sorensen. How the cinema has portrayed the city.

History

The Concise Pepys by Samuel Pepys. Read a first-hand account of the Great Fire of London and find out about daily life in 17th-century England
Dr Johnson's London by Liza Picard. Brings 18th-century London to life.
London: The Biography by Peter Ackroyd. Anecdotal and entertaining history.
London: A Social History by Roy Porter. Less quirky than Ackroyd but a telling account of how badly the capital has been governed over the centuries.
The Story of the British Museum by Marjorie Caygill. A fascinating tale, authoritatively told, featuring an astonishing variety of heroes and villains.
London Villages by John Wittich. A walker's notes on his travels through village London.

Memoirs

The Shorter Pepys by Samuel Pepys. A distillation of 11 volumes of diaries describing London life, including the Great Fire, from 1660 to 1669.
84 Charing Cross Road by Helene Hanff. Touching book-lover's correspondence with a London book seller.
London Orbital by Iain Sinclair. A walk round the M25, exploring little-known parts of London's periphery.
The Oxford Book of London edited by Paul Bailey. A bran-dip of observations by famous visitors over eight centuries.

FEEDBACK

We do our best to ensure the information in our books is as accurate and up-to-date as possible. The books are updated on a regular basis, using local contacts, who painstakingly add, amend and correct as required. However, some mistakes and omissions are inevitable and we are ultimately reliant on our readers to put us in the picture.

We would welcome your feedback on any details related to your experiences using the book "on the road". Maybe we recommended a hotel that you liked (or another that you didn't), as well as interesting new attractions, or facts and figures you have found out about the country itself. The more details you can give us (particularly with regard to addresses, e-mails and telephone numbers), the better.

We will acknowledge all contributions, and we'll offer an Insight Guide to the best letters received.

Please write to us at:
Insight Guides
PO Box 7910
London SE1 1WE
United Kingdom
Or send e-mail to:
insight@apaguide.co.uk

Art & Architecture

A Guide to London's Contemporary Architecture by Ken Allinson and Victoria Thornton. Covers buildings since the 1980s; black-and-white pictures.
London Under London by Richard Trench and Ellis Hillman. Traces the astonishing maze of railway lines, sewers and utilities that lies beneath the streets.

Other Insight Guides

The **Insight Guides** series includes several titles on London. ***Insight Guide: Museums and Galleries of London***, which provides reviews of more than 130 venues, together with background features and lavish illustration. ***Insight Guide: Shopping in London*** contains 128 pages of shop listings and shopping tips in compact format. A companion volume is the 176-page ***Insight Guide: Eating in London***, which reviews hundreds of restaurants. The new **Insight Smart Guides** series provides a full run-down of London's sights in an easy-to-use A–Z format.

Insight FlexiMaps to *London* and to *London's Museums and Galleries* are fold-out laminated maps that are both easy to use and long-lasting.

London Street Atlas

The key map shows the area of London covered by the atlas section. An index of street names and places of interest shown on the maps can be found on the following pages. For each entry there is a page number and grid reference.

Map Legend

Motorway with Junction	Airport	Motorway	Underground
Motorway (under construction)	Church (ruins)	Dual Carriageway	Docklands Light Rail (DLR)
Dual Carriageway	Monastery	Main Roads	Bus Station
Main Road	Castle (ruins)		Tourist Information
Secondary Road	Archaeological Site	Minor Roads	Post Office
Minor Road	Cave		Cathedral/Church
Track	Place of Interest	Footpath	Mosque
International Boundary	Mansion/Stately Home	Railway	Synagogue
County Boundary	Viewpoint	Pedestrian Area	Statue/Monument
National Park/Reserve	Beach	Important Building	Tower
Ferry Route		Park	Lighthouse

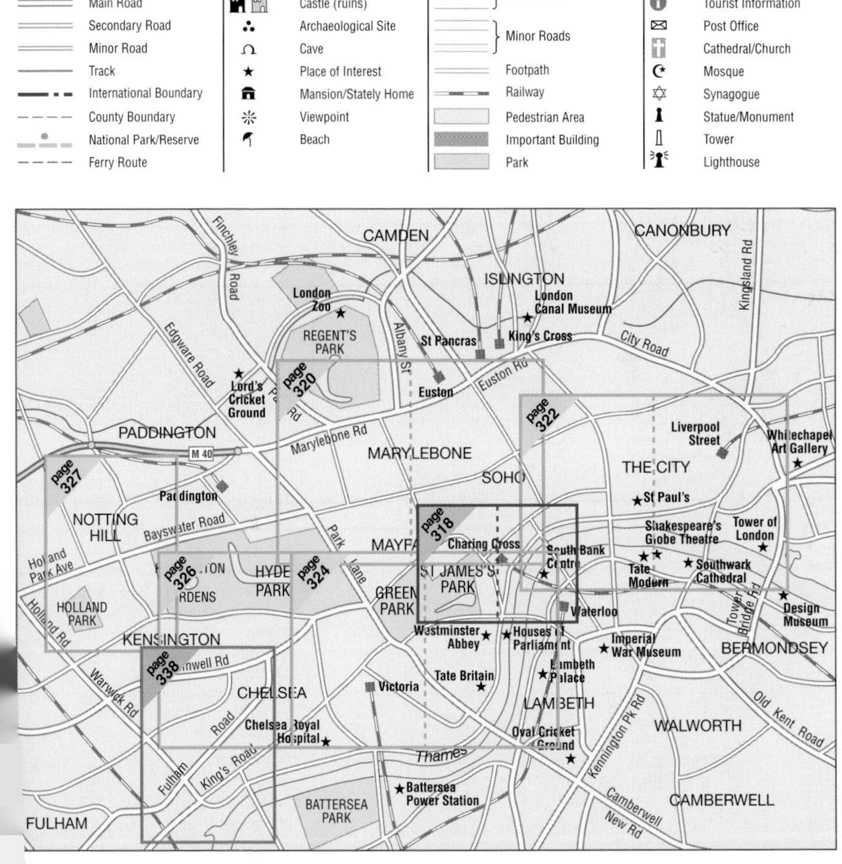

321

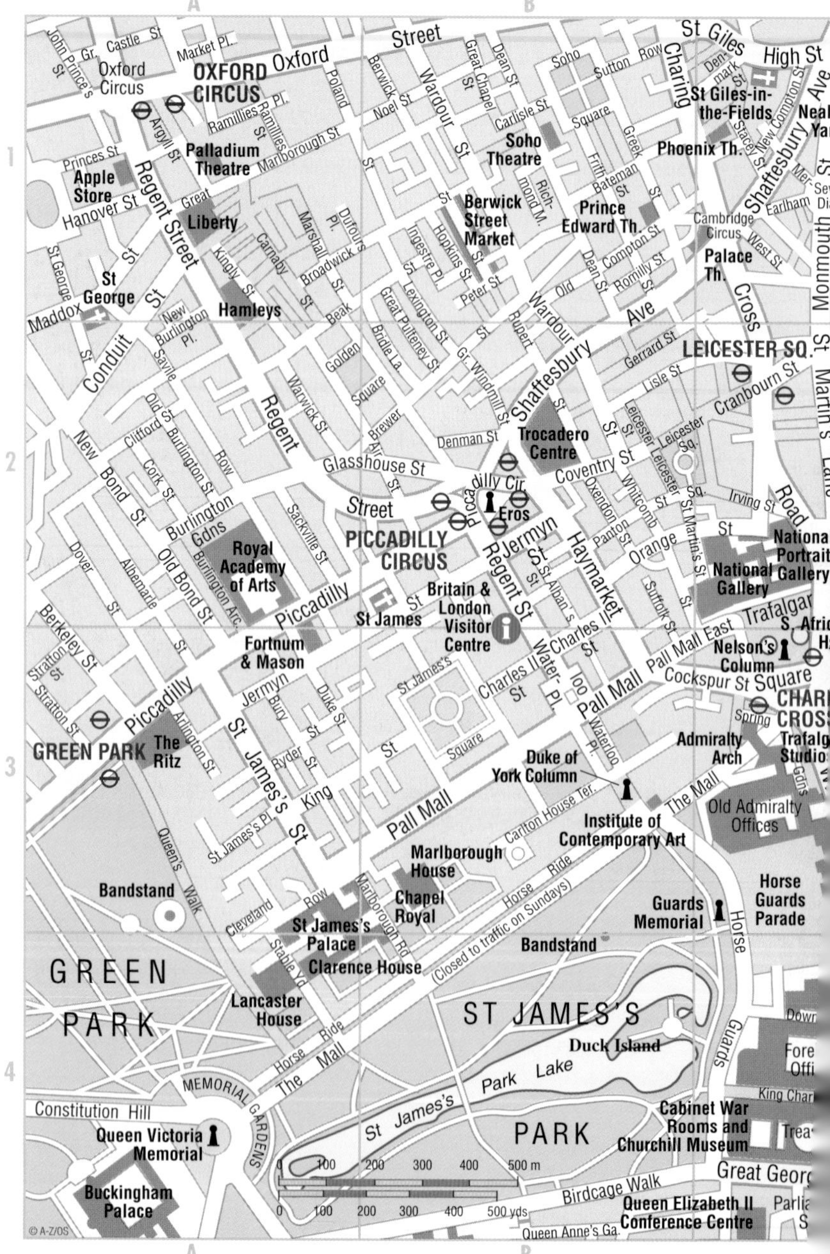

A
B
C
1
2
3
4
OXFORD CIRCUS
Oxford Circus
Oxford Street
John Prince's St
Gr. Castle St
Market Pl.
Ramillies Pl.
Ramillies St
Poland St
Berwick St
Noel St
Wardour St
Great Chapel St
Dean St
Soho Square
Sutton Row
Carlisle St
St Giles
Charing Cross Road
Denmark St
High St
St Giles-in-the-Fields
Neal's Yard
New Compton St
Stacey St
Shaftesbury Ave
Phoenix Th.
Soho Theatre
Frith St
Greek St
Bateman St
Richmond M.
Berwick Street Market
Prince Edward Th.
Princes St
Argyll St
Palladium Theatre
Marlborough St
Apple Store
Hanover St
Regent Street
Great Marlborough St
Liberty
Carnaby St
Kingly St
Marshall St
Dufours Pl.
Broadwick St
Ingestre Pl.
Hopkins St
Peter St
Lexington St
Great Pulteney St
Bridle La.
Old Compton St
Romilly St
Cambridge Circus
West St
Earlham St
Seven Dials
Monmouth St
Palace Th.
St George St
St George
Maddox St
Hamleys
New Burlington Pl.
Beak St
Golden Square
Conduit St
Savile Row
Warwick St
Brewer St
Gt. Windmill St
Rupert St
Wardour St
Shaftesbury Ave
Gerrard St
LEICESTER SQ.
Lisle St
Cranbourn St
St Martin's Lane
Old Burlington St
Clifford St
Cork St
New Bond St
Regent St
Air St
Glasshouse St
Denman St
Trocadero Centre
Coventry St
Leicester St
Leicester Sq.
Oxendon St
Whitcomb St
Irving St
Charing Cross Road
Burlington Gdns
Piccadilly Cir.
Eros
Street
Royal Academy of Arts
Sackville St
PICCADILLY CIRCUS
Jermyn St
Panton St
Orange St
St Martin's St
National Portrait Gallery
National Gallery
Dover St
Albemarle St
Old Bond St
Burlington Arc.
Piccadilly
St James
Britain & London Visitor Centre
St Alban's St
Haymarket
Suffolk St
Trafalgar Square
Berkeley St
Stratton St
Fortnum & Mason
Duke St
St James's Square
Charles II St
Waterloo Pl.
Pall Mall East
Nelson's Column
S. Afric H
Cockspur St
CHAR CROS
Spring Gdns
Arlington St
Bury St
Ryder St
King St
St James's St
GREEN PARK
The Ritz
Duke of York Column
Admiralty Arch
Trafalg Studio
The Mall
Pall Mall
Carlton House Ter.
Institute of Contemporary Art
Old Admiralty Offices
St James's Pl.
Queen's Walk
Marlborough House
Bandstand
Cleveland Row
Chapel Royal
Horse Ride
(Closed to traffic on Sundays)
Horse Guards Parade
Guards Memorial
St James's Palace
Marlborough Rd
Stable Yd
Clarence House
Bandstand
Horse Guards Rd
GREEN PARK
Lancaster House
ST JAMES'S PARK
Duck Island
St James's Park Lake
Fore Offi
King Char
MEMORIAL GARDENS
Constitution Hill
Queen Victoria Memorial
Cabinet War Rooms and Churchill Museum
Treas
0 100 200 300 400 500 m
0 100 200 300 400 500 yds
Great Georg
Birdcage Walk
Buckingham Palace
Queen Elizabeth II Conference Centre
Parlia S
Queen Anne's Ga.
© A-Z/OS

324

325

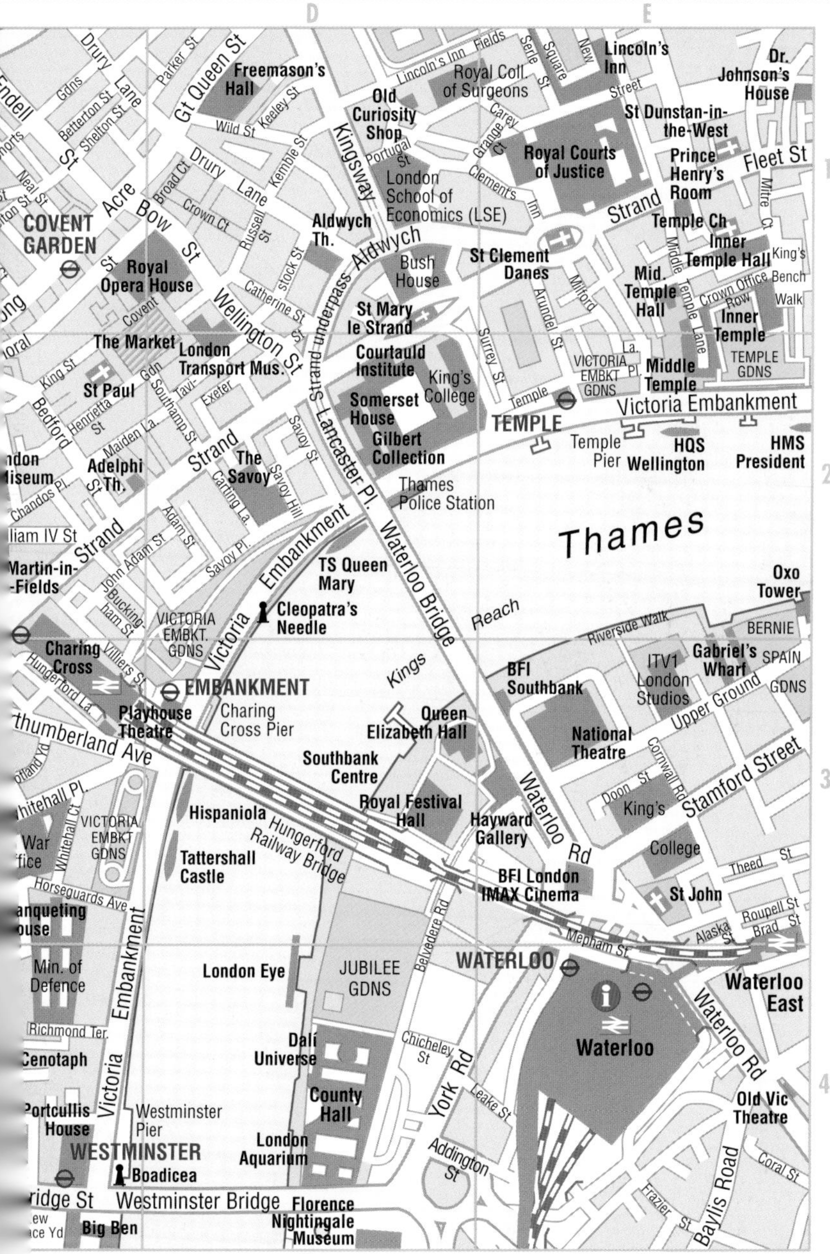
COVENT GARDEN
Royal Opera House
The Market
St Paul
London Transport Mus.
Freemason's Hall
Old Curiosity Shop
Royal Coll. of Surgeons
Lincoln's Inn
Royal Courts of Justice
London School of Economics (LSE)
Aldwych Th.
Bush House
St Clement Danes
St Mary le Strand
Courtauld Institute
King's College
Somerset House
Gilbert Collection
TEMPLE
Temple Pier
HQS Wellington
HMS President
Thames Police Station
Thames
The Savoy
Adelphi Th.
TS Queen Mary
Cleopatra's Needle
VICTORIA EMBKT. GDNS
Charing Cross
EMBANKMENT
Charing Cross Pier
Playhouse Theatre
Queen Elizabeth Hall
Southbank Centre
Royal Festival Hall
Hayward Gallery
BFI Southbank
National Theatre
ITV1 London Studios
Gabriel's Wharf
Oxo Tower
Hispaniola
Tattershall Castle
Hungerford Railway Bridge
BFI London IMAX Cinema
St John
WATERLOO
Waterloo
Waterloo East
London Eye
JUBILEE GDNS
Dalí Universe
County Hall
London Aquarium
Florence Nightingale Museum
Old Vic Theatre
Min. of Defence
Cenotaph
Portcullis House
WESTMINSTER
Westminster Pier
Boadicea
Big Ben
Westminster Bridge
Victoria Embankment
Waterloo Bridge
Strand
Fleet St
Kingsway
Aldwych
Dr. Johnson's House
St Dunstan-in-the-West
Prince Henry's Room
Temple Ch
Inner Temple Hall
Mid. Temple Hall
Inner Temple
Middle Temple
TEMPLE GDNS
322

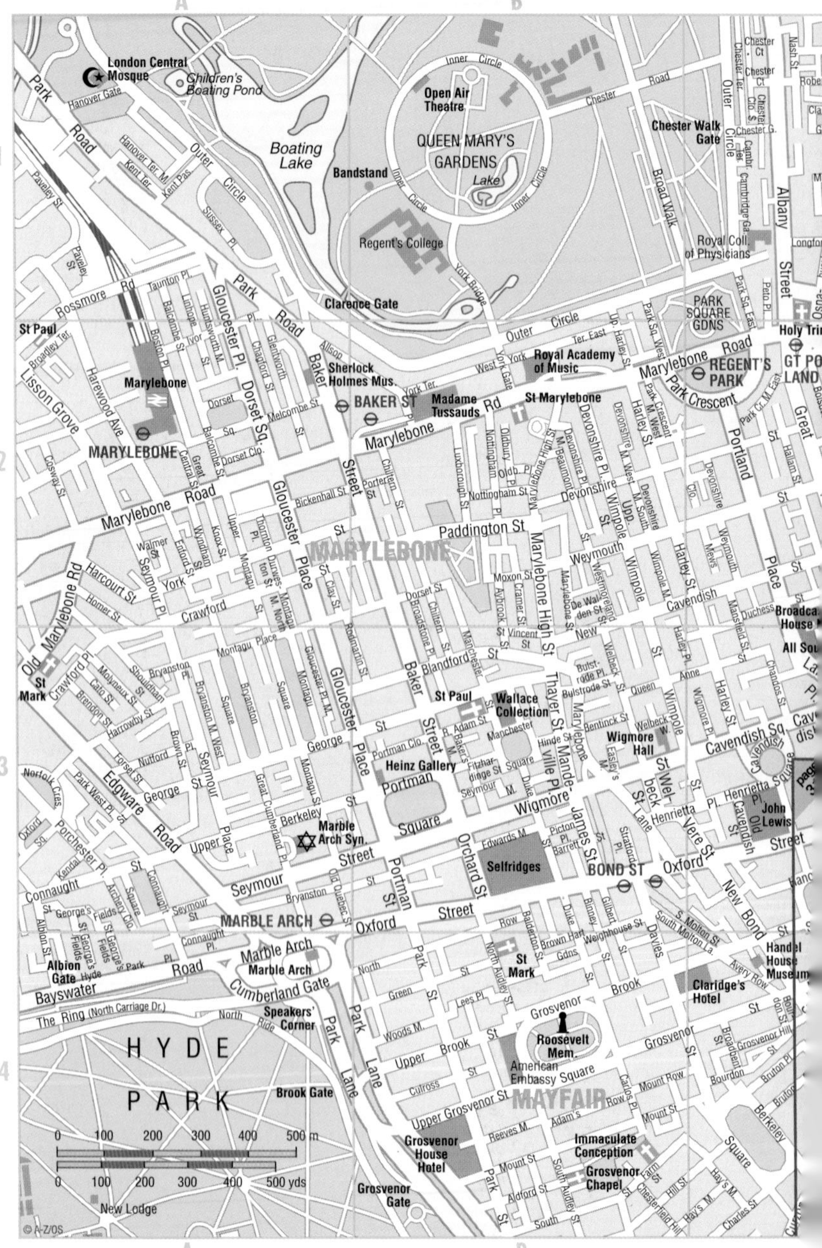
London Central Mosque
Children's Boating Pond
Boating Lake
Open Air Theatre
QUEEN MARY'S GARDENS
Lake
Bandstand
Regent's College
Clarence Gate
Chester Walk Gate
Royal Coll. of Physicians
PARK SQUARE GDNS
REGENT'S PARK
Holy Trin
GT PORTLAND
St Paul
Marylebone
MARYLEBONE
Sherlock Holmes Mus.
BAKER ST
Madame Tussauds
St Marylebone
Royal Academy of Music
MARYLEBONE
Broadcasting House
All Souls
St Mark
St Paul
Wallace Collection
Wigmore Hall
Heinz Gallery
Marble Arch Syn.
Selfridges
BOND ST
John Lewis
MARBLE ARCH
Marble Arch
Albion Gate
St Mark
Handel House Museum
Claridge's Hotel
Speakers' Corner
Roosevelt Mem.
HYDE PARK
Brook Gate
MAYFAIR
Grosvenor House Hotel
Immaculate Conception
Grosvenor Chapel
Grosvenor Gate
New Lodge
0 100 200 300 400 500 m
0 100 200 300 400 500 yds
© A-Z/OS

324

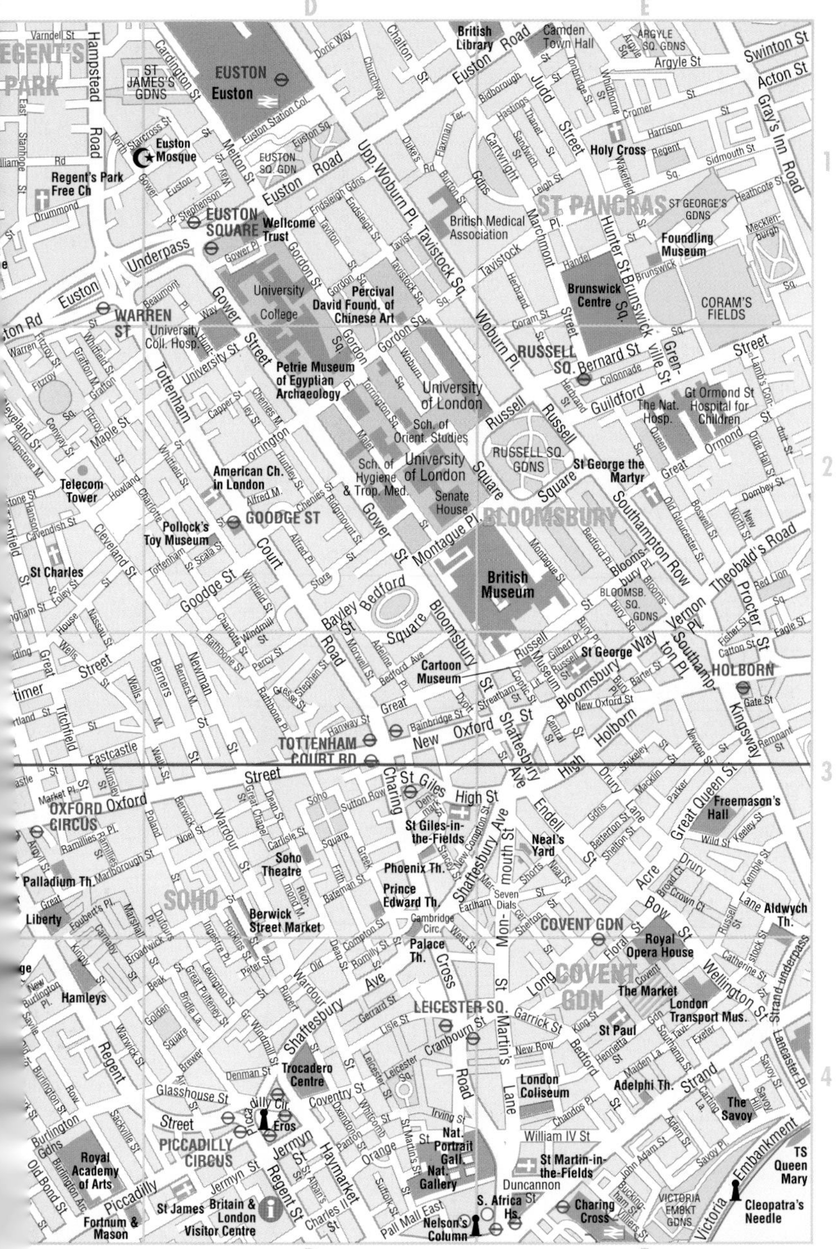
D
E
1
2
3
4
Regent's Park
Hampstead Road
St James's Gdns
Euston
Euston Mosque
Regent's Park Free Ch
Euston Square
Wellcome Trust
Warren St
University College
University Coll. Hosp.
Percival David Found. of Chinese Art
Petrie Museum of Egyptian Archaeology
British Library
Camden Town Hall
Argyle Sq. Gdns
Argyle St
Swinton St
Acton St
Gray's Inn Road
Holy Cross
St Pancras
St George's Gdns
British Medical Association
Foundling Museum
Brunswick Centre
Coram's Fields
Russell Sq.
University of London
Sch. of Orient. Studies
Russell Sq. Gdns
St George the Martyr
The Nat. Hosp.
Gt Ormond St Hospital for Children
Telecom Tower
American Ch. in London
Goodge St
Pollock's Toy Museum
Sch. of Hygiene & Trop. Med.
Senate House
Bloomsbury
British Museum
St Charles
Bloomsb. Sq. Gdns
Theobald's Road
Cartoon Museum
St George
Holborn
Tottenham Court Rd
New Oxford St
Kingsway
Oxford Circus
St Giles-in-the-Fields
Freemason's Hall
Soho Theatre
Neal's Yard
Phoenix Th.
Palladium Th.
Prince Edward Th.
Soho
Liberty
Berwick Street Market
Covent Gdn
Aldwych Th.
Palace Th.
Royal Opera House
Covent Gdn
The Market
London Transport Mus.
Hamleys
Leicester Sq.
St Paul
Trocadero Centre
London Coliseum
Adelphi Th.
The Savoy
Eros
Piccadilly Circus
Nat. Portrait Gall.
Nat. Gallery
St Martin-in-the-Fields
Royal Academy of Arts
St James
Britain & London Visitor Centre
Fortnum & Mason
S. Africa Hs.
Nelson's Column
Charing Cross
Victoria Embkt Gdns
TS Queen Mary
Cleopatra's Needle
Victoria Embankment
Strand
Regent St
Haymarket
Piccadilly
Shaftesbury Ave
Charing Cross Road
St Martin's Lane

322

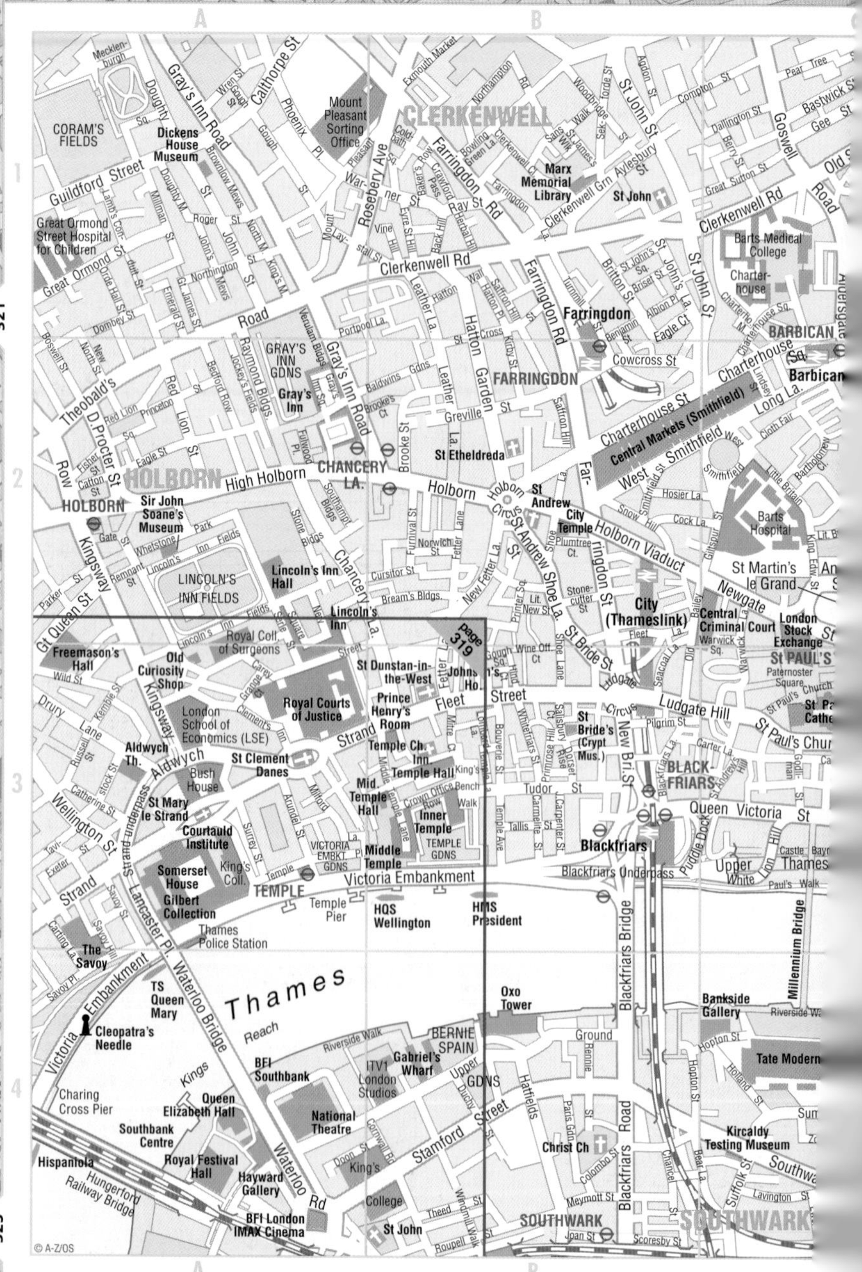

A B

321

1

CLERKENWELL
Mecklenburgh Sq.
CORAM'S FIELDS
Doughty St
Gray's Inn Road
Wren St
Gough St
Calthorpe St
Phoenix Pl.
Mount Pleasant Sorting Office
Exmouth Market
Northampton Rd
Rosebery Ave
Farringdon Rd
Dickens House Museum
Brownlow Mews
Guildford Street
Lamb's Conduit St
Millman St
Doughty M.
Roger St
John St
North M.
Kings M.
Great Ormond Street Hospital for Children
Great Ormond St
Orde Hall St
Emerald St
Gt. James St
Northington St
John's Mews
Dombey St
Warner St
Vine Hill
Eyre St Hill
Back Hill
Herbal Hill
Ray St
Coldbath Sq.
Bowling Green La.
Clerkenwell Cl.
Farringdon La.
Clerkenwell Grn
Aylesbury St
Marx Memorial Library
Sans Walk
St James's Row
Woodbridge St
Sekforde St
St John St
Agdon St
Compton St
Pear Tree St
Bastwick St
Dallington St
Gee St
Goswell Road
Berry St
Great Sutton St
Old St
St John
Clerkenwell Rd
Barts Medical College
Charterhouse
Leather La.
Hatton Wall
Saffron Hill
Hatton Pl.
Turnmill St
Britton St
St John's Sq.
Briset St
Albion Pl.
St John's La.
Eagle Ct
Benjamin St
Farringdon
Charterhouse M.
Charterhouse Sq.
Aldersgate
BARBICAN
Barbican
Portpool La.
Boswell St
New North St
Road
Verulam Bldgs
GRAY'S INN GDNS
Gray's Inn
Gray's Inn Sq.
Raymond Bldgs
Jockey's Fields
Bedford Row
Red Lion St
Princeton St
Red Lion Sq.
Theobald's Road
Baldwins Gdns
Brooke's Ct
Hatton Garden
Cross St
Kirby St
Cowcross St
FARRINGDON
Charterhouse St
Central Markets (Smithfield)
Lindsey St
Long La.
Cloth Fair
Greville St
Saffron Hill
St Etheldreda
Brooke St
Fulwood Pl.
Eagle St
Fisher St
Catton St
D.Procter St
Row

2

HOLBORN
High Holborn
CHANCERY LA.
Holborn
Holborn Circus
St Andrew
City Temple
Far-ringdon St
West Smithfield
Smithfield
Hosier La.
Bartholomew Cl.
Little Britain
Snow Hill
Cock La.
Giltspur St
Barts Hospital
Lit. Britain
Sir John Soane's Museum
Gate St
Whetstone Park
Lincoln's Inn Fields
Southampton Bldgs
Stone Bldgs
Furnival St
Fetter Lane
Norwich St
Shoe La.
Plumtree Ct.
Holborn Viaduct
St Martin's le Grand
Kingsway
Remnant St
Parker St
LINCOLN'S INN FIELDS
Lincoln's Inn Hall
Chancery La.
Cursitor St
Bream's Bldgs.
New Fetter La.
St Andrew St
Printer St
Lit. New St
Stonecutter St
City (Thameslink)
Old Bailey
Newgate St
Central Criminal Court
London Stock Exchange
Warwick Sq.
Warwick La.
ST PAUL'S
Paternoster Square
St Paul's Church
Gt Queen St
Freemason's Hall
Wild St
Old Curiosity Shop
Portugal St
Royal Coll. of Surgeons
Lincoln's Inn
Serle St
Carey St
Grange Ct
Clement's Inn
Royal Courts of Justice
St Dunstan-in-the-West
Johnson's Ho.
Gough Sq.
Wine Off. Ct
Shoe Lane
St Bride St
Fleet La.
Ludgate Circus
Seacoal La.
Ludgate Hill
Pilgrim St
Carter La.
St Paul's Cath.
Drury Lane
Kemble St
Kingsway
London School of Economics (LSE)
Fleet Street
Prince Henry's Room
Mitre Ct
Whitefriars St
Salisbury Ct
Bouverie St
St Bride's (Crypt Mus.)
New Bri. St
Blackfriars La.
Strand
Temple Ch. Inn.
Temple Hall
King's Bench Walk
Primrose Hill
Dorset Rise
Russell St
Aldwych Th.
Aldwych
St Clement Danes
Bush House
St Mary le Strand
Catherine St
Wellington St
Strand underpass
Courtauld Institute
Surrey St.
Arundel St.
Milford La.
Mid. Temple Hall
Middle Temple La.
Crown Office Row
Inner Temple
Tudor St
Carmelite St
Carpenter St
Tallis St
Temple Ave
BLACK-FRIARS
Queen Victoria St
St Andrew's Hill
Puddle Dock
Godliman St

3

Tavistock St
Exeter St
Somerset House
King's Coll.
VICTORIA EMBKT. GDNS
Middle Temple
TEMPLE GDNS
Blackfriars
Blackfriars Underpass
Upper Thames St
White Lion Hill
Castle Baynard St
Paul's Walk
Strand
Savoy St
Lancaster Pl.
Gilbert Collection
Temple
TEMPLE
Victoria Embankment
Temple Pier
HQS Wellington
HMS President
Carting La.
Savoy Hill
The Savoy
Thames Police Station
Waterloo Bridge
Blackfriars Bridge
Millennium Bridge
Savoy Pl.
Victoria Embankment
TS Queen Mary
Thames
Reach
Oxo Tower
Bankside Gallery
Riverside Walk
Cleopatra's Needle
Riverside Walk
BERNIE SPAIN
Gabriel's Wharf
Ground
Rennie St
Hopton St
Tate Modern
Holland St

4

Kings Reach
BFI Southbank
ITV1 London Studios
Upper GDNS
Duchy St
Hatfields
Charing Cross Pier
Queen Elizabeth Hall
National Theatre
Stamford Street
Paris Gdn
Southbank Centre
Cornwall Rd
Christ Ch
Blackfriars Road
Sumner St
Kircaldy Testing Museum
Hispaniola
Royal Festival Hall
Doon St
King's College
Colombo St
Chancel St
Bear La.
Suffolk St
Southwark St
Hungerford Railway Bridge
Hayward Gallery
Waterloo Rd
Theed St
Windmill Walk
Meymott St
Lavington St
BFI London IMAX Cinema
St John
Roupell St
SOUTHWARK
Joan St
Scoresby St
SOUTHWARK

325

A B

page 319

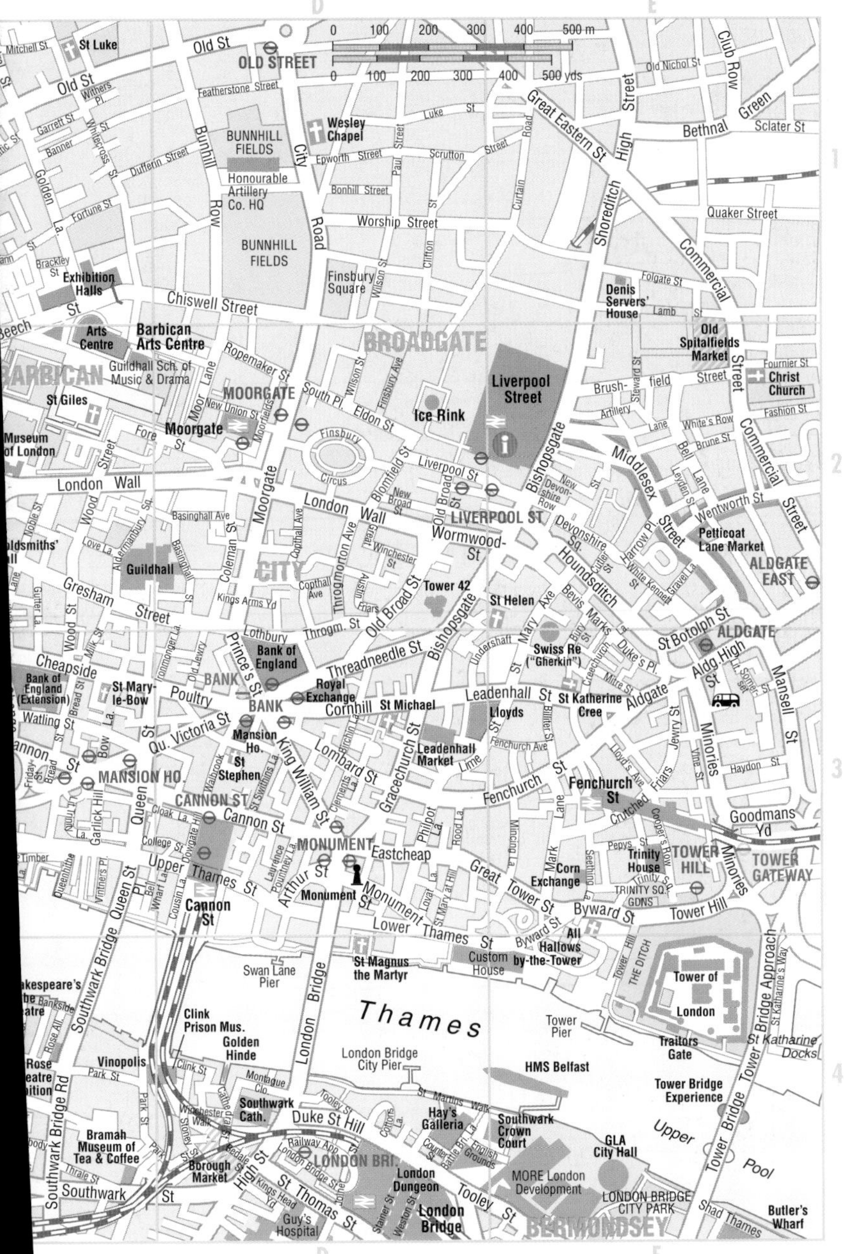
D
E
0 100 200 300 400 500 m
0 100 200 300 400 500 yds
1
2
3
4
Old St
OLD STREET
St Luke
Mitchell St
Central St
Old St
Withers Pl.
Garrett St
Whitecross St
Banner St
Golden La.
Fortune St
Brackley St
Dufferin Street
Featherstone Street
Bunhill Row
BUNHILL FIELDS
Honourable Artillery Co. HQ
BUNHILL FIELDS
City Road
Wesley Chapel
Luke St
Epworth Street
Paul Street
Scrutton Street
Bonhill Street
Worship Street
Curtain Road
Great Eastern St
Shoreditch High Street
Old Nichol St
Club Row
Bethnal Green
Sclater St
Quaker Street
Commercial Street
Folgate St
Denis Servers' House
Lamb St
Old Spitalfields Market
Exhibition Halls
Chiswell Street
Finsbury Square
Wilson St
Clifton St
Beech St
Arts Centre
Barbican Arts Centre
BARBICAN
Guildhall Sch. of Music & Drama
Ropemaker St
BROADGATE
Liverpool Street
MOORGATE
Moor Lane
New Union St
Moorfields
South Pl.
Eldon St
Ice Rink
St Giles
Museum of London
Moorgate
Fore St
Wood Street
Finsbury Circus
Liverpool St
Bishopsgate
Brushfield Street
Steward St
Artillery Lane
White's Row
Fournier St
Christ Church
Fashion St
Brune St
Middlesex Street
Bell Lane
Leyden St
Wentworth St
London Wall
London Wall
Blomfield St
New Broad St
Old Broad St
LIVERPOOL ST
New Devonshire Row
Devonshire Sq.
Petticoat Lane Market
Harrow Pl.
Noble St
Aldermanbury Sq.
Basinghall Ave
Coleman St
Copthall Ave
Throgmorton Ave
Great Winchester St
Wormwood St
Houndsditch
Cutler St
White Kennett St
Gravel La.
ALDGATE EAST
Goldsmiths' Hall
Love La.
Guildhall
Basinghall St
CITY
Austin Friars
Tower 42
St Helen
St Mary Axe
Bevis Marks
Gresham Street
Kings Arms Yd
Copthall Ave
Old Broad St
Gutter La.
Wood St
Lothbury
Throgm. St
Bishopsgate
Swiss Re ("Gherkin")
Undershaft
Bury St
Duke's Pl
St Botolph St
ALDGATE
Aldgate High St
Mansell St
Ironmonger La.
Old Jewry
Milk St
Cheapside
Prince's St
Bank of England
Threadneedle St
Creechurch La.
Mitre St
Bank of England (Extension)
St Mary-le-Bow
Poultry
BANK
BANK
Royal Exchange
Cornhill
St Michael
Leadenhall St
St Katherine Cree
Aldgate
Lt. Somerset
Bread St
Watling St
Bow La.
Qu. Victoria St
Mansion Ho.
Birchin La.
Gracechurch St
Lloyds
Lime St
Billiter St
Jewry St
Minories
Cannon St
MANSION HO.
St Stephen
Walbrook
St Swithins La.
King William St
Lombard St
Leadenhall Market
Fenchurch Ave
Lloyd's Ave
Vine St
Haydon St
Friday St
Queen St
Garlick Hill
CANNON ST
Clements La.
Fenchurch St
Fenchurch St
Lane
Friars
Cloak La.
Cannon St
Philpot La.
Rood La.
Mincing La.
Crutched Friars
Cooper's Row
Goodmans Yd
College St
Dowgate Hill
MONUMENT
Eastcheap
Mark Lane
Pepys St
TOWER HILL
TOWER GATEWAY
Timber
Queenhithe
Vintners Pl.
Upper Thames St
Laurence Pountney La.
Arthur St
Great Tower St
Corn Exchange
Seething La.
Trinity House
Trinity Sq.
TRINITY SQ. GDNS
Minories
Queen St Pl.
Whar La.
Cousin La.
Cannon St
Monument
Monument St
Lovat La.
St Mary at Hill
Byward St
Byward St
Tower Hill
Lower Thames St
All Hallows by-the-Tower
Southwark Bridge
St Magnus the Martyr
Custom House
Tower Hill
THE DITCH
Tower Bridge Approach
St Katharine's Way
Swan Lane Pier
London Bridge
Tower of London
Shakespeare's Globe Theatre
Bankside
Thames
Tower Pier
Clink Prison Mus.
Golden Hinde
Traitors Gate
St Katharine Docks
Rose All.
Rose Theatre Exhibition
Vinopolis
London Bridge City Pier
HMS Belfast
Park St
Clink St
Montague Clo.
Tower Bridge Experience
Cathedral St
St Martins Walk
Southwark Cath.
Tooley St
Winchester Walk
Duke St Hill
Cottons La.
Hay's Galleria
Southwark Crown Court
Upper Pool
Southwark Bridge Rd
Bramah Museum of Tea & Coffee
Stoney St
Park St
Bedale St
Railway App
LONDON BRI.
Counter St
Battle Br. La.
English Grounds
GLA City Hall
Tower Bridge
Thrale St
Borough Market
High St
London Bridge St
London Dungeon
MORE London Development
Southwark St
Kings Head Yd
St Thomas St
Joiner St
Tooley St
LONDON BRIDGE CITY PARK
Guy's Hospital
Stainer St
Weston St
London Bridge
BERMONDSEY
Shad Thames
Butler's Wharf
D
E

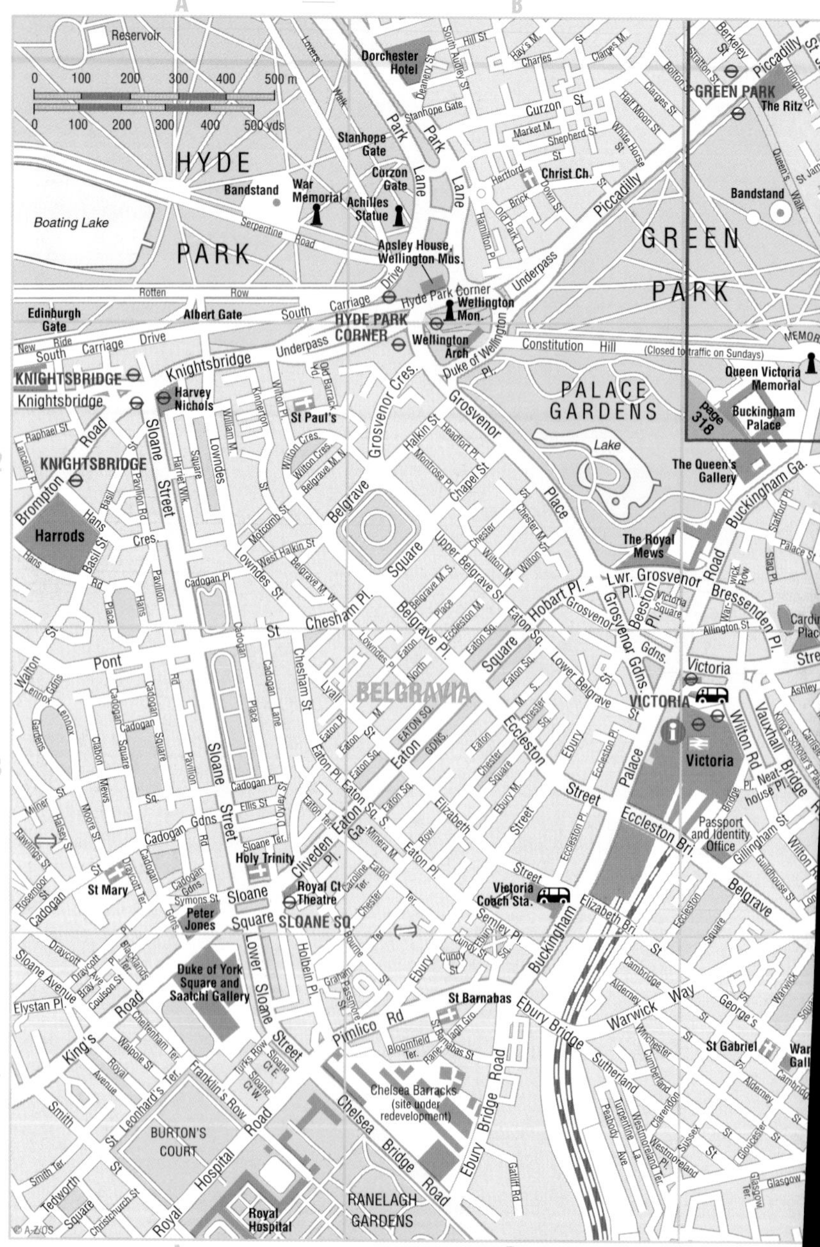
320
326
page 318
A
B
C
1
2
3
4
0 100 200 300 400 500 m
0 100 200 300 400 500 yds
Reservoir
HYDE
PARK
Boating Lake
Serpentine Road
Bandstand
War Memorial
Achilles Statue
Stanhope Gate
Curzon Gate
Dorchester Hotel
Lovers' Walk
Park Lane
Apsley House, Wellington Mus.
Rotten Row
South Carriage Drive
Edinburgh Gate
Albert Gate
Hyde Park Corner
HYDE PARK CORNER
Wellington Mon.
Wellington Arch
New Ride
Knightsbridge
KNIGHTSBRIDGE
Harvey Nichols
Harrods
Brompton Road
Sloane Street
St Paul's
Grosvenor Cres.
Belgrave Square
Halkin St
Chapel St
Grosvenor Place
Constitution Hill
(Closed to traffic on Sundays)
PALACE GARDENS
Lake
GREEN PARK
GREEN
PARK
The Ritz
Piccadilly
Bandstand
Curzon St
Christ Ch.
Queen Victoria Memorial
Buckingham Palace
The Queen's Gallery
The Royal Mews
Buckingham Ga.
Lwr. Grosvenor Pl.
Bressenden Pl.
Victoria St
VICTORIA
Victoria
Passport and Identity Office
Wilton Rd
Vauxhall Bridge Rd
Upper Belgrave St
Eaton Sq.
Chesham Pl.
Chesham St
Cadogan Pl.
Pont St
BELGRAVIA
Lowndes Sq.
Eaton Place
Ebury St
Eccleston St
Elizabeth St
Victoria Coach Sta.
Buckingham Palace Rd
Cadogan Gdns
Holy Trinity
St Mary
Peter Jones
Royal Ct Theatre
SLOANE SQ.
Sloane Square
Lower Sloane Street
Duke of York Square and Saatchi Gallery
Sloane Avenue
King's Road
Pimlico Rd
St Barnabas
Ebury Bridge
Ebury Bridge Road
Warwick Way
St Gabriel
Chelsea Barracks (site under redevelopment)
Chelsea Bridge Road
Royal Hospital Road
BURTON'S COURT
Royal Hospital
RANELAGH GARDENS
Franklin's Row
St Leonard's Ter.
Smith St
Tedworth Square
© A-Z/OS

A
B
C
1
2
3
4
326
0 100 200 300 400 500 m
0 100 200 300 400 500 yds
A40
Westway
Tavistock Road
McGregor Road
St Luke's Road
All Saints Rd
Basing St
Lancaster Road
St Luke's Mews
Leamington Road Villas
Aldridge Road Villas
Westbourne Park Villas
ROYAL OAK
Westbourne Park Rd
St Stephen's Gardens
Shrewsbury Road
Dartmouth Close
Cornwall Close
Chepstow Road
Talbot Road
Portobello Rd
LADBROKE GROVE
Westbourne Park Road
Portobello Road Market
Powis Terrace
Powis Gardens
Powis Square
Ledbury Road
Talbot Road
Courtnell St
Moorhouse Rd
Sutherland Place
Northumberland Place
Bridstow Place
Hereford Road
Hatherley Grove
Queensway
Bishop's Bridge
Kensington Park
Talbot Road
Colville Road
Terrace
Artesian Mews
Newton Rd
Bayswater
Blenheim Crescent
Colville
Colville Mews
St John's Mews
Head's Mews
Botts Mews
Westbourne Grove
Whiteley's Shopping Centre
Ladbroke
Portobello Road
Lonsdale
Road
Westbourne Grove
Pembridge Villas
Garway Road
Kensington Gardens Square
Redan Place
Inverness Place
Elgin Crescent
Road
Westbourne Grove
Ledbury Road
Hereford Road
Queensway
Porchester Gardens
Grove
Arundel Gardens
Denbigh Terrace
Denbigh Rd
Denbigh Close
Chepstow Villas
Chepstow Crescent
Pembridge Place
Chepstow Road
Reds Place
Leinster Square
Princes Square
Princes Square
Queen's Mews
Salem Rd
Terrace
Lansdowne Road
Ladbroke Gardens
Pembridge Crescent
Dawson Place
Prince's Mews
Greek Orthodox
BAYSWATER
Inverness Place
NOTTING HILL
Stanley Crescent
Stanley Gardens
Kensington Park Road
Portobello Road
Pembridge Square
Moscow Road
St Petersburgh Place
St Petersburgh Mews
Bark Place
Poplar Place
Caroline Place
Orme Court
Queensway
Inverness Terrace
Lansdowne Crescent
Lansdowne Rise
Kensington Park Gardens
Pembridge Road
Pembridge Gdns
Linden Gardens
Clanricarde Gardens
Ossington Street
Place Court
QUEENSWAY
St John's Gardens
Lansdowne
Ladbroke Grove
Ladbroke Square
Hornbury Mews
Hornbury Crescent
Road
Bayswater Road
Diana Memorial Playground
Ladbroke Terrace
Ladbroke
Willby Mews
Victoria Gardens
Bulmer Place
NOTTING HILL GATE
Kensington Palace Gardens
Elfin Oak
Lansdowne Walk
Road
Ladbroke Walk
Notting Hill Gate
Kensington Mall
Palace Gardens Mews
KENSINGTON GARDENS
Portland Road
Clarendon Road
Ladbroke Road
HOLLAND PARK
Campden Hill Square
Hillsleigh Road
Campden Hill Road
Hillgate St
Kensington Place
Palace Gardens
The Broad Walk
Princedale Road
Holland Park Avenue
Aubrey Road
Holland Walk
Aubrey Walk
Peel Street
Campden Street
Kensington Church Street
Brunswick Gardens
TENNIS COURTS
Bedford Gardens
Sunken Garden
Holland Park
Holland Park Mews
Holland Park
Airlie Gardens
Sheffield Terrace
Tor Gardens
Vicarage Gate
Kensington Palace
Woodstock Square
Campden Hill
KENSINGTON
Gloucester Walk
Campden Grove
Hornton
The Dial Walk
HOLLAND
Sheldrake Place
Pitt St
Duke's Lane
Palace Grn
Palace Avenue
Royal Garden Hotel
Duchess of Bedford's Walk
Holland
Street
Kensington Road
PARK
Addison Road
Abbotsbury Road
Abbotsbury Close
Upper Phillimore Gardens
Campden Hill Rd
Kensington Town Hall
Drayson Mews
St Mary Abbots
Holland House
Phillimore Place
Argyll Road
HIGH STREET KENSINGTON
Young St
Kensington Court
Kensington Court
Somerset Square
Essex Villas
Stafford Terrace
Walk
Shopping Arcade
Kensington Square
Thackeray Street
Albert Place
Addison Cres
Oakwood Lane
Oakwood Court
Ilchester Place
Holland Walk
Phillimore Gardens
Phillimore
Street
Adam and Eve Mews
Wright's Lane
Douro Place
Park Close
High
St Albans Grove
Melbury Road
Melbury Court
Kensington
Abingdon Rd
Allen Street
Iverna Gardens
Marloes Road
Scarsdale Place
Stanford Road
Cottesmore Gardens
Addison Road
Leighton House
Holland Park Road
Earls Court Road
Pater St
Cope Place
Abingdon Villas
Kelso Place
Eldon Road
Kensington (Olympia) Station

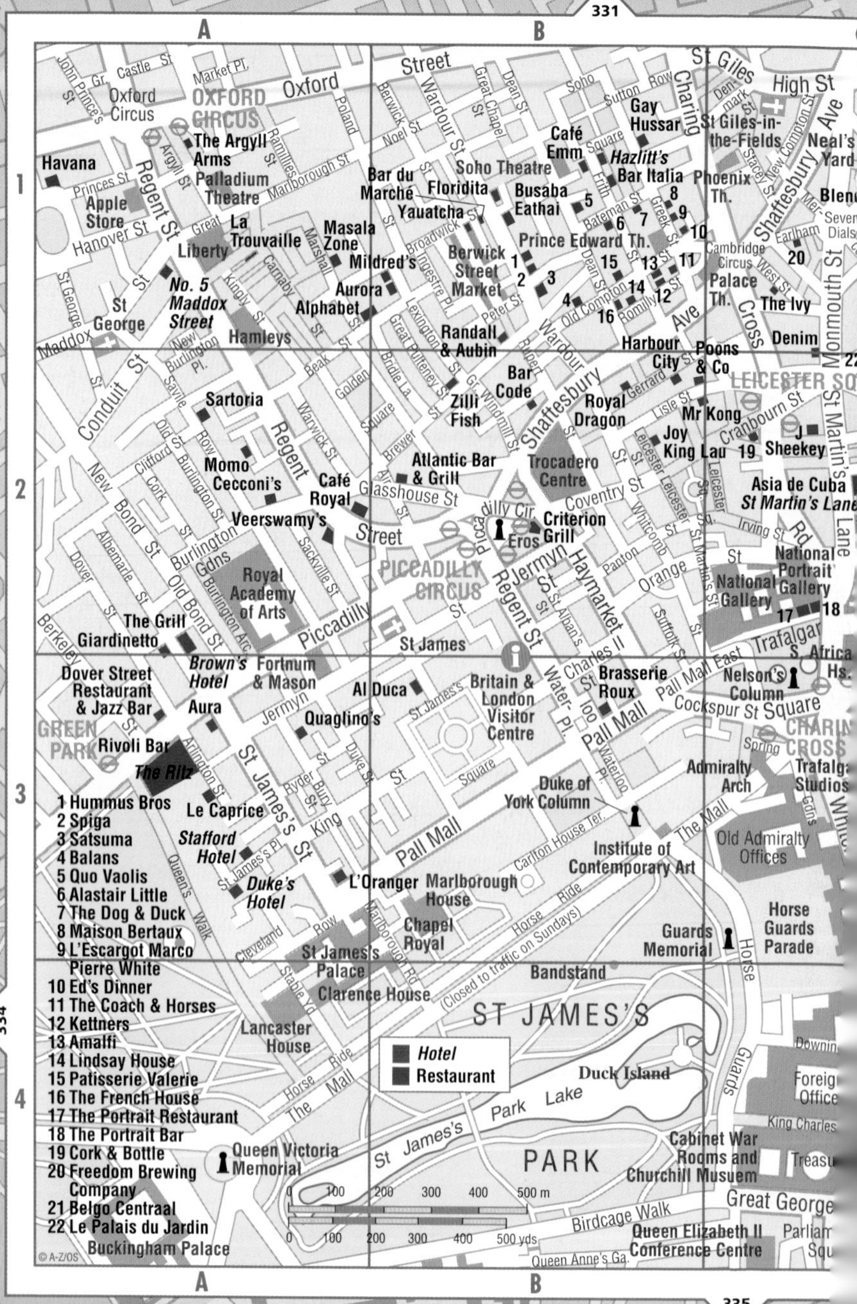
331
A
B
1
2
3
4
Oxford Circus
OXFORD CIRCUS
The Argyll Arms
Palladium Theatre
Havana
Apple Store
Liberty
La Trouvaille
No. 5 Maddox Street
St George
Hamleys
Masala Zone
Mildred's
Aurora
Alphabet
Bar du Marché
Floridita
Yauatcha
Soho Theatre
Berwick Street Market
Café Emm
Busaba Eathai
Gay Hussar
Hazlitt's
Bar Italia
Prince Edward Th.
St Giles-in-the-Fields
Phoenix Th.
Neal's Yard
Seven Dials
Cambridge Circus
Palace Th.
The Ivy
Denim
Randall & Aubin
Harbour City
Poons & Co
LEICESTER SQ
Sartoria
Momo
Cecconi's
Zilli Fish
Bar Code
Royal Dragon
Mr Kong
Joy King Lau
J Sheekey
Café Royal
Atlantic Bar & Grill
Trocadero Centre
Veerswamy's
Criterion Grill
Eros
Asia de Cuba
St Martin's Lane
National Portrait Gallery
National Gallery
Royal Academy of Arts
PICCADILLY CIRCUS
The Grill
Giardinetto
St James
Dover Street Restaurant & Jazz Bar
Brown's Hotel
Fortnum & Mason
Al Duca
Britain & London Visitor Centre
Brasserie Roux
Nelson's Column
S. Africa Hs.
Aura
Quaglino's
GREEN PARK
Rivoli Bar
The Ritz
CHARING CROSS
Admiralty Arch
Trafalgar Studios
Duke of York Column
Le Caprice
Stafford Hotel
Duke's Hotel
L'Oranger
Marlborough House
Institute of Contemporary Art
Old Admiralty Offices
Chapel Royal
Guards Memorial
Horse Guards Parade
St James's Palace
Clarence House
Bandstand
(Closed to traffic on Sundays)
Lancaster House
ST JAMES'S
PARK
Duck Island
Hotel
Restaurant
Queen Victoria Memorial
Cabinet War Rooms and Churchill Museum
Buckingham Palace
Queen Elizabeth II Conference Centre
0 100 200 300 400 500 m
0 100 200 300 400 500 yds
1 Hummus Bros
2 Spiga
3 Satsuma
4 Balans
5 Quo Vaolis
6 Alastair Little
7 The Dog & Duck
8 Maison Bertaux
9 L'Escargot Marco Pierre White
10 Ed's Dinner
11 The Coach & Horses
12 Kettners
13 Amalfi
14 Lindsay House
15 Patisserie Valerie
16 The French House
17 The Portrait Restaurant
18 The Portrait Bar
19 Cork & Bottle
20 Freedom Brewing Company
21 Belgo Centraal
22 Le Palais du Jardin
© A-Z/OS
334
335

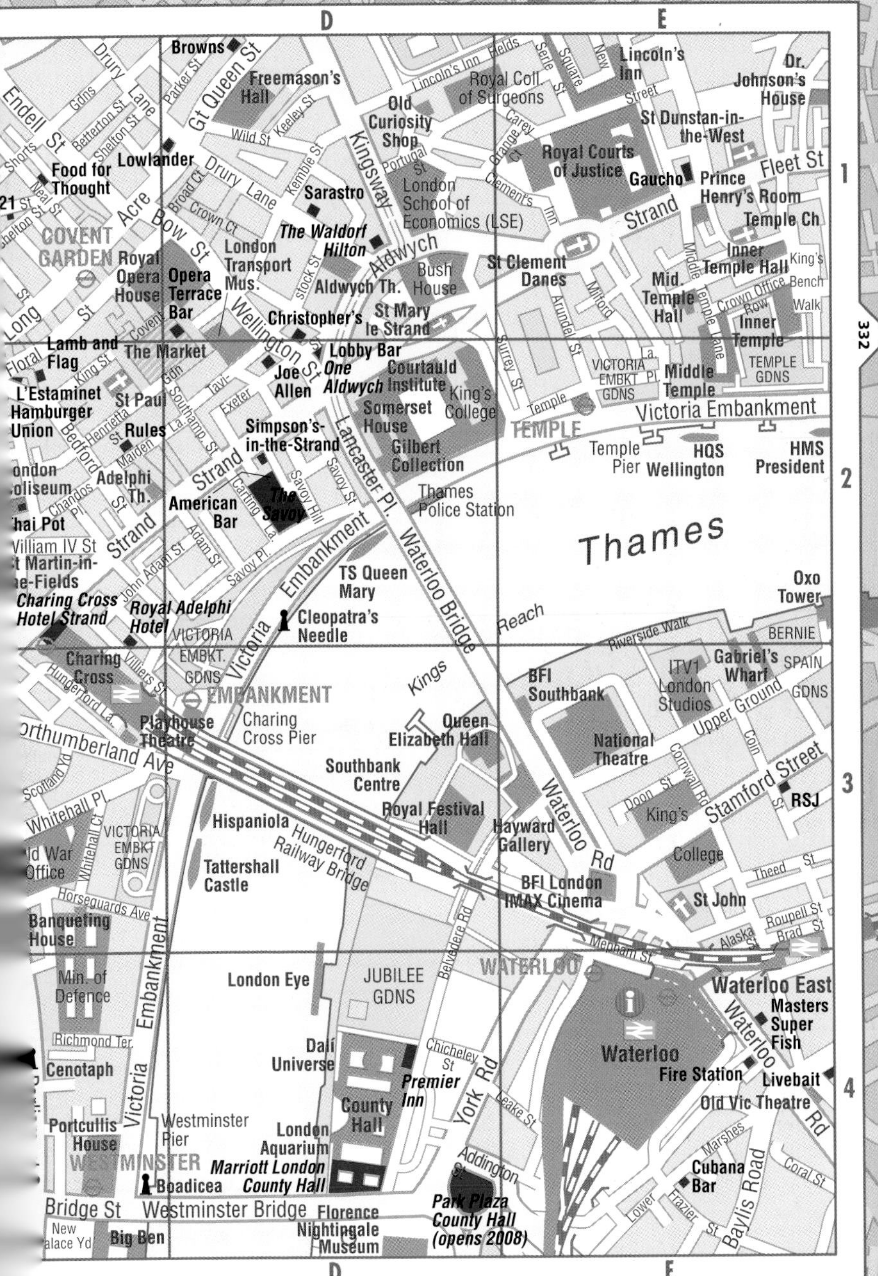
D
E
1
2
3
4
332
Browns
Freemason's Hall
Lincoln's Inn
Dr. Johnson's House
Royal Coll. of Surgeons
Old Curiosity Shop
St Dunstan-in-the-West
Lowlander
Food for Thought
Royal Courts of Justice
Gaucho
Prince Henry's Room
Fleet St
Sarastro
London School of Economics (LSE)
Temple Ch
COVENT GARDEN
The Waldorf Hilton
Inner Temple Hall
Royal Opera House
Opera Terrace Bar
London Transport Mus.
Aldwych Th.
Bush House
St Clement Danes
Mid. Temple Hall
Inner Temple
Christopher's
St Mary le Strand
Lamb and Flag
The Market
Lobby Bar
One Aldwych
Courtauld Institute
Joe Allen
King's College
Middle Temple
TEMPLE GDNS
L'Estaminet
Hamburger Union
St Paul
Rules
Somerset House
VICTORIA EMBKT GDNS
Victoria Embankment
Simpson's-in-the-Strand
TEMPLE
Gilbert Collection
Temple Pier
HQS Wellington
HMS President
Adelphi Th.
The Savoy
American Bar
Thames Police Station
Thames
Strand
Aldwych
Kingsway
Lancaster Pl.
Waterloo Bridge
TS Queen Mary
Oxo Tower
Charing Cross Hotel Strand
Royal Adelphi Hotel
Cleopatra's Needle
Reach
VICTORIA EMBKT. GDNS
Riverside Walk
BERNIE SPAIN GDNS
Charing Cross
EMBANKMENT
BFI Southbank
ITV1 London Studios
Gabriel's Wharf
Playhouse Theatre
Charing Cross Pier
Queen Elizabeth Hall
National Theatre
Upper Ground
Northumberland Ave
Southbank Centre
Stamford Street
RSJ
Whitehall Pl
Royal Festival Hall
Hayward Gallery
King's College
Hispaniola
Hungerford Railway Bridge
Waterloo Rd
Tattershall Castle
BFI London IMAX Cinema
St John
Banqueting House
WATERLOO
Min. of Defence
London Eye
JUBILEE GDNS
Waterloo East
Masters Super Fish
Waterloo
Fire Station
Livebait
Dalí Universe
Premier Inn
Cenotaph
Old Vic Theatre
County Hall
York Rd
Westminster Pier
London Aquarium
Portcullis House
WESTMINSTER
Marriott London County Hall
Cubana Bar
Boadicea
Park Plaza County Hall (opens 2008)
Baylis Road
Bridge St
Westminster Bridge
Florence Nightingale Museum
Big Ben
Victoria Embankment

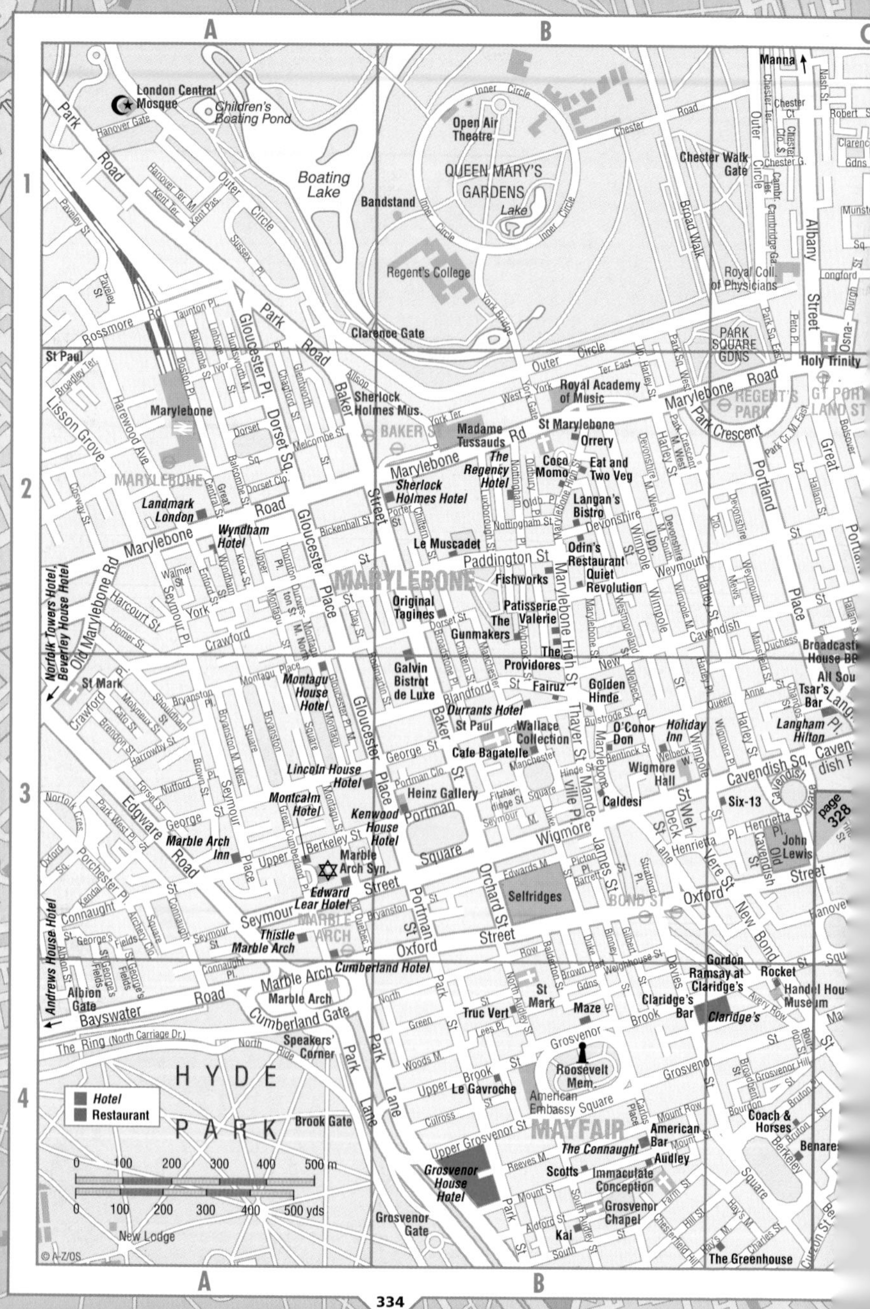
A
B
C
1
2
3
4
Manna
London Central Mosque
Children's Boating Pond
Hanover Gate
Park Road
Hanover Ter. M.
Kent Ter.
Kent Pas.
Outer Circle
Boating Lake
Bandstand
Inner Circle
Open Air Theatre
QUEEN MARY'S GARDENS
Lake
Chester Road
Chester Walk Gate
Broad Walk
Regent's College
York Bridge
Royal Coll. of Physicians
Albany Street
Robert St
Nash St.
Chester Ct
Outer Circle
Chester Pl.
Clarence Gdns
Munster Sq.
Longford
Osnaburgh St
Peto Pl.
Pavelev St
Sussex Pl.
Rossmore Rd
Taunton Pl.
Gloucester Pl.
Park Road
Clarence Gate
Outer Circle
PARK SQUARE GDNS
Park Sq. West
Park Sq. East
Holy Trinity
St Paul
Broadley Ter.
Lisson Grove
Harewood Ave.
Boston Pl.
Marylebone
Balcombe St.
Ivor Pl.
Huntsworth M.
Dorset Sq.
Chagford St.
Glentworth St.
Melcombe St.
Allsop Pl.
Baker Street
Sherlock Holmes Mus.
BAKER ST
York Ter.
Madame Tussauds
Royal Academy of Music
St Marylebone
Orrery
Marylebone Road
REGENT'S PARK
GT PORTLAND ST
Park Crescent
Bolsover St
Great Portland Street
MARYLEBONE
Landmark London
Conway St.
Great Central St.
Marylebone Road
Wyndham Hotel
Marylebone Rd
Sherlock Holmes Hotel
Porter St.
Chiltern St.
The Regency Hotel
Nottingham St.
Coco Momo
Eat and Two Veg
Langan's Bistro
Devonshire St
Bickenhall St.
Le Muscadet
Paddington St
Odin's Restaurant
Quiet Revolution
Weymouth St
Wimpole St
Harley St
Portland Place
Fishworks
Walmer St.
Enford St.
Knox St.
Upper Montagu St.
Thornton Pl.
Gloucester Place
MARYLEBONE
York St
Seymour Pl.
Harcourt St
Old Marylebone Rd
Original Tagines
Patisserie Valerie
The Gunmakers
Marylebone High St
Cavendish St
Crawford St
Homer St.
Norfolk Towers Hotel, Beverley House Hotel
St Mark
Crawford Pl.
Bryanston Pl.
Montagu Place
Montagu House Hotel
Galvin Bistrot de Luxe
The Providores
Broadcasting House BBC
All Souls
Tsar's Bar
Langham Pl.
Langham Hilton
Durrants Hotel
Blandford St
Fairuz
Golden Hinde
Bulstrode St.
O'Conor Don
Holiday Inn
Wallace Collection
St Paul
Cafe Bagatelle
George St
Thayer St
Bentinck St
Wigmore Hall
Cavendish Sq.
Cavendish Pl.
Lincoln House Hotel
Portman Clo.
Heinz Gallery
Manchester Square
Caldesi
Six-13
Nutford Pl.
Montcalm Hotel
Kenwood House Hotel
Portman Square
Wigmore St
Henrietta Pl.
John Lewis
page 328
Norfolk Cres.
Edgware Road
George St
Marble Arch Inn
Upper Berkeley St
Marble Arch Syn.
Edward Lear Hotel
Selfridges
Orchard St
James St
Stratford Pl.
Oxford Street
BOND ST
New Bond St
Connaught St
Seymour Place
Seymour St
MARBLE ARCH
Thistle Marble Arch
Oxford Street
Portman St
Andrews House Hotel
Albion Gate
Connaught Pl.
Cumberland Hotel
Marble Arch
Bayswater Road
Cumberland Gate
Gordon Ramsay at Claridge's
Rocket
Handel House Museum
St Mark
Brown Hart Gdns
Maze
Claridge's Bar
Claridge's
Truc Vert
Brook St
Speakers' Corner
North Ride
The Ring (North Carriage Dr.)
HYDE PARK
Park Lane
Grosvenor Square
Roosevelt Mem.
Upper Brook St
Le Gavroche
American Embassy Square
Grosvenor St
Hotel
Restaurant
Brook Gate
Culross St
Upper Grosvenor St
MAYFAIR
American Bar
Coach & Horses
The Connaught
Audley
Benares
Grosvenor House Hotel
Scotts
Immaculate Conception
Mount St
Grosvenor Chapel
Berkeley Square
0 100 200 300 400 500 m
0 100 200 300 400 500 yds
Grosvenor Gate
New Lodge
Kai
South St
Chesterfield Hill
The Greenhouse
© A-Z/OS

334

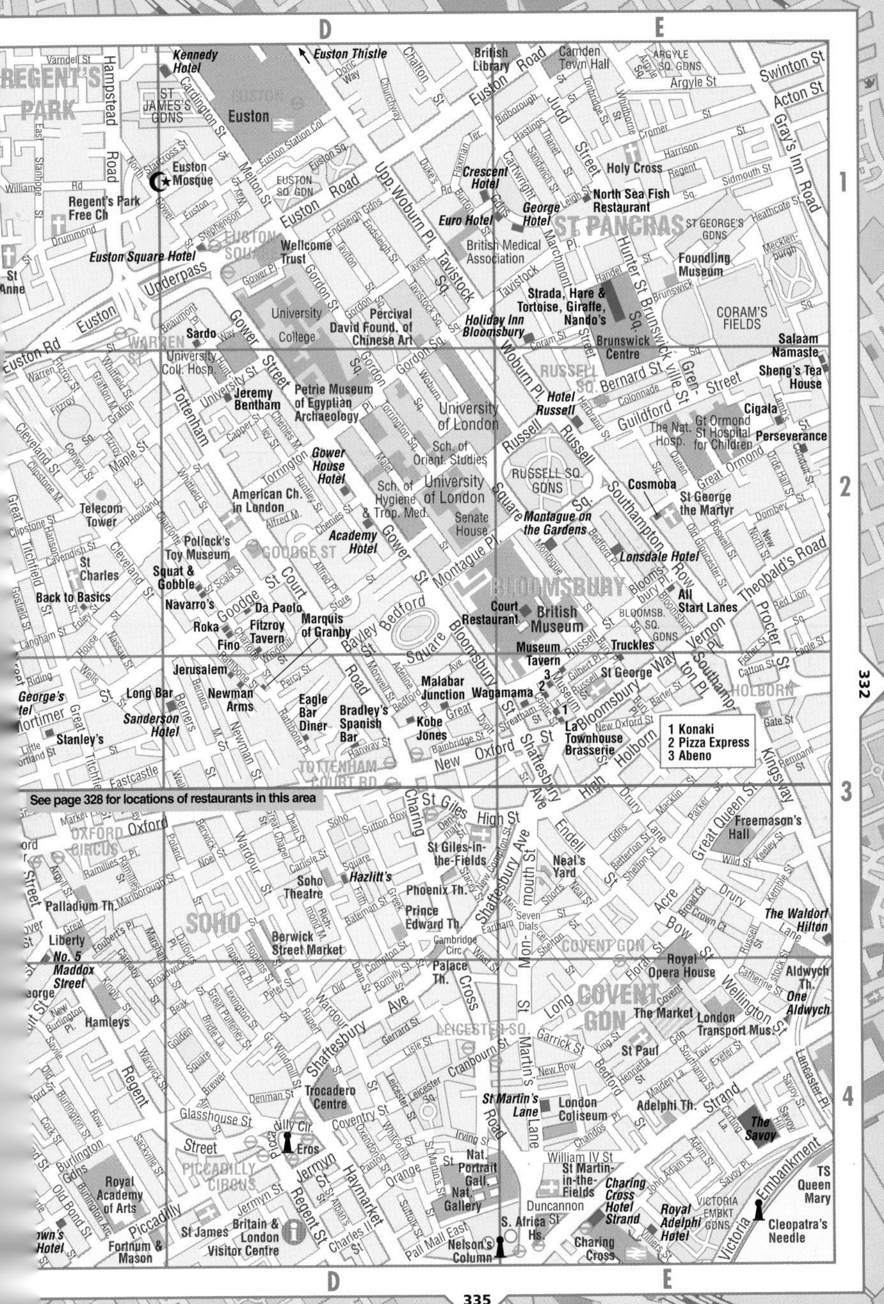
D
E
1
2
3
4
332
Kennedy Hotel
Euston Thistle
British Library
Camden Town Hall
REGENT'S PARK
Euston
Euston Mosque
Regent's Park Free Ch
Euston Square Hotel
Wellcome Trust
Crescent Hotel
Euro Hotel
George Hotel
North Sea Fish Restaurant
Holy Cross
ST PANCRAS
British Medical Association
Foundling Museum
CORAM'S FIELDS
Strada, Hare & Tortoise, Giraffe, Nando's
Brunswick Centre
Holiday Inn Bloomsbury
University College
Percival David Found. of Chinese Art
Sardo
University Coll. Hosp.
Salaam Namaste
Sheng's Tea House
Jeremy Bentham
Petrie Museum of Egyptian Archaeology
University of London
Hotel Russell
RUSSELL SQ.
Cigala
Perseverance
Gt Ormond St Hospital for Children
The Nat. Hosp.
Sch. of Orient. Studies
Gower House Hotel
Sch. of Hygiene & Trop. Med.
RUSSELL SQ. GDNS
Cosmoba
St George the Martyr
American Ch. in London
Telecom Tower
Senate House
Montague on the Gardens
Pollock's Toy Museum
GOODGE ST
Academy Hotel
Lonsdale Hotel
St Charles
Squat & Gobble
BLOOMSBURY
Back to Basics
Navarro's
Da Paolo
Fitzroy Tavern
Marquis of Granby
Roka
Fino
Court Restaurant
British Museum
All Start Lanes
Truckles
Museum Tavern
Jerusalem
St George
HOLBORN
George's Hotel
Long Bar
Newman Arms
Malabar Junction
Wagamama
Sanderson Hotel
Eagle Bar Diner
Bradley's Spanish Bar
Kobe Jones
Stanley's
La Townhouse Brasserie
1 Konaki
2 Pizza Express
3 Abeno
TOTTENHAM COURT RD
See page 328 for locations of restaurants in this area
OXFORD CIRCUS
St Giles-in-the-Fields
Freemason's Hall
Hazlitt's
Soho Theatre
Neal's Yard
Palladium Th.
Phoenix Th.
Prince Edward Th.
SOHO
The Waldorf Hilton
Liberty
No. 5 Maddox Street
Berwick Street Market
Seven Dials
COVENT GDN
Royal Opera House
Aldwych Th.
Palace Th.
One Aldwych
Hamleys
COVENT GDN
The Market
London Transport Mus.
LEICESTER SQ.
St Paul
Trocadero Centre
St Martin's Lane
London Coliseum
Adelphi Th.
The Savoy
Eros
PICCADILLY CIRCUS
Nat. Portrait Gall.
Nat. Gallery
St Martin-in-the-Fields
Charing Cross Hotel Strand
Royal Adelphi Hotel
TS Queen Mary
Cleopatra's Needle
Royal Academy of Arts
St James
Britain & London Visitor Centre
S. Africa Hs.
Nelson's Column
Charing Cross
Fortnum & Mason
Town's Hotel
VICTORIA EMBKT GDNS

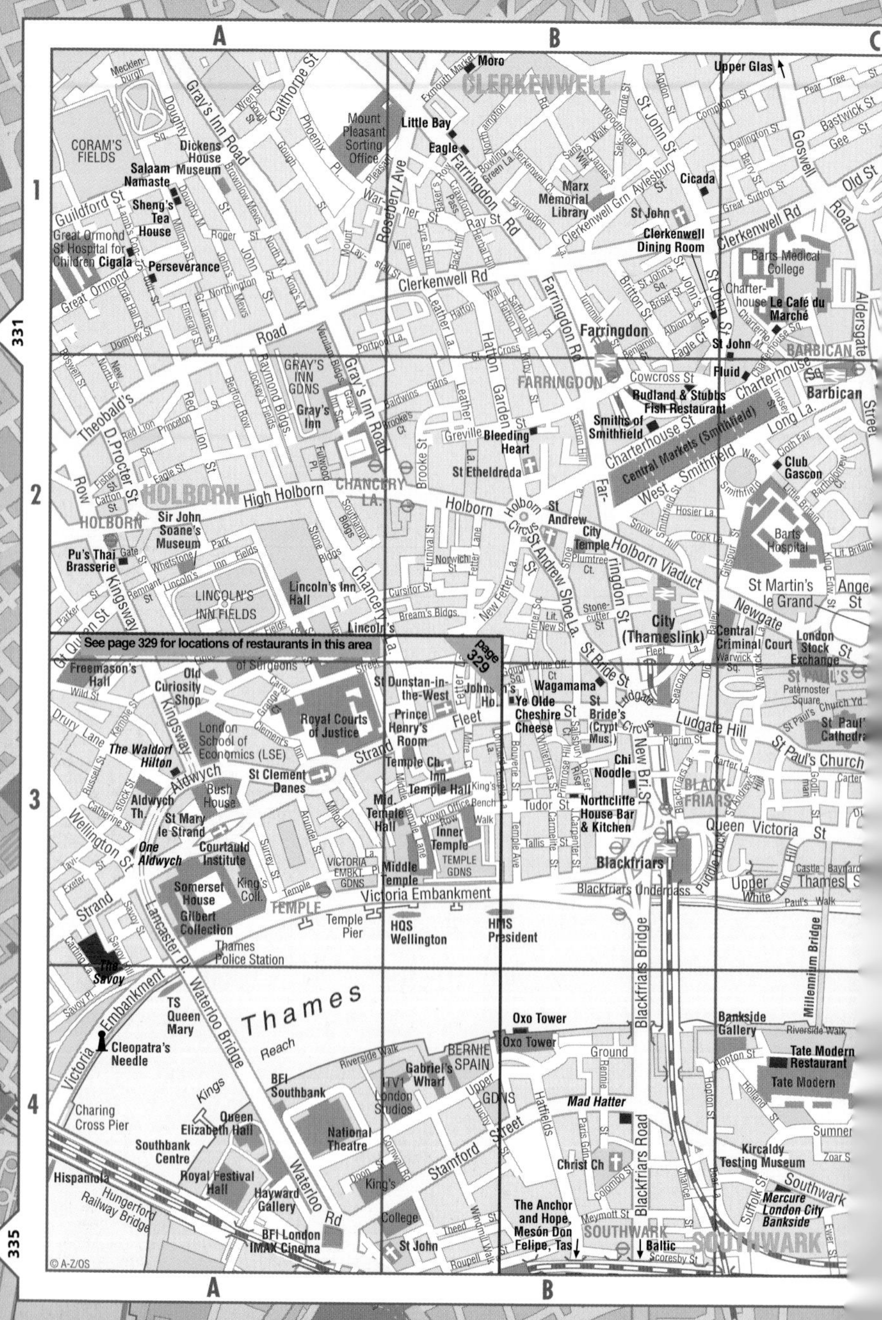
Moro
Little Bay
Eagle
Cicada
Upper Glas
Salaam Namaste
Sheng's Tea House
Cigala
Perseverance
Clerkenwell Dining Room
Le Café du Marché
St John
Fluid
Rudland & Stubbs Fish Restaurant
Smiths of Smithfield
Bleeding Heart
Club Gascon
Pu's Thai Brasserie
See page 329 for locations of restaurants in this area
Wagamama
Ye Olde Cheshire Cheese
Chi Noodle
Northcliffe House Bar & Kitchen
The Waldorf Hilton
One Aldwych
The Savoy
Oxo Tower
Tate Modern Restaurant
Mad Hatter
Mercure London City Bankside
The Anchor and Hope, Mesón Don Felipe, Tas
Baltic
Hispaniola
CLERKENWELL
HOLBORN
FARRINGDON
BARBICAN
CHANCERY LA.
TEMPLE
BLACKFRIARS
ST PAUL'S
SOUTHWARK
Thames
331
335
© A-Z/OS

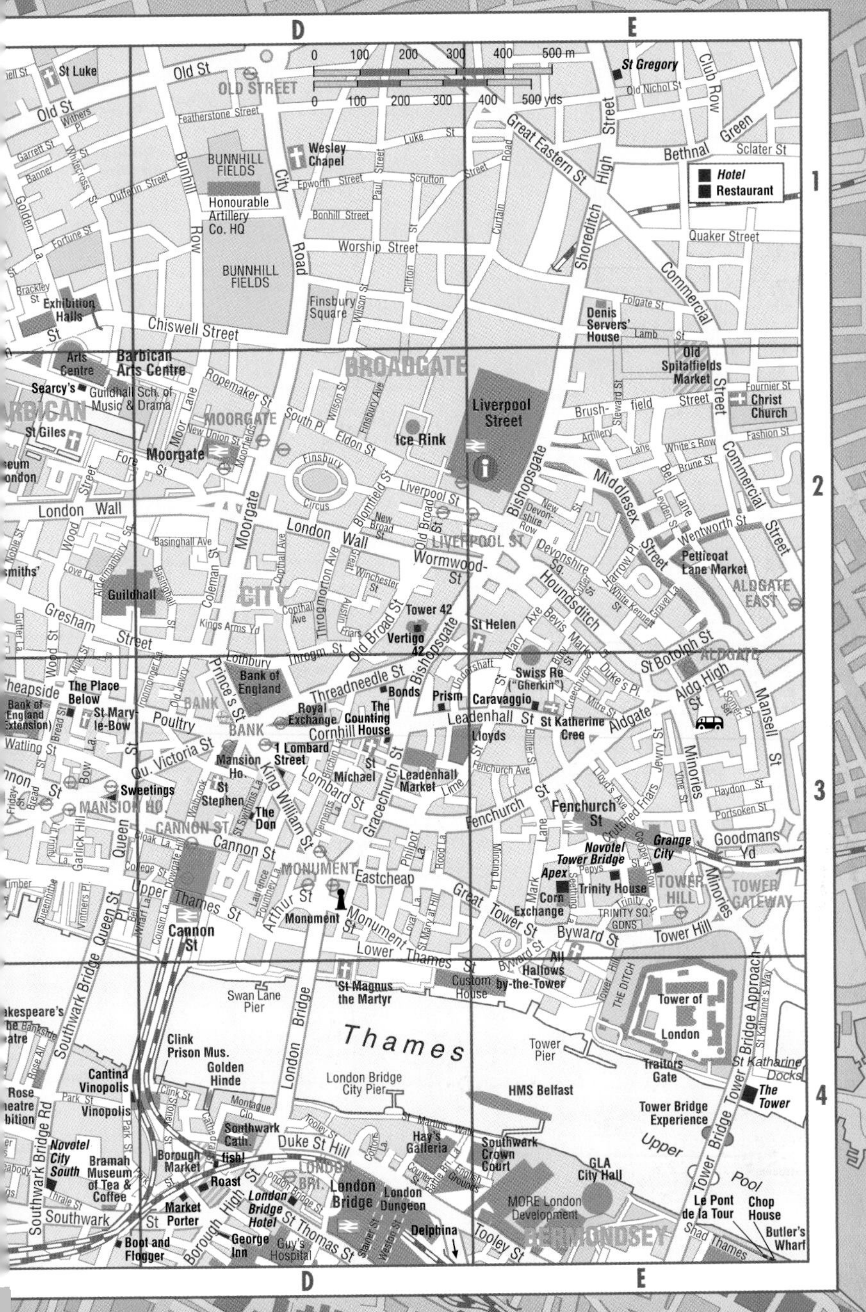

Hotel
Restaurant
St Gregory
Wesley Chapel
Honourable Artillery Co. HQ
Bunnhill Fields
Exhibition Halls
Denis Servers' House
Old Spitalfields Market
Christ Church
Barbican Arts Centre
Searcy's
Guildhall Sch. of Music & Drama
St Giles
Liverpool Street
Ice Rink
Broadgate
Moorgate
Guildhall
Petticoat Lane Market
Tower 42
Vertigo 42
St Helen
Swiss Re ("Gherkin")
Bank of England
The Place Below
St Mary-le-Bow
Royal Exchange
The Counting House
Bonds
Prism
Caravaggio
St Katherine Cree
Lloyds
Mansion Ho.
1 Lombard Street
St Michael
Leadenhall Market
St Stephen
Sweetings
The Don
Fenchurch St
Novotel Tower Bridge
Grange City
Apex
Trinity House
Corn Exchange
Monument
Cannon St
All Hallows by-the-Tower
St Magnus the Martyr
Custom House
Tower of London
Thames
Tower Pier
Traitors Gate
HMS Belfast
The Tower
Tower Bridge Experience
Clink Prison Mus.
Golden Hinde
Cantina Vinopolis
Vinopolis
Southwark Cath.
fish!
Borough Market
Roast
Novotel City South
Bramah Museum of Tea & Coffee
London Bridge Hotel
London Bridge
London Dungeon
Hay's Galleria
Southwark Crown Court
GLA City Hall
MORE London Development
Le Pont de la Tour
Chop House
Butler's Wharf
Market Porter
Boot and Flogger
George Inn
Guy's Hospital
Delphina
Bermondsey

330

336

page 328

Hotel
Restaurant

0 100 200 300 400 500 m
0 100 200 300 400 500 yds

Reservoir
HYDE PARK
Boating Lake
Bandstand
War Memorial
Achilles Statue
Serpentine Road
Rotten Row
South Carriage Drive
Edinburgh Gate
Albert Gate
Stanhope Gate
Curzon Gate
Apsley House, Wellington Mus.
Hyde Park Corner
HYDE PARK CORNER
Wellington Mon.
Wellington Arch

Dorchester Hotel
Dorchester Bar
China Tang
Park Lane
London Intercontinental Hotel
London Hilton on Park Lane
Metropolitan
Met Bar
Nobu
Christ Ch.
El Pirata
The Four Seasons Hotel
Hard Rock Café
Mirabelle
Ye Grapes
Miyama
Fakhreldine
The Ritz
Curzon St
Piccadilly
GREEN PARK
Bandstand

Mandarin Oriental Hyde Park
Mandarin Bar
Library Bar
Pizza on the Park
Blue Bar
Berkeley Hotel
Lanesborough Hotel
Halkin Hotel
Fifth Floor
Harvey Nichols
Knightsbridge
KNIGHTSBRIDGE
Isola & Isola Bar
Knightsbridge Green Hotel
Basil Street Hotel
Capital Hotel
Harrods
St Paul's
Grenadier
Constitution Hill
(Closed to traffic on Sundays)
PALACE GARDENS
Lake
Queen Victoria Memorial
Buckingham Palace
The Queen's Gallery
The Royal Mews
The Rubens
41
Goring Hotel
Goring Dining Room
Royal Westminster Thistle Hotel
Victoria
VICTORIA

Belgrave Square
Sloane Street
Cadogan Hotel
BELGRAVIA
Eaton Square
Ken Lo's Memories of China
Tophams Hotel
Boisdale
Thomas Cubitt
Victoria Coach Sta.
Passport and Identity Office
Victoria Park Plaza
Holy Trinity
St Mary
Royal Ct Theatre
Peter Jones
Sloane Square
SLOANE SQ.

The Willett
Duke of York Square and Saatchi Gallery
Chelsea Kitchen
King's Road
La Poule au Pot
St Barnabas
Fox and Hounds
Orange Brewery
La Fontana
Georgian House Hotel
Airways Hotel
Grapevine Hotel
Elizabeth Hotel
New England Hotel
Hanover Hotel
Dover Hotel
St Gabriel
Chelsea Barracks (site under redevelopment)
BURTON'S COURT
Royal Hospital Road
Chelsea Bridge Road
Ebury Bridge Road
RANELAGH GARDENS
Gordon Ramsay
Royal Hospital
Surprise

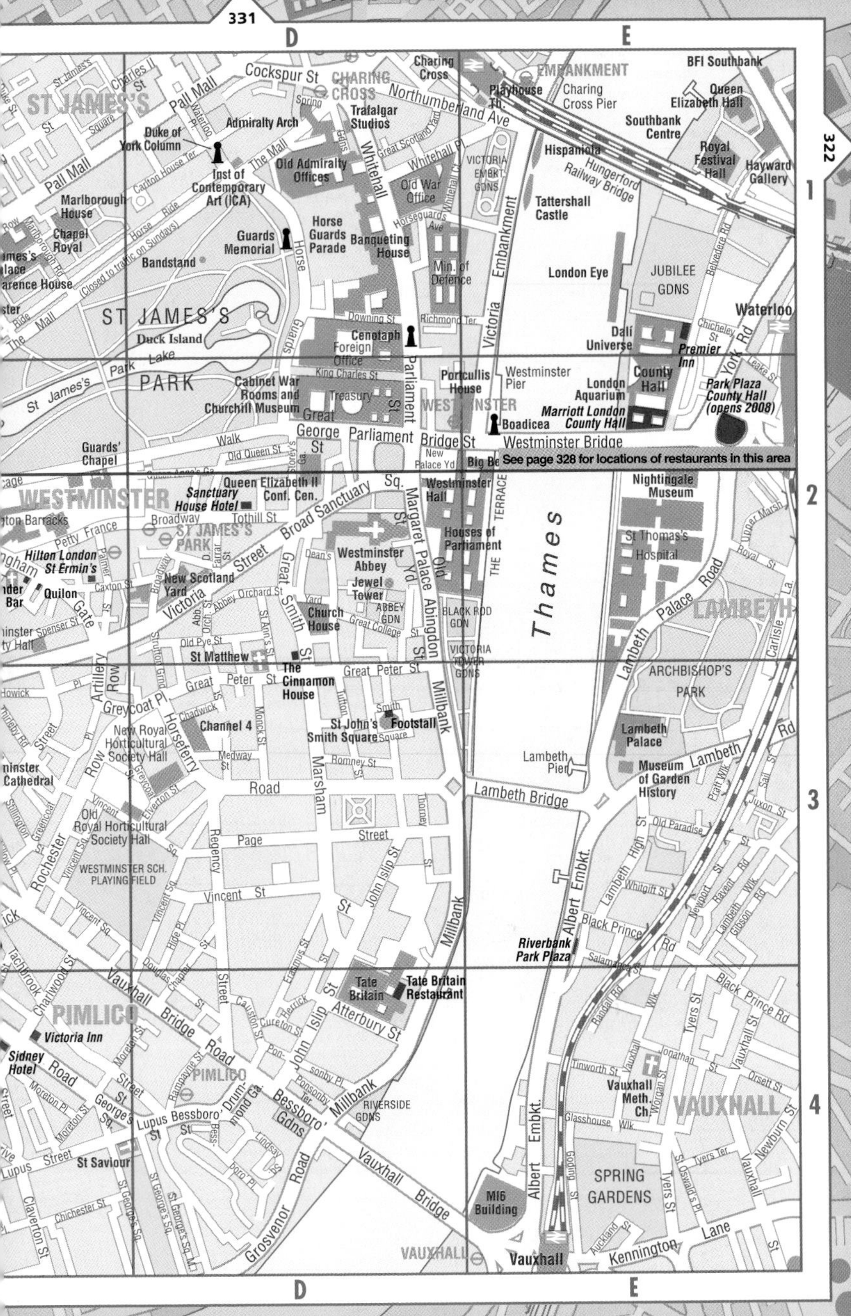
331
322
D
E
1
2
3
4
St James's
Pall Mall
Cockspur St
Charing Cross
Northumberland Ave
Embankment
Playhouse Th.
Charing Cross Pier
BFI Southbank
Queen Elizabeth Hall
Southbank Centre
Royal Festival Hall
Hayward Gallery
Duke of York Column
Admiralty Arch
Trafalgar Studios
Old Admiralty Offices
Whitehall
Great Scotland Yard
Hispaniola
Hungerford Railway Bridge
Inst of Contemporary Art (ICA)
The Mall
Marlborough House
Chapel Royal
Old War Office
Victoria Embkt Gdns
Tattershall Castle
Guards Memorial
Horse Guards Parade
Banqueting House
Min. of Defence
London Eye
Jubilee Gdns
Bandstand
Clarence House
St James's Park
Duck Island
Lake
Downing St
Richmond Ter
Cenotaph
Foreign Office
Victoria Embankment
Waterloo
Dalí Universe
Premier Inn
York Rd
Cabinet War Rooms and Churchill Museum
King Charles St
Treasury
Portcullis House
Westminster Pier
London Aquarium
County Hall
Park Plaza County Hall (opens 2008)
Marriott London County Hall
Boadicea
Westminster
Great George St
Parliament St
Parliament Bridge St
Westminster Bridge
Guards' Chapel
Birdcage Walk
Old Queen St
New Palace Yd
Big Ben
See page 328 for locations of restaurants in this area
Queen Elizabeth II Conf. Cen.
Sanctuary House Hotel
Broad Sanctuary
Westminster Hall
Nightingale Museum
Tothill St
Broadway
St James's Park
Houses of Parliament
Thames
St Thomas's Hospital
Petty France
Hilton London St Ermin's
Westminster Abbey
Jewel Tower
Quilon
New Scotland Yard
Victoria Street
Caxton St
Great Smith St
Church House
Abbey Gdn
Great College St
Black Rod Gdn
Lambeth Palace Road
Lambeth
Old Pye St
St Matthew
The Cinnamon House
Victoria Tower Gdns
Abingdon St
Millbank
Archbishop's Park
Great Peter St
Artillery Row
Greycoat Pl
Horseferry
Channel 4
St John's Smith Square
Footstall
Lambeth Palace
New Royal Horticultural Society Hall
Lambeth Pier
Museum of Garden History
Westminster Cathedral
Marsham St
Road
Lambeth Bridge
Old Royal Horticultural Society Hall
Page Street
Regency St
Westminster Sch. Playing Field
Vincent Sq
Rochester Row
Vincent St
John Islip St
Albert Embkt
Lambeth High St
Black Prince Rd
Riverbank Park Plaza
Tate Britain
Tate Britain Restaurant
Atterbury St
Pimlico
Vauxhall Bridge Road
Victoria Inn
Sidney Hotel
Vauxhall Meth. Ch.
Vauxhall
Riverside Gdns
Bessboro' Gdns
Lupus Street
St Saviour
Grosvenor Road
Vauxhall Bridge
MI6 Building
Spring Gardens
Kennington Lane
Claverton St

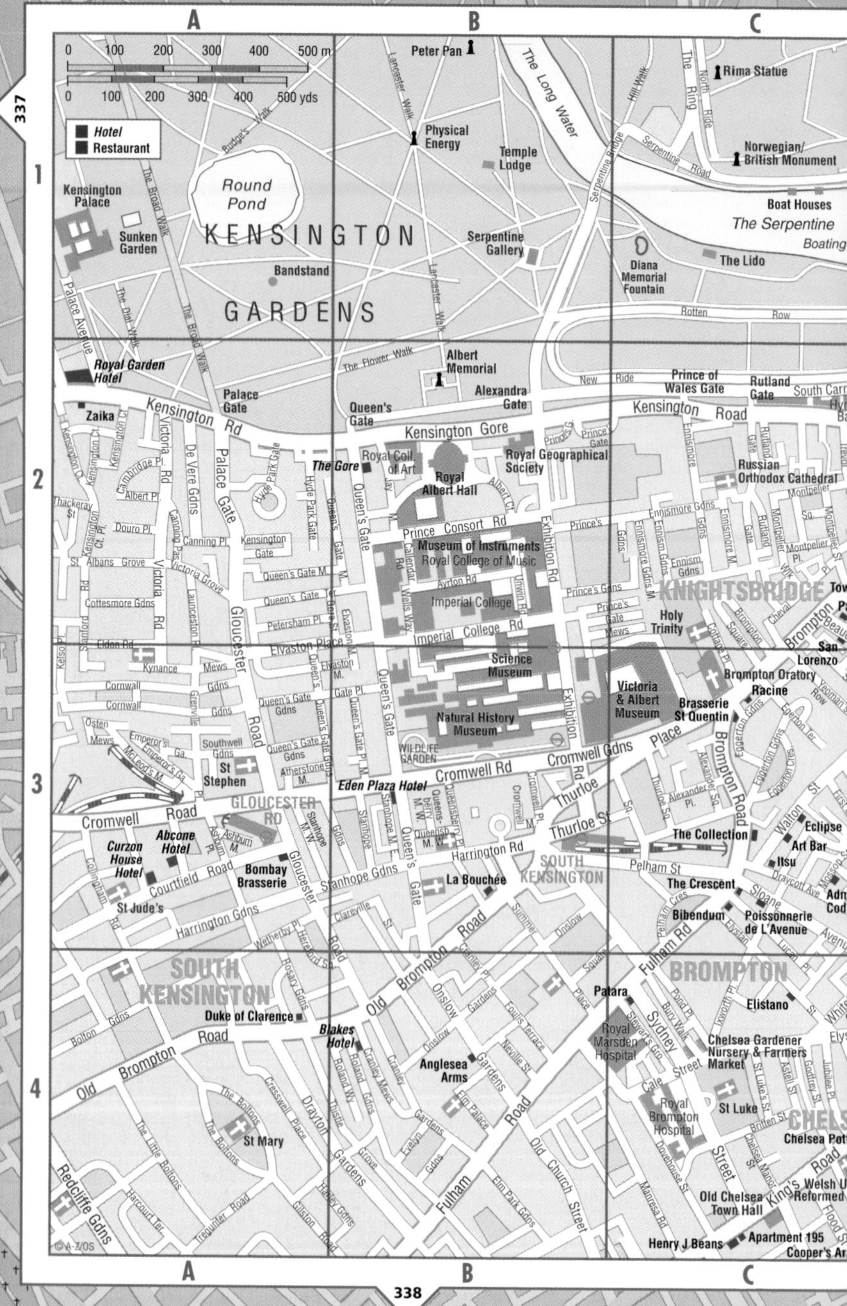
A
B
C
1
2
3
4
0 100 200 300 400 500 m
0 100 200 300 400 500 yds
Hotel
Restaurant
337
338
KENSINGTON
GARDENS
Round Pond
Kensington Palace
Sunken Garden
Bandstand
Peter Pan
Physical Energy
Temple Lodge
Serpentine Gallery
Rima Statue
Norwegian/ British Monument
Boat Houses
The Serpentine
Boating
The Lido
Diana Memorial Fountain
The Long Water
Albert Memorial
Alexandra Gate
Queen's Gate
Palace Gate
Prince of Wales Gate
Rutland Gate
Royal Garden Hotel
Zaika
Kensington Rd
Kensington Gore
Kensington Road
The Gore
Royal Coll. of Art
Royal Albert Hall
Royal Geographical Society
Russian Orthodox Cathedral
Prince Consort Rd
Museum of Instruments
Royal College of Music
Imperial College
Imperial College Rd
Science Museum
Natural History Museum
Victoria & Albert Museum
KNIGHTSBRIDGE
Holy Trinity
Brompton Oratory
San Lorenzo
Racine
Brasserie St Quentin
Eden Plaza Hotel
Cromwell Rd
Cromwell Road
Cromwell Gdns
GLOUCESTER RD
St Stephen
Abcone Hotel
Curzon House Hotel
Bombay Brasserie
St Jude's
SOUTH KENSINGTON
La Bouchée
The Collection
Eclipse
Art Bar
Itsu
The Crescent
Bibendum
Poissonnerie de L'Avenue
BROMPTON
Patara
Elistano
Royal Marsden Hospital
Chelsea Gardener Nursery & Farmers Market
Royal Brompton Hospital
St Luke
Duke of Clarence
Blakes Hotel
Anglesea Arms
St Mary
Old Brompton Road
Fulham Road
Old Church Street
Old Chelsea Town Hall
King's Road
Henry J Beans
Apartment 195
Cooper's Ar
Chelsea Pot
Welsh Reformed
© A-Z/OS

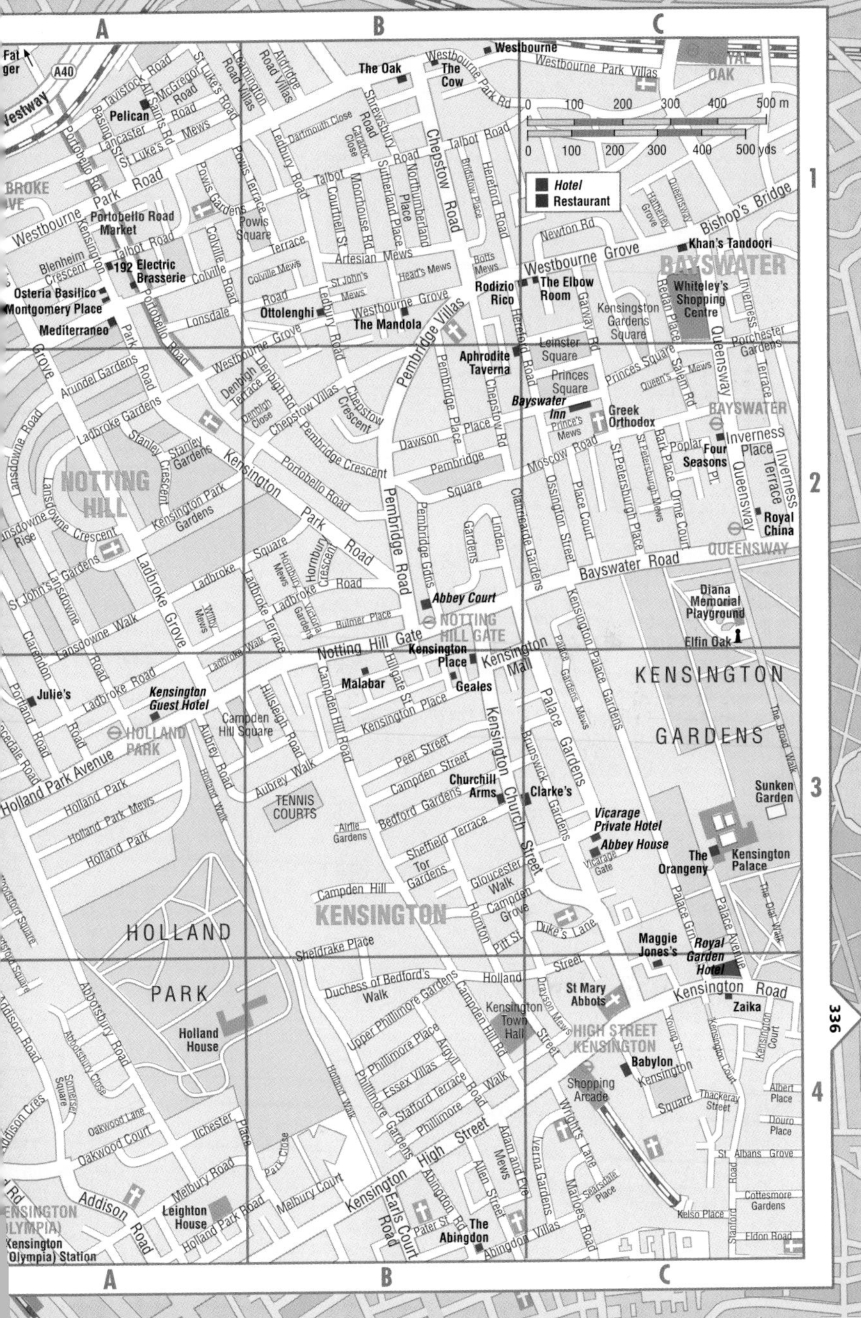
A
B
C
1
2
3
4
Hotel
Restaurant
0 100 200 300 400 500 m
0 100 200 300 400 500 yds
Westbourne
The Oak
The Cow
Pelican
Portobello Road Market
192
Electric Brasserie
Osteria Basilico
Montgomery Place
Mediterraneo
Ottolenghi
The Mandola
Rodizio Rico
The Elbow Room
Khan's Tandoori
BAYSWATER
Whiteley's Shopping Centre
Aphrodite Taverna
Bayswater Inn
Greek Orthodox
Four Seasons
Royal China
QUEENSWAY
ROYAL OAK
NOTTING HILL
Abbey Court
NOTTING HILL GATE
Kensington Place
Malabar
Geales
Diana Memorial Playground
Elfin Oak
KENSINGTON GARDENS
Julie's
Kensington Guest Hotel
HOLLAND PARK
Campden Hill Square
TENNIS COURTS
Churchill Arms
Clarke's
Vicarage Private Hotel
Abbey House
The Orangery
Kensington Palace
Sunken Garden
KENSINGTON
HOLLAND PARK
Holland House
Maggie Jones's
Royal Garden Hotel
St Mary Abbots
Zaika
Kensington Town Hall
HIGH STREET KENSINGTON
Babylon
Shopping Arcade
Leighton House
The Abingdon
KENSINGTON OLYMPIA
Kensington (Olympia) Station
Westway
Westbourne Grove
Westbourne Park Road
Bayswater Road
Notting Hill Gate
Holland Park Avenue
Kensington Church Street
Kensington High Street
Kensington Road
Ladbroke Grove
Pembridge Road
Queensway
Bishop's Bridge Road
336

336
A
B
C
1
2
3
4
Hotel
Restaurant
Kynance
Abcone Hotel
Curzon House Hotel
Enterprise Hotel
Oliver Plaza Hotel, My Place Hotel
Barkston Hotel
Bombay Brasserie
Eden Plaza Hotel
La Bouchée
Duke of Clarence
Blakes Hotel
Anglesea Arms
Patara
Bardo
The Stockpot
Buona Sera at the Jam
Front Page
Ed's Easy Diner
Eight Over Eight
Pig's Ear
Vivienne Westwood
Mokssh
Chutney Mary
Lots Road Pub and Dining Rooms
Blue Kangaroo
606 Club
Conrad International
Science Museum
Natural History Museum
Victoria & Albert Museum
Imperial College
SOUTH KENSINGTON
CHELSEA
WEST BROMPTON
BROMPTON CEMETERY
WORLD'S END
WALHAM GREEN
SANDS END
EARL'S COURT
GLOUCESTER ROAD
Royal Marsden Hospital
Chelsea & Westminster Hospital
Stamford Bridge Chelsea F. C.
Kensington & Chelsea College
Thames
Cromwell Road
Fulham Road
King's Road
Old Brompton Road
Chelsea Creek
Chelsea Wharf
Cremorne Wharf
Battersea Bridge

Art & Photo Credits

Akg-images London/Erich Lessing 259tr117
Alamy 11tl, 84bl, 167c&BR, 245b, 246br, 260cl&bl,
Apa Publications 5br, 6tl, 7tl, 22tr, 44b, 75cl, 78cl, 83tr, 93tl, 101bl, 102bl, 125tr, 139br, 152tl, 152b, 162b, 163tl, 167cr&br, 169b, 192tr, 244cl, 280, 292tr, 306, 312, 313
Art Archive 27, 28cr, 36bl, 37c, 38bl, 165tl,
Natasha Babain/Apa 94tr, 192br, 259cl, 289, 315tl
Bank of England Museum 170c
Clive Barda/ArenaPAL 40/41
David Beatty/Apa 43b, 266, 270b, 273, 291, 301tr
Martin Black/Impact 115br
Ian Bradshaw 155tl
Bridgeman Art Library 28tl, 29tr, 31tl, 37tl & tr, 38bl, 207bl, 208cr, 226tr, 238bl, 262tr
Britain on View 70
British Library 36tl
British Library/HIP/TopFoto 36cr
British Museum 7cr
Julian Calder 150
Cannizaro House 290
Mark Cator/Impact 83cl
Piers Cavendish/Impact 303
David Churchill/Arcaid/Corbis 58b
Corbis 33t&br, 35tl, 44tl, 74t&b, 252bl
Andrew Eames 20
English Heritage 235br
Alyse Dar/Apa 30b, 161t, 163tr&br, 164tl&cl, 173bl,
Linton Donaldson/Apa 256, 257tr&bl, 258t&bl, 261cr&b,
Mary Evans Picture Library 27,
Florence Nightingale Museum 184tr
Freud Museum 245tr
Geffrye Museum, London 251t
Glyn Genin/Apa 3, 4, 6br&bl, 7tr, cl, c&bl, 8tr, 9tl&cr, 25tl,tr&cl, 42, 43tl, 45, 57 all, 58tl,tr&cr, 60/61, 72t, 73tr, 75b, 81t, 82b, 83b, 84br, 88, 89, 91br, 92tr, 93b, 94br, 96br, 97, 99, 100bl, 101br, 102br, 112, 114cr, 115tr, 117tr&br, 119b, 121br, 124, 126tl, 128b, 129bl, 130, 134, 135, 138tr, 140bl, 141, 146, 151b, 152bl&cr, 154br, 156tl, 158, 159, 160, 161b, 163bl, 164b, 165b, 168bl, 169tr, 171tl,tr&b, 172tl, c &b, 173br, 182, 183, 184bl, 185cl, 186, 187tr&bl, 188tl,bl&br, 189b, 193cr&br, 194tr&bl, 202, 205tr, 206tl,cr, bl&br, 207tr, 220, 222tl, 223bl&br, 225tl, bl&br, 226cl&bl, 227, 232, 233, 242, 244b, 246bl, 250, 254tr, 255b, 262bl, 269t&b, 270t, 271bl, 274, 276, 278tl&br, 279, 286tl, 288, 299tl&br, 300, 307, 309, 314, 315br
Getty Images 16/17, 34t&b, 35tr, 39t&br, 71, 252tr, 303tr
Tim Graham 24
Tony Halliday/Apa 101tr, 190b, 191b
Halkin Hotel 283
B. Herman/Network 9bl
Historic Royal Palaces, Crown copyright 210tr, 240tl
i-Stock 7br
Indexstock/Photolibrary 195
Britta Jaschinski 91tl
Britta Jaschinski/Apa 8bl, 10cr, 18, 23, 47 all, 48 all, 49tr, 50all, 51t, 85cr&bl, 94bl, 95tl&br, 96tl, 103tr, 105br, 106, 107, 113, 114tl, 116tr&b, 118br, 119cl, 120, 121tl, 128br, 131tl&br, 137cl, 142, 143, 157, 174bl, 175tl, 197tl,tr&cr 213br, 221, 223tr&cr, 224b, 228, 229tl&br, 243b, 248, 281, 285, 292bl, 293t&br, 294tl&br, 295tl&br, 296tl&br, 297tl&br, 301BR, 310
Michael Jenner 272B
Caroline Jones/Apa 268, 272TR
Richard Kalina/Shakespeare's Globe 298
Keats House 245TR
Alex von Koettlitz/ArenaPAL/TopFoto 304
John Kegan 1
The Lanesborough 286BR
Rachel Lawrence/Apa 253tl&tr, 254b, 255t
Pavel Libera 11CR
Tom Le Bas/Apa 73B, 76BR, 78TR, 79TR & B, 80TL, 84TL, 154TL &BL, 155BR, 156BL
Sian Lezard/Apa 8CR, 51B, 203, 204, 205TR, 207BR, 208BL, 209TR,BL & BR, 210TL & BL, 211cr&b, 212, 213tl, 234, 235TL & TR, 236TL, BL & BR, 237BR & TR, 238BR, 239C & BR, 241, 249
London Aerial Photo Library 62/63
London Borough of Southwark 138BL
London Transport Museum
Alisdair Macdonald 156tl
Neil Meneer 22B, 224T
J. Miller/Robert Harding Picture Library 259B
Alastair Muir/Rex Features 43CR
Museum of London/HIP/TopFoto 39BL
Museum of St. Bartholemew's Hospital 162TL
National Gallery, London 100TR
National Maritime Museum 258BL
Richard Nowitz 14/15, 179BL & BR, 240B
Tony Page 237TL
Clare Peel/Apa 103BL, 104TR, BL & BR, 105TR, 189TR, 191TR & C, 192CL & BL, 196BL
Jo Potts/Apa 93TR
Ray Roberts/Collections 156TR
Ronnie Scott's Jazz Club 92BL
Royal Airforce Museum 247B
Sauce Communications/Gordon Ramsay @ Claridges 49TL
Savoy Hotel 10TR
Brian Shuel/Collections 166
Dorothy Stannard/Apa 25BR, 137BL & BR, 140BR, 311
SuperStock 56L, 59
Sarah Sweeney/Apa 125, 127BR
Liba Taylor/Collections 303BL
TopFoto 43
Ray Tang/Rex Features 44TR
Jonathan Trapman/Acestock 240CR
Visit London 98, 103BR
The Waldorf 284
Bill Wassman/Apa 118TL, 267,
The William Morris Gallery 247TR
Roger Williams 77TR
Corrie Wingate 10BL, 253B
Adam Woolfitt 22TL, 168BR
Adam Woolfitt/Robert Harding 46, 64
Crispin Zeeman/Apa 271R

STREET INDEX

A

B

C

Picture Spreads

Pages 52/53: 52TR, 53CL Glyn Genin, 52BL & BR, 53br, BL, CL& BCL Britta Jaschinski, 52/3 TC Sian Lezard, 53TCL Getty Images, 53TCR Nils Jorgensen/Rex Features, 53CR Pierre Verdy/AFP/Corbis.
Pages 54/55: 54TL & BR, 54/5TC, 55TR & BL Glyn Genin, 54bl, 55CL & TCR Corrie Wingate, 55BR Sian Lezard.
Pages 86/87: all pictures by William Beckett except top centre Glyn Genin.
Pages 108/109: all pictures Bridgeman Art Library/National Gallery except 100BR National Gallery.
Pages 110/111: all pictures National Portrait Gallery.
Pages 122/123: 122BL Alamy, 122TL Brian Shuel/Collections, 122BR Liba Taylor/Collections, 123TR Apa, 123CR Glyn Genin, 123BL Rex Features.
Pages 132/133: all picture Brian Bell except 133TR, CR&BR courtesy Madame Tussauds.
Pages 145/149: 145, 146, 148CL,CR & TR all courtesy British Museum, 147/48 all TopFoto/HIP/British Museum except 147CR Apa, 147BR Werner Forman Archive.
Pages 178/181: all pictures Historic Royal Palaces, Crown Copyright except 178/9TC Britain on View, 179TR Bridgeman/Guildhall Library/Corporation of London, 180TR Corbis, 181BR Getty Images.
Pages 198/199: all pictures ©Tate, London except 199BR Apa.
Pages 200/201: all pictures Imperial War Museum except 200BR Clare Peel, 200/1TC, 201TRGlyn Genin.
Pages 214/215: all pictures Glyn Genin except 215BL Science & Society Photo Library.
Pages 216/217: 216/7TC Derry Moore/V&A, 216BR, 217BR V&A ,216/7BC Bridgeman Art Library/V&A, rest Glyn Genin.
Pages 218/219: all pictures Glyn Genin.

Map Production: Stephen Ramsay, Mike Adams, Neal Jordan-Caws & James Macdonald

Production: Linton Donaldson, Mary Pickles

General Index

D

E

F

MAYOR OF LONDON

24 hour travel information
020 7222 1234